Central Asia

Central Asia
Since Independence

Editors

K. Warikoo
Mahavir Singh

Maulana Abul Kalam Azad Institute of Asian Studies, Kolkata

SHIPRA

ISBN: 81-7541-164-3

First Published in India in 2004

Central Asia Since Independence

Published by:
SHIPRA PUBLICATIONS
115-A, Vikas Marg, Shakarpur
Delhi-110092, INDIA
Phone: 91-11-55277210, 22500954
E-mail: info@shiprapublications.com
www.shiprapublications.com

Laser Typesetting by:
Sunshine Graphics
Delhi-110032

Printed at:
Chaudhary Offset Process
Delhi-110051

Preface

Stretching from the Caspian Sea in the west to the western frontiers of China in the east, Central Asia has played important role in the history and politics of Eurasia. In its past history, Silk Route system provided a trans-continental bridge facilitating multilateral exchanges between Central Asia, Russia, China, West Asia and the Indian sub-continent. During the 19th and early 20th centuries, Central Asia was a zone of triangular contest between Britain, Russia and China, which has been romanticized as the 'Great Game'. The disintegration of former USSR and the subsequent emergence of independent Central Asian Republics, all having predominantly Muslim population, changed the balance of power in this region. Due to its geographical proximity to China, Russia, West Asia and South Asia, this region emerged as a distinct geopolitical entity stimulating global attention and interest. Neighbouring countries like Russia, China, Iran, Turkey, Pakistan and India have been pursuing competing strategic, economic and cultural interests in the region. They have been in the forefront of building new linkages with the independent Central Asian Republics. On their part the Central Asian Republics have moved into a multilateral network of international relations, by becoming members of CIS, ECO, OIC, OSCE, UN etc. These Republics, keen to be self-reliant perceive the involvement of such international institutions in Central Asia as guarantee for their independence. The political regimes in Central Asia have played their cards well by establishing regional system of collective security with the help of Russia, USA, European Union etc.

Central Asian Republics have been in transition passing through a stage of transformation into a new political, social and economic order. Though, post-Soviet Central Asia did witness rise of Islamic militancy, trans-border terrorism, inter-ethnic tensions and ethno-religious resurgence, the conflict in Afghanistan and in Tajikistan helped in blunting the appeal of Islamic fundamentalism and its politics in Central Asia. Language, race and religion are seen as symbols of nationhood and necessary components of cultural revivalism that has taken place throughout the region. Local writers, artists and academics have idealised local history and culture. Old leaders/personalities who were either purged by Soviets under Stalin or discarded for corruption have been resurrected as national heroes. Whereas public squares, institutions and streets have been renamed, local languages have been declared as official language. Nation-building process in Kazakhstan has banked upon consolidation of Kazakh ethnic-national identity in terms of their demographic growth, new emphasis on Kazakh language, shifting of capital from Almaty to the north and marginalisation of non-Kazakhs from the power structures. But due to several decades of secularisation and non-existence of clerical hierarchy, Islam remained generally limited to spheres of spiritual faith and cultural identity. Economic and infrastructure development is gaining primacy in policies and programmes in Central Asian Republics.

At the dawn of independence, these Republics were faced with numerous problems of nation and state building, rural unemployment, environmental degradation and inter-ethnic problems. Ethnic complexities in Central Asia, its colonial past, historico-cultural identity of titular nationalities, different ethnic groups settled across the borders, problem of Slavic minorities and competition for pipeline routes and energy resources have been the key issues prevalent in post-Soviet Central Asia. As the borders of Central Asian Republics do not coincide with the linguistic and cultural affinities of different groups living in respective states, there have been lingering inter-state territorial disputes. Though the problem of borders and disputes over water sharing remain, yet no Balkanisation of the region or secession of any one part has taken place. However, concerns have been expressed over the progress of democratisation and sustainable economic development. Apprehensions of any breakdown of the sovereign statehood of the Central Asian Republics have been proved wrong, with the consolidation of their national identity overcoming the difficulties of transition. These countries successfully completed their transition to sovereign independent statehood.

While conducting its external relations, Turkmenistan claimed to have scored success in its principles of 'positive neutrality', on the domestic front the country has witnessed the consolidation of Presidency with the Turkmenbashy Saparmurat Niyazov having been awarded the life time Presidency. Kazakhstan looks itself as a bridge between Europe and Asia with its emphasis on establishing multilateral economic and relations with all countries, within the CIS, with Russia, US, European Union, China etc. Kazakhstan has evinced interest in the establishment of a common economic space in the Eurasian landmass. Whereas there have been misgivings about regional integration in Central Asia, the Inter State Council of Kazakhstan, Kyrgyzstan, Tajikistan and Uzbekistan is an example of regional cooperation in Central Asia. However, the emphasis of Central Asian Republics throughout the period of their independent statehood has been on making bilateral relationships viable and effective.

Afghan crisis influenced all the Central Asian Republics during the period. Rise of Taliban to power variously affected these countries, which sought to build secular democratic states. Though they followed different approaches to the Afghan conflict, there was unanimity among the Central Asian Republics over the threats posed by Islamist extremism of Taliban, terrorism and drug trafficking. Security of Tajik-Afghan border remained the crucial issue. Tajikistan witnessed bloody civil war and conflict during the early and mid-1990s, which fragmented the society and polity, besides causing severe economic damage to the country. In the late 1990s, the country moved forward towards reconciliation between opposition and the government.

Afghan conflict accompanied with trans-border terrorism, arms and drug trafficking caused instability in the region. The crisis deepened during the Taliban period when Osama bin Laden and Al Qaeda turned Afghanistan into the hub of terrorism and narco-trafficking, adversely affecting security in the entire region. However, in the post-September 11 period, when Taliban were defeated and a new broad based government was formed, the Central Asian Republics felt relieved. Demise of Taliban has relaxed the security concerns of Central Asian countries and with new hopes of building secular and democratic polity in Afghanistan, Central Asian Republics are looking towards peace and security in the region. Due to its rich energy resources, Central Asia-Caspian region has emerged as the focus of great power interest, with various countries seeking to establish their influence in the region.

In view of the momentous changes taking place in the post-Soviet Central Asia, Maulana Abul Kalam Azad Institute of Asian Studies, Kolkata and Central Asian Studies Programme, Centre for South, Central and South East Asian Studies, Jawaharlal Nehru University, New Delhi organised an International Seminar at New Delhi on 21-22 November 2001, to review the experience of the Central Asian Republics during the first decade of their independence. This book is based on the papers presented at this Seminar, which have, however, been updated. Developments in all the five Central Asian Republics of Tajikistan, Uzbekistan, Turkmenistan, Kyrgyzstan and Kazakhstan have been dealt with in this book.

The experience of Central Asian Republics in their transition to sovereign independent nationhood and market economy, has been appraised by Prof. Devendra Kaushik. Whereas, Prof. Ondjik Musayev of Turkmenistan highlights the achievements of Turkmenistan during its ten years of independence, Dr. Rafis Abazov from Kyrgyzstan makes a critical analysis of Kyrgyzstan's struggle for democracy, stability and economic development. Kazakhstan's experience of state-building during the past decade has been reviewed by Prof. Ajay Patnaik. And the priorities of foreign policy of independent Kazakhstan have been detailed by Bulat Sultanov. Complexities of inter-ethnic relations in Central Asia have been examined by Prof. P.L. Dash.

The bilateral and multi-lateral relationships evolved by the Central Asian Republics in the post-Soviet era both within the CIS and outside with the West, NATO, OSCE and the UN have been explained by Mohammad Munir Alam. Impact of Afghanistan factor over Central Asian domestic and external politics has been analysed by Prof. K. Warikoo. The extent and pattern and future prospects of India-Uzbekistan relations, particularly in the economic realm have been explored by Fatih Teshabaev from Uzbekistan and Prof. Shri Prakash of India. The dynamics of Iran's multilateral relationship with the Central Asian Republics during the past decade or so, has been explained by Prof. S. P. Singh. Whereas Prof. Sheel K. Asopa outlines the linkage between the Afghan cauldron and Tajikistan, Dr. Suchandana Chatterjee makes an analysis of the politics and society in Tajikistan highlighting the conflictual relationship between the Tajik government and the opposition as well as the reconciliation between the two sides in the aftermath of Tajik civil war.

M.N. Sabirov provides an authoritative inside account of the process of regional cooperation in Central Asia, and the problems and prospects of regionalisation, regionalism and regional cooperation have been analysed by Anita Sengupta. Leila Muzapparova of Kazakhstan draws attention to the basic directions of economic cooperation of Central Asian Republics. Whereas the geo-economic and geopolitical importance of the Caspian-Central Asian region for USA has been reviewed by Laura Yerekesheva, the potential of conflict over the utilisation of energy resources in the Caspian region in the post-Soviet era has been addressed by Prof. R.G. Gidadhubli. Prof. A. Gafurov, A. Urinov and Dr. Hakimov, all economists from Uzbekistan have detailed the process of socio-economic development as well as the structural changes introduced into the economy of Uzbekistan following its independence. Prof. Kh. Umarov and J. Makhmadshoev, both from Tajikistan have highlighted the problems of socio-economic development in Tajikistan mainly due to civil war. Dustobaev of Tajikistan addresses the issues of ecology and development in Central Asia.

The study presents an integrated view of the developments in post-Soviet Central Asia adopting an inter-disciplinary and comparative study approach. Almost all well known Indian specialists in this field have contributed to this volume. The contributions by eminent scholars from all the five Central Asian Republics provide rich insights into the processes of nation building, democratisation, economic development, regional cooperation and building of bilateral and multi-lateral linkages. As such the book not only consolidates the Indian scholarly contribution in the field of Central Asian studies but also provides the Central Asian experiences as presented by the scholars from Tajikistan, Uzbekistan, Turkmenistan, Kyrgyzstan and Kazakhstan.

New Delhi **Editors**

Contents

1

Central Asia Since *Ozodi*

An Appraisal

Devendra Kaushik

The year 2001 marked the completion of a decade of independence of the five former Soviet Central Asian Republics of Kazakhstan, Kyrgyzstan, Uzbekistan, Turkmenistan and Tajikistan. These Republics attained their independence in the wake of disintegration of the USSR. Strangely, in the March 1991 referendum 90 to 95 per cent of the electorate in the Central Asian Republics had supported the preservation of the USSR as against only 53.5 per cent in the Russian Republic favouring its continued existence. However the situation started changing following the abortive coup in Moscow in August 1991. The Supreme Soviet of Uzbekistan and Kyrgyzstan declared the independence of their respective republics on 31 August 1991. On 9 September 1991, Tajikistan was also declared an independent republic by its Supreme Soviet. Kazakhstan, declared its independence on 16 December by a resolution of its Supreme Soviet. Only Turkmenistan proclaimed its independence on 26 October 1991 following a referendum in which 94.1 per cent of the electorate favoured such a course.

Independence caught the Central Asian Republics unawares (it came as a consequence of bitter in-fighting among two rival groups of Metropolitan Russian elite headed by Gorbachev and Yeltsin). The Central Asian Republics have successfully faced the stupendous task of completing their transition to sovereign independent statehood. At the dawn of independence they were confronted by numerous problems of state and nation-building in a difficult milieu wherein various groups of elites competed for political power in an economy set on a course of steep decline on account of sudden severance of strong economic ties with Russia and consequent stoppage of Union subsidies. The acute problem of rural unemployment and environmental degradation further contributed to aggravation of inter-ethnic relations. A host of analysts and experts in the West in fact forecast a bleak future for the newly independent Central Asian states. Thus a study edited by Ali Banuazizi and Myron Weiner published in 1994 from London and New York which carried contributions from scholars associated with the M.I.T, Harvard and other leading American universities and research organisations like the Rand Corporation, advanced an interesting hypothesis about the disintegration of the major empires resulting inevitably in civil wars or regional conflicts. Banuazizi and Weiner linked the future course of this territory, equal to half the size of the United States and the whole of the Western and Eastern Europe, with the historical, ethno-linguistic and religious ties of its 60 million people with the 300 million people living in the four Muslim countries, namely, Afghanistan, Turkey, Iran and Pakistan. It became fashionable to analyse the developments in the post-Soviet Central Asian Republics in a geopolitical rather than a national framework. It was argued that more Azeris live in Iran (15 million) than in Azerbaijan (7 million) and the same was true of Tajiks residing in Afghanistan (4 million).

The demise of the northern neighbour Russia was taken for granted and in the 20th century version of the "Great-Game", Turkey and Iran were projected as replacement for Britain and Russia. After rejecting the two scenarios of filling up the Central Asian vacuum by either Turkey or Iran (the former under Pan-Turkism and the latter under Pan-Islamism) because of lack of economic resources in both these countries and limited appeal of Islam in the Central Asian Republics except in parts of Tajikistan and Ferghana valley, the contributors of this volume reached a rather grim and foreboding scenario. Through a process of elimination a most pessimistic note was struck by American scholar, former CIA analyst, Martha Brill Olcott, who concluded that "the Central Asians were left with an independence for which they had not prepared, which they did not want, and which was not likely to bring them any tangible benefit for a long time, if ever"[1]. Sharing this pessimism another Western scholar, Nancy Lubin, made a spine-chilling forecast about emergence in Central Asia of a new Columbia with nuclear weapons, pointing to a rapid expansion of opium-poppy cultivation in Central Asia. Banuazizi and Weiner in an effort to moderate the above-mentioned pessimistic scenario observed that Central Asia's future might not be a mere replication of the Balkan's past or present though there are parallels which should not be summarily dismissed."[2]

With all their faults and failings, the Central Asian leaders have proved wrong the Western apprehensions of their region going the Balkan way after breakup of the Austro-Hungarian empire in the 19th century. The Central Asian Republics have preserved intact their national independence and sovereignty and carved out a dignified place for themselves in the comity of nations. They have taken several positive diplomatic and political initiatives at the U.N. and other international fora. President Niyazov must get due credit for obtaining the U.N. recognition for the positive neutrality of Turkmenistan. The Central Asian Republics are presently members of several international and regional organisations. If through their voluntary membership of the C.I.S. they have preserved their essential links with Russia on a new basis, they are also striving to expand their ties with their Islamic neighbours—Turkey,Iran and Pakistan—through their participation in the E.C.O. They have tried to reach out to the European Community, the United States and even to the distant centres of economic power like Japan and South Korea. Their religious belief has not come in the way of developing mutually beneficial relations with Israel. The Central Asian Republics have cordial relations with China and India. They are with the exception of

Turkmenistan members of the Shanghai Cooperation Organisation (SCO) and the C.I.S Collective Security Treaty Organisation (CSTO) with the exception of Uzbekistan, which have contributed greatly to improvement in the regional security environment. All of them except Turkmenistan are also members of the Central Asian Cooperation Organisation (CACO). Their success in resolving the bloody internal conflict in Tajikistan by peacefully integrating the Islamic opposition into the mainstream politics of the Republic is a creditable achievement. They have also evolved a strong joint response together with Russia and China to the threat of cross-border terrorism and drugs and arms peddling.

So far as the progress of Central Asian Republics in the direction of democratization and transformation of their economy is concerned, the balancesheet of *Ozodi* leans more to the debit side in general though the picture differs from Republic to Republic. Yet in this regard one has to be patient and need not be overly pessimistic. The growing influence of democratic international public opinion and increasing global integration of the Central Asian Republics, as also their slow but steady advance towards a market economy, are bound to help their transformation into a democratic polity. The slow progress towards democracy as it is understood in the West may also be explained besides the important factor of absence of democratic norms, values, institutions, and political culture by the continuing threat from religious extremism from the South.

The Central Asian states have moved from a single party authoritarian system to a personalized authoritarianism of their Executive Presidents—Niyazov, Karimov, Nazarbayev, Akaev and Rakhmonov. All these Republics have not succeeded in forging an effective party system of their own though efforts in this direction were made. All power is concentrated in the hands of the President and he alone exercises it, quite often arbitrarily, and at times in violation of the constitution which is changed to suit the drive towards concentrating power in the hands of the Executive President. Checks and balances, independent judiciary, free press and media and democratic rights of the citizens are conspicuous by their absence.

Some analysts may not agree with this largely negative assessment of the political processes unfolding themselves in the region. But the fact remains that the little progress made in the direction of political pluralism during the later period of *Perestroika* (1989-91) has been subsequently scrapped in favour of personalized authoritarian rule. The only consolation is that the present day Central Asian polity has not degenerated into an extremist type of totalitarianism of the communist or fundamentalist variety. One is encouraged to harbour the hope that this oriental guided-democracy experiment will be nudged in the desirable direction of minimal democracy of free and fair competitive elections and formation of multiple political parties under conditions of freedom of speech and assembly and observance of basic human rights. The growing influence of democratic public opinion against the backdrop of intensified foreign interaction is likely to help the process towards democratisation of the Republics.

The most populous Central Asian Republic—Uzbekistan—is rated quite low just above Turkmenistan so far as democratisation and popular political participation is concerned. President Karimov consolidated his position initially by taking over the main planks of the agenda of the opposition movement *Birlik,* such as, Uzbek as state language, reduction of cotton cultivation and protection of health and environment. He managed to split the opposition into *Birlik* and *Erk* party by driving a wedge between Mohd. Salih and Pulatov. To enhance his legitimacy he accomplished the rehabilitation of Sharaf Rashidov who was denigrated posthumously during the later period of Perestroika. In the fall of 1991 the *Erk* party led by Mohd. Salih was registered and its leader allowed to contest against Karimov for the President's office.

The Islamists became active in the Namangan district of the Ferghana valley. In November 1991 following a public demonstration they seized the Communist Party's provincial office. Their demands for legalisation of Islamic Renaissance Party and establishment of the Islamic Republic were rejected by Karimov who however allowed the party office building to be converted into Islamic centre. The demonstration in Namangan was suppressed. For the next five years there was to be no relaxation in Karimov's authoritarian rule. Karimov got elected as President of Uzbekistan in December 1991 defeating his only rival Salih by a big margin of votes. The 16 January 1992, students riot in Tashkent caused by rise in bread prices and non-availability of bread at the fair price shops was put down with a heavy hand. Vice-president Mir Saidov was sacked and Salih was forced to flee abroad. The more radical oppositionist Pulatov who tried to stage a demonstration was physically assaulted on 28 May 1992.

Karimov changed the name of the Communist Party of Uzbekistan to People's Democratic Party (PDP) which legally inherited the property of the Communist Party of the Soviet Union in Uzbekistan. The party had a membership of 3,51,000 as against 3,000 members of *Erk*. In 1993 a new constitution was promulgated which gave the President power to exclude a member of parliament on ground of participation in unconstitutional acts directed at destabilising the socio-political situation. Censorship of press was strengthened and *Erk* paper was closed down. The paper of *Birlik* appeared irregularly form Moscow. Karimov encouraged businessmen and bankers to form a new opposition party *Watan Tarrakkiyati* (Progress of the Homeland) in May 1997 to replace the only legal opposition party *Erk*. This pocket opposition party is led by a poet named Azim.

New elections were held to the parliament (*Oliy Majlis*) in December 1994. The PDP founded by the President as a substitute for the Communist Party won 69 seats, polling 28 per cent of votes. The newly formed opposition party *Wattan Tarrakkiyati* polled 14.6 per cent votes. In 1995 Karimov initiated a policy of relaxing political control. Justice Minister of Uzbekistan travelled to the United States to meet Salih and Pulatov. Newspapers in Uzbekistan began to write about expansion of rights of public associations and unions. A new political party named as *Adalat* Social Democratic Party appeared under the leadership of Anvar Jorabayebv, editor of a government paper *Kholo Sozi*. Forty Seven deputies from the PDP joined the new party. A new mass organisation under the name of *Birlik* also began to function. In March 1995 the *Oliy Majlis* decided to hold a referendum to extend President Karimov's term until 2000. It was due to expire in 1997. Of the 99.6 percent of the voters who participated in this referendum 99 percent approved the extension of the President's term. A new political party, *Fidokorlar National Democratic Party*, appeared in December 1998 with the blessing of President Karimov. Its leader is Erkin Norbotayev.

Elections to the *Oliy Majlis* were held in December 2000. The PDP secured the largest representation with 48 seats. Non-party local councils' nominees however gained 110 seats. *The Fidokorlar National Democratic Party* was the second largest party with 34 seats. With *Watan Tarrakkiyati* Party, the *Odolat Social Democratic Party* and *Millie Tiklinish Democratic Party* also achieved representation in the *Oliy Majlis* winning, 20, 11, and 10 seats respectively. The O.S.C.E sent only a limited number of observers alleging that Uzbekistan had reneged on earlier commitments to make the elections free and fair.

President Karimov won an overwhelming victory in Presidential elections held on 9 January 2000, beginning his new five year term. He secured 91.9 percent of the total votes cast. His sole opponent, his personal friend and leader of the PDP Abdul Khafiz Jalalov polled only 4.2 percent of votes. In all 95 percent of the total electorate participated in the poll. Both the O.S.C.E and the United States government criticised the election as undemocratic owing to the fact that opposition parties had been barred from nominating candidates.

Abdul Khafiz Jalalov, Presidential candidate against Karimov, told the author whom he received in Tashkent in October 2000 that throughout his entire election campaign he never criticised President Karimov. When he was asked why he did not criticise his opponent, his reply was that his purpose behind contesting the election was to educate the people of Uzbekistan about the kind of society and polity for which they should aspire. He gave them his vision of social reconstruction based on spiritual values and asked them to vote for him if they were in agreement with his ideas.

By yet another referendum held on 27 January 2002 President Islam Karimov's term was extended to 2007 by amending the constitution of Uzbekistan to allow for 7-year presidential term. The referendum also approved the creation of a bicameral parliament. Rejecting the demand in the West for a quicker transition to democracy, Karimov stated, " At a certain stage of historical change you need a strong will and a certain figure... and you have to use some authoritarian measures at times". Karimov argued, " Authoritarian power would diminish with the rise of political consciousness". Some of the presidential powers such as the right to appoint certain senior officials have been transferred to the upper chamber which will also represent the country's territorial unit. Subsequently a draft law adopted by the Uzbek Parliament at its 27 April 2003 session gave the President of the Republic immunity from prosecution even after he had left the office.

The territory-wise largest Central Asian Republic—Kazakhstan—is often described as "ethnic tinder box". In 1989 the Kazakhs formed 39.7 per cent and Russians 36.8 per cent of the Republic's total population. However, in 1996, the Kazakhs formed 48.1 per cent and Russians were 34.1 per cent of the total population. In December 1991 Nazarbayev became President through an uncontested Presidential election. The opposition parties were not allowed to contest Nazarbayev made three unsuccessful attempts to form a national political party, namely, the Nevada-Semipalatinsk Movement led by Olzhas Suleimanov, the Socialist Party led by Anur Alimzhanov which inherited the CPSU property but failed to make a headway in the 1994 elections, and the Union of People's Unity for Kazakhstan later renamed People's Unity Party which he agreed to join in 1993. Nazarbayev launched two constitutions in 1993 and 1995. He dismissed the parliament and got elected a new one. A series of scandals rocked his administration leading to the fall of Tereshenko government in 1994. Nazarbayev's reputation was adversely affected by the controversy around his nephew's firm which acquired 10 percent of vouchers.

In March 1994 elections the parliamentary constituencies were gerrymandered to create a Kazakh majority. Faced with a no confidence vote in his Prime Minister Tereshenko, Nazarbayev nominated A. Kazhegeldin as the new Prime Minister. In a style reminiscent of President Yeltsin of Russia, he packed off his Parliament in March 1995 after a stand-off with the speaker A. Kekibayev. Through a referendum held in April 1995 Nazarbayev got his term extended upto the year 2000.

In September 1998 in his annual 'state of the nation' address to parliament, Nazarbayev outlined proposals for political reforms, including amendments to electoral procedures, enhanced powers for the legislature, and measures to ensure the independence of the judiciary. The President also affirmed his determination to eliminate corruption and tax evasion, together with a rationalization of government structures and increased accountability of public servants. Nazarbayev turned down the parliamentarians' demand for a Presidential election before expiry of his extended mandate in 2000. In his opinion an early poll would not be conducive to further economic development and democratic reforms. Nazarbayev's proposal for transfer of some of the Presidential powers to the Parliament was viewed by the latter as an attempt to mitigate the former's responsibility in the event of any future economic crisis. In October 1998 both Houses proposed constitutional reforms and passed by an overwhelming majority of votes an amendment preponing the Presidential election to January 1999. The minimum age for holding the office of President was raised from 35 to 45 years and the maximum age of 65 was abolished. The political parties henceforth required to receive at least 7 percent of the votes cast in order to secure representation (previously 10 percent). Despite reports that Nazarbayev accepted early election under threat of impeachment, it was believed by many that the parliament's opposition was orchestrated by Nazarbayev's supporters to facilitate his election with an extended mandate. An early poll left insufficient time for preparation by several potential candidates.

During November 1998 the Central Electoral Commission disqualified several oppostion figures from contesting the Presidential election in accordance with a Presidential decree of May. The most prominent of the disqualified opposition figures was former Prime Minister Kazhegeldin. He was disqualified on ground of a recent conviction for attending a meeting of unauthorized political organizations. Kazhegeldin formed a new political party, the Republican People's Party of Kazakhstan. In late1998, the Organization for Security and Cooperation in Europe (OSCE) voiced serious concern at the conduct of the election campaign in particular the exclusion of Kazhegeldin and other opposition candidates. Despite appeals for postponement Presidential election was held on 10 January 1999. Nazarbayev won receiving an overwhelming majority of votes—81.7 per cent of total votes cast. The candidates of the Communist Party of Kazakhstan, Serikbolsyn Abdildin came second polling 12.1 percent of the votes cast. On 20 January 1999, Nazarbayev was sworn in as President for a new term of office. A new government under Prime Minister Balgymbaev was formed two days later. Balgymbaev resigned in October 1999 on the eve of Parliamentary elections to return to his former position as chief of the Kazakh Oil. He was replaced by K. Tokayev, a former Foreign Minister. Kazhegeldin and his wife, who were charged for tax evasion in April 1999 were arrested at Moscow airport in early September 1999, following a visit to the United Kingdom. He was released following criticism of his detention by the OSCE but barred by Ministry of Justice from registering as a candidate for the Parliamentary elections.

In May 1999 nine opposition parties and social movements signed a memorandum urging the establishment of a 'single bloc' of democratic forces against authoritarianism and dictatorship in Kazakhstan. The document denounced the Presidential election as a 'farce' and criticized measures adopted by Nazarbayev in recent years to extend his Presidential powers. In June 1999 Nazarbayev requested Parliament extension of his legislative powers during the summer recess of the lower house in order to expedite passage of outstanding legislation before the parliamentary elections. He, however, withdrew this request in the face of opposition by the Speaker of the *Majlis* Marat Ospanov. Elections to the *Majlis* were held in October 1999. 65 candidates from nine political parties contested 10 seats allocated for the first time according to votes on the basis of party list system while about 500 candidates contested for the remaining 67 seats from single member constituencies. All the 10 party-list seats were filled in the first round of elections (the pro-President *Otan* Party winning 4 seats, and the Communist Party of Kazakhstan, the Agrarian Party of Kazakhstan and Civic Party of Kazakhstan each won 2 seats). Of the 67 directly contested seats, 20 were filled in the first round of elections and 'run-off' elections were held for 47 seats. Finally, *Otan* Party emerged as the largest party in the *Majlis* with 23 seats. The

Civic Party won 13 seats. Three other parties registered their token presence. The independent candidates numbered 34. The OSCE which monitored the elections cited numerous breaches of the election law. It may be recalled that the President of Kazakhstan was granted immunity from prosecution even after he had demitted the office long before such legislation was passed by the Uzbek Parliament in 2002. He was in fact a pioneer in this direction.

In the latest election to the lower house of Kazakh parliament (*Majlis*) held in October 2004 President Nazarbayev's party *Otan* (Fatherland) won seven out of the ten seats allocated on the basis of overall votes for a given party and 35 of the 67 single seat constituencies giving it 42 out of 77 seats in the lower house. The rest of the seats with a single exception went to the party called *Asar* led by President's daughter Dariga and to several other small partiess of President's loyalists. Only one seat in the 77-member parliament went to an opposition party *Ak Zohl.* Protesting against the alleged irregularities in elections the lone opposition member subsequently resigned from the membership of the lower house. The parliamentary election in Kazakhstan were criticised by the O.S.C.E observation mission for falling short of international standards. A spokesman of the U.S State Department also agreed with the criticism of serious shortcomings in voter lists, candidates' access to media and the tabulation of the results.

After attaining independence Kyrgyzstan under the leadership of Askar Akaev gained reputation as an "oasis of democracy" in the sprawling desert of authoritarianism in Central Asia. However, by 1995 this image began to fade. The leadership resorted to anti-democratic measures to beef up its eroding authority in the face of an economic crisis. During the summer of 1994 President Akaev suppressed two opposition-oriented newspapers and dissolved the Parliament several months before its terms. The February 1995 elections were marred by electoral fraud and corrupt practices. The results of the Parliamentary elections came as a big disappointment for both President Akaev and democratic opposition. Akaev was now forced to forge an alliance with the *Akimy*, the regional heads of administration in the six regions of the country.

This condominium of the President and the *Akimy* (regional administration heads) slowly started tilting in favour of the President. The Parliament refused to extend the term of the President by holding a referendum on it. Akaev accepted the challenge and won in the election for Presidency held in December 1995 against the Speaker M. Sherimkulov and former Communist Party Secretary A. Masaliev polling 71 percent of the votes cast. After the victory Akaev expanded the Presidential powers through a referendum. Thus Akaev through frequent use of the institution of referendum gradually converted the Kyrgyz political system from Parliamentary Democracy which the 1993 constitution conceived to Executive Presidential system. As the economic crisis caused by reforms and their faulty execution by a corrupt administration deepened, the leadership in the newly independent Republics where the democratic traditions were already either non-existent or weak on account of decades of single-party rule, started reneging on the process of democratisation unleashed in the later period of *Perestroika* and *Glasnost* and embodied in a nascent form in constitutions adopted after independence. Thus one finds the Central Asian Republics' Presidents ridiculing the Western model of democracy and extolling the indigenous institutions of *mohalla*, that is, neighbourhood committees, and councils of elders and religious divines. President Akaev of Kyrgyzstan cautioned against canonizing the principle of separation of powers advocated by Montesquieu and Locke. He also debunked the maxim that the parliamentary regime was the most democratic form of rule by pointing out to the degeneration of the Senate in Athens and the National Convention in the time of the French Revolution and quoting American President Thomas Jefferson about 'legislators' tyranny'[3] .

Like other Central Asian Republics in Kyrgyzstan parliamentary elections were also held on 20 February 2000, followed on 12 March 2000, by a run-off. On both the occasions the turnout-was not high, with 57.8 per cent of the electorate casting vote in the first round and 61.86 per cent in the second round; direct elections were held for 45 seats in the Legislative Assembly (*Ek Okuldor Jyiyny*) and 45 in the people's Assembly (*Myizam Chygaruu Jyiyny*) and another 15 seats in the Legislative Assembly were allocated on the basis of proportional representation. Most of the candidates running in single seat electoral districts failed to win 50 per cent of the votes required to be elected. Only the former leader of the Kyrgyz Soviet Communists, Turdakum Usubaliyev, and Kyrgyz President Askar Akaev's brother got through the first round of the elections.[4] Those who made it to the parliament represented the *El* (People) party the Communist Party, the *Ata-Mekum* (Fatherland Party, and the *Kairan El* party.[5] Observers were highly critical of the elections. As Mark Steven, head of an OSCE Observer Mission commented, "The recent parliamentary elections in Kyrgyzstan did not reflect the Kyrgyz authorities' commitment to the Organisation for Security and Cooperation in Europe." [6] Similarly in the Presidential election, which was held on 20 October 2000, the incumbent President Akaev secured 74.45 per cent of the votes. His main challenger Omurbek Tekebayev secured 13.85 per cent of votes.[7] Like in the case of parliamentary elections, the OSCE criticized the presidential elections and in a press release pointed out that "the Kyrgyz presidential elections fell short of the country's commitment to the OSCE". The report also pointed out that international standards of equal, free and fair election were not adhered to."[8] President Akaev who has by now been in power for the last 14 years has changed the constitution several times to his advantage, most recently in February 2003, when he won lifetime guarantee of immunity from prosecution. As a result of the February 2003 referendum the new constitution proposed by President Akaev was approved by 75 per cent of the votes polled. The referendum also approved the abolition of its bicameral parliament and favoured President Akaev completing his term due to expire in 2005. The voting in the referendum was criticised by the Kyrgyz Committee for Human Rights which stated that " ballot boxes were carried from door to door to boost the turnout total".

Turkmenistan is perhaps the least changed former Soviet Republic ruled by its powerful President Saparmurad Niyazov, the First Secretary of the Communist Party of Turkmenistan since 1985 who was elected unopposed as executive President of Turkmenistan for the first time on 27 October 1990 with 98.3 percent of the votes cast. The Communist Party of Turkmenistan changed its name to that of Democratic Party of Turkmenistan in December 1991 with Niyazov as its Chairman. Promotion of his personality cult by the President led to the resignation in August 1992 of Foreign Minister Abdy Kuliyev. The new constitution adopted in May 1992 further enhanced presidential authority making Niyazov head of Government besides his position of head of state. In June 1992 he was re-elected unopposed with 99.5 percent of the votes cast in a direct election. Through the creation of a People's Council (*Khalk Maslakhaty*) by 1992 constitution as the supreme representative body of popular power to be headed by the President, Niyazov further enhanced his authority when it conferred the rank of General on him at its first session held in December 1992.

The President's 'personality cult' has been further strengthened in the subsequent years with numerous institutions, streets, public buildings air and sea ports renamed Turkmenbashy (Head of the Turkmens) a new tribal mode of address favoured by President Niyazov. In November 1993 the Democratic Party of Turkmenistan proposed that Presidential election scheduled for 1997 be cancelled. The following month the *Majlis* (Parliament) voted extension of the term of Niyazov's office until 2002 on the ground that the Republic's political and economic stability depended on realization of Niyazov's 10 years of prosperity programme of reforms. The extension of Niyazov's Presidency was endorsed by 99.99 percent of the electorate in a referendum held on 15 January 1994. Recently he has been made President for life but he is reported to have announced that he would not continue beyond 5 years, i.e., 2007. Niyazov has completed his magnum opus *Ruhnamah* (the spiritual edict) which is a sort of second *Shariat*

Despite results of the referendum extending the President's term of office, opposition to Niyazov has grown both inside and outside Turkmenistan. Former Foreign Minister A. Kuliev is operating through his Turkmenistan Foundation from Moscow. In November 1994 two Turkmen opposition leaders in exile were arrested in Moscow for plotting to assassinate Niyazov but they were released following protest by Russian human rights groups. In June 1995 two other opposition members were arrested in Tashkent for plotting to overthrow Niyazov's rule. They were extradited to Turkemenistan and sentenced to12 and 15 years prison term by the Supreme Court. In July 1995 a protest rally took place in Ashgabat in which 1,000 demonstrators criticised Niyazov's leadership and continuing economic hardships. In August 1995 in response to this protest Niyazov sacked 10 of the Republic's 50 administrative leaders for their failure to meet the state order for wheat in their regions. At a meeting of the People's Council in October 1995 the President dismissed a number of senior Ministers by publicly drawing attention to their mistakes and lapses before the TV cameras. The Presidential axe recently fell on the longest surviving Deputy Premier and Foreign Minister, Boris Shikmuradov who after serving for a while as a special envoy of the President was dispatched to China as ambassador and sacked later. Shikmuradov was charged with the attempt to assassinate the President. He was sentenced to life imprisonment for trying to seize power through a coup. President Niyazov and siege power through coup. Niyazov's systematic purging of Ministers and regional administrators which has had several rounds acquired an alarming character when in September 1998 following an attempted military revolt the Minister of Defence was sacked. All this, however, did not prevent the growth of his personality cult. In December 1998 a giant ceremonial arc surmounted by a revolving gold-plated statue of the President was inaugurated in Ashgabat. Despite the President's promise that the new *Majlis* elections scheduled for 1999 would be held on a multi-party basis and after the elections greater powers would be vested in the *Majlis* and also in the People's Council, the Democratic Party of Turkmenistan was the only Party which put up candidates in the *Majlis* elections held in December 1999. According to official reports 99 percent of the electorate participated in these elections. The new *Majlis* extended the President's term indefinitely. With the endorsement by the *Majlis* President Niyazov announced that creation of opposition political parties was not possible before 2010 by which time the political consciousness of the Turkemen people would be fully formed. In March 2000, the leader of the unregistered popular front *Agzybirlik,* Nurberdy Nurmamedov was sentenced to five years imprisonment on charges of hooliganism when he protested against the constitution as undemocratic. In January 2000 President Niyazov dismissed several Ministers including three Deputy Premiers for alleged professional shortcomings.

However in February 2001, Niyazov announced in Parliament (*Khalk Maslakhaty*) that he would not like to continue beyond 2010 when the election for the next President would take place. This pronouncement of the Turkmen President has not been seen as a renewal of his commitment to democratisation. In fact, his declaration that election for the post of President due in 2002 would now take place in 2010 is tantamount to a life time presidency for Niyazov. Who knows he would not change his mind about not contesting the 2010 election any time before that year.

Tajikistan's case appears to be a peculiar one when it comes to appraisal of the democratic transformation process in this Republic. Generally speaking it also belongs to the category of hard authoritarianism like Uzbekistan and Turkmenistan. Only difference is that it is tempered with the power of the field commanders—the regional warlords. The rivalries between the field commanders—Yakub Salimov, Sohrab Kassimov, Biomotov and Khudaibardiev—which posed a serious threat to peace and stability in this republic has been skilfully exploited by President Emomali Rakhmonov who has also used the recession of the threat from the Tajik group of Afghan Mujahideen from across the frontier where they were for a long time locked in a grim fight with the Taliban. He has also used this situation in Afghanistan to contain the Islamic opposition in Tajikistan. The biggest feather in the cap of Rakhmonov is the conclusion of the General Agreement on Peace and National Accord in Tajikistan signed by him and Nuri, the leader of the United Tajik Opposition in Moscow in 1997 ending the five year old civil conflict.

In September 1994, 72 per cent of the voters endorsed constitutional amendments proposed by President Rakhmonov which included formation of a bicameral legislature, extension of Presidential term from 5 to 7 years and the legalization of religion-based political parties. 92 per cent of the voters participated in this referendum. The Islamic Renaissance Party of Tajikistan was renamed the Islamic

Rebirth Party of Tajikistan and was officially registered with the Ministry of Justice. In mid-October the United Tajik Opposition again withdrew from the National Reconciliation Commission alleging that the government had not honoured its assurances. The UTO sought a postponement of the impending presidential election as three of its candidates had been prevented from contesting the election on procedural grounds. Later, a ruling of the Supreme Court enabled the Minister of the Economy and IRP member, Davlat Usmonov, to contest the election for the office of the President. A split took place in the IRP in mid-October 1999 when the First Deputy Prime Minister and deputy leader of the UTO, Akbor Turojonzoda was expelled from the organization and its largest constituent Party, the IRP. Turojonzoda was critical of the demand for postponement of the Presidential poll.

The Presidential election took place on 6 November 1999. President Rakhmonov received 97 per cent of the votes cast and his rival Davlat Usmonov got just 2 per cent. 90 per cent of the electorate participated in voting. The UTO decided to return to the National Reconciliation Committee and participate in the Presidential election after the government released about 90 UTO fighters. The OSCE declined to send its observers alleging widespread malpractices. After taking his oath of office following his reelection as President, Rakhmonov formed a new government with a new Prime Minister Akil Akilov. Elections were held for both the chambers of the Tajik Parliament in February and March 2000. In the elections to the new Assembly of Representatives held in February 2000 President Rakhmonov's party PDPT won 64.5 per cent of total votes polled along with its allies, bagging 45 out of 63 seats. The Communist Party received around 20.6 per cent of the votes winning 13 seats. The Islamic Rebirth Party did not fare well. It received about 7.5 per cent votes gaining just two seats. In June 2003 fifty-six changes were incorporated in the constitution of Tajikistan through a referendum in which 96.39 per cent of the registered voters took part and 93.13 per cent of those who voted favoured the changes in the constitution. The most significant change related to the dropping of restriction on the number of terms the President may serve and the removal of guarantees for free health care and education. The Tajik President Rakhmonov can now theoretically remain in office until 2020. His current term is due to expire in 2006 and he will now be eligible to run for two additional seven-year terms.

From the above discussion of the unfolding political scenario in the Central Asian Republics since their independence it is evident that their transition from single-party authoritarian rule to a multi-party democracy has not made much headway. This chequered transition to democracy has often been attributed to the objective need for giving priority to stability. The fragile character of stability based on a personalised authoritarian rule has been exposed in Indonesia under the Suharto rule. The intense concentration of power by the existing ruling elite makes it impossible for new political leadership or ideas to emerge in a peaceful manner. By thwarting the development of institutions like free press, competing political parties and an independent judiciary, the present leaders of the Central Asian Republics have eliminated the possibilities of political change being effected without a convulsion. The unpredictability of succession only breeds instability. The unimpressive performance of opposition candidates in the Presidential election can not be solely explained in terms of election malpractices, rigging of polls, intimidation of voters or discriminatory electoral regulations. The presidential elections have underscored the absence of viable opposition parties or movements in the region.

The Central Asian Republics will be facing the problem of leadership succession during the first decade of the new millennium. In all likelihood the old guard, former communist elite, which has been in power continuously since mid or late eighties of the previous century is going to be replaced by a younger generation of nationalists who might be more sympathetically inclined towards the forces representing tradition and religion (radical Islam, not completely ruled out) atleast in the three republics—Uzbekistan, Tajikistan and perhaps Turkmenistan. This scenario might not be applicable to Kyrgyzstan and Kazakhstan on account of their predominantly nomadic cultural heritage and stronger presence of people of European stock. The changing situation in Afghanistan largely on account of resolute action by international community against radical Islam represented by the

Taliban cannot but tilt the balance in Central Asia in favour of moderate Islam influencing the succeeding generation of elite.

Two trends appear to be quite likely. The new elite expected to succeed the present day rulers in Central Asia will in all probability lean heavily on Islam as is evident from recent developments in Turkey, Algeria, post-Shah Iran and post-Suharto Indonesia. It is however going to be a long way in developing a civil society in Central Asia with democratic institutions. The new political elite in Central Asia will be somewhat similar to the former state and party nomenklatura with a highly circumscribed reformist potential. At least for a generation this elite is most likely to emerge from "big families" of Central Asia. In this respect one cannot but agree with the prognosis offered by Vitaly Khlyupin, a former official of President's Archives of Kazakhstan, now a consultant of the Russian State Duma.[9] The prevailing Central Asian political culture which is strongly conditioned by the Soviet period excludes the possibility of succession by a really democratic elite.

Several models of succession and leadership change are being discussed by specialists on political developments in the region. The Russian model of succession determined by the incumbent President in favour of a capable and dependable person from outside the family seems to be ruled out in view of the fact that President Nazarbayev, President Karimov and President Akaev have already devised an elaborate constitutional mechanism to guarantee their immunity from being prosecuted for acts of omission and commission not only for their term in office but even beyond when they are not in power by nominating themselves as life-long members of the Senate. The other two models under discussion are those of Azerbaijan and Georgia. The election of President Aliev's son Ilham Aliyev who became Speaker of the Parliament during his father's tenure in office succeeding him through a rigged presidential election, to which western democracies turned a blind eye is being discussed in connection with the likely succession of President Nazarbayev's daughter, Dariga, whose candidature has been zeroed in with the exclusion of her husband Rakhat Aliyev and nephew Kairat Saltybaldy form the contest. Dariga, who is the Chairperson of *Khabar* media group has started a movement called *Asar* which has been converted recently into a political party. This party contested the parliamentary election held in October this year. Dariga has already contested and won a seat in parliament, and as the observers believe, she would be appointed as Senate Chairperson who is the first-in line of succession under the Kazakh constitution, if the President were to resign, die or otherwise become incapable of carrying out his duties. Dariga has contradicted the speculation that she would run in 2006 presidential election by saying that "Nazarbayev's rivals can relax for next 10 years". It is believed that she would be contesting for the post of President in 2013 only. Her husband Rakhat has been sent to Austria as ambassador.[10]

In Uzbekistan, too, the Azeri model is being looked upon as easily applicable. Gulnora, the daughter of President Karimov is believed by many to be ready to takeover once her father decides to lay down office. Since there is no worthwhile opposition she need not even take the route to presidency through election as Member of Parliament and Speaker. But Gulnora is not popular with the different groups which form the mainstay of the Uzbek regime and her candidature might cause dissensions. The recent appointment of Mirzoyev former Governor of Samarkand and Jizzak region as the new Prime Minister in place of Sultanov has given rise to speculations about his being a likely successor, an indication of Russian model of succession.

President Akaev's term in office which expires next year in 2005 has also led to speculation about his successor. Akaev has said that he will not seek re-election. Observers are discussing the possible candidates whom Akaev might choose to succeed him. Some see the new pro-government coalition as an instrument for promoting such a figure. However, opposition figures have dismissed the new government bloc *Alga Kyrgyzstan* as an empty shell with no political weight. In this connection succession from the family of the President is also being discussed. Akaev's daughter, Bermet, and her mother Mairam Akaeva appear to have political ambitions. Bermet is a smart and intelligent person who is heading the Aga Khan Foundation in Kyrgyzstan. But her young age {30 plus} and the popular prejudice against woman heading the state are likely to prove a stumbling block in her way. A popular movement demanding resignation of Akaev has also raised its head. A demonstration organised by it resulted in police firing leaving 6 persons dead. The names of heads of security and law enforcement agency have also figured in the list of likely successors to President Akaev. Former Interior Minister Temirbek Akmataliyev and General Bolat Januzakov, a former Chairman of the National Security Service and others are being considered as potential presidential candidates in case of emergency and political instability.[11]

The problem of succession in Turkmenistan is considered by analysts to be the most difficult one. The change is most likely to emerge from within the incumbent elite, succession from the President's family is ruled out, as his son and wife are non-resident. In the opinion of some observers, Niyazov does not have a successor and any change is likely to be volatile and swift. Many experts have compared succession in Turkmenistan with Zaire and Haiti.[12]

It is too early to discuss succession in Tajikistan where the regime headed by Emomali Rakhmonov has just consolidated itself through reining in the various warlords and the Islamist opposition. Of late, President Rakhmonov has also started moving along the path of personalized authoritarianism. He is reported to have inducted some of his close relatives into key political offices. Like his Kyrgyz counterpart he too has skilfully manipulated the powerful groups and factions by doling out to them goodies from the large foreign aid received to run the country.

The Georgian model of succession stage-managed by the U.S through a Velvet Revolution cannot also be ruled out. The Open Society Foundation run by George Soros and the Aga Khan Foundation have been actively involved in imparting training for carrying out the Velvet Revolution. This pattern of political change has been successfully tried out in Yugoslavia and Georgia where popular movements have been organised through the NGOs in the name of fighting corruption of the political elite.

Before eventually facing the problem of ensuring a smooth succession the present leadership of the Central Asian Republics will be called upon to meet the threat posed to the stability (imparted by them through strong authoritarian rule) by their non-performance on the economic front. During the ten years of independence (*Ozodi*) the leaders have on the whole performed poorly. Living standards fell sharply as savings were devoured by run-away inflation in the first half of the 90s. There has been a gradual deterioration of the social welfare, health-care and education system. Disease and malnutrition have taken a heavy toll. Disparities between the rich and the poor sections of population along with corruption rampant at all levels of administration are further eroding the so-called stability. No doubt the economies of the Central Asian Republics did start somewhat looking up from 1995, but this improvement did not last long as the 1998 economic crisis in Russia had its adverse impact.

The Central Asian Republics have witnessed a decline in real terms of both the annual GDP and per capita GNP. In Kazakhstan the per capita GNP declined at the rate of 7.4 per cent per year in spite of population having decreased at an average rate of 0.5 per cent. The GDP in the Republic decreased in real terms at an average rate of 6.9 per cent in the1990-98 period. Real GDP declined by 8.2 per cent in 1995, but increased by 0.5 per cent in 1996 and by 1.7 per cent in 1997. It decreased by 1.9 per cent in 1998 before rising by 1.7 per cent in 1999[13]. The economy of Uzbekistan was not so badly affected by the collapse of the USSR in 1991 owing to the country's near self-sufficiency in energy resources and agricultural products. However a poor cotton harvest in 1996 resulted in weakening of monetary policy as the government sought to meet the debts incurred by cotton producers by printing more money leading to depreciation of the national currency and a rise in inflation.[14] The fall in the GDP with 1991 index of 100 as the base year in the case of Uzbekistan remained at about 83 in 1993 and 1997 as against 62 for Kazakhstan, 61 for Kyrgyzstan, 42 for Tajikistan and Turkmenistan in 1997.[15] In Turkmenistan during the period 1990-1997 per capita GNP declined in real terms at an average of 14.6 per cent annually while the GDP decreased by 9.6 per cent per year. The population increased at the rate of 3.4 per cent per year.[16] In Tajikistan the per capita GNP for the same period declined annually at the rate of 16.1

per cent, the population increased by an annual average of 1.8 per cent. The annual rate of decline in GDP was 16.4 per cent in real terms.[17] The figures for decline in GNP and GDP for the period 1990-1997 in the case of Kyrgyzstan were 9.7 per cent and 7.3 per cent respectively, while the population grew at the rate of 0.8 per cent per year.[18]

After independence GDP plummeted throughout the Central Asian Republics. Only in Uzbekistan and Turkmenistan it was able to recover its pre-independence level by the mid or late 1990s. According to a U.N.D.P study, in Kyrgyzstan the proportion of the poor people went up from a third on the eve of independence to over 55 per cent in 1999, dropping to just half in 2001.In Tajikistan, more than 80 per cent of the population fell below the official poverty line and 17 per cent lived on less than $ 1 a day. According to the World Bank the average wage in this Republic covers only one-third of the minimum needed to survive. One child in three is chronically malnourished.[19] In Kazakhstan the richest country in the region nearly one person in four lives below the poverty line. The situation has somewhat improved since 1996 when this figure was one in three. There are vast disparities not only between urban and rural areas but also among the regions. In Mangystau province of Kazakhstan bordering on the Caspian Sea 95 per cent of the rural population lives in poverty, whereas the figure for Astana was only 2 per cent. Tajikistan and Kyrgyzstan are saddled with debt and heavily dependent on foreign aid. The gas wealth of Turkmenistan has gone mostly for marble palaces of the President, grand mosques and public monuments leaving the population little better off than before. The economic development of the Central Asian Republics has been largely lopsided mainly confined to one sector alone. In Kazakhstan oil and gas contributed to over a quarter of the GDP as well as of government revenues in 2001 and over half of the foreign investment was in energy sector. In Tajikistan 70 percent of export revenue depend upon aluminum and cotton. The latter also makes up 27 percent of exports from Uzbekistan. In Kyrgyzstan production of gold from Kumtor mine makes up about 40 percent of the Republic's industrial production. Thus the Central Asian economies still have a long way to go and reducing poverty must be seen as vital to stability in the region. The only way out is to expand employment through small and medium-sized enterprises, which have failed to forge ahead on account of excessive bureaucratic controls and heavy taxation.[20]

A weak legal system and all-pervading corruption have acted as a disincentive for foreign investment. In the Kazakhgate scandal hefty payments are alleged to have been made into the Swiss bank accounts for the benefit of the top Kazakh politicians including the President.[21] Allegations of corruption and nepotism have appeared from time to time in the western press against the Presidents of Turkmenistan, Uzbekistan, Kyrgyzstan and Tajikistan as well. It is however difficult to vouch for the veracity of these allegations. But the disquieting aspect of the matter is the widespread circulation of such rumors among the people of the region which certainly bodes ill for its stability.

In an interview given on his birthday on 6 August 1997 to the newspaper *Yegemen Kazakhstan,* President Nazarbayev strongly denied the allegations aired by *Financial Times* (London), that he belongs to the 25 super rich persons in the world, followed by another British paper *Guardian* in 1998 placing him among 8 richest persons in the world which was also reported by Arab Information Agency in July 1998. Interestingly, the President of Kazakhstan admitted having three houses in Naples, London and on the Mediterranean coast in Turkey, the last one being a present from the Turkish construction company *OKAN Holding* as a token of its gratitude for multimillion contracts for building the new Kazakh capital in Astana. He, however, denied that these three villas abroad were luxurious by any standards, and also stated that it was difficult for him to remember about all the presents made to him from time to time on the occasions of festivals.

However, the performance of the Central Asian Republics in transition to a market economy need not be subjected to a harsh criticism. It should be remembered that the market though a necessary condition for transformation is not a sufficient one without a strong state. The Central Asian Republics being new states were expected to discharge their traditional functions namely providing public goods, basic social services and infrastructure; protect vulnerable people and the environment, establish the rule of law and order. They were themselves in transition from overall dominance over society and economy to fair and democratic redistribution of its function between the government and the market.[22] The step-by-step gradual state-led transition as practiced in Uzbekistan, Turkmenistan and Tajikistan has several merits. In the case of Tajikistan a devastating civil war also had an adverse impact on the economic progress of the republic.

The threat of Islamic fundamentalism in the Central Asian Republics has been keenly debated by specialists in the field. Some have argued that in view of 70 years of modernisation under Soviet rule, promotion of secular ideas and institutions by it, and the great advance in emancipation of women, near total literacy, lack of knowledge of the Arabic language even among the Central Asian clergy, and the weak hold of Islam over the nomadic culture of the Kazakhs and Kyrgyzs, there are not much prospects of emergence of religions extremist forces in the Central Asian society. However, it cannot be denied that the decay and disappearance of Soviet ideology has left a vacuum in the belief and value systems. Much as Christianity is spreading in Russia, so can Islam be expected to acquire deeper roots among the masses in the Central Asian Republics. The Islamic revival in this region has thus gained a wide sweep involving millions of peoples. The Islamic revival is of course not Islamic fundamentalism, but it has far-reaching implications in terms of Islamization of public life. Under conditions of social tensions caused by problems of transition to a free-market economy and democracy, there persists a danger of easy conversion of 'folk Islam' into 'political Islam', and through the exploitation of the latter by international vested interests and internal opposition, into 'fundamentalist Islam'. The Islamist fundamentalist forces are striving to come to power in Central Asia through coercion and outside armed intervention by the Taliban in Afghanistan resulting in civil strife and turbulence in Tajikistan, Uzbekistan and the southern part of Kyrgyzstan.

The success of the on-going unified international action against the fundamentalist forces in Afghanistan is bound to have a salutary effect on the neighbouring Central Asian Republics. The rising threat of religious extremism from the South to the security of these republics has been obviously acting as a big impediment in the democratization of these republics. As this threat starts receding an atmosphere more conducive to the development of democratic institution is likely to be created. The pacification of the strife-torn Afghanistan and the growing unity displayed by the great-powers in their struggle against the dark forces of medievalism is expected to help integrate the economy of the land locked Central Asian Republics into the global economy by providing them access to the sea and international market. But realization of this hope for the better economic prospects for the Central Asian Republics will eventually depend on the willingness of the great powers, particularly the United States, to bury once and for all their power rivalries, thus preventing the recurrence of a "Great Game" in the new millennium. However, much will depend on the U.S. withdrawal from the military bases it has recently set up in Uzbekistan, Tajikistan and Pakistan after solving the Afghan tangle. The new developments in and around Central Asia in the wake of 9/11 incident in 2001, leading to the military presence of the U.S. in the region will most likely have an impact on the leadership succession in the Central Asian Republics. There are two viewpoints on this matter. According to some analysts this would strengthen the stability of the present regimes in Central Asia while some are of the opinion that American military presence would only aggravate social tensions which are likely to be exploited by regional terrorist and radical Islamist groups like the Islamic Movement of Uzbekistan and the *Hizbut Tahrir al Islami* (HTI) as well as the suppressed political parties.

India's economic and security interests require that the Central Asian states consolidate their newly attained independence without interference from outside powers in the name of religion or ethnicity and develop balanced friendly relations with their neighbours both in the north and the south, including India and Pakistan as well as with all the major and great powers in Europe, America and the Pacific on equal and mutually advantageous basis. It is in India's interest that the Central Asian states grow into stable secular democracies. The Central Asian states' efforts to forge a balanced relationship with their neighbours in the north and the south by seeking to develop economic cooperation with Islamic neighbours in the south and west within the framework of the E.C.O; with Russia in the north through the C.I.S and China in the east through the Shanghai Cooperation Organisation. While trying to consolidate the ties at the Central Asian regional level by establishing the Central Asian community and developing economic relations with the non-Muslim Western and East Asian powers as a countervailing factor have met with understanding in India's circle of foreign policy elite.

The growing international competition for influence in Central Asia causes a serious security concern for the region in general and for India in particular. New Delhi cannot remain an indifferent onlooker winking at the blatant attempts by outside powers to change the geopolitical balance in Central Asia which is fraught with grave consequences for the strategic balance in South and West Asia. Even though India's frontier are not contiguous with Central Asia, its close proximity, long standing historical, cultural and economic ties have earmarked Central Asia as an area of high priority for the country's foreign policy.

NOTES

1. Ali Banuazizi and Myron Weiner, (eds.), *The New Geopolitics of Central Asia and its Borderlands* I.B.Tauris, London/New York, 1994, p. 45.
2. *Ibid.*, 15.
3. Askar Akaev, *Kyrgyzstan on the way to Progress and Democracy*, reproduced by Narendra Kumar in his book *President Akaev of Kyrgyzstan: A Political Biography* New Delhi 1998, pp. 40-41.
4. *SWB*/SU/3772/G/1, 24 February 2000.
5. Rafis Abazov, "Democracy in Kyrgyzstan: In the Context of Recent Elections", *Contemporary Central Asia*, Vol. 4, No. 1 & 2, 2000. p. 52.
6. *SWB*/SU/3789, G/1, 15 March 2000.
7. *SWB*/SU/3986/4/1, 1 November 2000.
8. *Ibid.*, p. G/2.
9. Alexei Malashenko, "Central Asia: Liberals and Conservatives", *Nezavisimiya Gazeta*, Supplement, No. 5, May, 1999, p. 3.

10. Aldar Kusainov, "Wheels set in motion for Dynastic transition in Kazakhstan", 16/09/2003, http:www.eurasianet.org/departments/insight/articles/leav0916103-pr.shtml
11. Rafis Abazov, "Kyrgyzstan: The Political Succession Game", *Central Asia and Caucasus Analyst,* 24 September 2003, pp. 5-6.
12. Michael Ochs, " Niyazov's Turkmenistan: A Sultanistic Regime?", http://www.geocities.com/WestHollywood/Park/6443/Turkmrnistan/cummings.pdf.
13. *The Europa Year Book–2000,* 41st edition, London, p. 2090.
14. *Ibid.*, p. 3976.
15. *UNDP, Central Asia 2010. Prospect for Human Development,* p. 14.
16. *The Europa Year Book–2000, op cit.*, p. 3654.
17. *Ibid.*, p. 3509.
18. *Ibid.*, p. 2193.
19. "A Survey of Central Asia" *The Economist,*26 July 2003, p. 11.
20. *Ibid.*
21. *Ibid.*, p.13
22. Bakhtior Islamov, "State-led Transformation and Economic Growth in Central Asia; From Plan to Industrial Policy", *Hitosuboshi Journal of Economics,* December, 1998, p. 106.

2

Neutral Turkmenistan

Ten Years of Independence

Ondjik Musayev

October 27, 2001 has been celebrated as the 10th anniversary of neutral Turkmenistan. Turkmen people have full confidence in the country's leader Saparmurat Turkmenbashy, who is considered as the creator of our independence. His energy, consistency, decisiveness and clear political understanding, which are bestowed on him by Allah the Great, helped him to bring independence peacefully without any kind of social tremors, victimization and peoples' sufferings in Turkmenistan. It is worth mentioning that since the second half of the 1980s when the gradual process of USSR's collapse as a totalitarian regime was taking place, the head of Turkmenistan Saparmurat Atayevich Niyazov managed to get support from the Union organs for the legal economic interests of the Republic and began to carry out the process of national revival, thereby returning to the progressive tradition of Turkmen people.

In the historic process of Turkmenistan's independence Saparmurat Turkmenbashy's theoretical talent of being a great strategist and wise tactful person became evident. At the beginning of October 1991, Turkmen President S.A. Niyazov took the initiative of passing a resolution on the domestic and foreign affairs of the country. In this document the necessity of political stability in the country as an important means of successful economic development and settlement of urgent social problems was stressed. The significance of the political stability was highly appreciated and the strengthening of a young sovereign state began to take place without any shocks or chaos. Only political stability in all the stages of formation of independent Turkmenistan allowed us to avoid negative impact of the transitional period which brought so much sufferings to peoples of the other post-Soviet states.

On 26 October 1991, a referendum on the legal establishment of Turkmenistan as an independent state took place and the next day on 27 October 1991 Turkmenistan was solemnly declared as an independent state and became subject to international law. This day has been the turning moment in the long history of the Turkmen people. Every year we celebrate it as Independence Day. After gaining independence the main task to be accomplished was to carry out democratic reform in the society and building up a new democratic, secular, legal type of State. That is why immediately the process of reforming the political system of the society began. First of all, on 18 May 1992, a new Constitution of independent Tukrmenistan as the main Law was adopted which was the product of direct guidance and participation of President S.A. Niyazov. In this significant document, a constitutional structure was designed which included the main rights and duties of a citizen, the system of authority and management, and also the voting system in the country.

The Constitution stipulates that the state administration in Turkmenistan is to be carried out under the Presidential form of Government. President as the highest symbol of the state administration has thus become the guarantee who takes care of the people in this complex transitional period and consolidation of the society in accordance with the constitutional rights, given to him as well as interaction of administrative branches. All the layers of the society support the head of the State, whom they respect and trust very much. Elections of the first President of Independent

Turkmenistan in accordance with the new Constitution of the country took place on 21 June 1992. Saparmurat Atayevich Niyazov was unanimously elected as the President of Turkmenistan.

Great authority of the State head can be seen clearly by the fact that the session of the *Madjlis* of Turkmenistan, held on 1 October 1993, fulfilling the will of the people who acknowledged S. Niyazov as their leader and head, unanimously gave the President of the country a respected name of Saparmurat Turkmenbashy. Further, a national referendum was held on 15 January 1994 by which Presidential rights of Saparmurat Turkmenbashy were extended to one more term without holding an election. In December 1999, at the IX Joint Session of the Council of Elders, the participants on behalf of the whole nation strongly urged to take a decision of giving life-time Presidency to S. Niyazov. This national forum supported the proposal and authorised *Madjlis* to adopt the law. On the memorable day of December 28, 1999, *Madjlis* of Turkmenistan adopted a historic Constitution Law which provided the first President of Turkmenistan Saparmurat Atayevich Niyazov with exceptional right to head the State for his life-time. The people of Turkmenistan accepted this constitutional law "On exceptional rights of the first President of Turkmenistan Saparmurat Turkmenbashy" with warm approval.

In full accordance with the Constitution, various governmental bodies consisting of People's representatives have been formed and are functioning in Turkmenistan. The highest authoritative body of the people is *Halk Maslahati* (People's Council) of Turkmenistan. Unlike in most parts of the world, such kind of people's authority has a wide range of rights and it includes both the people's representatives as well as deputies of the *Madjlis* of Turkmenistan. Besides, in accordance with the main law of Turkmenistan the executive bodies are also functioning which include Cabinet Ministers headed by the President. There are also *Hakims* of cities and Etraps who are the representatives of the State head at local levels. On the basis of the political system of neutral Turkmenistan, a Turkmen model of democracy was outlined by President Saparmurt Turkmenbashy. It presupposes gradual introduction of democratic norms and principles as and when necessary objective conditions arise.

In order to keep the independent and sovereign status of Turkmenistan intact, the process of democratization of society is being deepened and national legal system is being perfected. Besides, more effective measures to observe human rights are also taken. One of the significant steps in this direction was the opening of Turkmen National Institute of Democracy and Human Rights by the President of Turkmenistan in 1996. Apart from political changes it was also necessary to solve another complicated task, i.e., implementation of economic reforms or transition to market economy. Typical feature of Saparmurat Turkmenbashy's policy in this sphere is gradual transition to market economy without making a direct jump, thereby refusing the notorious method of 'shock therapy'. In fact, his policy aims at providing a system of measures oriented towards effective social care of population. He thinks that only such methods of reforms in the economy can benefit the people as a whole and do not harm their living condition.

In the process of implementing programs for the growth of economy, particularly concerning the rational use of rich natural resources, the Turkmen leader looks ahead by taking into account the perspective and consequences of the decisions made. This signifies his wide-range thinking ability that can be seen through big projects like oil and gas pipelines, railway lines and automobile highways. Our country has never seen such a wide-range transport infrastructure as in the epoch of Saparmurat Turkmenbashy. Some pipelines such as Korpedje–Kurtkuyi, railway lines like Tedjen–Serahs–Meshhed and Turkmenabat–Atamurat are already functioning, while intensive construction of the highways connecting Ashgabat–Karakum–Dashoguz, Ashgabat–Turkmenbashy and Ashgabat–Mary–Turkmenabat are being taken up now. There are other prospective projects as well. It is worth remembering that the Garagum lake construction is intended to develop the region by solving issues like watering the desert land and it's amelioration. Much work is being done in order to give lands on lease and also for private use to the farmers as well as privatisation of industrial and trade enterprises. All these changes have paved the way for achieving the target set for national economy. In this respect much has been achieved during the last 10 years of independence. It is worth mentioning that the reconstruction of Turkmenbashy and Seydi Refineries has contributed much to the national economy. Besides, setting up of several textile enterprises in all the Velayats of the country enabled us to process a great part of Turkmen cotton and produce ready-made cotton products of world standards and also export them with high quality fabric samples. By the 10th anniversary of the independence of Turkmenistan many other textile and industrial enterprises have also been put into operation. Turkmen farmers have grown and produced more than 2 million tons of golden wheat thereby providing the country with food security, besides producing the same amount of record cotton – 2 million tons of white gold.

Progress in Turkmenistan economy has been tremendous. It is worth mentioning that in the year 2000, Turkmenistan reached the level of highest growth of gross output in the world – 17.6 per cent. This high rate of growth has been observed in 2001 too. In the first 6 months, the gross output growth has been recorded as 15 per cent, while as the industrial growth touched 24 per cent. Moreover, in some branches of economy like oil and gas sector the index reached upto 34 per cent.

Remarkable achievements during the years that followed independence of Turkmenistan can also be seen in the course of national revival conducted by Saparmurat Turkmenbashy the Great, particularly in spiritual development and perfection of moral attention to our cultural legacy inherited from our forefathers. Much has been done towards the revival of Turkmen tradition, religion, and culture. It began with functioning of the mother tongue as an official and state language as well as creation of a new alphabet in order to objectively study the history of the ancient Turkmen people.

The tenth anniversary of independence was marked with an auspicious occasion when on 18 February 2001 at the joint session of the State Council of Elders (*Halk Maslahati* of Turkmenistan and All National Movement *Galkinish*), Saparmurat Turkmenbashy acquainted its participants with the first version of his genius creation – sacred *Ruhnama*, which is going to become the textbook of Turkmens. *Ruhnama* is a book on unity which can become such a force that could unite the Turkmen nation in time and space. In the creative history of Turkmens precious sayings, scattered as aphorisms and proverbs, have been widely used, but they haven't yet been able to unify the nation as a whole. *Ruhnama* should cover this gap. Turkmen people consider sacred *Ruhnama* as the spiritual light of the nation. In the 21st century it will serve to light up the way of the Turkmen people towards spiritual-moral perfection as well as provide an impetus to strengthening of great independence and prosperity of our beloved motherland – the county of Saparmurat Turkmenbashy.

The policy of positive neutrality elaborated and carried out by Saparmurat Turkmenbashy further promotes strengthening of independence and growth of international status of Turkmenistan. It is necessary to stress that Turkmen leaders are realising this policy firmly. In a historic appeal to the people of Turkmenistan made during the session of *Halk Maslahati* on 14 December 1992, Saparmurat Turkmenbashy underlined four main bases of our government including the open door policy, positive neutrality and good neighbourly relations.

Thorough analysis of the reasons of the Turkmen state to choose the policy of positive neutrality is given in Asparmurat Turkmenbashy's speech in March 1995 at the meeting of the Member States of Economic Cooperation Organisation in Islamabad. During his speech he made an appeal for international recognition of Turkmenistan as a neutral state and peace-loving center in the region. This appeal was supported not only by the leaders of ECO member countries but also by other international organisations such as ASEAN and the Non-alignment Movement. Of great significance was another speech of Saparmurat Turkmenbashy made in the United Nation General Assembly session on 23 October 1995 in which he elaborated the essence of positive neutrality policy of Turkmenistan and stressed that it was being realised in practice.

Theoretical and organisational activities of the Head of the Turkmen government and the truthfulness of his approach brought its results. For the first time in the 50 years history of the United Nations, the issue of positive neutrality of independent Turkmenistan was considered in the session of the General Assembly. On 12

December 1995, 185 member countries of this world community unanimously voted for the resolution in which the General Assembly acknowledged and supported the positive neutrality status of Turkmenistan. This neutrality status allows Turkmenistan to more actively carry out its peaceful policy in every possible way to promote peace and stability in the region. It is widely known that the country has played an important role in the process of solving internal conflict in Tajikistan as well as in holding talks between opposing sides in Afghanistan. Turkmenistan with its beautiful capital Ashgabat has really become an oasis of peace and stability in the Asian continent.

The neutrality status along with constructive foreign policy of Saparmurat Turkmenbashy has created favourable conditions to strengthen equality and mutually beneficial cooperation with foreign countries. Such constructive and peaceful policy of independent and neutral Turkmenistan naturally enhances the international status of our motherland and its leader Saparmurat Turkmenbashy. Turkmen people always rally around the creator of the independence of our motherland, Saparmurat Turkmenbashy. This highest authority of his being leader of our nation is the result of his wise and long perspective policy, his close and organic connection with the people and his fatherly care about the welfare and prosperity of the country.

3

Kyrgyzstan's Struggle for Democracy and Stability

RAFIS ABAZOV

When in December 2001 President Akayev of Kyrgyzstan joined the leaders of Central Asian republics and other former Soviet republics in Moscow to celebrate 10th anniversary of the dissolution of the USSR and formation of the Commonwealth of Independent States (CIS), he talked about continuity of strong political and economic relations within the grouping. The talks, topics and environment in this gathering did not change significantly. However, back home Kyrgyzstan had been very different. During 10 years of independence, the republic has undergone significant political, economic, and social changes. If in 1991 the political landscape was still dominated by single ruling party, the Communist Party of Kyrgyzstan, in 2001 there were more than 32 active political parties and hundreds of NGOs. If in 1991 almost all people were employed in the State-controlled enterprises and collective farms, in 2001 approximately 70 per cent of people were employed in private sector, in their businesses or worked on their family owned farms. And most importantly, if in 1991 police on the streets and military in the barracks were largely controlled from Moscow, in 2001 on the outskirts of Bishkek the US personnel were hastily building a first-ever US military base and the US military was talking about cooperation with and assistance to the independent Kyrgyz defence forces.

This article is an attempt to examine the political changes, economic reforms and nationality policy as well as foreign policy of Kyrgyzstan during the first decade after independence in 1991 and it focusses on the impact of these transformations on consolidation of the Kyrgyz national identity and institutions.

FOREIGN AFFAIRS: DEALING WITH FORCES OF GLOBALISATION

Kyrgyzstan achieved its independence in a very difficult time. The regional security was undermined by internal and cross border ethnic conflicts, disputes over the delimitations of national boundaries and militant threats, illicit drugs and terrorism spill over from troublesome Afghanistan. On top of it, the national economy was on the wake of collapse due to sudden disruption of the Soviet subsidies and breakdown of trade ties with the former Soviet Republics. Therefore Kyrgyzstani policy maker, turned to international community for assistance, support and bilateral and multilateral cooperation.

Throughout the 1990s in its international relations, Kyrgyzstan focussed on what President Askar Akayev once described as "Equitable partnership, friendship and cooperation with all Great Silk Road countries are the most important components of [Kyrgyzstan's foreign policy] principle."[1] Initially, Kyrgyzstani diplomacy focused on three priorities. One was maintaining cooperation, coordination and sustainable multilateral relations with the former Soviet republics, especially with neighbouring countries — Kazakhstan, Uzbekistan and Tajikistan. The other was concerning security issues through bilateral and multilateral cooperation. The third was establishing international political and economic relations with the so-called far-abroad countries (outside the CIS), including the USA, countries of western Europe, Japan and Turkey.

In order to proceed peacefully in resolving disagreements over the USSR's legacy, Kyrgyzstan joined the Commonwealth of

Independent States (CIS) in December 1991. From the beginning the CIS has been a temporary compromise among the former Soviet republics, than an integration mechanism. However, it allowed to resolve peacefully (in sharp contrast to Yugoslavia) most sensitive and disputable issues, as the Alma-Ata Declaration, the CIS's binding document, highlighted five major principles: 'assuring the territorial integrity and inviolability of the national boundaries; creation of a system of political security; creation of a military system of security, and last but not least, stabilisation of inter-ethnic relations within the former USSR'.[2] The Commonwealth has become largely a ceremonial institution due to the intense disagreements among Moscow's policy makers over Russia's attitudes towards the CIS and absence of resources to re-assert Russian influence in the region. The CIS neither fulfilled the hopes of those members of the Central Asian elites who favoured a closer economic integration, nor confirmed the apprehensions of those who feared resurgence of the Muscovite dominance and the Russian imperial pressure. By 2001, the CIS sank from supra-regional integrational organisation into a club of several members who discussed issues of political and economic development on the territory of the former USSR but who had no desire to be bound by any agreements.

Kyrgyzstan was among the founding members of the Central Asian Union (CAU), which was created in 1990 as a consultative body for the CARs' leaders. The official declarations stated that this forum was created with the general objective to enhance a greater inter-republic cooperation and integration. This included an idea of developing cultural contacts among those people, who shared cultural, historical and linguistic traditions, and promoting economic cooperation and financial self-reliance (khozras'chet). The unspoken agenda was a desire to coordinate Central Asian political stand toward increasingly destabilising Kremlin's reforms and to increase bargaining position for greater autonomy in the internal affairs and greater share of the federal subsidies. As the USSR was dissolved, the CAU was on the brink of collapse, mainly due to the CARs differences in their approach to integration and to course of domestic political and economic changes. Only in 1994 Kazakhstan, Uzbekistan and

Kyrgyzstan changed their approach to multilateral regional cooperation and formalised some common principles of the integration, and in April 1994 they re-launched the CAU as the Central Asian Economic Union (CAEU) (Tajikistan joined in 1998). The CAEU helped in some degree to promote coordination between the members in resolving trade, transportation and border issues, and proposed to establish a regional bank for development and several regional coordination commissions at the ministerial level. But by 2001 it was reduced to an informal meeting point undermined by personal rivalries and dislikes and differences in policy approaches. During the January 2001 meeting of heads of states, President Karimov weighted his bold criticism of the CAEU declaring that very few out of hundreds of documents and treaties are enforced and actually worked. He suggested the re-organisation the CAEU into the Central Asian Economic Forum (CAEF). The Forum would replace the CAEU serving as a summit of the Central Asian leaders, businessmen and intellectuals, and not as a regional cooperation institution. The idea of the Forum effectively buried the idea of political-economic integration between the Central Asian republics in near future.

In another development, Kyrgyzstani leaders were attracted by the so-called "Turkey's secular model of development."[3] In 1992 Kyrgyzstan joined a summit of Turkic nations in Istambul and agreed to extend economic and cultural relations and consider closer political cooperation. This opened the doors for growing trade, investments and travel, and for cooperation in education and cultural issues between the two countries. In 1997 Kyrgyzstan and Turkey signed the 'eternal friendship agreement' and in 1999 they also signed a joint statement "Kyrgyzstan and Turkey together into the 21st century".

Yet, in the security area, Kyrgyzstan largely relied on Russian support. The republic joined the CIS Security Treaty (Tashkent Treaty) in 1992 and signed several bilateral agreements on military cooperation; and Russian border guards patrolled Kyrgyzstan's borders with China until 1998. In an effort to resolve border disputes, in 1996 Kyrgyzstan joined the 'Shanghai Five' organization (it includes

China, Kazakhstan, Kyrgyzstan, Russia, Tajikistan and, since 2001, Uzbekistan). Several years of intensive consultations culminated in a 'Shanghai Five' summit in Bishkek in August 1999. The most important outcome of this summit was signing an agreement between China, Kazakhstan and Kyrgyzstan that Akayev called "a final point in difficult border issues" in delimiting the borders between the three countries. The heads of the states also signed 12-point Bishkek Declaration pledging demilitarisation of borders between the states, confirmed existing agreements on border issues, mutual respect of the territorial integrity and sovereignty, and cooperation against terrorism, illegal drug and arms trafficking, national separatism and religious extremism. Security issues have also been high in the agenda since the outbreak of the Civil War in the neighbouring Tajikistan in 1992-1997 and the spread of the conflict to the territory of Kyrgyzstan in 1999. Radical militants from Tajikistan entered the Kyrgyzstani territory in 1999 and again in 2000, forcing Kyrgyzstan's government to turn to its neighbours for help in order to create the regional security institutions. In June 2001 President Akayev joined the representatives 'Shanghai Five' meeting in Shanghai, as the grouping was relaunched into 'Shanghai Cooperation Organisation', declaring its primary focus on joint efforts against international terrorism, drugs and arms trafficking, and further political and military cooperation.

In economic area, during the 1990s Kyrgyzstan put its special attention to increase and diversify of foreign trade and attract foreign (primarily Western) investors. Kyrgyzstan maintained slow but steady growth of its export from 288.6 million US$ in 1992 to 531.1 million US$ in 1996, and to 631 million in 1997, although it slid to 505 million in 2000. Kyrgyzstan managed to develop its international trade and economic relations with countries outside the former Soviet Union. The international trade turnover with countries outside the CIS grew from the virtual zero to almost 55 per cent. Kyrgyzstan has limited natural resources (unlike Kazakhstan with its oil and Turkmenistan with its gas) and their development needs large capital investments. In 1992-1997 Kyrgyzstan managed to attract estimated US$ 450 millions, Canada being the largest foreign investor (45%

of total investments), and Turkey being the second largest investor (20%), followed by USA (12%) and China (10%).

The international economic relations, especially at regional level, were often rocked by conflicts and disagreements. Despite joining the CAEU and maintaining positive relations with the CIS members, Kyrgyzstan's trade was adversely affected in 1998 and 1999 due to 'custom war' erupted on its borders with Kazakhstan and Uzbekistan when high tariffs were imposed by Kazakhstan for the Kyrgyzstani goods. The 'custom war' originated from the disagreement over taxation and other policies and Kazakhstan's anger over unilateral Bishkek's negotiations on the WTO entry in 1998. In an attempt to calm down the tensions, in October 2000 Kyrgyzstan joined the Eurasian Economic Community (EEC), which consisted of the CIS Customs Union members (Belarus, Kazakhstan, Kyrgyzstan, Russia and Tajikistan). The EEC declared that it aimed to simplify the customs border control between the member states, unify taxation, and enact other legislation to increase economic cooperation between member states. However, in 2001 the EEC was overshadowed by the Shanghai Cooperation Organisation.

It is common place to talk about Russia's overwhelming predominance over Central Asian republics, especially over Kyrgyzstan's foreign policies. However, the truth is that geographical distance, disagreements within the Russian policy making elite and economic and political mess within the Russian Federation left plenty of space for manoeuvring and implementing foreign policy in Kyrgyzstan like in other Central Asian republics. This is evident in Kyrgyzstan's growing relations with the Western world.

Kyrgyzstan's relations with western countries took an uneasy path in the 1990s. Initially, Akayev's efforts to bring radical political and economic changes into the Republic received substantial support from the US and other developed countries as well as from international funding organisations. Between 1991 and 1997 Kyrgyzstan received sizeable international assistance (one of the highest in the CIS in per capita term) and was dubbed as a 'Central Asian Island of Democracy'. However, since 1998 Akayev's administration has been under increasing pressure and criticism from the Western governments and international organisations over its handling of the opposition and elections. Controversies over these issues contributed to considerable cooling off in relations between Kyrgyzstan and the West.

However, the September 11 terrorist attacks on New York became a turning point for the relations between the Bush administration and the Kyrgyzstani government. Akayev immediately expressed his condolences to American people and his full support for the US actions against "international terrorism and extremism"[4] and agreed to offer Kyrgyzstan's airspace for the American actions in Afghanistan.[5] The United States' government instantly signalled that it valued Kyrgyzstan's support in its struggle against international terrorism and that it would extend its assistance to Kyrgyzstan. There was a report that a group of US military experts visited Kyrgyzstan, Tajikistan and Uzbekistan in November 2001 in order to assess the possible use of the former Soviet air bases to station the US troops. In December 2001 after secret negotiations between Kyrgyzstan and the US government the military leaders finally confirmed that the US would establish a permanent military base near Bishkek international airport.

EXPERIMENTING WITH DEMOCRACY

During the last decade, much of the efforts in political arena were focussed on transforming the Soviet one-party political system into a pluralistic and democratic society. President Akayev-led government declared that it had chosen the Western liberal democracy as a 'model', attempting to build Western style political institutions and civil society in this small largely rural country with strong traditions of the totalitarian state and deep rooted patronage and tribal and communal differences.

Among the first steps of the newly independent Kyrgyzstan was the introduction of political reforms. This inevitably included dismantling the Soviet-style one party political system, building institutions of a sovereign State, preparing a new constitution and building legitimacy of the Jogorku Kenesh and the presidential power and in Gregory Gleason words "seeking to develop European-style democratic institutions".[6] On the top of it there was a need to establish political equilibrium among various political parties and nationalist movements in order to avoid a civil war similar to that of Tajikistan and to build national consensus over the direction of the future development of the Republic.

Already in 1990 the Kyrgyzstani leadership was exposed to what E. Huskey called "serious rift in the republic" and "fault lines emerged within the elite itself".[7] The government was forced to remove an article in the Constitution, which formulated the dominant position of the Communist Party of Kyrgyzstan (CPK). Instead, it introduced the Law on Public Organisations. In October 1990, following the constitutional changes, the *Jogorku Kenesh,* the Parliament, introduced the post of the President of the Republic. The President was to be initially elected by the parliamentarians. The hopes of Apsamat Masaliyev, the CPK candidate, to become the first elected President were not realised as he could not obtain the decisive majority. After several rounds of elections a political compromise was found and Dr. Askar Akayev, the former head of the Kyrgyzstan's Academy of Sciences, was elected the first President. Akayev was elected with the support from the Democratic Movement of Kyrgyzstan (DMK). However, he decided not to join this movement, or any other political party. The President presented himself as a technocrat and strong leader, who had no ideological commitments to the CPK and had a clear idea of where to lead his country in the time of the economic turmoil, emphasising the establishment of a democratic, pluralistic society and of a liberal democratic multi-party political system.

The first tough test of the President's credentials happened in August 1991, when an attempt of the anti-Gorbachev military putsch in Moscow provoked a dramatic confrontation between the Kyrgyz President and democratic parties on the one hand and the Communist Party of Kyrgyzstan (CPK) on the other hand. The CPK, which supported the anti-democratic forces, was banned and its property was confiscated. And Kyrgyzstan declared its independence from the USSR. The CPK re-emerged in 1993 under a new moderate leadership of B. Amanbayev. A number of political parties and independent mass media emerged on the eve during the first years of independence as Kyrgyzstan established one of the most liberal political environments in the Central Asian region. This earned the title of the 'Island of Democracy' for the Republic and millions of dollars of international assistance from Western donors and international organisations.

On 5 May 1993 Kyrgyzstan adopted its first post-Soviet Constitution that provided a legislative framework for further democratic transition. New Kyrgyzstan's Constitution embraced the constitutional ideas of the modern western liberal democracies as the Constitution strengthened the division of powers between the executive, legislature and judiciary. Unlike some Baltic states, Kyrgyzstan guaranteed citizenship and full political rights to all people of the Republic without discriminating on language or ethnic basis. The Constitution gave substantial power to the President but provided the Parliament with a mechanism to check and balance the presidential power. According to the Constitution, the President is the head of State, he has the power to appoint the Prime Minister and the members of the Constitutional Court (with the approval of the Parliament). He also has the right to initiate new laws, and to veto the decisions of the Jogorku Kenesh. However, the Jogorku Kenesh has preserved its power, including the final say on the state budget, ratification of international treaties and the ability to deter presidential decisions.[8]

As the next step, the Soviet style single-chamber 350-seat Jogorku Kenesh was dismissed by presidential decree in October 1994, sparking a constitutional crisis and sharp criticism from the political opposition. This dismissal was justified by an argument that it would have helped to consolidate the political support and institutional strength of the government necessary for the implementation of radical economic reforms and in order to reflect what Akayev called "tradition and culture of people".[9] On 6 December 1994, the President suggested changes to the Constitution, replacing the old single-chamber Jogorku Kenesh with a new, two-chamber Jogorku Kenesh. It was suggested that the new Parliament would consist of 35 seats in the *El Okuldor Jyiyny* (the Legislative Assembly) and 70 seats in the *Myizam Chygaruu Jyiyny* (the Assembly of the People's Representative). The parliamentary elections were held on 9 February 1995, becoming one of the hottest contested elections as a total of 1,021 candidates representing approximately 40 parties and organisations were standing for 105 seats. The Social Democratic Party won the largest number of seats, followed by *Asaba*, Unity of Kyrgyzstan, *Erkin Kyrgyzstan*, *Ata-Meken*, Communist Party of Kyrgyzstan and Republican Party.

In the same year, Akayev called for early presidential elections (the elections were initially planned for 1996). These were the first competitive popular presidential elections (in 1991 Akayev was the only candidate in the popular elections), and two opposition candidates Apsamat Masaliyev and Medetkan Sherimkulov were registered by the Electoral Committee. The worsening economic situation in the country forced Akayev to change the focus in his platform. Although Akayev still emphasised the democratic orientation of the Republic, the main stress was laid on further intensification of economic reforms. He argued that only radical economic reforms, mass privatisation and structural adjustments recommended by the World Bank and IMF, may have transformed this small mountainous country into what he called 'Switzerland of Asia'.[10] He also appealed to the ethnic minorities by elevating Russian language to the status of the official language despite the resistance of some nationalistic parties and some members of the Jogorku Kenesh (Kyrgyz language had the status of the state language). The other two candidates for the presidency critically approached his policy from the position of the left. Masaliyev emphasised the values and achievements of the Soviet era, which, in his opinion, were lost. The other candidate into the presidency, Sherimkulov, put forward a political platform emphasising the necessity to preserve social guaranties, to lower taxes and to develop socially oriented policy. He built up a considerable part of his election platform on the criticism of economic and social policies of President Akayev.

The presidential elections were held on 24 December 1995 demonstrating high participation of the electorate: 81.1 per cent of the people participated in the elections. President Akayev won the elections receiving 71.6 per cent of the votes. The candidate of CPK Masaliyev received 24.4 per cent of the votes, and Medetkan Sherimkulov received 1.7 per cent of the votes.

The years following the 1995 elections were among the most difficult for independent Kyrgyzstan as the economic difficulties continued and the political environment deteriorated. The parliamentary elections of 2000 became an important benchmark for testing public support for the President and government's policies. Pro-presidential political parties hoped to strengthen their presence in the *Jogorku Kenesh,* underlining the extensive political and economic changes and success of economic stabilisation. Meanwhile, the opposition hoped to establish a powerful political base for the Autumn 2000 presidential elections utilising general dissatisfaction with the falling standards of living, consolidating numerous small groups and parties and overcoming the deep division rooted in regional rivalry. This rivalry between the north and south regions was also complicated with an increasing role of the tribal division of the society in political mobilisation.

The parliamentary elections were held on 20 February 2000, followed, on 12 March, by a run-off. On both occasions the turnout was extremely low, at 57.8 per cent of the electorate casting votes in the first round and 61.86 per cent in the second round. Direct elections were held for 45 seats in the Legislative Assembly (El Okuldor Jyiyny) and 45 in the People's Assembly (*Myizam Chygaruu Jyiyny*), and other 15 seats in the Legislative Assembly were allocated on the basis of proportional representation.

There were a number of candidates in the elections (230 for the 45-seat Legislative Assembly, and 186 for 45-member People's Assembly), and a second round was needed. Ultimately, just seven opposition candidates made their way to the new Kyrgyz Parliament wining in direct elections. Several prominent opposition politicians — Daniyar Usenov and Omurbek Subanaliev, both powerful and popular, and both being viewed as potential presidential candidates, were simply disqualified on legal grounds. General Feliks Kulov, another opposition leader, had good results in the first round, but lost in the second round. Those, who did make it to the Parliament represented the *El* (People) Party, the Communist Party, the *Ata-Meken* (Fatherland) Party, and the *Kairan El* (Never-Do-Well People's) Party.

The pressure on the opposition before and irregularities during the parliamentary elections led to widespread criticism from the opposition and international observers. The OSCE observers, led by Marc Stevens, noticed that the Kyrgyz authorities "did not fulfil their commitment to organise fair parliamentary elections and the elections were neither democratic nor fully lawful".

During the same year 2000, the parliamentary elections were followed by the presidential elections as the *Myizam Chygaruu Jyiyny* (People's Assembly) announced the date for the presidential elections. According to the electoral procedures, it established the deadline for nomination and registration of candidates, and passing a special Kyrgyz language examination.

In the presidential election campaign, the incumbent president and his team emphasised Akayev's capability to preserve political stability in the country and deliver results. Meanwhile, the opposition focused on allegations of corruption during privatisation process and growing nepotism and social cost of the 'shock therapy' approach to the economic reforms and of IMF designed structural adjustment program. The Electoral Committee officially registered five candidates, including Akayev. They were Omurbek Tekebayev, the Chairman of the *Ata-Meken* (Fatherland) Party; Almazbek Atambayev, an industrialist; Melis Eshimkanov, journalist and one of the leaders of the *Asaba* party; Tursunbay Bakir Uulu, one of the leaders of the *Erkin* (Free) Kyrgyzstan Party; and Tursunbek Akunov, a human rights activist. However, two strongest candidates, Felix Kulov, the former Vice-President, and Daniyar Usenov, the former parliamentarian and chairman of the opposition People's Party, were barred from the elections. Daniyar Usenov was barred on the legal ground (due to past criminal conviction on charges that he always denied). General Felix Kulov decided not to take the Kyrgyz language exam (his spoken Kyrgyz was very weak), and gave his support to Omurbek Tekebayev, the chairman of the moderate opposition *Ata-Meken* (Fatherland) Party.

According to the results published by the Electoral Committee, the turnout at the polls on 29 October 2000 was 77.3 per cent. Like incumbent presidents in Kazakhstan in 1999 and in Russia in 2000,

Kyrgyzstani President Askar Akayev won in the first run, securing 74.4 per cent of votes. The alliance between Omurbek Tekebayev and Felix Kulov surprisingly received only 13.9 per cent of votes; Almazbek Atambayev received 6.0 per cent; Melis Eshimkanov received 1.1 per cent; Tursunbay Bakir Uulu received 1.0 per cent, and Tursunbek Akunov received 0.4 per cent.

Although the incumbent President won the election, the price was extremely high as the irregularities in both the parliamentary and presidential elections tarnished the image of the 'Island of Democracy'. In 2000 according to the Freedom House, Kyrgyzstan was ranked in the 20th place out of 28 transitional countries of the CIS and Eastern Europe, just behind the Ukraine, Albania and Armenia, but ahead of Bosnia, Kazakhstan and Azerbaijan.[11] In short term, it seems that international sponsors, on whom the Republic is heavily dependent, will accept the situation as it is. However, in the longer term, it could be more difficult to get extended political support and economic assistance as the democratic experiment fades.

THE ECONOMIC CHANGES

The greatest paradox of initial stage of Kyrgyzstan's economic reforms was that in order to integrate with the international market its economic policy aimed at cutting its ties with the CIS partners. After acquiring independence in 1991, the Kyrgyzstan government viewed that overcoming dependency on Moscow, decentralising and restructuring economic, and building national economy were the three main tasks of the reforms. This was an especially urgent task since the Soviet system, which emphasised centralised control and distribution of the resources and created a highly specialised industrial and agricultural base in Kyrgyzstan, experienced steep recession between 1989 and 1991. Therefore Kyrgyzstan's government led by the first post-independence Prime Minister Chyngyshev focused on building national economy and financial systems, large scale privatisation and restructuring.

After dissolution of the Soviet Union in December 1991, many experts including those from the IMF and World Bank, thought that Kyrgyzstan might rapidly undergo transition similar to that of Western

Europe countries after the Second World War under the Marshal Plan. This plan channelled massive financial and technical assistance enabling war-torn Germany, France and other countries to modernise their economies in less then a decade. Independent Kyrgyzstan was among IMF's favourites. In 1990 it was ranked 31st in UNDP Human Development Index (HDI), ahead of many Asian countries, it was positioned 4th in the RBEC ranking, and it had GDP per capita of US$ 1,160, slightly similar to the South East Asian countries in the late 1980s. Kyrgyzstan's economic structure was also similar to economies of rapidly transforming Eastern Europe countries as according to the IMF, Kyrgyzstan's industrial sector contributed 32 per cent to the national GDP, its agriculture contributed 42 per cent to the national GDP and other sectors made up remaining 26 per cent.[12] The literacy rate, which was close to 99 per cent both among men and women, was among the highest in Asia. The strong education was backed by the well-established and free tertiary educational system. The Republic was led by newly elected and democratically oriented President Dr. Askar Akayev, who defeated the Communist leadership in the 1990 presidential elections. The government and the President were unhindered with links to Communist leadership and were open to free market-oriented reforms and changes.

From the early days of independence, the Kyrgyzstani government accepted and steadily followed the 'shock therapy' approach, in line with the recommendations of the IMF and the World Bank. In 1992 the government introduced the 'Program of Economic Reforms', which the IMF described as a program designed "to transform the economy from one dominated by central planning and administrative control of resource allocation to one in which economic decisions are determined primarily by market forces".[13] The Republic fully liberalised economic activities in the domestic market and its foreign trade, expecting that the foreign direct investments would flow into the country's economy. Kyrgyzstan's rich reserves of mineral resources, such as gold, uranium and some others, were considered valuable assets and attracted foreign investors from Canada, Turkey, the United States and Germany. International funding organisations also noted advantage of the small size of the country's population, that stood at around 4.4 million in 1991, and of country's economy that could require smaller amounts of international assistance. Under pressure from the IMF, Kyrgyzstan's government tightened its belt in order to achieve macro-economic and financial stabilisation, cutting government and social welfare expenditures.

Kyrgyzstan together with the Baltic states was among the few former Soviet Republics that abolished most of its central planning institutions by the end of 1992. It also withdrew subsidies to major state-owned enterprises and simultaneously liberalised virtually all consumer prices. In 1991 and 1992, the Kyrgyzstani government adopted a program of mass privatisation, initially aiming at privatisation of the housing, small enterprises in the retail and service sectors. Later, the government moved towards privatisation of medium and large enterprises and of the banking and finance sector, retaining the state control over the so-called strategic enterprises (the energy and military sector). Between 1991 and 1998, the government privatised the major segments of the public assets. According to an official report, almost 80 per cent of industrial enterprises, 97.2 per cent of trade and food services and 100 per cent of household services were privatised by 1998.[14] In November 2000 the Jogorku Kenesh approved privatisation of the largest enterprises such as Kyrgyztelekom, Kyrgyzenergo, Kyrgyzgaz and the National Airline.

Kyrgyzstan was first among the Central Asian Republics (CARs) to leave the Rouble zone under the pressure of 1,300 per cent inflation in the Russian Rouble zone. In May 1993 it introduced its own currency, the *Som*. Gradually, Kyrgyzstan's government stabilised macro-economic situation cutting inflation from around 1,200 per cent in 1993, to 278 per cent in 1994 and to 45 per cent in 1995 and kept it below 35 per cent between 1997 and 2001. As part of the liberalisation program, the government maintained free exchange of the *Som* for hard currency, liberalised its international trade regime, and opened several Free Trade Zones for foreign investments. After five years of steady decline, the exchange rate of Kyrgyzstan's *Som* stabilised at 49 *Som* per one US$ in July 2001.

Throughout the 1990s, Kyrgyzstan's government targeted opening its economy for globalisation and for free trade, focussing on attracting foreign investors, establishing trade relations with developed countries and diversifying its trade.[15] After achieving its independence the Republic lifted all trade restrictions of the Soviet era and began to trade directly with China, Turkey, Germany, United States and other countries. The average annual trade turnover is stabilised around US$ 1.2 billion with the principal exports in non-ferrous metallurgy (mainly gold), electricity, agricultural and light industry products and principal imports in machinery, oil and gas. According to the EIU Country Report, for instance, in the year 2000 the exports increased by around 5 per cent and amounted to US$ 482.0 million, while imports grew by around 6 per cent valued at US$ 579.0 million with the current account deficit at US$ 167.0 million. However, foreign investments arrived in Kyrgyzstan at much slower rate than expected, forcing the government to rely heavily on international loans and credits. The foreign debts increased from zero in 1991 to US$ 1.4 billion in 2001, although the Kyrgyzstani government managed to repay or renegotiate its debt obligations, avoiding default and remaining moderately indebted country.

Kyrgyzstan's government continuously attracted attention of leading international organisations and individual states and received substantial international assistance for its radical economic and political reforms. In 1993 the IMF and World Bank provided financial backing for introduction of the *Som*. Also in 1993, Turkey together with other major donors agreed to support an initial aid program of US$ 400 million designed to increase Kyrgyzstan's capacity to import investment goods and industrial and agricultural inputs. From 1994 until 1997 Kyrgyzstan received funding and international expertise crucial for its structural economic reforms. In 1999 alone Kyrgyzstan received 27 million of the 100 million dollars under the three-year enhanced structural adjustment facility from the IMF and 45 million dollars from the Asian Development Bank. On 27 May 1999 the World Bank announced its plan to provide 13 million dollars to the private sector development program promoting export-oriented private businesses.

The economic restructuring came with heavy social cost for most of the population creating sharp regional and social disparities. In

Kyrgyzstan, like in many developing countries, the business activities and investments were mainly concentrated in the major urban centres such as Bishkek, while other regions, especially small towns and villages in the south and east of the country experienced steep economic decline. Many industrial enterprises were closed because they lacked managerial expertise and know-how, and could not compete with cheap foreign products. The official statistics insisted that the unemployment remained at around 3.1 per cent or 59,000 registered unemployed throughout the 1990s. Meanwhile, the local experts produced unemployment figures between 20 to 25 per cent of the labour force, insisting that in remote rural areas the rate may be between 30 to 35 per cent. In 2001 average monthly income stood at around 1,203 *Som* (US$ 25), placing them among lowest in the CIS countries. However, these figures do not reflect social polarisation in the country as some people had significantly profited from the 'Shadow Economy'. There are no reliable local studies on this phenomenon; however, the Economist Intelligence Unit estimates that the 'Shadow economy' might account for almost 40 per cent of GDP, which is among the highest in the CIS.[16]

The policy of radical reforms helped to restructure the national economy. However, it failed to generate promised economic growth. For five consecutive years from 1991 until 1996 Kyrgyzstan's economy depreciated at an average annual rate between 15 to 25 per cent. The Republic began to experience a moderate economic recovery in 1996 and 1997 at an average annual rate of 5 per cent, but was heavily hit by the Asian and Russian financial downturns. In July 1999, the World Bank together with the Kyrgyzstani government launched a joint project 'Integrated Basis of Kyrgyzstan Development on 2000-2010', and in December 2000 President Akayev presented a 'New National World-Outlook', a five-point 'Strategy' of the economic and social development of Kyrgyzstan until 2010 and reshuffled his government. These steps were considered by the local experts as important through belated response to criticism of the lack of long term planning for transitional reforms in the Republic.

The radical measures produced some results and in the year 2000 and 2001 Kyrgyzstan's economy showed positive signs of stabilisation and of economic recovery. In 2000 and 2001, Kyrgyzstan's GDP, according to the government's estimates, grew at annual average 5.0 per cent (up from 2.0 per cent in 1998 and 3.6 per cent in 1999). The output in the industrial sector grew around 10.3 per cent, helped by increase in gold, electricity and cotton-fibre production (which are also the among largest hard currency earning contributors). Meanwhile, in the year 2000 the agricultural production grew around 3.4 per cent. In this important sector of Kyrgyzstani economy, which provides employment to 55 per cent of the labour force, the grain harvest in 2000 was slightly lower than in the previous year, but tobacco and vegetables production (important export items) rose significantly. Overall, in 2001 Kyrgyzstan's GDP remained below the 1991 level and most probably it would fully recover from the so-called 'transitional recession of the 1990s only by 2010. According to the World Bank's classification Kyrgyzstan belonged to a group of low-income economies (US$ 755 or below).

According to the international experts several problems undermine the attraction of Kyrgyzstani economy for international investors, including lack of respect to the property rights, red tape and corruption. In 2001 the Heritage Foundation ranked Kyrgyzstan at 124th place among 161 countries in its Index of Economic Freedom, taking into consideration 10 major scoring factors (property rights, regulation, black market, etc). Corruption and bureaucracy's incompetence was also a big problem. In 1999 the Transparency International ranked Kyrgyzstan together with Pakistan at 87th place among 99 countries in its Corruption Perceptions Index, far behind such countries like Turkey, Bulgaria, China, Russia and Kazakhstan, but ahead of Azerbaijan and Uzbekistan. Another problem, which discourages investors, is small size of the local market and a shrinking purchasing power of the population. Kyrgyzstan slid from 31st place in 1991 to 98th place in 2000 in the UNDP Human Development Index,[17] behind Kazakhstan, Jordan, Albania and Iran, but ahead of China, Turkmenistan and Uzbekistan.

NATIONALITY POLICY AND CULTURAL CHANGES

Pre-independence years were marked by high inter-ethnic tensions and communal unrest in summer 2000, in which between 300 and

1,000 people were killed. Therefore, consolidation of all ethnic groups on the territory of the country into Kyrgyzstani nation has been the major objective of Kyrgyzstan's official policy after gaining independence. There was no unanimity, however, in the ethnic policy approach among the Kyrgyz elite. One view was that like the Baltic Republics of the former USSR, Kyrgyzstan's government should move towards an ethnocentric state. It should also declare that the land belongs to Kyrgyzs, and should demand compulsory knowledge of Kyrgyz language from all people who seek the Kyrgyzstani citizenship, irrespective of their ethnic origin. The other view was that Kyrgyzstan's government should have a moderate stand. The ethnic policy should be based on development of the Kyrgyzstani identity and loyalties of all citizens to the newly independent state; unification of all ethnic groups within the territory of the nation-state into one Kyrgyzstani nation, and maintenance of the multi-cultural nature of the society and moderate Islamic revivalism. The government should move towards a civil state, which guarantees equal opportunities to all citizens of the Republic without ethnic or religious discrimination.

The decision on the policy choice was difficult for several reasons. Firstly, the multi-ethnic composition of the country: in 1991 the Kyrgyzs, or the titular nation of the Republic, constituted roughly 52 per cent of the population, there were around 22 per cent Russians and the Uzbeks represented 13 per cent of the population. Secondly, inter-ethnic relations in the Republic were especially tense at the beginning of the 1990s because of the inter-ethnic conflicts in the southern regions of the Republic in 1989 and 1990. Thirdly, the Kyrgyzs themselves lacked national cohesiveness and they often defined themselves as members of different tribes or tribal groups with distinct dialects, dress and political affiliations.

Already in 1989 the Law on Language suggested that the Kyrgyz language should become the state language (Article 1), symbolising Kyrgyzstan's sovereignty (Article 2) and replacing Russian. It also required compulsory usage of the Kyrgyz language by management and administrative personnel (Article 8) and gradual translation of all documentation in the state and regional administrative institutions into Kyrgyz. The Law also required translation of signs in all public places, cities and streets into Kyrgyz. During public debates on the Law some members of public suggested to change the script of Kyrgyz language from Cyrillic to Latin, following example of Turkey. The Law (Article 22) suggested to 'create conditions for researching opportunities of changing Kyrgyz alphabet' to the Latin script. The Law on Land, adopted in 1991, declared that the land and natural resources should be exclusive possession of the Kyrgyz people.

Akayev's government chose to implement very moderate nationality policy, emphasising a civil identity, guaranteeing citizenship to all people who live on the territory of the Republic and maintaining multi-ethnic nature of the state. The government argued that in this multinational state, where the native Kyrgyz people constituted slightly more than half of the population in 1991, the strict ethno-centric policy would provoke escalation in the inter-ethnic tensions. The government suggested moderation of the wording in the Law on Land and in the Law on Languages. At the same time the government re-introduced the cultural references to Kyrgyz traditional symbols changing names of the streets, squares, public place, cities and towns. Thus, for example, the name of the main street in the capital was changed from 'Lenin street' to 'Chui street'. The names of the Przhevalsk and Rybach'ye were changed to Kyrgyz names Karakol and Issyk-Kul respectively. The new Kyrgyz flag and emblem, which symbolically refer to traditional Kyrgyz colour and symbol, were introduced along with the new national anthem, national currency, passport, etc. The Manas epic was elevated to the status of national symbol and in 1995 Kyrgyzstan celebrated the 1,000th anniversary of its national hero. The idea of changing the Kyrgyz script from Cyrillic to Latin was postponed due to scarce financial resources, although a number of Kyrgyz students began studying Turkish in various Turkish universities and in colleges and in the Turkish Manas University and International Ataturk Alatoo University in Bishkek. Kyrgyzstan's government also lifted restrictions of religious practice and a number of mosques and madrassahs were built or rebuilt in the Republic. Islam came to prominence and most of Kyrgyzs would highlight that the *Hanafi Mazhab*, which they belong, has been the most liberal school in Islamic thought.

Also, there were serious demographic changes due to the economic recession, fears of conflicts and collapse of the social welfare system. One of the consequences of these changes was the mass emigration of people from the Republic. According to official statistics, more than 590,000 people (or almost 15 per cent of the Republic's population), mainly Russians, Ukrainians, Jews, Germans and some other ethnic groups as well as some Kyrgyzs left Kyrgyzstan between 1989 and 1995. According to the 1999 population census, the Russian population declined from 21 per cent in 1989 to around 12 per cent in 1999. It is expected that it would further decline to 6 per cent within next 15-20 years (according to a recent survey 20.4 per cent of the respondents expressed their desire to leave the Republic 'forever'). As some ethnic groups moved out, others moved in. There were reports that up to several thousand Chinese settled in Kyrgyzstan, although there is no reliable statistics available at present. Nevertheless, the preliminary results of the 1999 Census in Kyrgyzstan indicated that the ethnic composition of the Republic is still changing. Kyrgyzstan is slowly becoming ethnically more monolithic with the proportion of Kyrgyz approaching 68 per cent in 2001 as against 52 per cent in 1989. However, the reality is that the country will maintain its multi-ethnic composition for decades to come, especially with the growing proportion of the Uzbeks and Chinese in Kyrgyzstan.

VISION 2010

Independence brought a number of changes to Kyrgyzstan. The government succeeded in dismantling its centralised political system, introducing democratic institutions and democratic procedures in the Republic. Political opposition and independent mass media can freely express themselves, although during last few years the government became less tolerant to criticism. Despite some quarrels in the domestic affairs, during the 1990s the country remained politically stable and relatively democratic. However, Kyrgyzstan is still undergoing difficult transition and struggling to become a nation with strong institutions, stable political environment and viable democracy, although the Republic has undergone a number of changes in economic, political and international relations spheres.

Kyrgyzstan managed to consolidate society and introduce a civic identity and new nationality policy without calamities, which haunted many other young nations after gaining their independence. But from a historical perspective, ten years is a very short period and it is still too early to arrive to any firm conclusion. The social, demographic and migration indicators are constantly changing as the process of forming the 'Kyrgyzstani' nation is far from being complete. Nevertheless, some changes found firm ground in the society. First, the nostalgia over the Soviet past is gone almost entirely and the people accept the post-Soviet realities, acknowledging that the disintegration of the Soviet Union is an irreversible fact. Second, the majority of the population understands that Kyrgyzstan is their only home country, regardless of their ethnic background, and the people perceive themselves as the citizens of this state. However, a considerable number of people in the Republic are still uncertain about their future, indicating their desire to migrate. Third, there has been a strong shift in the people's identities and loyalties towards the Republic and a growing acceptance that they are citizens of Kyrgyzstan, although the post-Soviet development reveals that the legacy of the Soviet past still strongly affects the people's perception of the ethnic policy and the nation-state.

The economic changes in Kyrgyzstan demonstrated that there was no easy and quick way to sustainable economic growth. It also showed that the country will need to re-adjust its economic program, taking into consideration new realities and difficult lessons from the past 10 years of reforms and changes. It also needs to put more attention to improving its competitiveness, rules of law and property rights as well as the regional trade liberalisation and economic cooperation. As President Akayev said, evaluating a decade of independent development, "although we declared independence and declared that we accepted market economy, at the same time we have still preserved some negative features of the Soviet mentality and corruption... we have difficult tasks before us."[18]

The decision to set up a US military base and a permanent US presence in Kyrgyzstan sparked further diplomatic rivalry between the US and Russia in the Central Asian region. It remains to be seen how

President Akayev would maintain the fragile balance between the competing interests of the US, China and Russia and if the great powers would be able to resolve their differences. It seems that if Russia and the US would be unable to find a common ground in the region, the century old so-called Great Game in Central Asia would enter a new round. This diplomatic and political rivalry would provide Kyrgyzstan important space for manoeuvring and diplomatic intrigues.

CONCISE CHRONOLOGY OF HISTORICAL EVENTS

1985	Turdakun Usubaliev, long standing Kyrgyzstan's leader, is dismissed from his position.
1986	Dinmuhamed Kunayev, long standing Kazakh leader is dismissed and replaced by Genaddii Kolbin.
1986	Students in Alma-Ata organise unsanctioned meetings and demonstrations. Students in Bishkek warned to restrain from any political activities.
1989 (Aug.)	Draft of a Kyrgyzstan's Law on Languages is published in main newspapers, sparking hot heated debates.
1989 (Sept.)	Jogorku Kenesh (Parliament) passes the Law on Languages, declaring Kyrgyzs the official language of the Republic.
1990 (June)	Inter-ethnic conflicts in Osh region of Kyrgyzstan
1990 (June)	Leaders of Central Asian Republics gather in Bishkek (then Frunze) and agree to establish a Central Asian Union.
1990	Jogorku Kenesh elects Dr. Askar Akayev as a first President of the Kyrgyz Soviet Socialist Republic.
1991 (Aug.)	Jogorku Kenesh (Parliament) declares political independence of Kyrgyzstan.
1991 (Oct.)	Dr. Askar Akayev is elected as a Kyrgyzstan's President by popular vote.
1991 (Dec.)	Belarus, Russian Federation and the Ukraine, founding members of the USSR, sign a treaty dissolving the Soviet Union.
1991 (Dec.)	Kyrgyzstan joins the Commonwealth of Independent States (CIS)

1992 (Feb.)	Kyrgyzstan joins the Economic Cooperation Organisation (ECO).
1992 (April)	Suleyman Demirel visits Central Asian Republics
1992 (May)	Kyrgyzstan signs the CIS Security Treaty in Tashkent
1992 (June)	Kyrgyz President visits Turkey.
1993 (March)	Turkic Orthographical Conference calls for the change from Cyrillic to Latin script for all Central Asian Turkic languages.
1993 (April)	Kyrgyzstan receives the status of a 'developing nation'.
1993 (May)	Jogorku Kenesh (Parliament) adopts a new Kyrgyzstan's Constitution
1993 (May)	Kyrgyzstan introduces its currency, the *Som.*
1995 (Dec.)	Dr. Askar Akayev wins the Presidential elections.
2000	Parliamentary elections held in Kyrgyzstan.
2000 (Oct)	Dr. Askar Akayev wins the Presidential elections.

REFERENCES

1. Askar Akayev, (1998), *Diplomacy of the Silk Road* (Bishkek: Ministry of Foreign Affairs), p. 11.
2. *Kazakhstanskaya Pravda*, 24 December 1991.
3. John Anderson, (1997), *The International Politics of Central Asia* Manchester: Manchester University Press, Anderson, 1997, p. 193
4. *Slovo Kyrgyzstana*, 13 September 2001.
5. *Slovo Kyrgyzstana*, 27 September 2001.
6. Gr. Gleason, (1997), *The Central Asian States: Discovering Independence,* Boulder, CO: Westview Press, p. 94.
7. Eugene Huskey, (1995), "*The Rise of Contested Politics in Central Asia: Elections in Kyrgyzstan, 1989-1990*", Europe-Asia Studies, vol. 47, No. 5, p. 821.
8. *Kyrgyz Respublikasynyn Konstitutsiasy* (Bishkek), 1996, pp. 19-41.
9. *Slovo Kyrgyzstana*, 7 December 1994.
10. *Slovo Kyrgyzstana*, 14-15 December 1995.
11. *Nations in Transit, 1999-2000, Civil Society,* Democracy and Market, Freedom House, 2001, p. 19.
12. IMF, *Kyrgyz Republic: IMF Economic Reviews* (Washington DC: International Monetary Fund, 1993), pp. 6-11.

13. *Ibid.*, p. 2.
14. Kyrgyz Republic Foreign Investment Agency. *Kyrgyz Republic: Information for Prospective Investors* (Bishkek: FIA, May 1998), pp. 12-14.
15. R. Abazov, (1999), "Policy of Economic Transition in Kyrgyzstan", *Central Asian Survey*, vol. 18, No. 2, pp. 204-09.
16. EIU, *Kyrgyzstan: Country Report*, London, January 2001, p.18.
17. UNDP, *Kyrgyz Republic: Human Development Report*, 2000.
18. *Slovo Kyrgyzstana*, 12 December 2000.

4

State-Building in Kazakhstan

Review of a Decade's Experience

AJAY PATNAIK

Kazakhstan, in many ways, has been uniquely more diverse than other Central Asian states. Existence of multiple identities – ethnic, sub-ethnic, religious, linguistic, regional etc.- have necessitated a very complex state-building endeavour in the post-Soviet period. While independence created some momentum, like in the rest of the post-Soviet successor states, to create a model of nation-state based on the titular national identity, soon the heterogeneity of the society impinged upon the process to make it more integrative rather than exclusive.

At the time of independence the majority of population in the Republic were non-Kazakhs. Sub-national identities that continued to exist in informal ways during Soviet days have become more conspicuous. There were strong regional divisions – the north and east of the country had a strong Russian majority. The southern part of the country had been comparatively more traditional. Not only were there substantial Russian speakers, there also were substantial Russophone Kazakhs.

The initial impulse under these circumstances was to create a nationalizing state of the Kazakhs, in which non-Kazakhs would only enjoy certain basic citizenship rights. There was a fear that Kazakhs would lose significance in their historical homeland if the existing situation is allowed to continue even after independence. The titular language was elevated to the status of 'state language', arousing fears among the non-Kazakhs that they would be discriminated in jobs on the basis of language. It was also envisaged as an instrument to keep the Russians particularly out of the top positions. The law of Kazakhstan requires a fluent knowledge of the Kazakh language for the President, the Vice-President, the Chairman of the Supreme Soviet and the Chairman of the Constitutional Court.[1] Resurgence of Islam and emphasis on reinterpreting history, changing place names etc. created the impression that Kazakhstan is well on its way to create a nation-state based on Kazakh identity alone. There were also policies aimed at strengthening the demographic base of the titular population.

This paper seeks to argue that despite early impulses to Kazakhize the state, subsequently there has been realization that state-building can dialectically combine both the processes of nation-building and integration of non-Kazakhs in the new states by creating equal stakes for them.

NATIONALIZING THE STATE

When Kazakhstan acquired its independence, the problem facing the nation-builders was the numerical position of the Kazakhs and the internal division that confronted the titular group. Kazakhs constituted only 39.5 per cent of the population in 1989, while the Russians nearly equaled them with 37.7 per cent. The demographic situation was even more unfavourable to the Kazakhs given the concentration of Russians in north and east of the country, where they constituted 61.7 per cent and 64.2 per cent of the population in those regions. Even in the then capital Almaty, situated in the south, Russians constituted 56 per cent of the population.[2]

The Kazakh national rhetoric has harped on the theme of numerically and culturally Kazakhs being in the danger of becoming inferior in their historical homeland. The Kazakh state was under mounting pressure to adopt the nation-state model. Even President Nazarbaev in 1994 made his choice clear and said, "the interests of the Kazakhs shall receive special emphasis... in matters pertaining to the revival of the national culture and language, the development of spiritual and cultural ties with the Kazakh diaspora, and the creation of a proper environment for the repatriation of persons forced to leave Kazakhstan".[3] Even the constitution declared Kazakhstan as the homeland of the Kazakh people first and foremost. Despite widespread resentment among the Slavs against the 1992 Declaration on Language, which made Kazakh the state language, Nazarbaev failed to persuade the parliament in January 1995 to make Russian the second state language. The other issue of Russian grievance has been that of dual citizenship, which was accorded only to Kazakhs. Changing the capital from Almaty to Akmola, in the north-east, which has a heavy concentration of Russians, provided credence to charges of asserting political control by Kazakhs over Russian areas.[4] The government justified the move without any allusion to the ethnic dimension: growth potentiality of Alamaty has been exhausted; it is far removed from country's industrial and geographical centre due to its location in the extreme south-east corner; Almaty lies in an earthquake zone and plagued by air pollution, and so on.[5]

Thus, it has been said that at the core of Nazarbaev's state-building scheme has been the policy of 'Kazakhisation'—reviving the Kazakh language, restoring traditional names to cities and landmarks, revising history to reflect a Kazakh national perspective, and observing Kazakh and Islamic holidays etc. The replacement of Russian and Soviet toponyms by Kazakh ones has been an important way to assert the pre-eminence of Kazakh culture and history in the new state. A multitude of regions, cities, streets, squares, collective farms and, even settlements founded by Russians prior to the Soviets, have been renamed or are scheduled to be renamed.[6]

Some have pointed to the definition of the state in the constitution as a sign of 'Kazakhisation' of the state. Though the1993 Constitution opened with the reference to 'We, the people (*narod*) of Kazakhstan', clearly a non-ethnic entity, Art.1 of the constitution hailed the republic of Kazakhstan as 'the form of statehood of the

Kazakh nation (*natsiya*). The official view was that whatever else Kazakhstan was, it was also a national state of the Kazakhs. This view was reflected in several Kazakhstani laws and other official documents.[7]

The officially outlined 'conception of the establishment of an historical consciousness in the republic of Kazakhstan', which was approved by the President's National Council on State Policy in June 1995 stressed that the Kazakhs are autochthonous on the territory of modern day Kazakhstan. "The statehood of the Kazakhs is the continuation of the statehood of the major nomadic empires and individual Khanates which have existed on the territory of Kazakhstan since antiquity", the document stated. Thus, state policy has mandated the primordial and perennial bond of the Kazakhs to the territory of the state, with the implicit assumption that they should occupy a pre-eminent status therein.[8]

The post-Soviet nationalization policy also entails a process of spatial and social mobility for ethnic Kazakhs and seeks to keep the reins of government firmly in their hands.

THE DEMOGRAPHIC TRANSFORMATION

One of the favourite themes in the Kazakh nationality debate is demography. In the nationalist discourse, this development will remove a major obstacle to Kazakhification of the state. This thinking also in a way was reflected in state policy in the initial years of independent statehood. The law on citizenship, for example, allowed dual citizenship for ethnic Kazakhs living abroad, but for no other groups. Government encouraged immigration of Kazakhs from CIS states, Mongolia, Turkey, Iraq and China. It has attempted to entice these new immigrants, along with Kazakhs living in the south of the country to settle in the north with offers of subsidized housing, work and Kazakh-language schools. This effort cooled due to expenses involved apart from Russian opposition and lack of interest or ability to emigrate on the part of the diaspora.[9]

The government actively pursued a carefully designed national policy aimed at significantly boosting Kazakhstan's Kazakh population. Kazakhs from outside are automatically recognised as refugees and have preferential status with regard to returning and finding a home and a job, free college admission and free accomodation to travel within the territory of the republic. The number of Kazakhs settled in northern Kazakhstan increased from 30,000 in 1991 to 45,000 in 1993. By September 1994, half of the 120,000 Kazakh families in Mongolia were believed to have moved to Kazakhstan. Also moving into Southern Kazakhstan were many families from Iran and Karakalpakstan and from China and Turkey.[10]

Demographic gains for Kazakhs have also been as a result of large-scale exodus of Slavic and other nationalities from Kazakhstan. This trend was visible even in the later part of Soviet period and accelerated especially in the early years following the adoption of the language law. In 1989 and 1990, there was a net emigration of 31,000 Russians per year. The number increased rapidly after independence, peaking up in 1994 at 2,51,000 before declining in 1995-96. Kazakhstan's Russian population declined by about 10 per cent. Ukrainians and Belarussians had roughly the same rates of emigration as the Russians. The net emigration of 5,37,000 Germans from Kazakhstan in 1989-96 nearly equaled the corresponding total of

Table 4.1: Population Change by Nationality in Kazakhstan, 1989-96

	Population by Nationality				*Change from 1989 to 1996*			
	Percent		*Thousands*				*of which*	
	1989	*1996*	*1989*	*1996*	*Percent*	*Total*	*Natural Increase*	*Net Migration*
Kazakhstan	100.0	100.0	16,536	16,544	0.0	8	1321	-1313
Kazakhs	39.5	47.0	6,535	7,781	19.1	1,246	1,047	160
Russians	37.7	33.9	6,228	5,615	-9.8	-612	62	-678
Germans	5.8	2.6	957	426	-55.5	531	29	-537
Ukrainians	5.4	4.8	896	797	-11.0	-99	7	-100
Tatars	2.0	1.9	328	313	-4.6	-15	10	-23
Uzbeks	2.0	2.3	332	382	15.1	50	77	-23
Belarussians	1.1	1.0	183	167	-8.6	16	4	-12
Azeris	0.5	0.6	90	104	15.3	14	16	-2
Others	6.0	5.8	988	958	-3.1	-30	69	-98

Source: Tim Heleniak, "The Changing Nationality Composition of the Central Asian and Transcaucasian States", *Post-Soviet Geography and Economics*, Vol. 38, No. 6, 1997. p. 369.

Russians in absolute terms. In percentage terms, however, the emigration of Germans was half of country's German population. In 1997, the number of Germans declined further to 3,00,000. Since independence, 1,60,000 Kazakhs returned from other regions of FSU as well as from abroad. The government organized the return of some 70,000 Kazakhs from Mongolia, Iran and Turkey. Half of this migration occurred in 1992, the first year of independence. In 1997, the share of Kazakhs in the total population reached 51 per cent and the share of Russians went down to 32 per cent of the total.[11]

Debates related to demography are largely redundant for a number of reasons. Firstly, even without an overt state policy encouraging Kazakh diaspora to return, the share of Kazakhs was steadily increasing due to a higher birth rate among the indigenous population and outflow of Russians even a decade prior to the independence of Kazakhstan. Similarly, neither the influx of the diaspora nor the out-migration of the Russian-speaking population could continue beyond a level since the people are loathe to migrate out of their familiar settlements unless there is excessive discrimination against them and also because the capacity of the receiving countries is limited in material terms. It has been reported that many immigrants to the Russian Federation did not find it easy there and in 1994 alone, some 70,000 returned to Kazakhstan, of whom 30,000 were ethnic Russians. Customs, pace of life and even heavy drinking habits in Russia disturbed many. They were also politically isolated from the new quasi-democratic Russia. The economic situation in Russia had limited the capacity of the Russian government to accommodate increasing number of immigrants, who also faced a not-too welcoming population in areas in which they were settled due to economic hardships faced by the local population there already. Thus many Russian-speakers stayed behind, some unable to emigrate and others still unsure of any viable future outside.[12]

In the case of the Kazakhs the higher natural growth trends compared to Russians ensures increase in their share, while in case of Russians, the state will increasingly take care to prevent the emigration of educated and skilled cadres. Emigration was of particular concern to Kazakhstan where the first to leave were the skilled personnel, affecting the industrial sector and the sphere of education and welfare. For example, in 1993 alone, 1,000 doctors left. In 1994, in the single oblast of Ust-Kamenogorsk in Kazakhstan 302 teachers and 55 doctors left.[13]

It will not be easy to force the issue of demography beyond a point. There are several problems facing the Kazakh community including falling birth rate among women because of deteriorating living standards etc. There are other problems in the republic's population front like 2,00,000 abortions annually, single-women problems and covert tolerance of bigamy by the state since women outnumber men by almost 5,20,000, demographic depopulation; depopulation of the republic evident in the fall in the total number of the population from 17,324,000 in 1992 to 15,671,800 in 1998.[14]

Table 4.2: Russians in Kazakhstan, 1989-95

	Total number of Russians in the beginning of 1989 (thousands)	1989	1990	1992	1993	1994	1995	1995	Total Number of Russians 1997 (in thousand)	Net Russian out-migration 1989-1996 (in thousand)	Percentage decrease of Russians 1989-96
Kazakhstan	6228	6200.1	6165.9	6140.3	6058.0	5953.6	5719.3	5575.5	5477.3		
		25.9	36.2	25.6	82.3	104.4	234.3	143.8	98.2	750.7	
Decrease by % of Russians in Kazakhstan		0.4%	0.6%	0.4%	1.3%	1.7%	3.9%	2.5%	1.8%		12.1%

Source: Graham Smith, Vivien Law, Andrew Wilson, Annette Bohr and Edward Allworth (eds.), *Nation-Building in the Post-Soviet Borderlands*, CUP, Cambridge, 1998.

The overall depopulation of the country was mostly the result of emigration of the non-indigenous population. The demographic shift in favour of Kazakhs also endangers the labour situation. In 1993, according to official statistics, non-Kazakhs constituted 75.8 per cent of the total workforce of the country. Given the fact that 16,52,700 persons left the republic between 1993-98, especially from the northern provinces to Russia, there could be catastrophic consequences for the economy.[15]

Fearing the alienation of the Russian minority and its economic and political consequences, Nazarbaev has taken care to couple his nation-building efforts to a policy that he dubs 'harmonisation'. This is intended to encourage the participation of Russians in facets of Kazakh life and integrate them in the new state. Automatic citizenship, wide tolerance of Russian language and culture and government subsidies to the Russian-dominated industrial sector are all components of this policy.[16]

Thus, though both the 1993 constitution and the 1995 constitution declare that 'Kazakhstan was created on the basis of Kazakh self-determination', equal rights for all citizens, regardless of race, nationality, language or religion have been guaranteed. The new constitution grants automatic citizenship to all who desire it, with no language or residence requirement whatsoever. Art.5 of the new draft expressly forbids the establishment of any social organization that seeks to forcibly change the constitutional order, undermine state security, violate territorial integrity, or promote 'social, racial, national, religious, class, or tribal discord'. The new constitution supplemented the legislation by an absolute ban on any propaganda or campaign directed towards the above aims.[17]

LANGUAGE ISSUE

It has been pointed out by many scholars that the adoption of the language law making Kazakhs the state language has symbolized the growing marginalization of the Russians in the new state and some have even gone to the extent of suggesting that language issue has been responsible for out-migration of Russian-speakers from the republic. It has been pointed out earlier that out-migration from the republic has been an ongoing process since early 1980s. The exodus of Russian-speaking population intensified in the years of uncertainty, when a number of riots rocked the Central Asian region and the resurgence of radical Islamic movement in the region. Subsequent economic problems accelerated this process. However, neither the Russians have been targeted by state for discrimination, nor has the state embraced nationalism and Islam as defining identities. In the case of Kazakhstan especially, Russian language has been accorded better status than anywhere else in Central Asia. The leadership, having realized the need for protecting the multi-ethnic character of the society, has ostensibly been discouraging any nationalizing zeal.

There has been further evidence that the state-building policy is not going to be based on a mass linguistic transformation. While the 1993 constitution accorded Russian the status of 'language of inter-ethnic communication', the 1995 constitution conferred "official" status upon it as well (though not state language). The dual-language policy has so far ensured a balance. In the summer of 1995, Russian-language newspapers still outnumbered Kazakh ones, if barely, and Russian language television continued to dominate airwaves. Of all the successor states, Kazakhstan has the second largest number of schools in which classes are conducted in Russian. 1.9 million students attending these schools constitute more than half of all school children in the state.[18] In 1993-94 school year, 57.2 per cent of the students in Kazakhstan were studying in Russian schools compared to 40.1 per cent in the Kazakh schools.[19] In this republic about 40 per cent of Kazakhs, according to one survey hardly spoke their native language and even the draft constitution was written and published in Russian.

In 1996, the Information Analysis Centre of the Supreme Council, in collaboration with the Committee on Languages under the Cabinet of Ministers of Kazakhstan, carried out a sociological survey for the purpose of studying the place of the state language and other languages in the social and communication spheres, factors exerting an influence on how they function and the socio-linguistic interests and motives of representatives of the principal ethnoses–in short, the present language situation and the social and cultural factors that condition it.

The study concludes that the place that Kazakh language occupies in the social-communicative realm is not in accordance with its proclaimed status. It hardly performs official functions, or performs them only formally. The number of persons who are fluent in Kazakh has not increased very much, and basically it is among Kazakhs.

Kazakh's function continues to be limited to the household and traditional culture, and the farther from this sphere one goes, the more the Russian language assumes the main communication role. As market relations become more established, the Kazakh language will likely yield even more ground; one example is in advertising. Among Russian-speaking citizens, for the most part, it is assumed that it will be simply unnecessary in future. And the system of school and higher education has proved to be incapable of providing high-quality instruction of Kazakh in educational institutions.[20]

The study also indicates that the most favoured is the preservation of the present language situation, and, in this way, encourages the functional development and expansion of the range of social use of the language of the Kazakhs. One positive change has been the increase in the number of Kazakhs who are perfectly fluent in Kazakh while the level of fluency in Russian has not gone down. As a result, overwhelming majority of Kazakhs has developed genuine bilingualism. There has been a steady expansion of the network of pre-school and school institutions where the upbringing is conducted in Kazakh, although it has not been sufficient yet to satisfy completely the needs of society. It was also concluded by the researchers that language was not instrumental in emigration of non-Kazakhs. Persons who were preparing to leave Kazakhstan cited economic motives rather than factors of language and ethnic discrimination.[21]

Thus language-based nationalization in the complex situation is a difficult exercise. In any case, as the above study shows language policy has helped the promotion of Kazakh language which was losing its place among the urban Kazakh elite. In the mid-1980s, Almaty, the former capital, had only one or two titular-language schools to serve a titular population of 138,000. Around 1990, between 25 per cent and 40 per cent of the republic's Kazakhs had little or no mastery of their titular language.[22]

There is a genuine fear that giving Russian the status of 'state language' in the present context will stall the progress of Kazakh language since independence. Thus Kazakhstan's language policy is less oriented to discriminate Russian and more to encourage it at least among the local population. According to Fierman, state identity as represented through language issue was unlikely to become the political issue that causes conflict, given the fact that there is high level of fluency in Russian among Kazakhs which was over 60 per cent in 1989. The enormous impact of Russian in Kazakhstan is also illustrated by the fact that the most famous contemporary Kazakh writer, Olzhas Suleimanov, composes mostly in Russian.[23]

INDIGENIZATION OF POWER

There have been trends since independence that have resulted in the shrinking demographic base of Russians to control political processes and structures in Kazakhstan. The loss of power by the Russians in the political and administrative sphere is near total. Even though they still form a substantial segment of the population, they are poorly represented. At the republican level, Kazakhs have come to dominate the top positions in most major ministries. Even the premiership that had been given to an ethnic Russian since independence was finally handed over to a Kazakh in October 1994. More dramatically, administrations of regions heavily populated by Russians have become increasingly Kazakh-dominated. Karaganda Oblast, with a population that was less than 20 per cent Kazakh, had six of its top eight administrative positions filled by Kazakhs in early 1994. In Pavlodar (30 per cent Kazakh), Kazakhs outnumbered Russians in top administrative positions, the ratio of which was 6 to 3; and in the city of Almaty (less than 25 per cent Kazakh), the ratio was 9 to 2 in 1994.[24]

Attention has been drawn to practices of tacit nationalizing policy through the steady displacement and exclusion of the non-titular nationalities from the public and social service spheres, through 'covert' methods in the employment, firing and promotion of personnel. Generally lay-offs have taken place, after which many of the same positions were restored and priority was given to titular nationals during the rehiring process. Another common practice used by state-run organizations has been the issuance of official memorandums specifying that knowledge of the state language is required in order to qualify for employment or promotion. Similarly, perquisites have been given to those who possess a knowledge of the state language: in 1996 in Kazakhstan's Semipalatinsk region (which was merged with East Kazakhstan region in May 1997) – where ethnic Russians constituted approximately one-third of the population – government employees who had passed the Kazakh language test received an automatic pay increase of 15 per cent.[25]

In the March 1994 elections, 218 candidates were disqualified. The ethnic breakdown of those that remained revealed a clear anti-Russian bias – out of 756 candidates, 77 per cent were ethnic Kazakhs; only 18 per cent were Russians. Moreover, a quarter of the parliamentary seats were reserved for candidates from the state list – a slate of 64 nominees personally drawn up by Nazarbaev, from which 42 deputies were to be elected. The state list allowed the President to manipulate the new legislative body's ethnic composition – in many cases, forcing the election of at least one Kazakh from a Russian-dominated oblast and vice versa, and putting up for election representatives of other ethnic groups that would be unlikely to otherwise gain representation. The election results showed that Kazkahs were overrepresented, filling 59 per cent (105) of the parliamentary seats. Russians, on the other hand, managed to take only 48 seats, or 27 per cent.[26]

Table 4.3: Ethnic Composition of Parliament

	Total				*Party/Self-Nominated*				*State List*			
	Nominated		*Elected*		*Nominated*		*Elected*		*Nominated*		*Elected*	
Kazakhs	567	75%	105	59%	530	77%	80	59%	37	58%	25	60%
Russians	128	17%	48	27%	113	16%	39	29%	15	23%	9	21%
Others	61	8%	24	14%	49	7%	16	12%	12	19%	8	19%
Total	756	100%	177	100%	692	100%	135	100%	64	100	42	100

Source: Ian Bremmer and Cory Welt, "The Trouble with Democracy in Kazakhstan", *Central Asian Survey*, 15(2), 1996, p. 190.

The 1994 elections resulted in the formation of a Parliament that consisted of 21 per cent Russian and 58 per cent Kazakh. In 1995 election to the lower house (*Majlis*) 67 Kazakhs and 31 Russians were elected (in 1989 Kazakh Supreme Soviet, Kazakhs comprised 46.7 per cent compared to 41.8 per cent Russians and in first multicandidate elections in 1990, Kazakhs won 49.3 per cent of seats from territorial districts as compared to 33.0 per cent Russians). The former had 69.3 per cent of candidates elected by public organisations as compared to 15.9 per cent Russians. As a result, in the legislature as a whole the Kazakh share was 54.2 per cent as compared to 28.8 per cent of the Russians.[27]

The political clout of the Kazakhs is clearly running ahead of their demographic weight. In 1994, Kazakhs filled 60 per cent of the seats in the Kazakh Supreme Soviet. Only 49 Russians (28%) and 16 other Europeans were elected. In the December 1995 elections to the new two-chamber Parliament 26 Kazakhs and 12 Russians were elected/appointed to the Upper House (the Senate), while 42 Kazakhs, 19 Russians and five representatives of other nationalities took seats in the Lower House (the *Majlis*). Even more glaring disproportions could be found in the state bureaucracies, centrally and regionally.

The Supreme Court ruling that the previous year's election violated constitutional regulations, led to the dissolution of the Parliament in March 1995. In the elections that followed on 9 December 1995, Russians composed 25 per cent of the 274 candidates.[28] Kazakhs occupy more than two-thirds of the seats in the Upper House and in the Kazakhstani Parliament (the Senate) elected in late 1995 and early 1996 (32 of 47), while Russians hold less than one-third (13 seats). Similarly, Russians hold only 28 per cent of all seats in the Lower House (the Majlis), while the Kazakhs hold 65 per cent (although they made up only 46 per cent of the population in 1995).[29]

In 1994 a group of researchers from the semi-official Institute for the Development of Kazakhstan computed the ethnic composition of the top echelons of executives in two key bureaucracies – the apparatus of the Cabinet of Ministers and the Presidential apparatus.

This is one aspect of state-building which really bothers the non-Kazakhs. They fear that lack of fair representation in the decision-making process might harm their economic and cultural interest. This issue needs to be seriously addressed by the present leadership of Kazakhstan.

Table 4.4: First and Second Echelon Executives in Kazakhstani State Organs (%)

	1993			*1994*		
	Slavs	*Kazakhs*	*Minorities*	*Slavs*	*Kazakhs*	*Minoritie*
Cabinet of Ministers	24.9	73.1	6.5	22.8	74.3	3.1
Presidential Apparatus	25.8	67.7	6.5	22.8	74.3	3.1
Share of total population	43.4	42.8	13.7	43.0	44.3	12.7

Source: Timothy Edmunds, "Searching for a Nationalism: Foci for Kazakh Identity in the 1990's", *Central Asia Monitor*, No. 2, 2000.

A NEW ORIENTATION IN THE MAKING?

Kazakh statehood in the Soviet period was largely defined in the context of, and in relation to, the omnipotent Soviet state. With its removal, many Kazakhs found themselves bereft of the ideological and political structure that had defined the parameters of both their national identity and their statehood. In its place the Kazakhs have had to refashion their own context for an independent statehood. Some of the major foci that have helped to dictate this new agenda since independence are language, demographic consolidation and political pre-eminence of the titular group.

The move to ensure political pre-eminence to the titular nations which provides special protection for their cultures, however unwritten, finds manifestation in certain formulations in the constitutions and certain policies of the state. However, in general, the message conveyed by Nazarbaev and reflected in official pronouncements of Kazakhstani state authorities is distinctly different from the rhetoric used in the unofficial, Kazakh-language discourse on ethnicity and state-building. Nazarbaev has asserted that Kazakhstan is both a multinational society and a homeland for the ethnic Kazakhs. In a sense, he has tried to avoid making a choice between an ethnic and civic nation concept.[30]

At a large conference in Almaty in May 1993, Nazarbaev fleshed out the main goals and elements of a new 'Kazakhstani state ideology'. A major task, he declared, would be 'to combat every chauvinism, nationalism and separatism'. This should be done by the inculcation of 'Kazakhstani patriotism'. The nation-building model outlined by him was indisputably civic, the prototype being the United States.[31]

Another landmark in Nazarbaev's thinking on nation-building and ethnic integration was his remarkable speech to the Kazakhstani Supreme Soviet on 9 June 1994 "We should not close our eyes to the fact that very many people start to think about leaving the country at the moment when they begin to feel a psychological discomfort. This feeling of theirs is caused by a number of factors, first and foremost related to excesses and an unreasonable speed in the implementation of complex socio-cultural programmes."[32]

In this speech he criticized as simplistic the conventional Kazakh view that Russians were leaving the country for economic reasons only. In particular, Nazarbaev singled out the 'destructive policy' of changing Russian toponyms. "The mass renaming of streets, towns and even major cities has had a one-sided tendency. It has not taken into consideration the public sentiment or the ethnic composition of the population. Sometimes it has disregarded even centuries-old traditions and, worst of all, it has ignored the mass psychology of the inhabitants".

He further claimed, the problems were caused by 'distortions in personnel policy'. Such distortions could be found both locally and in the capital. He insisted, "for instance, 30 Kazakhs as against only three Russians, two Uighurs and one Azeri are working in the Language Committee. And this is an agency which deals with the development of all of our languages, not only with Kazakh."

After this came the new constitution in May 1995. The phrase defining Kazakhstan as 'the form of statehood of the self-determining Kazakh nation' was deleted, as was the special right of the Kazakh diaspora to hold dual citizenship. Russian was elevated to a status of an "official" language "to be used on par with the state language in state organs and in organs of local administration".

In May 1996 a new official 'Concept for the Forming of a State Identity of the Republic of Kazakhstan' was published in Kazakhstan media. The Concept, while performing a delicate balancing act between an ethnic and civic idea of the nation, nevertheless must be regarded as a retreat from the studious ethnic neutrality of the 1995 constitution.

The Concept noted that the 'ethnic centre' of the Kazakhs was Kazakhstan since nowhere else in the world did Kazakhs possess a statehood which was concerned about the preservation of the Kazakh as an ethnic group, or about the development of Kazakh culture, language, traditions and life style. "When we define Kazakhstan as a national state, it is this quality of the state we primarily ought to have in mind". Acknowledging that Kazakhstan certainly also was a multi-ethnic state, the Concept nevertheless stated that the other ethnic groups in the country could not adduce similarly strong claims to be attached to this state as the Kazakhs could.[33]

Nazarbaev has made conciliatory gestures like inviting one of the ethnic Russian leaders, Mikhail Golovkov, to serve as one of the presidentially nominated senators. In another example, the Central government did not push the issue when the city administration of Petropavlovsk refused to acknowledge a directive to change the city's name to its Kazakh variant.

The leadership of Kazakhstan has come to realize that creation of a model of nation-state in a multi-ethnic society like Kazakhstan is not the best form of state. The presence of large minorities, who are educated and skilled is an asset for the new state. Any attempt to prevail over ethnic minorities by the dominating majority can threaten the social stability of the emerging state. There was a need to redress the imbalances of the previous years. At the same time, some amount of nationalizing would be helpful in creating a sense of national solidarity among the Kazakhs who are faced with certain resurgence of sub-national identities

Attention has been drawn by many experts to the increasing importance of traditional tribal institutions like the *Zhuz* (horde) in contemporary Kazakh life. While in the early Soviet period a concerted effort was made by the centre to eliminate the traditional Kazakh *Zhuz* based power structures, and replace them with Soviet ones, many aspects of the clan-based politics the *Zhuz* structure typified remained. Since independence, these networks have largely assumed control of the national and local administration, while at the same time intensifying the competition for power between them. According to Timothy Edmunds, the most important division that has emerged in Kazakhstan since independence is not between ethnic groups, but amongst Kazakhs themselves, at least at the political level. This influence in itself, however, may be problematizing the future development of a unified Kazakh, indeed Kazakhstani, national identity. Nazarbaev himself expressed concern as early as October 1993 and observed that, "… dangerous trends towards a national split have lately emerged in Kazakhstan's society … this is due to the fact that the relative independence of the regions is being taken advantage of by the local elite to establish tribal ideology and clan-based protectionism."[34]

This dilemma between a nationalistic urge to create a nation-state based on Kazakhisation and a Kazakhstani state based on multiple ethno-national identities has hunted state-builders since independence. While there is a need to strengthen the core ethnic group by some amount of national consolidation and nationalization of the state and society, it could not be carried on beyond a level given the ethno-demographic and linguistic reality of the country. The economic compulsions and the nature of human resources that the non-indegenes represented made it even more urgent to draw a balance between various ethnic concerns in the state-building process.

In Kazakhstan, people are divided on the issue of whether the state in future is to be a multinational state, a half-Russian, half-Kazakh hybrid or an exclusively Kazakh homeland. Thus so far Nazarbaev has managed to avoid defining Kazakhstan by asserting that it is all three. He has found it difficult to increase the role and prominence of Kazakh culture, language and history in the republic without alarming the non-Kazakh population, especially the Russians.

One of the ways in which Nazarbaev is seeking to achieve a stable political base is through the ideas of Kazakh poet and public figure Olzhas Suleimenov, who in 1976 advanced the thesis that the Turkic and Slavic tribes of early mediaeval times had shared one culture, and so were a kind of brother peoples. If widely accepted, this thesis would provide the ideological underpinnings necessary for stabilizing Kazakhstan's binational makeup. Suleimanov has actively argued that Turks and Slavs can and should work together to create a great confederation of separate states, or a single secular state, based on their shared heritage, history and culture.[35]

The recent trends show that Kazakhstan's leadership has begun to clearly spell out a direction that will possibly go beyond harmonization and usher in a phase of integration of national minorities. Now that the demographic, language and cultural concerns of the national intelligentsia has been taken care of, there is hope that Russians, the 'significant other' of Kazakhs would not feel insignificant in the new state. After an uncertain phase of state-building, Kazakhstan has entered a period, which most likely would result in integration of all the communities living within its borders and contributing to its stability and prosperity.

REFERENCES

1. *CDPSP*, Vol.XLVI, No.13, p. 10.
2. Robert Kaiser and Jeff Chin, (1995) "Russian-Kazakh Relations in Kazakhstan", *Post-Soviet Geography*, Vol. 36, No. 5, p. 260.
3. Adam Dixon, (1996), "Kazakhstan:Political Reform and Economic Development", in Roy Allison (ed.), *Challenges for the Former Soviet South*, Washington, D.C., p. 76.
4. *Ibid.*, pp. 76-77.
5. Graham Smith, Vivien Law, Andrew Wilson, Annette Bohr and Edward Allworth (eds.), *Nation-building in the Post-Soviet Borderlands*, Cambridge, 1998.
6. *Ibid.*
7. Pal Kolsto, (1998), "Anticipating Demographic Superiority: Kazakh Thinking on Integration and Nation-building", *Europe-Asia Studies*, Vol. 50, No. 1, p. 56.
8. Graham Smith, Vivien Law, Andrew Wilson, Annette Bohr and Edward Allworth (eds.), *op. cit.*
9. Ian Bremmer and Cory Welt, (1996), "The Trouble with Democracy in Kazakhstan", *Central Asian Survey*, 15(2) .
10. Jiger Janabel, (1996), "When National Ambition Conflicts with Reality: Studies on Kazakhstan's Ethnic Relations", *Central Asian Survey*, 15(1), pp. 7-8.
11. Anatoli Vishnevskii and Zhanna Zaionchkovskaia, (1993), "Waves of Migration", *Russian Social Science Review*, Vol. 34, No. 4.

12. John Glen, (1999), *The Soviet Legacy in Central Asia*, Basingstoke.
13. *Ibid.*
14. Azamat Sarembayev, (1999), "Imagined Communities and Kazakh Nationalism", *Central Asian Survey*, 18(3), p. 335.
15. *Ibid*, p. 336. Kendirbaeva, Gulnar, (1997), "Migration in Kazakhstan: Past and Present", *Nationalities Papers*, Vol. 25, No. 4, pp. 741-51.
16. Ian Bremmer and Cory Welt, (1996), "The Trouble with Democracy in Kazakhstan", *Central Asian Survey*, 15(2), p. 182.
17. *Ibid.*
18. *CDPSP*, Vol. XLV, No. 11, 1993, p. 23.
19. Robert Kaiser and Jeff Chinn, "Russian-Kazakh Relations in Kazakhstan", *Post-Soviet Geography*, Vol. 36, No. 5, p. 263.
20. M.M. Arenov and S.K. Kalmykov, (1997), "The Present Language Situation in Kazakhstan", *Russian Social Science Review*, Vol. 38, No. 3.
21. *Ibid.*
22. *Ibid.*
23. William Fierman, (1997), "Language, Identity, and Conflict in Central Asia and Southern Caucasus", *Perspectives on Central Asia*, August , Vol. II, No. 5, (Centre for Political and Strategic Studies, Washington).
24. Ian Bremmer and Cory Welt, (1996), "The Trouble with Democracy in Kazakhstan", *Central Asian Survey*, 15(2).
25. Graham Smith, Vivien Law, Andrew Wilson, Annette Bohr and Edward Allworth (eds.), *op. cit.*
26. *Ibid*, pp. 188-189.
27. Martha Brill Olcott, (1997), "Democratization and Growth of Political Participation in Kazakhstan", in Karen Dwaisha and Bruce Parrott (eds.), *Conflict, Cleavage, and Change in Central Asia and the Caucasus*, Cambridge, pp. 213-14, 231, 219-20.
28. Ian Bremmer and Cory Welt, "The Trouble with Democracy in Kazakhstan", p. 193.
29. Graham Smith, Vivien Law, Andrew Wilson, Annette Bohr and Edward Allworth (eds.), *op. cit.*
30. Pal Kolsto, *op. cit.*, p. 56.
31. *Ibid.*
32. *Ibid*, 57.
33. *Ibid*, 58.
34. Timothy Edmunds, (2000), "Searching for a Nationalism: Foci for Kazakh Identity in the 1990's", *Central Asia Monitor*, No. 2.
35. Martha Brill Olcott, (1994), "Kazakhstan", in Mohiaddin Mesbahi (ed.), *Central Asia and the Caucasus after the Soviet Union*, Florida, p. 128.

5

Foreign Policy of the Republic of Kazakhstan

BULAT SULTANOV

Ever since the Republic of Kazakhstan gained its independence, its foreign policy has been creating favourable conditions to properly integrate itself into the world community as a sovereign state and find its place there. Earlier a number of strategic and tactical issues came up before the government, which are as follows:

1. Formation of National Security Concept
2. Development of Foreign Policy Doctrine
3. Selection of allies (in the international, military, defence fields, particularly on the issues of national and regional security) as well as trade and economic partners.

On December 2, 1991, at a press conference devoted to the results of the Presidential elections, Nursultan Nazarbayev for the first time outlined Kazakhstan's foreign policy and identified its numerous directions. He noted that Kazakhstan must become a bridge between Europe and Asia due to its geographical location. When asked about whether Kazakhstan was oriented to Europe or Asia, Nursultan

Nazarbayev indicated about openness of Kazakhstan and emphasized that first of all the country would like to establish multilateral economic and political contacts with all countries. Stressing that Kazakhstan would not be limited to the Asian continent only, the President said that "the country should strike a reasonable balance between Europe and Asia. But it is going without saying the Kazakh people have very deep roots with the Turkic nations".

Further, at the inauguration ceremony held on December 10, 1991, President Nursultan Nazarbayev specified his vision for sovereign Kazakhstan's foreign policy. He said that during the Presidential elections his people voted for a free sovereign democratic state and so "Kazakhstan is not willing to become a closed system but to serve as a unique bridge between Asia and Europe, i.e., between the great cultures of the West and the East".

The Kazakh leadership also demonstrated a well-considered approach towards events in the former Soviet Republics. It prevented the ex-USSR from splitting into the Slavic and Turkic alliances when Turkmenistan proposed to establish the Central Asian Confederation in response to the decisions made in the Belovezhskaya forest. Making reference to it, President Nazarbayev stressed that "today many of us do not remember those events, but indeed we've been on the threshold of creating the two alliances – Slavic and Turkic – with participation of Turkmenistan". He further went into specifics of the independent days by saying, "History made a provision for Kazakhstan to find itself in the very epicentre of the world policy during collapse of the bipolar world. The new States replaced the ex-powers, and special attention was paid to our country. Twist of fate made the attention justified mainly by the fact that the USSR had placed a great portion of its nuclear potential in our country. Initially, ignorance of our specifics formed a negative image of Kazakhstan as an Islamic nation having the nuclear weapons and threatening the entire world community. That negative image became a disturbance not only for us, but for our future partners as well."

In view of the above mentioned concern, the priorities during the first stage of the Republic of Kazakhstan's foreign policy, have been:

1. Maintenance of overall economic, cultural and humanitarian space with the CIS.
2. Integration into the modern international relations and processes through the UN, OSCE and other international organizations. A share in the achievements of the world civilization in political economic, social, humanitarian, scientific and educational fields. Involvement of the world community in the transition processes from centrally planned economy to the market-based relations in Kazakhstan, and provision of necessary assistance and support.
3. Due to refusal of its nuclear status Kazakhstan wanted the nuclear powers – the USA, Russia, Great Britain and China, to provide guarantee for Kazakhstan's security, sovereignty, independent territorial integrity and inviolability of borders;
4. International cooperation with the principal financial organizations – International Monetary Fund, World Bank, European Bank for Reconstruction and Development
5. Bilateral cooperation. In doing so the priorities were the establishment and development of cooperation with the neighbouring nations – Russia, China, Uzbekistan, Kyrgyzstan, Turkmenistan and Tajikistan.

Respect and recognition received by Kazakhstan from the world community further gave rise to its willingness to forego the nuclear status and sign Strategic Offensive Weapons Treaty-1, Treaty on non-proliferation of nuclear weapons and Treaty on overall prohibition of nuclear tests.

Initiated by Kazakhstan and Russia, signing of the Collective Security Treaty by the five leaders of the CIS nations in Tashkent on January 15,1992, played an important role in creating the collective security system in the former Soviet Republics. The member-states confirmed their commitment to abstain from using the force or traits of the force in their inter-State relations. Besides, they also made a commitment to settle any disputes which might arise between them in a peaceful manner. One of the provisions made in this Treaty was that in case if "any member-State is exposed to aggression by any state or a group of states, then such actions will be considered aggression against all the member-states". This provision occupied principal importance.

Thus, in the first half of 1990s, based on the foreign policy doctrines and national security concept formulated by the government, the Kazakh diplomacy has been able to deal with the main challenge – proper integration of the Republic of Kazakhstan into the world community as a new sovereign State. However, in the second half of 1990s, Kazakhstan's foreign policy was affected not only by the geopolitical factors, but also by the international transformation process due to intensification of globalization and direct threats to the national security of the country originating from the "southern arc of unstability".

At the turn of the century the nations are facing new challenges and problems due to global re-arrangement of the current world system. While addressing the 7th Summit of the Turkic Nations' Heads in Istanbul held on April 25-27, 2001, President Nazarbayev identified the threats of global nature arising out of increasing disproportion in the social and economic development of the countries as threat of nuclear proliferation, aggressive national and religious radicalism, drug trafficking and international terrorism.

According to President Nazarbayev, there is need to study the potential negative consequences of globalization for all the nations – rich, developing, poor – in order to eliminate them timely. The Kazakh leader paid special attention to the fact that if globalization benefits only a small group of highly developed nations (20 per cent), this will inevitable result in the confrontation, conflict and social cataclysm.

However at the end of 20th and beginning of the 21st century, the world political situation and role and importance of Kazakhstan and Central Asia in the world policy significantly changed. As we see it, the milestones of changing geopolitical situation can be guaged from the following events:

1. Russian-American Relations.
   (*a*) In the second half of 1990s, on the one hand, Russia got rid of pro-west orientation in its foreign policy, which was

initiated by A. Kozyrev, former Foreign Minister of the Russian Federation. On the other hand, the country preferred to cooperate with the CIS States as a principal foreign policy direction.

(*b*) Current trend in the Russian government policy is to get back its position in the Caspian and Central Asian regions.

(*c*) Russia's interest has also developed in increasing cooperation with the states which are called "the scoundrel-states" in the USA.

2. American-Chinese Relations

(*a*) Increasing American-Chinese competition further complicated by the tragic events of unilaterally victimising the citizens of the People's Republic of China (bombing of one of the buildings of Chinese Embassy in Belgrade in 1999 and clash of US reconnaissance aircraft with Chinese fighter in 2001).

(*b*) Re-organization of the US military force as Defence Secretary Donald Rumsfeld believes that the Pacific Ocean is likely to become an area of large-scale US military operations given the fact that "China is getting transformed into a powerful state and Russia is still losing its position".

(*c*) As a result, increasing military budgets of the two nations.

3. Growing dissatisfaction among some nations with the only-leader-role the USA seems to play in the world politics and its negative consequences. A glaring example can be the military campaign against Yugoslavia initiated by the United States and its NATO partners. As a result, the Balkan crisis has not been resolved, on the contrary it is getting worse. The current situation of tension in Macedonia can prove it.

4. Growth of international terrorism, religious extremism and drug trafficking based in Afghanistan.

5. The oil factor in the Caspian-Central Asian region and potential oil transportation routes to the world market.

(*a*) USA is interested to fix its positions in the region due to geopolitical interests, and strategically control the routes located between its hypothetical rival China and its potential partner Russia, and also to increase its own energy security.

(*b*) Contrary to the USA, Russia is interested in restoring its influence in the region, which the Kremlin considers as a zone of its vital interests.

(*c*) Based on its short-term and long-term domestic and foreign policy programs, China is interested to cooperate with the Central Asian Republics under the following considerations: Firstly, it wants to take joint action against terrorism, extremism and separatism in Xinjiang-Uighur Autonomous Region. Secondly, its position is based on its economic interests. And thirdly, in order to obtain a safe rear in case the situation in the Asia-Pacific region worsens.

Therefore, the foreign policy efforts of the Kazakh diplomacy are directed towards the establishment of efficient institutions at the UN and at the international regional organizations like the EU and OSCE. Such institutions will help eliminate the social and economic problems which may otherwise lead to conflicts among the nations. Recently we have got acquainted with the new alarming phenomena of various kinds of problems like international terrorism, organized crime, militant separatism, religious extremism, inter-ethnic conflicts, drugs and weapon trafficking. The leadership of Kazakhstan believes that the events witnessed in Kyrgyzstan and Uzbekistan clearly prove that (*a*) the old security system of the late 1980s and early 1990s went into oblivion, and (*b*) operations by international terrorists had the definite targets. The crises in Afghanistan, Central Asia, Chechnya and Xinjiang are interlinked.

Having suffered from the civil war, Afghanistan has become the epicentre of international terrorism. Earlier, at the UN Millennium Summit held on September 6, 2000, President Nazarbayev stressed the need to organize an extra session of the UN Security Council to review the situation in Afghanistan and Central Asia and develop mechanism for stabilizing the situation in these regions. In order to counteract international terrorism, religious extremism and other dangerous phenomena threatening the stability and security in Central Asia, the leadership of Kazakhstan has taken a number of measures ensuring national security in the new conditions.

The Shanghai Five member-states are actively engaged in developing their relations. The process of executing various programmes within the Organisation has become a regular feature. It is already a common practice that the Shanghai Five leaders hold regular meetings. At their meetings, they discussed a wide range of issues and even went far beyond the "Agreement on confidence building in the military field in the border areas" and "Agreement on reduction of military forces in the border areas". Therefore, this is not by chance that having resolved the border issues the Shanghai Five leaders commenced discussion on the new challenges facing the region and created the Shanghai Cooperation Organisation (SCO) at a meeting held on June 14-15, 2001.

While addressing summit meeting of the Shanghai Cooperation Organisation its leader President Nazarbayev outlined principal targets of the Organisation containing the following:

1. Provision of stability and security in the region in general and SCO member-states in particular. A special consideration shall be given to counter terrorism, extremism, drug trafficking, illegal migration and weapon trafficking;
2. Economic interaction;
3. Environmental interaction, particularly in the border areas;
4. Consideration and review of the regional social and economic issues mainly the trans-border rivers, migration, diasporas;
5. Creation of efficient regime to interact with the structures like ASEAN, Collective Security Treaty, CICA and others.

The unprecedented merciless terrorist attacks in the USA on September 11, 2001, which killed many people, have drastically changed the situation in the world. As a result, the discussions on bi-polar or multipolar world, Russia's potential cooperation with China, Iran and North Korea, competition between the USA and China, etc. were temporarily put on the back burner and how to counter terrorism became the main subject of discussion. Currently, the world community has one common enemy – terrorism.

Kazakhstan takes a clear and principal stand on the issue of international terrorism. Just after the September 11 terrorist attacks

President Nursultan Nazarbayev expressed his condolences to the US people. In his message to President George Bush. He noted: "We are filled with indignation by the terrorist attacks, which have killed and injured many people. Such actions against the mankind shall not be forgiven. The civilised community shall join its efforts to combat international terrorism".

A statement by Kazakhstan's Ministry of Foreign Affairs described the September 11 terrorist attacks as a challenge to the entire world community and called for a "joint effort to fight against the global evil". Besides, it stressed upon the need of taking "efficient and coordinated measures by all the stages, governments and international organizations" against the terrorists. It was also emphasized that Kazakhstan is ready to provide any reasonable assistance to the United States America to overcome the consequences of the tragic events and to take joint measures to counteract terrorism in all its forms.

It is to be noted that successful fight against terrorism, extremism and separatism depends in many ways on cooperation of the Central Asian Republics with Russia, the USA, the European Union and China. However, cooperation with Russia in particular, is very important for national and regional security of Kazakhstan as well as other Central Asian nations. Moreover, Russia being in neighbourhood with "the southern arc of unstability" is also interested in such cooperation. This will help in the development of the economic, military and political integration process in Eurasia, creation of Eurasian Economic Community and a new level of development of the Collective Security Treaty.

As such, any policy prepared within the framework of regional and sub-regional systems together with the bilateral relations should be brought to the forefront in order to combat terrorism, religious extremism and separatism. This can be achieved through the Eurasian Economic Community, Shanghai Cooperation Organisation, Central Asian Economic Unity and Collective Security Treaty.

6

Central Asia: Managing Inter-Ethnic Relations

P.L. Dash

The first ever ethnic conflict of the Gorabchev era had occurred in the then Kazakh capital, Alma Ata, in December 1986. It had clear ethnic undertones because Kazakhstan was a Soviet republic, where titular population were a minority. This had generated considerable apprehensions about the Kazakh nation becoming extinct in due course of time. Secondly, at that point of time, the replacement of the Kazakh leader, Din Mukhammed Kunaev by Genady Kolbin, a Russian, as the republic's Party Secretary had suddenly provoked native wrath. People took to the streets to demonstrate their feelings and the result was a mob-cop clash in the streets of Alma Ata that had left dozens killed, others maimed and many more injured. What had followed this event elsewhere in the erstwhile Soviet Union was the rapidly spreading virus of ethno-national conflicts, leading to secession of republics as sovereign entities, and to their emergence as independent countries.

However, with the advent of independence in 1991, managing ethnic relations in the post-Soviet space became a paramount duty of governance in all successor states of the former Soviet Union. In the southern fringe in general, and in the Central Asian states in particular, multi-ethnic composition of the population was a complex bequeathal of statehood, based on formation of ethnonyms on these territories. Their subsequent subjugation by Tsarist and Soviet rules, spanning over a century has added a new dimension to contemporary problems. New states and their leaders, largely inexperienced and mostly avid to affirm their statehood on the debris of socialism, have been grappling with the monumental burden of ensuring ethnic harmony among the population living on their respective countries. But to their dismay, the hot spots of ethno-national conflicts that had erupted in the Perestroika years have only shifted gears from high volatility to continuing low intensity conflicts. From Alma Ata through Osh to Tajikistan, it is a saga of conflicts that have never ended. Their memories are stark reminders to an uneasy calm prevailing over the surface of ethnic cohesion. The very fear that violence might occur on the basis of ethnic belongingness makes everyone think that managing ethnic relations in Central Asia is an important task for now and for the future. And in the context of ongoing globalization, the future of democracy in a multi-ethnic and multi-cultural Central Asia depends on how the present leaders project their countries in the scheme of things to come, especially in the changing context of Central Asia's importance in the light of ongoing developments in Afghanistan. This paper is an attempt to highlight the issues and factors that affect optimal management of ethnic relations in post-Soviet Central Asia.[1]

BACK TO THE ROOTS

A paramount aspect of inter-ethnic relations in present day Central Asia is rooted in the core of its settled and peripatetic populations, who visited and inhabited the region over centuries. They came as nomads, first from Iran and then from Turkey, when Central Asia had no pronounced ethnic making. Over the centuries, when ethnonyms took definite shape much before the advent of Islam, they evolved yet into a broad divide based on Iranian and Turkic communities. Language and religion played a pivotal role in this divide. Yet, Central Asia remained by and large homogeneous, with Sunni sect of Islam predominating in all five countries, save the sole exception of Ismailis and Zoroastrians in Tajikistan. Rest of the peoples from contiguous countries, who subsequently migrated to the region whether Slavic or Chinese or Germans or Meshkhetians, have had only peripheral impact on native ethno- national composition of the region, rather than anything deep that might threaten the native fabric. Since assimilative choices were restricted only to inter-community marriages, and immigration and emigrations were largely under centralized state control, the population remained by and large homogeneous in each country. Yet, historically, the pattern of settlement in Central Asia, the specifics of each tribe that came from outside to make the region their permanent home, and the differences among those tribes plus their ethno-linguistic and national loyalty to various ethnoses made Central Asia's ethnic mosaic fairly complex. Thus, back in history, lay the ethnic vivisection of the reality that sets the countries and their ethnic communities apart from one another.

In Kazakhstan, The Kazakhs were united mainly in three tribal confederations or *Juzes*: senior, middle and junior or *Ulu*, *Orta* and *Kishi*. What made the Kazakh situation more difficult was the inner structure of each of the *Juzes*. The chief of each *Juze* was an elected Khan; and each Khan had a tentatively defined nomadic territory: the junior in the northwest, the senior in the east and the middle in the central part of Kazakhstan. In turn, the sub-divisions were more complex: the *Ulu* fell into ten clans, the *Orta* into four tribes consisting of forty three clans and the *Kishi* into two major tribes further branching out to include as many as twenty five clans.[2]

Similarly, in Turkmenistan, we find strong ethno-tribal loyalty to the local chieftain. The Turkmen are divided mainly into seven large tribes: *Teke*, *Ersari*, *Yomut*, *Saryk*, *Chovdur*, *Geklen* and *Salyr*. Their defined mode of settlement in preferential areas snowballed over the years into territorial distinction and each of them have clear ethno-territorial status.[3]

The Kyrgyz case too typifies a unique tribal structure divided into two wings: the right wing having twenty one tribes and the left having eight. Large Kyrgyz tribes such as *Sarybagyshese*, *Bugu*, and *Salto* are all in the right wing. Besides, there is large tribal group called *Ichkilik*, consisting of ten tribes and some seven other tribes of mixed non-Kyrgyz origin.[4]

Throughout the past century, the nomadic Uzbeks also had tribal system along the line of Turkic ethnoses. Some of them, for instance, were "the *Mangytes*, which produced the dynasty of Bukhara Amirs of 1753-1920, the *Kungrats*, whose tribe chieftain, Muhammad Amin founded a new Khiva dynasty in 1763 and others. Among the Karakalpaks, there were two major sections subdivided into tribes and clans. Although settled life in Central Asia existed alongside the peripatetic life style of nomadic tribes, mainly on the territories of Uzbekistan and Tajikistan, nomads had always intermingled with the settled populations, thus thinning out the line between natives and non-natives. Therefore, the distinctive differences of native versus non-natives that confronts Central Asia today is a recent phenomenon seen after the advent of the Russians in the 1860s.

The complexity of contemporary Central Asian situation is further compounded by the overlapping multi-ethnic settlements across one another's territories. In this sense, not only the five countries of the region, but also migrant populations from afar provide a definite multicultural pattern of ethnic plurality across the border areas of all contiguous countries. This is discernible in Uzbeks living in Tajikistan and vice versa, Kazakhs living in Russia and Kyrgyzstan, Uighurs living in China and Kazakhstan and many other clear ethnic groups residing beyond the boundaries of their autochthonous territories. Thus, while managing ethnic relations in multi-ethnic Central Asia, it is the root that matters most, plus the innumerable branches that have sprang up over the years.

BINDING COMMONNESS

While ethnogenesis and growth of nation states made Central Asia a diverse region, there are some discernible commonalities facing the region as a whole. There are several common features that demonstrate this unity in diversity. First of all, a colonial past has been bequeathed to all the post-Soviet Central Asian countries. Settlement of many post-colonial disputes is prolonged by an extraordinary transition through which the erstwhile colonies and metropolis have been passing through simultaneously and together. Although difficulties are the same, the solutions very often tend to be dissimilar. Metropolis Russia is in no position to substantially help the former colonies in their pursuit of independence. Yet, Central Asia's cooperation with Russia, willy-nilly, remains a cornerstone of all evolving relationships in the region and beyond.

Secondly, all countries of Central Asia have Turko-Iranian cultural roots. This makes them hark back to their past in search of national identity. In this context, ethnic affinity to the roots is obviously looked upon as a cementing factor of closeness on the basis of Islam, rather than an element of mutual hostility. Evolving relationship with the Islamic world is as much important as relations with the rest of the non-Islamic world. In view of its advanced level of education, Central Asian countries in the post-Soviet space are better placed to turn adversity into opportunity by interpreting the benign teachings of Islam to their advantage in state building as well as in resolving nagging ethno-national problems. Political prudence coupled with tenacity to project Islam as a peaceful religion could go a long way to dispel the fear of Islamic extremism and fundamentalism. Here a common approach by all countries seems more than timely and inevitable.

Thirdly, all countries face the related problems of cross-border settlements. Due to historical reasons, overlapping populations reside across the border areas of all countries. At the forefront of cross-border settlers are the Uzbeks, the most numerous ethnic group in Central Asia, totalling over 19 million. "Ethnic Uzbeks constitute a diaspora in neighbouring countries: 24 per cent of the population in Tajikistan, 16 per cent in Kyrgyzstan, 9 per cent in Turkmenistan and 2 per cent in Kazakhstan."[5] With Uzbekistan having borders with all other states and nurturing ambitions of a regional hegemon, a lot depends on how the Uzbeks behave vis-à-vis other ethnic groups, particularly in Tajikistan and Kyrgyzstan; and most specifically in the Ferghana valley, where ethnic frictions are quite evident. Here, once again, a collective approach to reducing ethnic tensions is the need of the hour.

Fourthly, all Central Asian countries have the problem of the Slavic diaspora. Despite a post-Soviet shrinkage, the Russians constitute the second largest ethnic group in Central Asia, varying considerably from one republic to the other: in Kazakhstan 33.9 per cent of the population, in Kyrgyzstan 15.5 per cent, in Turkmenistan 6.6 per cent, in Uzbekistan 5.6 per cent and in Tajikistan 3.4 per cent.[6] These figures bounce upward if the number of Ukrainians and Belorussians is taken into account. The problem is too delicate to be handled overnight by any individual republic. Only a balanced and collective approach to this issue could iron out existing discord with Russia and the Russians to the advantage of the Central Asians.

Two more areas where all Central Asian states have common grounds to work on are evolving a democratic polity of their own and building their nascent armies. All of them profess democracy on the ruins of authoritarian yesteryears. After a decade of independence, all of them have achieved varied level of democracy: in Kazakhstan and Kyrgyzstan, it is more democratic and less authoritarian, while in Uzbekistan and Turkmenistan, reverse is the case. Tajikistan teeters on the brink of a United Tajik Opposition. Insufficient democratic experience and lack of firm political commitment are the obstacles to overcome the past communist legacy, once again requiring political will and coordination among the Central Asian leaders.

The second area is building national armies in respective countries and overcoming the post-Soviet security fragility. Individually weak and collectively faltering, the Central Asians have been facing a dilemma how soon to overcome the Russian legacy. All of them save Turkmenistan are signatories to CIS collective security system. All of them have bilateral defence cooperation agreements with Russia (except Uzbekistan, which withdrew from it in 1999). At the same time all of them have been trying hard to build their own national armies. Success in this regard are varied, but efforts are under way. Recent developments in Afghanistan have reinforced the urgency of the question regarding national armies in these countries by adding an international dimension to their native importance. Issues germane to regional defence cooperation have been discussed collectively at the CIS platform and at bilateral and multilateral levels among groups of countries. Artificial borders of the Soviet era are perhaps the only impediment on which regional defence collaboration stumbles on and should anyone venture to redraw it, a Pandora's box will be opened and bloodshed will be perpetuated.

Finally, what changes the social fabric of Central Asian countries is the outpouring number of migrants to urban areas, where Russians and Slavic population still constitute the majority. Indigenization of cities by Central Asian natives, who migrate to urban pockets in search of jobs and better living conditions, face the privation of everything they yearn for. The point of friction culminates when natives see non-natives living better and the delicate moments come when these frictions create tension and hostility, leading ultimately to ethnic clashes. Social hardships provoke bitterness and mutual distrust that finally create a cleavage between the Europeans and the Central Asians. And its reflections mirror on rural regions, creating commotion in those areas from where the migrants came to cities. In turn, it generates a new rural-urban contrast far beyond the ken of the authorities to effectively handle it.

RALLYING POINTS

Many dominant post-Soviet tendencies are current in the independent countries of Central Asia. First of all, each of them separately and all of them together, endeavour to assert their national independence. National pride has visited each country with a difference. However, definite manifestations of symbols and heroes whose glorified past has revived strong native feelings of respective populations are discernible. Hero worshipping Babur in Uzbekistan is a good example. The precarious economic situation has not deterred the fun-loving Central Asians to restage their past heroes. Toys of heroes are available for sale in shops. In the summer of 1991, a pompous ceremony, dedicated to Ablay Qan of the Middle Horde was held in Kokshetaw oblast. Chief among the speakers was the then President of Kazakh Academy of Sciences, U.M. Soltanqazin, who delivered an eulogy in praise of the Qan, presumably to have united the three Hordes of Kazakhstan in 18th Century.[7] Similar instances are far too common in other countries in recent times.

Secondly, there is a strong monoethnic tendency sweeping across the area. Apart from each state trying to strengthen its nationhood, evident is a concurrent trend of expressive proclivity to cling to one's national culture as far as possible. Years of privation of native feelings in an alien land has generated the urge among the Central Asian Germans to migrate to Germany, the Koreans to Korea, Meshkhetians to Georgia, the Russians to Russia, the Ukrainians to Ukraine and so on. Whether it is the fear of reprisal of non-natives by natives or mismanagement of inter-ethnic relations in a pluralistic context by the authorities is a matter of debate. What remains explicit is the emigration of non-eponymous nationals from Central Asia—too widespread a phenomenon to be ignored.

Thirdly, there has ever been a growing fear of radical Islamization. Central Asian states stood at the crossroads, where their Soviet past met with radical ilk of Islam spreading from across the borders with Khomeini's Iran and Talibanized Afghanistan. But they had a distinct advantage of being socially and educationally advanced and, therefore, better equipped to judge the situation themselves. As a result, although Islam has spread, the radical spirit is counterbalanced by relatively high level of understanding. Despite increasing number of mosques and popularity of the Koran, that have overwhelmed the region, a confessional compromise across the region is felt fairly in tune with what the authorities have desired to see. This has belied the hopes and "proved wrong the Western apprehensions of Central Asia going the Balkan way after the break-up of the Austro-Hungarian empire in the 19th century".[8]

Finally, the popularity of the Islamic heritage and spread of mosques across republics have not been uniform. Uzbekistan, Turkmenistan and Tajikistan are the republics where Islam has penetrated faster into the social fabric than in Kazakhstan and Kyrgyzstan. In a compact region measuring 4 million square kilometers and inhabited by 130 national and ethnic groups, Central Asia offers a mosaic of religious problems; more along the line of rediscovering Islam than anything pernicious. The inherent threat, however, could be read between the lines, when one republic (in this case Uzbekistan) took pride in setting up an Islamic University in Tashkent in September 1999 and provided official information that there are 1,700 religious organizations in the republic of which 1,566 were Islamic, and the rest belonged to other religions.[9] Armed with these figures, from the vantage point of fast growing Islamic institutions, one could visualize a more complicated picture, particularly relative to the situation in Afghanistan and Tajikistan; and wish Uzbekistan not to emerge as a forepost of Islam in Central Asia.

The cultural plurality of post-Soviet Central Asia clashes with the cultural proximity of such Islamic countries as Iran, Pakistan, Afghanistan and Saudi Arabia, professing radical Islam. The region is jinxed on two differing religious equations: Christanization of the northern part competes with the Islamization of the southern part, thus leading to a religious polarization that complicates the region's ethnic divide. The affairs are too delicate to be handled by a single leader. Therefore, there is need to create a specific space for communication on religious matters, where all affected countries of the region could chalk out strategies to deal with the situation of a pluralistic society.

PREVAILING SCENARIO

The fact that the current stage of nation state building in Central Asia rests on the roots of ethnogenesis, and the borders are artificial inheritance of the Soviet yesteryears, there are several, overlapping conflicting situations to be handled. These could be divided into two broad levels of dealing with ethnic differences: one within the republic; and the second beyond it. Some of the sharp features that precipitate ethnic friction, leading to hostility are evident in each republic. Similarly every state has regional differences within it as is prominently evident in Tajikistan. The presence of aliens and their intervention in Tajik affairs create here a peculiar precondition for conflict management. Clear regional demarcation with varied aspirations of the natives of Tajikistan openly clashes with the objectives of the non-natives, present in the republic in the guise of

CIS peace keepers. The civil war resulted in 50,000 casualties and more than 800,000 fleeing their homes to safer places.[10]

Similarly, regional ethnic differences in Kazakhstan are across a north-south divide: the north being predominantly Russified and the south largely Kazakhzed. What adds more complexities to the Kazakh problem is the differences among various Hordes. The third dimension of ethnic sharpness stems from the sizeable presence of Cossacks, settled in Kazakhstan for centuries. The fourth angle that throws Kazakhstan into a global jigsaw is the very central location of the state in Eurasia. This itself makes it a coveted place for international rivalry; the presence of any ethnic divide just sharpens that competition. The fifth, and possibly final perspective, could be the aspirations of the Uighurs for a unified territory of their own, snatching a bit of land from all three countries – Kazakhstan, Kyrgyzstan and China. Interestingly, the Uighur movement is the only organized nationalist mission in Central Asia, aiming at a separate state, more threatening China than Central Asian states.

Uzbekistan's problems are a wee bit different. First, there is a Uzbek-Tajik problem, a traditional inheritance that always simmers beneath placid bilateral ties. Secondly, Uzbekistan has a highly porous border with Afghanistan and the aftermath of September 11, 2001 has considerable significance on the role this major republic of Central Asia could play in fighting international terrorism. Its close linkages with Afghanistan are attested by the fact that, traditionally, in the fight against the Talibans, it had extended stoic support to General Dastum, an ethnic Uzbek in northern Afghanistan pitted against General Masood, an ethnic Tajik, who had received respective patronage from both their eponymous neighbours like Iran and Tajikistan. The third and most worrisome aspect is the Ferghana tinder box. In a compact territory, saddled with overpopulation and shortage of land, sharply divided by high living standard of the nomadic non-natives relative to the settled natives, Ferghana, at least on two past occasions, had epitomized Central Asia's ethnic bitterness in fierce battles with many reported deaths and casualties.

Turkmenistan singles out itself as a state of unlimited authoritarian principles. Held together by tribal loyalty from the grass root to republican level, it maintained "positive neutrality" in all matters of inter-state relations and largely avoided conflicting prospects. Pillars of its internal relations were state subsidies to woo people to support whatever Saparmurad Niyazov undertook on behalf of the state; and external policies anchored on exporting the huge oil and natural gas potential of the country. Whoever helped in those areas remained friends; others were treated neutrally. What remains specific to Central Asia in general is the political transformations of its polity. All republics have transformed themselves from a single party authoritarianism to what Devendra Kaushik says "a personalized authoritarianism of their executive presidents."[11]

CONFLICT MANAGEMENT LEVEL

As conflict itself arises at various levels, its management could take place at various levels too: local, provincial, regional, national and international. Corresponding to these territorial levels, conventional attempts have been made at all these levels in Tajikistan. Warring factions at the local levels taking up cudgels with provincial power barons had fought relentlessly until UN mediation and CIS-Russia peacekeepers arrived on the scene in Tajikistan to take control of the situation. Some of these methods have also been tried in other conflicting situations like those in Alma-Ata in Kazakhstan and Ferghana in Uzbekistan mainly through politico-diplomatic channels and only through the means of dialogue between conflicting parties and the authorities.

However, ethnic conflicts considerably differ from other types of conflicts. There are inherent difficulties in dealing with such conflicts because they encompass cultural ethos of nations in conflict. Overlooking any aspect—religious, linguistic, cultural, territorial et al—could lead to conflagration on ethno-national grounds. Therefore, the managers of ethnic conflicts ought not ignore sensitive nuances of ethno-nationalism. The Central Asian situation is all the more complicated in view of the sizeable cross-cultural, cross-linguistic, cross-border and cross-religious phenomena as shown in the following diagrams.

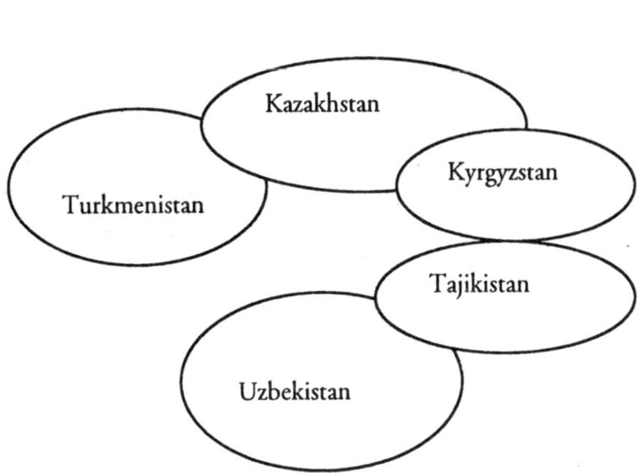

Fig. 6.1: Overlapping Ethno-Territorial Entities

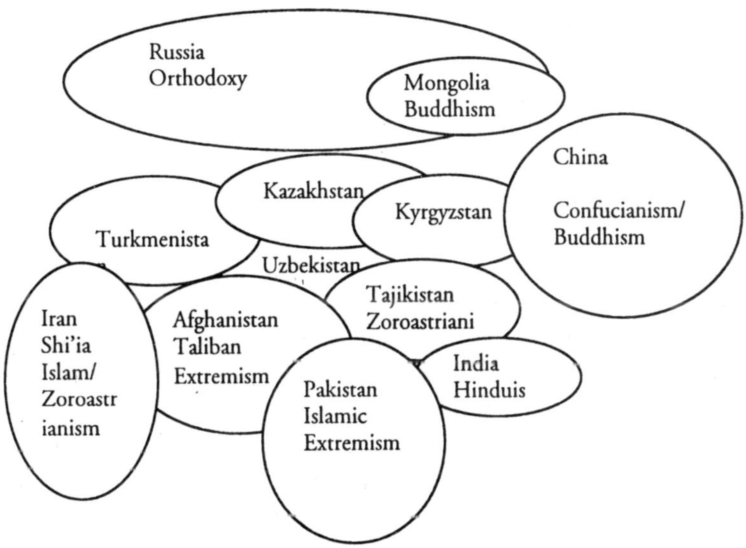

Fig. 6.2: Confessional Complexities of Neighbourhood States

The overlapping character of unresolved issues on a given territorial space ferments bickering within and among ethnic communities, leading largely to mutual hostility; and finally ending in bloodshed. The case study of ethnic conflicts in the Ferghana valley is a valid example. If we circle the territory of the valley which is the residence of the populations of three independent states – Uzbekistan, Tajikistan and Kyrgyzstan, we get the first level of politico-territorial conflicts. Overlapping population causes majority-minority differences based on which other acrimonies soon follow. If we draw further circles on linguistic lines, sharpness of the conflicts becomes more obvious. If we still add the Slavic dimension to the Ferghana region and circle that territory with possible Slav-Islam divide, we get a clear picture of religious animosity without even going into the sub-divisions of those religions.

Thus, on one plain, independent states such as Kazakhstan, Kyrgyzstan, Tajikistan, Turkmenistan and Uzbekistan form major conflicting circles. They vie with each other to affirm their nationhood, national supremacy and effective governance, but come into conflict when they embark on resolving inter-state disputes. Segmentation circles drawn on historical roots as enumerated above within the given space of each republic, provide us clues to visualize a complex regional ethnic scenario far too difficult to handle. In such a situation absence of cooperation leads to mutual differences, and lack of deference for one another's demands breeds the ground for inter-ethnic hostility.

If we further draw country-wise circles on the outer fringe of these states by involving countries of the Central Asian neighborhood such as Russia, Mongolia, Afghanistan, Pakistan, Iran, China and India, we get a mosaic of problems. Apart from ethnic differences, the more complicated aspect here is that of religion. Confucianism in China, Hinduism in India, Buddhism in Mongolia and China, Orthodox Christianity in Russia, Shi'ia Islam in Iran, Islamic extremism in Afghanistan and Pakistan and moderate Islam in the erstwhile space of Soviet Central Asia, all provoke us to believe as if all great religions of the world are thrust onto a small space on earth to fight out their own limits, strength and space.[12] In such a situation, hopefully, only the language of togetherness, brotherhood and cooperation could work, while anything else would end in fatality.

In the Central Asian context, the sub-national, national and supra-national levels of dealing with ethnic conflicts may not give desired results because situations and contexts overlap and overshadow individual interests, even if they are defined, thus putting forth common interests of the region to the fore. Handling narcotic trafficking, dealing with collective security issues, fighting the menace of terrorism are some of the regional issues that solicit collective remedy rather than micro level handling.

CLASH OF INTERESTS

Emergence of new states in Central Asia after the Soviet collapse precipitated the urgency of not only asserting independent statehood, but also diplomatically dealing with other countries of the world. As novices in the field of diplomacy, all the twenty one new post-communist multinational countries: six born out of the constituent republics of former Yugoslavia and fifteen constituent republics of the erstwhile Soviet Union, often looked to the outer world for appropriate support and a model to emulate. There was an array of choice before them ranging from western democracy to Chinese communism and from India's parliamentary model to Turkey's Ozal model of mixed economy. While the Central Asian states embarked on their quest to democracy, they found no path appropriately viable for themselves. The ideal model for them was initially thought to be Turkey, which subsequently became not so very alluring. The quest continued in the midst of trial and errors and what prevailed most was the care for national interests uppermost in the minds of Central Asian leaders. The diplomatic forays of Central Asian countries in the past decade attest their admirable overtures in cultivating ties with countries of the East and West alike, but first of all safeguarding their respective national interests.

In a distinct departure from the Cold War practice, when "the West would not and the East could not support multiethnic communist states", the post-Cold War equations have seen countries of the East and West, ironically, offering all possible help to Central Asia for economic reconstruction. Major countries of the world had quickly assessed their strategic and economic interest in Central Asia and had begun their pursuits immediately. The USA, Turkey, China, Japan and Russia et al had landed with their own agendas to be implemented. These agendas overtly implied taking full advantage of the fluid situation in the region. Exploitation of the Caspian oil reserve, finding a way out for Turkmen gas, eyeing on Uzbekistan's gold and getting a hold over natural and mineral resources in other countries were some of the tangible intentions.

The covert intentions, however, were the assumptions of Central Asia's weak predicament on the one hand, and strategic location on the other. And it was presumed that gaining a foothold in the area matters for the future. It was also assumed that, if possible, the unstable ethno-political situation could be harnessed to distinct western advantage. However, that did not happen. What followed were ambitious pipeline projects, memoranda of understanding and several cooperation agreements signed at bilateral and multilateral levels with many foreign countries. Simultaneously, visible too was an integration movement for regional cooperation. One observes a decade after the continuing clash of native interests with foreign interests and what has prevailed is not the clash of interest so much as new platforms of tangible cooperation in various fields without harming national interests of Central Asian countries. Central Asia's economic cooperation with the outer world has made progress without holding resolution of ethno-national conflicts hostage to it. The primacy of economic growth has overshadowed other imperatives. Economic growth has become a leading candidate for easing conflicts of all kinds because economic prosperity is regarded as a miracle drug for social and economic ills.[13]

CONFLICT RESOLUTION METHODS

Use of Force: Since most ethno-national movements incorporate violence into their agenda, and tend to be violent at the slightest provocation, authorities dealing with such movements treat them not peacefully. The normal recourse to contain such movements is "violence for violence or tit for tat". A case study of Central Asian ethnic hostilities, whether in Osh, Alma-Aty or Tajikistan tells us more about violent attempts of resolving it rather than anything peaceful. Use of force remains unfortunately a primary means of conflict resolution, although very often experience has shown that it brings damaging outcomes.

Force is used mainly at two levels: at the local level by the police to handle minor frictions, and at wider level by intervention of the army when situation goes out of hand. Both implementing agencies show scant regard for violation of human rights and never think of alternative strategies to obtain non-violent outcomes. Since ethno-national conflicts across the globe have become policy dilemma for governance, force is not perceived as the most efficacious means to deal with them effectively. Instead, countries facing ethno-national volatility prefer diplomacy to force as a panacea.

Negotiations: The number of sovereign states has continued to grow in the last fifty years. The United Nations had only 50 members, when it was founded in 1945; by 1999 its membership stood at 185.[14] No sooner a new state is born than it carves out its own political niche on the map, precipitating boundary issues to become patent within its parent territory. The imperatives of negotiations arise at this point to assuage collateral damages of an ethnic conflict involving two or more states. If the instruments of dialogue remain ineffective, objectives of the given ethno-national movement remain murky, rather blurred in the thick of violent twists and turns its people have just passed through.

Negotiations begin when violence ceases and violence starts where negotiations fail or falter. This unending ups and downs entwined within the action-reaction process of violence and negotiations make negotiations a paramount instrument of conflict resolution. The involved parties wrestle within their available social and political space to ventilate their national emotions, a cultural space to air their heritage, and finally, obtain a solution to clashing national interests. Success of negotiations depends on maturity of the movement, leadership qualities within the movement, ability and adroitness of those at the helm of affairs, their negotiating skills, mass appeal of their programs and most of all the level of public awareness about self-determination that stands to back the movement. A combination of all these makes negotiations a formidable instrument of conflict resolution in general, and ethno-national conflicts in particular.

Emigration as Solution: A case study of post-Soviet Central Asian ethnic situation throws light on ethnic proclivity getting strong in the face of mounting crisis. The outpouring desire demonstrated by the Slavic population to migrate from Central Asia while facing a crisis situation has brought to the fore emigration as means of resolving ethnic conflict. Why has such a fear overtaken the Central Asian Slavs? An interesting fact to note in this context is that only a negligible 3-5 per cent of the Slavic population in Central Asia knew very well the language of the republic of their residence compared to above 65 per cent of the natives knowing fluent Russian. Such a linguistic alienation accentuated by new language laws in favour of the natives has obviously led to a cultural cleavage, raising apprehensions about safety and security among the non-natives, who considered fleeing from the reality of a solution to their problem. A host of other reasons such as "the danger of being close to an area of conflict, the worsening inter-ethnic relations, urban over-crowding and difficulties in finding appropriate language schools for children" are cited for the mass exodus.[15] In any case, over the years, emigration has not resolved inter-ethnic problems. Proper handling of linguistic issues coupled with a strong political will may go a long way to tackle the problem.

The fact that Central Asian ethnic disputes have only ethnic undertones, and do not have self-determination agendas (except in the case of Uighurs), provokes us to search for unconventional solutions. Unlike Abkhazia, Chechnya, Tatarstan and other ethnic hot-spots, Central Asian states have problems within the republic, mostly stemming from cultural mismatch. The immediate task, therefore, is not independence but affirming statehood, and mitigating frictions, springing from intolerance, conflicting cultural roots and aspirations. These frictions need deft and tactful political handling by the republics themselves. One could also seek foreign aid to mitigate the economic plight of the people in order to moderate ethnic conflicts, not necessarily by outside intervention, but certainly by means of negotiations and cooperation among the countries of the region.

REFERENCES

---

1. The definition of Central Asia here is without any territorial prejudice and in accordance with the decision of the Heads of States meeting

held in Tashkent in January 1993 that encompasses Kazakhstan, Kyrgyzstan, Tajikistan, Turkmenistan and Uzbekistan.

2. Vitaly V. Naumkin (Ed.), (1994), *Central Asia and Transcaucasia: Ethnicity and Conflict*, London, Greenwood Press, p. 17.
3. S.P. Polyakov, (1980), *Istoricheskaya Etnographiya Srednei Ajii i Kazakhstana*, Moskva, Nauka, pp. 95-96.
4. *Ibid.*, p. 97.
5. Anara Tabyshalieva, (1999), "The Challenge of Regional Cooperation in Central Asia: Preventing Ethnic Conflict in Ferghana Valley", *Peace Works* No. 28, *US Institute of Peace*, Washington DC, p. 9.
6. Timothy Heleniak, (1997), "Going Home: Migration among the Soviet successor States", *Analysis of Current Events*, Vol. 9, No. 6, p. 5.
7. Jiger Janabel, (1996), "When National Ambition Conflicts with Reality: Studies on Kazakhstan's Ethnic Relations", *Central Asian Survey*, March, Vol. 15, No. 1, p. 15.
8. Devendra Kaushik, (2001), "The Central Asian Republics: The Balance Sheet of a Decade of Ozodi", *Eurasian Studies*, Summer, p. 5.
9. Uran Botobekov, (2000), "Situatsiya v Ferghanskoi Doline", *Rossiya i Mussyl'manskii Mir*, No. 11, p. 77.
10. "Tajikistan: Tajik Refugees in Northern Afghanistan", *Human Rights Watch*, Vol. 8, No. 6, p. 3.
11. Devendra Kaushik, *op. cit.*, p. 6.
12. For a scintillating discussion, please refer to P.V. Chernov, (1999), *Rossiya: Etnopoliticheskie Osnovi Gosudarstvennosti*, Moskva, Boctochnaya Literatura.
13. Michael Mandelbaum, (1999), "The Future of Nationalism", *National Interest*, No. 57, Fall, pp. 21-22.
14. *Ibid*, p. 18.
15. John B. Dunlop, (1994), "Will the Russians Return from Near Abroad?", *Post-Soviet Geography*, Vol. XXXV, No. 4, p. 208.

7

Central Asian Republics' Quest for Security in the Post-Soviet Period

MOHAMMAD MONIR ALAM

The disintegration of the Union of Soviet Socialist Republics was an unprecedented event of the twentieth century. As a result, five independent Central Asian Republics—namely Kazahkstan, Uzbekistan, Tajikistan, Kyrgyzstan and Turkmenistan emerged in the vast Eurasian space. All these five Republics occupy a vast territory extending from western Siberia in the north to Afghanistan and Iran in the south, from the banks of the Volga and the Caspian sea in the west to China in the east. They cover an area of 4 million square kilometeres, or almost one-sixth of the territory of the former Soviet Union.

From the very ancient period, the geographical location of Central Asia has been of importance particularly for trade. It was a vibrant part of the world economy, and formed a crucial corridor connecting East and West as well as South to North. Before the discovery of sea routes; all the main land trade routes connecting East and Central Asia with Eastern Europe and countries of the Near East lay across this territory.[1] The 'Great Silk Route' connecting Persia and China with the Roman empire also passed through the Central Asian region. During the 19th and early 20th centuries, this region was a zone of triangular contest between Britain, Russia and China which had been romanticized as "the Great Game". However, the 19th century "Great Game" over Central Asia which Britain played against Russia was mainly explained in terms of the strategic significance of the region because of its geographical location as the gateway to the Indian subcontinent and the Persian Gulf. Even then the geographical factor was merely a facade and the leitmotif was the economic driven imperialist rivalry between the European Great Powers.

At present, oil is a crucial source of energy all the world over and it is likely to remain so in the foreseeable future. Central Asia with its large hydrocarbon reserves and natural gas resources has undoubtedly become a region of critical strategic importance and an object of international activities and interests. According to Western experts, the real hydrocarbon reserves in Central Asia are staggeringly large, perhaps equal to those of Saudi Arabia and Kuwait combined if both the onshore and offshore Caspian Sea resources are included. The oil reserves in the Caspian shelf are estimated at 17 to 21 billion tons (the Russian experts, however, consider these estimates as exaggerated in order to justify extension of American and Western political influence to the Caspian and the Caucasus region). Central Asia is estimated to contain about 46 per cent of the world's gas reserves.

After the October Revolution of 1917 and the establishment of the Soviet power in Central Asia, the Soviet leadership always demonstrated its adequate concern for the security and stability of its southern territories, which formed its 'soft underbelly'. During the seven decades of Soviet rule, it remained free from internecine conflicts, and felt no threat to its security from neighbouring powers. But after the disintegration of the Soviet Union, all five Central Asian Republics have been thrown into the vortex of the international politics. A wide ranging debate covering such diverse issues as economic changes, ecological imbalances, democratization and human rights, ethno-nationalism, religious revivalism, arms proliferation, terrorism, regional stability and most important of all, the defense and security issues, have assumed importance.

THE FALLOUT OF THE DISSOLUTION OF THE SOVIET UNION FOR CENTRAL ASIAN SECURITY

Both geography and history have already combined to keep Central Asia as a landlocked area with a strife torn turbulent neighbour like Afghanistan in the south and powerful ones, like Russia in the north, Turkey and Iran in the west and south, and China in the east, as a region with an astonishing mix of geopolitical interests. Furthermore, after the disintegration of the Soviet Union, these newly independent states, with their weak economies, unstable political system and no independent strong defense capability, became vulnerable to external pressure and penetration. As a result, certain regional powers namely-Turkey, Iran, Saudi Arabia and Pakistan as well as other western powers, especially the United States of America, attempted to fill the power vacuum created by the Soviet withdrawal in the Central Asian Republics.

At first, Yeltsin's leadership failed to formulate a clear policy towards Central Asia. In the beginning, while giving preference to integrating the former Soviet Republics into the broad frame-work of the Commonwealth of Independent States (CIS) under Russia's leadership, Boris Yeltsin could not take viable steps to fill the vacuum that the collapse of the Soviet Union created for the Central Asian Republics. In fact President Yeltsin initially tried to build the CIS on the basis of an alliance with nuclear and mainly Slavic Ukraine and Belarus. However, when the struggle between two competing visions of Russia's foreign policy (the Euro-Atlanticist represented by Andrei Kozyrev, Yegor Gaider, Boris Yeltsin) and (the Neo-Eurasianists represented by Vice President Alexander Rutskoi, Ruslan Khasbutalov, Sergei Stankevich, Yuri Skanov, General Shaposhnikov and General Pavel Grachev)[2] intensified, Boris Yeltsin and Kozyrev embraced some of the formulations of their opponents by emphasizing the need for adaptation in the world community, with the maintenance of Russia's status as 'a greater power', with global and regional interests, and good relations with both East and West on the basis of what best served 'Russian national interest' as 'the only ideology of... foreign policy'.[3] Hence, after an initial phase of indifferent policy towards

Central Asian states, Russia made a concerted effort to deter all external and regional powers from filling the gap.

President Boris Yeltsin and his Foreign Minister Andrei Kozyrev personally realized that for all practical purposes and security considerations, Russia must maintain a determining influence in Central Asia. Subsequently, Russia made efforts to maintain close relations with its erstwhile components to secure a strong guarantee for regional security and stability. Russia's comprehensive and long standing relations with Central Asia also clearly indicate that protection of these states from external threats and internal instability, is, however, the sole responsibility of the Russian Federation. It is well justified that despite its withdrawal from Central Asia, Russia could not ignore its strategic concerns, geopolitical links and collective security interests in maintaining stability within the region. It had already ensured that no regional power can supplant Moscow's preferential status in Central Asia. At the same time, these newly independent states also harbored no military ambitions, but urgently needed an 'external stabilizing presence' in the region.[4] Central Asian elite still believe that Russia, the only external actor, is 'potentially capable for maintaining the existing degree of stability in the region'.[5]

The ethno-nationalistic fervor in the region, the secessionist movements, and the spread of Islamic radicalism both in Central Asia and Russia (Chechnya, Tatarastan and Dagestan) have been also identified as sources of grave concern for regional security. These factors pose serious threats not only to political stability of the Central Asian regions but also have serious repercussions for the security of Russia and the People's Republic of China. For all these perceived threats, Russia can only provide the 'front line of defense'. Moreover, the interface with the power vacuum factor immediately exposed the Central Asian Republics to regional power rivalries and Islamic influences. Of the regional powers, Iran, Turkey, Pakistan and Saudi Arabia now found a new area of influences. Instability in Afghanistan after the victory of the *mujahideen* over the Soviet backed government headed by President Najibullah in 1992, and subsequent seizure of Kabul and Mazar-i-Sharif by *Taliban* Islamic militia also raised the specter of what some of the Russians had feared.

Afghanistan, torn apart by internal conflicts, encouraged by religious extremism, ethnic intolerance, drug trafficking, illegal arms trade, is still a hotbed of instability. During the course of the Tajik civil war, the armed provocation on the Tajik-Afghan border, together with other manifestations of subversive activity from Afghanistan, seriously destabilized the situation in Tajikistan, and consequently the entire region. It also generated a wide ranging problem— the problem of refugees, illegal drug trafficking, international terrorism and arms proliferation. According to UN Report, Afghanistan has become not only one of the leading producers of raw opium, but it is the biggest transit point for drug delivery to the states of Central Asia and the west.

At present, the multi-national military campaign and war against global terrorism in Afghanistan against *Taliban* Islamic militia to pick-out Osama Bin-Laden, the prime suspect of September 11 terrorist attack on Washington and New York, and to crackdown his terrorist organisation *Al-Qaeda,* under the leadership of United States of America, has already created a situation of uncertainty and instability throughout the region. However, the success of military campaign against the Taliban Islamic militia has created a conducive situation for political stability in Afghanistan.

After the dissolution of the Soviet Union, there was a publicized upsurge in the U.S. concern under the former President George Bush about what was called the growth of 'Iranian backed Islamic fundamentalism' and vulnerability of the Central Asian Republics to it. Subsequently, the U.S. Secretary of State James Baker, in a well publicized tour, visited the Central Asian Republics in early 1992, and urged leaders to look towards Turkey for the best model of development rather than to Iran, which he declared, to be an 'outlaw state'.[6] The United States of America was also very much concerned about the proliferation of nuclear fissile materials of Central Asia into the hands of international terrorist groups.

However, the first alarm for security concern of Central Asian states was raised in early 1992, when the ruling elite of these Republics warned Moscow that its Euro-centric orientation dominated policy could pave the way for the predatory designs of the West Asian Muslim fundamentalist forces in their lands. Powerful economic lobbies also demanded Russia's continued and even enhanced 'strategic interest in Central Asia taking into account the need of protecting the Central Asian States'.[7] Subsequently, the ethno-nationalist conflict in Tajikistan in May 1992 proved instrumental in giving an assertive turn in pushing the Russian active policy towards the Central Asian States. Tajikistan became the venue for fierce power struggle between the ruling Communist Government of President Nabiev and the opposition, led by an alliance of the Islamists.

These all perceived radical Islamic threats and developments around the periphery forced the Central Asian elite to prepare for close ties with Russia. 'In Uzbekistan', said President Islam Karimov, 'fundamentalism can find no support. Russia guarantees the security and indivisibility of the borders of the Central Asian region, therefore Uzbekistan can not survive without it'.[8] Uzbekistan sees Russia as its only partner, which in spite of having its own interests in the region, is a lesser evil than the fundamentalist regimes of Iran or Afghanistan. It is only Uzbekistan among the Central Asian Republics, which with its authoritarian secular regime, has become the main obstacle to the expansion of Islamic fundamentalism in the region. All these developments (growth of Islamic radicalism, instability in Afghanistan, perpetuated by fighting among the *mujahideen* groups, and international rivalry of regional powers as well as European powers for influence in the region), have added to the importance of Russia as a real guarantor of peace, security and stability of the region. Besides the economic domination, military grip of Russia over Central Asia, though it may change with time, is still quite strong to meet the new challenges arising from the changing geopolitical conditions following the disintegration of the USSR and increasing outside interest in the energy resources of the region.

CENTRAL ASIAN REPUBLICS AND MULTI-LATERAL SECURITY ARRANGEMENTS WITHIN THE CIS FRAMEWORK

The Soviet Union was replaced by the Commonwealth of Independent States (CIS) grouping 12 of the former constituent republics of the Soviet Union in a loose alliance on December 21, 1991 at Almaty.[9] The formation of the Commonwealth of Independent States by the erstwhile components of the Soviet Union and their collective declaration on the various issues of socio-economic, strategic, defense and security cooperation was a landmark event towards their peaceful existence in the post-Soviet period. It was assumed by all members of the CIS that Russia, the real successor of the Soviet Union and having special as well as advantageous position, would play a pivotal role during the transitional phase of independence in the overall security of the newly emerged Commonwealth of Independent States. Hence, all the five Central Asian Republics, though having some differences with the Russian Federation, fully shared a common concern for their security on account of their mutual dependence. The leaders of Central Asian Republics emphasized that Russia, for all practical purposes within the institutional context of CIS, would be the sole guarantor of peace and security in the region.

After the formation of the Commonwealth of Independent States, the most significant development within the CIS with far reaching security implications for Central Asian Republics was the *Treaty on Collective Security* signed between Kazakhstan, Russian Federation, Kyrgyzstan, Tajikistan, Uzbekistan and Armenia, in Tashkent (Uzbekistan) on May 15, 1992.[10] The only Central Asian Republic-Turkmenistan was not the signatory to the Treaty.

The Tashkent Summit, attended by the Heads of the Government of all the participant members and chaired by Kazakh President Nursultan Nazarbayev, negotiated a five year collective security agreement providing for a collective response to aggression against any of its signatories. Other agreements signed by all participants at the summit included—

(*i*) agreement for reducing armed forces of the former Soviet Union,
(*ii*) reducing chemical weapons in accordance with international agreements,
(*iii*) creating a single air space, a single information space, and in principle, a CIS television and radio company,
(*iv*) agreement on border troops,

(*v*) social provision for servicemen, and
(*vi*) provision for formation of a collective Security Council consisting of the heads of participating states and the Commander-in-Chief of the CIS joint armed forces.

Article 1 and 4 of Treaty of the Collective Security signed at the Tashkent Summit clearly states: 'The participating states shall not enter into military alliances or participate in any groupings of states, nor in actions directed against any other participating state'; and furthermore, 'If one of the participating states is subjected to aggression by any state or group of states, this will be perceived as an aggression against all participating states to the treaty'. In the event of an act of aggression being committed against any of the participating states, all the other participating states will give it the necessary assistance, including military assistance, and will also give support with the means at their disposal by way of exercising the right to collective defense in accordance with article 51 of the United Nations' Charter.[11]

General V. Samsanov, Chief of the CIS Joint Armed Forces General Staff, pointed to the political significance of the Treaty: 'The treaty on collective security is the basis for forming a defence alliance' and '... the first and probably the most complex step towards creating on effective military and political structure capable of being a guarantee of security for the successful political and economic development of the subjects that form the CIS'.[12]

Thus, the Tashkent Summit provided the main security dimension of the Commonwealth of Independent States. The significance of the agreement did not primarily lie in its internal provisions, more importantly it provided an essential precondition and backdrop for the more detailed and substantive bilateral military agreements which Russia subsequently signed with all the Central Asian states including Turkmenistan..

Immediately after the Tashkent Summit, two agreements, equally but not more significant, were reached among the participant states in Moscow (July 6, 1992) and Tashkent (July 16, 1992) which provided more substantive support to the previous collective security agreement. The two meetings specifically addressed the twin significant issues—mechanism of the creation of the CIS 'blue helmet' peace keeping force (Moscow Summit) for rapid deployment in the areas of regional conflict within the CIS, and the issue of security of the southern border of the CIS (Tashkent Summit). The Moscow summit also defined 'the exterior border of the participant states as the border of the CIS and its defence within the jurisdiction of CIS Joint Armed Forces'.[13] Both Marshal Shaposhnikov, the Commander-in-Chief of the CIS Joint Armed Forces, and General V. Samsanov, CIS Chief of the General Staff, re-affirmed that the quick reaction to the threat posed against the 'outside borders of the commonwealth' is one of the key tasks of the CIS collective security agreement.[14]

Another very important summit of leaders of the Commonwealth of Independent States with far reaching security implication was held in the Byelarussian capital, Minsk, on January 22, 1993. After prolonged debate, a charter for closer political, economic integration, and defence alliance was prepared. The charter was signed by seven of the 10 former Soviet Republics represented at the meeting (Russia, Byelarus, Armenia, Kazakhstan, Uzbekistan, Kyrgyzstan and Tajikistan). Ukraine, Moldova and Turkmenistan refused to sign. A commitment was made within the CIS framework that Russia would be ready to guarantee the security and territorial integrity of Central Asian states and to defend it against external attack and internal instability.[15] The Charter of this Conference may be looked upon as a 'multilateral treaty' consisting of fifty articles. Article 3 maintains that the member states ought to build their relations on the principle of 'non-interference in one another's internal and external affairs'. Article 5, 4 and 29 stipulate 'the coordination of foreign-policy activity' and 'co-operation in the field of the defense industry and the protection of external borders'. The third section of the Charter envisages 'Collective Security and Military-Political Cooperation'. Article 4 may be viewed as an extension of the Collective Security Treaty signed at Tashkent.[16]

An extraordinary meeting of the Heads of Government of the Commonwealth of Independent States (CIS) was again held in Minsk on April 16, 1993. The summit was attended by all the CIS heads of state except Turkmenistan and Kyrgyzstan. Both Boris Yeltsin and the President of Kazakhstan, Nursultan Nazarbayev, emphasised the security cooperation and need to check growing intrigues of anti-government forces in Tajakistan.[17] The concept of collective security within the CIS appears to have gained ground since the Minsk Summit. On August 7, 1993, Russia and the Central Asian Republics of Kazakhstan, Tajikistan and Uzbekistan, decided to set up a regional security system 'in accordance with the agreement of collective security of the CIS states and bilateral agreements with Tajikistan'. President Islam Karimov of Uzbekistan justified the security pact on the ground that the militant Islamic fundamentalistic forces were working overtime to turn Tajikistan into a 'springboard' for spreading militant fundamentalism in the Central Asian Republics and other CIS states and that, therefore, it was necessary to 'prevent in their territories the activities of persons, groups and organisations' aimed 'at violating the security of those states'. It was also emphasised that the borders of Tajikistan were 'part of the common borders of the CIS', and Russia has a historic duty to guard the Tajik-Afghan border.[18]

Keeping in view the security of the exterior border of the Commonwealth of Independent States particularity Tajik-Afghan border, a communiqué was issued by the Foreign Ministers of Russia, Tajikistan, Kazakhstan, Kyrgyzstan and Uzbekistan following their meeting in Dushanbe on March 15, 1994. It demanded that peacekeeping forces of CIS in Tajikistan should be granted the UN status. Even Russian Foreign Minister, Andrei Kozyrev insisted that the CIS's peacekeeping role did not require 'international approval' and that Russia had 'a historic duty to guard the Tajik-Afghan border'.[19]

Another important CIS Summit was held in Moscow on January 19, 1996. President Boris Yeltsin, while addressing the meeting of the CIS Heads of State, proposed concentrating efforts on creating a single defence space and stronger system of collective security in the CIS. Boris Yeltsin stated: 'It is virtually impossible for the countries of the Commonwealth, acting individually, to ensure their national security, but we can achieve this through a system of collective security'.[20] The Russian President also stressed the importance of preserving the military systems which previously protected the territory of the Soviet Union, in particular the single air defence system, and of restoring joint production in the military industrial complex. [21]

Presidents of the five former Soviet Republics of Central Asia in a joint statement, issued on January 6 1998, following two days of talks in the Turkmen capital Ashkabad, agreed on an individual approach to CIS. All leaders agreed that the CIS is 'an acceptable model for cooperation at the transitional stage'. However, 'each member of the Commonwealth should determine its participation independently on the basis of domestic priorities and international commitments'.[22] Uzbek President Islam Karimov, in a news conference after the summit, highlighted the problems of poor decision making and excessive bureaucracy in the CIS, and expressed the opinion that each country should retain its own independent policy instead of 'setting up supra state structures'. He also stated that 'the CIS cannot act as an international legal entity, nor it exists as a military and political bloc'.[23]

A landmark summit of the Council of Heads of States of the CIS opened in Moscow on April 29, 1998 to discuss future of the Commonwealth. After the summit, the leaders decided against adopting any final declaration on the results of this CIS summit, and even President Nazarbayev of Kazakhstan commented: 'What is the sense (of taking a declaration) if nothing is decided'. He was backed by President Boris Yeltsin, who noted that 'a faulty practice is shaping up' whereby 'it is necessary by all means to adopt a certain document' after each meeting.[24]

President of Belarus, Lukashenko while criticizing Russia for not being ready for a 'full fledged union' with Belarus, stated that over 1,000 agreements have been signed within the CIS but none of them was working, That's why 'before any thing else, whatever has been signed must be implemented'. Moldavian President Lucinschi, while commenting on functions of the CIS, said: 'The Commonwealth is at a turning point, facing a dilemma – to be or not to be', and suggested that 'all 12 CIS states weigh their opportunities and sign a workable document' which should provide for 'transparent borders and the free flow of capital, people and commodities all over the CIS'.[25]

The Declaration on CIS Guidelines of Development adopted on April 2, 1999, by the Moscow meeting of Heads of States mentioned among others the "confirmation of our resolution to settle armed conflicts in Commonwealth member countries as soon as possible by peaceful means and with the use of UN and OSCE mechanisms and resources on the basis of undeviating compliance with territorial integrity, inviolability of state frontiers, and other universally recognised international legal norms and principles".

However, till now more than hundred agreements within the framework of Commonwealth of Independent States have been signed by all its constituent members, but in practice, not a single provision of the agreements has been implemented. Furthermore, for all practical purposes the Collective Security Treaty was already dead when President Islam Karimov openly declared in February 1999 that it would not renew its membership and gave formal notice for withdrawal of Uzbekistan from the Treaty. Moreover, the changing perceptions of leaders and the regional groupings and alliances by the members of the CIS, has also greatly affected the relevance of the Commonwealth of Independent States as collective organisation to look after collective security as well as various issues of the Commonwealth Republics.

RUSSIA AND CENTRAL ASIAN REPUBLICS: BILATERAL SECURITY AGREEMENTS

In the post-Soviet period, Russia has continuously accelerated the process of reintegrating former Soviet Central Asian Republics both through multilateral and bilateral security agreements. While the Treaty on Collective Security provided the security guarantee for the Central Asian Republics, its chances for survival and endurance have, however, been greatly enhanced by the series of bilateral 'friendship treaties' that Russia has signed with all the Central Asian Republics. It is this 'bilateral level' that provides the additional and perhaps real substance to the 'collective level' security agreements.

Kazakhstan

The Republic of Kazakhstan (until December 1991, the Kazakh Soviet Socialist Republic) is the largest and most prosperous among the five Central Asian Republics. Its unique geopolitical and strategic position by possessing former Soviet nuclear warheads (approximately 1,410) and regarded as the fourth largest nuclear power in the world, had greatly attracted Russia. At the time of disintegration of the Soviet Union, the most important Soviet strategic nuclear weapons on Kazakh territory were the Inter-Continental Ballistic Missile (ICBM) bases with 104-SS-18, each armed with ten warheads, 40TU-95 Bear bombers, the Semipalatinsk nuclear test site, the Baikanur space launch centre, and the Anti-Ballistic Missile (ABM) radar site. This was considered to be an important factor in forging the bilateral security agreements between Russia and Kazakhstan in the post-Soviet era.

Kazakhstan took the lead on May 25, 1992 for the bilateral security agreements. Following his trip to the United States, Kazakh President Nursultan Nazarbayev arrived in Moscow to sign the Treaty on Friendship, Cooperation and Mutual Assistance. Both the leaders, Nursultan Nazarbayev and Boris Yeltsin, signed a 25 years Treaty of Friendship and Cooperation providing for Russian assistance in establishing Kazakh armed forces, joint use of space and military bases, test sites, to render each other military assistance in case of aggression and other military infrastructures.[26]

The Treaty was characterised by Yeltsin's Press Office as 'a kind of political test site and verifying philosophy' of relations between newly independent states.[27] Boris Yeltsin and Nazarbayev expressed hopes that other CIS states will take the Treaty as a model to be followed. This first experiment in bilateral security within the CIS also had an additional regional significance, as it was taking place after the Ashkhabad Summit in which Central Asian leaders as well as the leaders of Iran, Turkey and Pakistan contemplated formation of an 'Asian Bloc'. The Ashkhabad Summit signifies the height of Russia's indifference and passive attitude towards the geopolitics of the southern republics. However, the Treaty with Kazakhstan was the beginning of Russia's 'Eurasian/ Eastern' shift and of the regaining of some of the lost ground in the region.

After the May 1992 agreement, a delegation headed by the Russian Armed Forces of General Staff, Colonel General Viktor Dubynin and Kazakhstan's Defence Minister, Colonel General Sagadat Nurmogombetov signed a famous accord on military agreements and assistance covering the transfer of personnel between two armed forces, training and military cooperation on August 19, 1992, at Alma-Aty. President Nursultan Nazarbayev and his counterpart, President Boris Yeltsin, issued a joint declaration and emphasized the importance of full scale economic cooperation, and coordinated security arms control and science policy regarding the former Soviet installation in space station at Baikanur and nuclear testing area at Semipalatinsk.[28]

Moving on to the question of military cooperation President Nazarbayev stated in Moscow on February 26, 1993, that as Russia and Kazakhstan had signed a collective security treaty, they regarded the territories of the two states as a "single defence space", and that in order to promote further unity of the armies of the two Republics it was necessary to set up joint contingents. A joint communiqué issued after the negotiations between President Boris Yeltsin and Nazarbayev on February 26, 1993, reiterated the commitment of both states to the implementation of the bilateral treaty signed in May 1992, and the enhancement of the treaty of collective security by a Kazakh-Russian decision to 'sign a treaty on military cooperation in order to set up a united defence space (common defence zone) and make joint use of military capabilities'. [29]

Another land mark important bilateral military agreement at the level of Defence Ministers, was signed in Alma-Aty, when Russian Defence Minister Pavel Grachev alongwith a delegation of senior military officials with the plan of joint military work of the two states for 1996, arrived in Kazakhstan on January 25, 1996. Kazakh Defence Minister, Alibek Kasymov, and his visiting Russian counterpart, Grachev, signed a package of 16 bilateral military agreements in Alma-Aty on January 26, 1996. The package included 'agreements on a consolidated air defence system, on Kazakhstan's national fleet which is to be set-up in the Caspian sea, and also documents regulating cooperation between the two countries defence ministers'.[30] Under a protocol on naval forces, Russia agreed to transfer five Cutters to Kazakhstan for carrying out coastal patrols, mainly used to combat drug trafficking and arms smuggling. Later on, this formed the basis of the Kazakhstan's new Caspian fleet to establish control and order in Caspian waters.

The package of agreement allowed Russia to give Kazakhstan SU-25, SU-27, and MIG-29 Combat aircrafts—'Several dozen' of each type to compensate for the transfer of 40 TU-95 MS strategic bombers from Kazakhstan to Russia. Pavel Grachev also agreed to help Kazakhstan in the consolidation of air defence system, to maintain and operate radar reconnaissance facilities along the Kazakh border to protect the CIS external borders. Kazakhstan also agreed to the withdrawal of a strategic Rocket Troops division from Kazakhstan to Russia within the first half of 1996. Both Ministers also discussed regional security and NATO's expansion. Grachev expressed his views and said that Russia 'categorically opposes' the expansion of NATO into Eastern and Central Europe. At the same time he welcomed cooperation with NATO according to the '16 + 9' formula—NATO plus the nine members of the CIS Collective Security Treaty, or the '16 + 12' formula—NATO plus the military and political structures of the CIS.[31]

The spirit of military cooperation between the two countries considerably enhanced and took a new shape by visualizing 21st century, when Russian President Boris Yeltsin, and his Kazakh counterpart, Nursultan Nazarbayev signed 'Declaration of Eternal Friendship and Alliance' in July 1998. The bilateral military cooperation was further strengthened by the visit of President Boris Yeltsin to Alma-Aty on October 12, 1998. Both President Boris Yeltsin and Nursultan Nazarbayev signed a number of bilateral military documents on border demarcation between Russia and Kazakhstan, a number of inter-governmental accords, including agreements on the Baikanur space complex and on cooperation in the fight against trans-border terrorism, drug trafficking and smuggling of illegal arms and ammunitions. President Nazarbayev, while commenting on bilateral agreements, stated: 'I pursue the policy of closeness and confidence towards Russia. We want to see Russia a prosperous country, and the Russian president shouldered the responsibility for the reforms which will put the country to a new road'.[32]

Uzbekistan

The Republic of Uzbekistan was the next to follow the model of Kazakhstan for bilateral security agreements with Russia. On May 30, 1992, Russia and Uzbekistan signed the 'Treaty on the Fundamentals of Interstate Relations, Friendship and Cooperation'. Both the Presidents Islam Karimov and Boris Yeltsin agreed that 'territories of Russia and Uzbekistan will form a common military strategic area'. They also granted each other "the right to use military facilities situated on their territories in case of necessity on the basis of military agreement".[33]

The Russian-Uzbek military and defence cooperation was further strengthened, when Russian Prime Minister Viktor Chernomyrdin visited Uzbekistan on July 28, 1995. After prolonged discussions with Islam Karimov on military technical cooperation, both leaders stressed the importance of the May 15, 1992 Treaty on Collective Security, and openly spoke in favour of forming a CIS Collective Security System on its basis. Both leaders also stressed Russia's and Uzbekistan's desire to continue 'strengthening cooperation and coordination of activity in the interests of ensuring peace and stability in Central Asia'.[34]

After the arrival of Boris Yeltsin in Tashkent, capital of Uzbekistan on October 11, 1998, the Russian President and his Uzbek counterpart, Islam Karimov, discussed bilateral military cooperation and the situation in Afghanistan. President Boris Yeltsin promised 'specific steps which we must take jointly to neutralize the threats to regional security and stability from Afghanistan'. After a long discussion on security cooperation President Karimov and his visiting Russian counterpart, Boris Yeltsin, signed a trilateral document on the military assistance pact. The document had been signed earlier by Tajik President Emomali Rahmonov. The declaration says that the sides 'intend to develop dialogue and collaboration in security and defence on the basis of equality, partnership and enhanced military-technical cooperation', and these three states also pledged to develop their cooperation, interacting with the UN, the OSCE and the CIS and also with other interested countries 'in the interest of total political stabilization in Tajikistan'. [35]

Kyrgyzstan

The Kyrgyz Republic is a small, landlocked state, situated in eastern Central Asia. After its independence, Kyrgyzstan joined the defence structures of the Commonwealth of Independent States (CIS) and along with other five member states signed the Collective Security Treaty in May 1992. Askar Akayev, President of Kyrgyzstan, was the next Central Asian leader to go to Moscow for a similar treaty with Russia. The two countries signed the Friendship, Cooperation and a Bilateral Assistance Treaty on June 10, 1992. According to Boris Yeltsin, this Treaty raised the bilateral relations to a new level putting the two states 'on an absolutely equal footing'. [36] Russia's role as the guarantor of Kyrgyzstan's security was reaffirmed. Kyrgyzstan's economic difficulties and inability to handle the financial responsibility of taking part in supporting CIS formations in Kyrgyzstan made this bilateral arrangement with Russia more appealing and more of a necessity.

In the beginning of 1996, a new impetus to the bilateral military cooperation was given, when Director of the Russian Federal Border Service Col. General Andrey Nikoloyev, who arrived in the Kyrgyz capital, Bishkek, on March 5, met President Askar Akayev. After discussing various issues related to defence cooperation, both signed two documents—one on the presence of Russian border troops in Kyrgyzstan, and another on extending the mandate of the Kyrgyz battalion currently serving in Tajikistan. They also signed 'Air Defence Accord', under which Russia agreed to supply Kyrgyzstan with arms, ammunition, spare parts and technical documentation, mutual exchange of information, and allowing Kyrgyz military units to carry out exercises at Russian test sites.[37]

On the basis of previous bilateral defence agreement, Kyrgyz troops and Russian border guards held a joint military exercise in Chon-Alay District in southern Kyrgyzstan on April 4-5, 1997, to prepare for possible trouble on the republic's border with Tajikistan. In this joint exercise, units of the OSR Motor-Rifle Brigade, the OSR Militia, a Directorate of the Republic's National Security Ministry and a Detachment of the Ministry for Emergencies were involved.[38] This military exercise was first of its kind to be held in the Republic. It was organized because the Kyrgyz leadership was alarmed by the possible spread of the inter-Tajik and inter-Afghan military conflicts to the territory of the Republic. Bishkek had repeatedly expressed fears that 'the growing influx of drugs and refugees from Tajikistan posed a threat to Kyrgyzstan, and that armed groups ousted into eastern Tajikistan would have easy access to Kyrgyz territory'.

Turkmenistan

The Republic of Turkmenistan was not a signatory to the CIS Collective Security Treaty of May 1992, but it remained within the collective security zone of CIS. The significance of the treaty with Turkmenistan was underscored by the intimate involvement of General Pavel Grachev, the Russian Defence Minister, who personally negotiated the agreement with Turkmen defence officials and Saparmurad Niazov, the President of the Republic. The treaty signed between Saparmurad Niazov and Russian Defence Minister, General Pavel Grachev on June 8, 1992, in Ashkhabad, was a unique one that envisioned the formation of a national army for Turkmenistan under joint command. The control of air force and air defence systems of Turkmenistan remained with the Russian Armed Forces (with some limited control by Turkmenistan).[39] Another military agreement with Russia, signed on September 2, 1993, allowed Russian citizens to take up military service in Turkmenistan, while enabling Turkmen officers to receive training at Russian military institutes. Turkmenistan also agreed to bear the cost of maintaining Russian forces on its territories after January 1, 1994. In return Russia would preserve some strategic bases in Turkmenistan.[40]

Turkmenistan's politico-military posture will continue to reflect the two key realities and preoccupations of its post-Soviet positions.

First, continuous and direct dependence on Russia for security of the new state vis-à-vis its neighbours. Second, the political desire and commitment to remain as independent as possible from Moscow and to avoid meaningful commitment in any regional politico-military bloc (i.e., CIS). Turkmenistan's continuous effort to enhance the political weight of its position in the command structure and decision making mechanisms of the 'joint command' of the army and its persistent relevant policy within the CIS – rejecting any notion of creating a 'supra state' structure of the Commonwealth – are reflective of Turkmenistan's dual predicament. Russia's forward politico-military position in Turkmenistan will thus continue to be affected by the inherent tension between Russian security designs and Turkmenistan's independent regional posture.[41]

Tajikistan

After the formation of the Commonwealth of Independent States, Tajikistan concluded a number of defence and security agreements with Russia. However, Russia's bilateral security treaties with Tajikistan are the most significant but more complex, because these directly dealt with the future security of the southern flank of the CIS.

After the collapse of the Najibullah regime in Afghanistan and victory of Islamic forces in that country, Tajikistan became vulnerable to the *Mujahideen* influence and border penetration. This development increasingly captured the attention of both Moscow and Central Asian states. Further, the ensuing 'Civil War' between northern and southern parts of Tajikistan after the victory of the democratic and Islamic coalition in Dushanbe, made the infiltration of arms and fighting groups from Afghanistan a potentially explosive issue. Islam Karimov, the Uzbek President, with a clear stake in the security of the 'southern flank' took the lead in addressing the issue in both the Tashkent and Moscow CIS summits.

Tajikistan's further incorporation into the security agreements was underscored by the request of President Nabiyev for deployment of CIS 'blue helmets' and 201st Motorised Rifle Division of Russia in Tajikistan's 'conflict zones' to dismantle the so called 'popular front' and to take over the task of ensuring the activities of the national economy's facilities and protection of the population. Russian security relations with Tajikistan, however, remained complicated because of domestic pressures generated by opposition forces in Tajikistan. Democratic and Islamic groups continued to be suspicious of Russian intentions and presence of its military contingent in the Republic.[42]

The invocation of a collective security agreement in the case of Tajikistan by the Alma-Aty meeting on November 4, 1992, was a clear indication that Russia and the Central Asian partners regardless of their intra–CIS differences would continue to hold the former Soviet Union's southern borders as the borders of the CIS and of Russia's sphere of influence. More significantly, it also indicated that the maintenance of the domestic stability of the Republic has been considered a legitimate security concern of the member states, which falls within the jurisdiction of the collective security agreements.

This was a clear message to all regional actors, including Iran, that inspite of the collapse of the Soviet Union, its geopolitical legacy will remain largely unchanged. Sergei Yastrzhemskiy, Head of the Foreign Ministry Press and Information Department, characterized Moscow's position rather frankly:

> The Russian Ministry proceeds from the premise that interference in the internal affairs of Tajikistan that is located in the area of the Russian Federation's important and versatile interest, can not be justified no matter from where it comes and what is motivated by ... Russia is ready to take all necessary measures to provide assistance to the fraternal Tajik people in stabilizing the situation in the country, to help it shore up its sovereignty and territorial integrity and ensure the security of the CIS's southern borders.[43]

Earlier, when Afghan crisis deepened in May 1997, after the Taliban's major victory in Afghanistan with the seizure of Mazar-i-Sharif, Russia along with other Central Asian States convened an emergency meeting in Moscow, and decided to put the Russian 201st Motor Rifle Division, which forms the core of the CIS peacekeeping force in Tajikistan on full combat alert. At the time of second seizure of Mazar-i-Sharif by the *Taliban* Islamic militia, which took place in early August 1998, all the Central Asian States (with the exception of Turkmenistan) together with Russia and China were ready to prevent the spillover effect of the forcible occupation of Afghanistan by the Taliban. As the Pakistan backed Taliban forces advanced towards the CIS borders, leaders of Russia and Uzbekistan declared their readiness to evoke the provisions of the 1992 Tashkent Collective Security Pact. This decision was taken after urgent consultation between the First Deputy Defence Minister and Chief of General Staff of Russia, General Anatoly Kvashniv, First Deputy Foreign Minister of Uzbekistan, General H. Tursunov, and A. Kamilov held in Tashkent on 5 August, 1998. They reserved their right to take all measures needed for strengthening security of their external borders in compliance with the Collective Security Agreement of 15 May 1992.

During his Moscow visit on April 16, 1999, President Emomali Rahmonov signed a treaty 'on joint cooperation between the Russian Federation and the Republic of Tajikistan oriented to 21st century. The Treaty which provides a military base to Russia in Tajikistan, signifies the establishment of a long-term strategic partnership between the two countries. At a press confrence in Dushanbe held on April 5, 1999, he called a functioning collective system of air defences which now embraces Russia, Belarus, Armenia, Kazakhstan and Kyrgyzstan and to be joined subsequently by Tajikistan as 'the key to CIS security'.

DIVERSIFICATION OF SECURITY RELATIONSHIP OF CENTRAL ASIAN STATES WITH WEST, NATO, OSCE AND THE UN

The Tashkent Collective Security and the separate bilateral and multi-lateral security agreements within the framework of the Commonwealth of Independent States with Russia have already provided the security guarantee to all the newly independent Central Asian states. But in the wake of active Russian foreign policy based upon the principle of the Euro-Atlantic Union (primarily represented by Mr. Andrei Kozyrev Russian Foreign Minister, Yegor Geydar the Russian acting Prime Minister and President Boris Yeltsin) and subsequently, newly formulated Russian military doctrine in the 'near abroad' of 1993, aimed at creating 'zones of influence' and declaring the whole of the former Soviet Central Asian territories as an area of 'vital interest' for Russia, the leaders of the Republics started exploring other avenues to ensure the security and stability of the Central Asian states.

While addressing the 48th Session of the UN General Assembly, Uzbekistan's President Islam Karimov emphasized over the regional security in Central Asia beyond the unified security structure of the Commonwealth of Independent States, and proposed to setup in Tashkent a 'Permanent United Nations Seminar' on issues of 'Regional Security and Cooperation'. Subsequently, a seminar on 'Security and Cooperation in Central Asia' was held on September 15-16, 1995, in the Uzbek capital, Tashkent, which was attended by the delegations representing the United Nations, the Organization for Security and Cooperation in Europe (OSCE), the Organization of Islamic Conference (OIC), Commonwealth of Independent States (CIS) as well as representatives from the permanent member states of the United Nations Security Council, and also from the neighbouring states of Turkey, Pakistan, Afghanistan, Iran and India.[45] While addressing the seminar, Islam Karimov, emphasized the need to work out a mechanism for cooperation principally between international organizations in order to strengthen peace and stability in the Central Asian region. He also stressed the need for international organizations such as OSCE, NATO, NACC, CIS, the U.N. and other international organizations and institutions to take an active interest in ensuring peace and security in the Central Asian region.[46]

After the Tashkent Seminar, a two-day international seminar on 'Regional Security in Central Asia', was organized in the Kazakh Capital, Alma-Aty, on December 7, 1995. It was attended by the Foreign Ministry officials from all the Central Asian Republics and experts from Kazakhstan, Tajikistan, Kyrgyzstan, the USA, Russia and Britain. It discussed the role of Central Asian states with regard to major regional and international issues. The seminar was sponsored by the Kazakh Foreign Ministry, Kazakh's Strategic Research Institute, and the London International Institute for Strategic Studies.[47] Another two day international conference on 'Security, Co-operation and Confidence Building Measures in Asia', was held in the Kazakh capital, Alma-Aty, on February 7,1996. Representatives from Azerbaijan, Afghanistan, China, India, Iran, Israel, Kazakhstan, Kyrgyzstan, Mangolia, Pakistan, Palestine, Russia, Tajikistan, Turkey and Uzbekistan participated. Observers from ten other countries, including Vietnam, Egypt, Indonesia and Japan also attended this conference along with representatives of the United Nations, the OSCE, and a number of other International Organizations.[48] Participants of this conference mainly discussed three draft documents, including a 'Declaration on the principles of relations between the member states of the Conference on Interaction and Measures of Trust in Asia (CIMTA)', 'Rules and procedures of conferences on interaction and measures of trust in Asia' and the 'structure and institutions of CIMTA'.[49]

To eliminate the possibilities of Russian domination over Central Asian States, the Central Asian leaders have tried to create a security space broader than the post-Soviet security space which would include the United Nations, Organization for Security and Cooperation in Europe (OSCE), and North Atlantic Treaty Organization (NATO) and other western international security structure. This could be designated as the Euro-Central Asian system of security space. Their active participation in the Partnership for Peace Programme as well as in the North Atlantic Cooperation Council (NACC) of the NATO, and staging of numerous NATO military exercises on the territory of Central Asia, are indicative of their desire to became self-reliant and independent of Russia's strategic security umbrella. Having gained full political sovereignty, the Central Asian regimes perceive the involvement of these various international institutions in their region as one of the basic guarantees for their stability and independence. On the other hand, the strategic objectives of NATO and Partnership for Peace Programme are to involve Central Asian states in the European Security structure based on cooperative processes and on mutual consultations in case of threat; to increase military cooperation and information exchange; to contribute to stability in the region through democratic control over the military and balanced civil-military relations and to increase interoperability for *inter alia* peace-keeping operations on the basis of a common conceptual approach.[50]

I. Central Asian States and Organisation for Security and Co-operation in Europe (OSCE): Towards an Euro-Central Asian Security Space

After the disintegration of the Soviet Union, the vast space stretching from the Caucasus to Central Asia is a region, where Organization for Security and Cooperation in Europe (OSCE) has been very active. Its role and responsibility on the territory covering Euro-Asian Russia, Trans-Caucasia and Central Asia (by geographic proximity one could describe this as the Euro-Central Asian region) is very high. The leaders of the Central Asian states believe that Euro-Central Asian system of security may place the Central Asian region in the European processes of security and extend to its territory the common principles of inviolability of frontiers and territorial integrity. The Central Asian states would like to enter into a broader security space than the post-Soviet space, which might reduce the domination of Russia in the Central Asian region, and would also increase opportunities of the OSCE to implement or control peace-keeping operations on its territory. Further, they argue that the Euro-Asian system of security may stop disputes about the possible expansion of NATO, diminish frictions between Russia and NATO, Russia and the USA, and Russia and the West as a whole, in connection with Russia's policy in Eastern Europe and the post-Soviet space. The border between the 'far' and 'near' abroad would be eliminated in favour of the single Euro-Central Asian space of security and after that there would emerge a reasonable balance of mutual relations between the OSCE, NATO, EU, and CIS, which as a whole under the aegis of the UN might characterise the Euro-Central Asian system of security.

To come closer and to integrate within the OSCE security structure, a seminar sponsored by the OSCE on 'Security and Confidence-Building Measures in Central Asia' was held in the Tajik capital Dushanbe, on 24 April 1996.[51] In yet another important summit of the Organization for Security and Cooperation in Europe (OSCE) subsequently organized in Lisbon on 2 December 1996, was participated by Kazakh President Nursultan Nazarbayev and Uzbek President Islam Karimov. While addressing a press conference soon after the Lisbon Summit, President Karimov disclosed that 'Our primary purpose in participating in this Organisation is to get security guarantees for Uzbakistan—for our people, for our country'.[52]

After a few months the Secretary-General of the OSCE, Jiancarlo Aragona, visited Uzbekistan on July 14, 1997, to discuss with President Islam Karimov regional and international security, the situation in Afghanistan and the prospects for cooperation between the OSCE and Uzbekistan. Subsequently, the Chairman-in-Office of the OSCE, Polish Foreign Minister Bronslaw Geremek, visited the countries of Central Asia on 14-20 April, 1998. It was the first CiO visit to the region. He was accompanied by members of the Troika and representatives of the OSCE Secretariat and institution. In each of the five countries he visited—Turkmenistan, Kazakhstan, Kyrgyzstan, Tajikistan and Uzbekistan, the Chairman-in-Office emphasised the importance of Central Asia as an integral part of the OSCE community, in accordance with the principle of indivisibility of the security in the OSCE area. He stressed the importance of their active participation in OSCE work, in all its dimensions. He also invited them to participate actively in the work on a document—charter on European security in order to ensure a proper link between European and Central Asian security. In his final report, CiO pointed out that OSCE is very much concerned about the Central Asia's internal and cross-border conflicts, inter-ethnic tensions, religio-political extremism, menaces of drug trafficking and international criminal activity, which are major possible threats for regional security of Central Asia. The gravity of these problems and others raised in his report suggest that the security situation in Central Asia and efforts to integrate more closely state of the region with the rest of the OSCE area should be given higher priority in the OSCE, including the document/charter on European security.[53]

In the opening statement, the OSCE Chairman-in-Office, Minister for Foreign Affairs of the Republic of Austria, Mrs. Benita

Ferrero-Waldner, made at the "International Conference on Enhancing Security and Stability in Central Asia: An Integrated Approach to Counter Drugs, Organised Crime and Terrorism" held in Tashkent, on 19th October 2000, emphasized the need for cooperation and coordination of OSCE in the security aspects of Central Asia. She also called for co-ordination at a national, regional, interregional and international level in order to adopt measures to prevent, control and eliminate the interrelated phenomena of drug trafficking, organized crime and terrorism. [54]

II. Central Asian States and NATO's Partnership for Peace' Programme

Relations with the North Atlantic Treaty Organisation hold the greatest importance for the Central Asian States' strategic relations with the West. Soon after the dissolution of the Soviet Union and at the beginning of the independent existence of Kazakhstan, President Nazarbayev declared that:

> ... The North-Atlantic Treaty has a suitable goal for our rapprochement to assist the democratic development of the states of Central and Eastern Europe and the CIS, and to prevent regional conflicts as far as possible. ... NATO member-states for the purposes of cooperation with these states have committed themselves to providing their accumulated experience and considerable expert potential in defence policy. ... Considering all this, we will broaden contacts with NATO, provided their sphere and limits are strictly determined and they are not damaging for military cooperation with the CIS framework or bilateral military ties.[55]

In December 1991, as part of a strategy to integrate members of the Warsaw Pact and the Soviet successor states within the Western Security structure, NATO heads of states and government responded by establishing the North Atlantic Cooperation Council. Later on this basis a completely new form of cooperation-programme 'Partnership for Peace' (PfP) was launched at the initiative of the American President Bill Clinton at the NATO summit in January

1994 at Brussels.[56] NATO has devoted considerable efforts to implement these objectives. Within a year of NATO inviting the new Central Asian states to cooperate under the Partnership for Peace programme, the framework document was signed with all Central Asian states except Tajikistan. Kazakhstan, Kyrgyzstan, Turkmenistan and Uzbekistan have participated in the 'Partnership for Peace' (PfP) programme. Thus NATO, for the first time, directly reached beyond the Ural mountains through the participation of Central Asian Republics' in the North Atlantic Cooperation Council (NACC) and Partnership for Peace (PfP) programme.[57]

Eversince the Partnership for Peace programme was initiated, military and civil representatives of the newly Central Asian states have taken part in the majority of events conducted within its framework—in seminars and conferences concerning security problems and the principles of constructing armed forces in democratic societies, and in various NATO training activities during which the objectives of peacekeeping activities have been elaborated. Military officers from Kazakhstan, Kyrgyzstan, and Uzbekistan have also visited different military schools of NATO member states.

Central Asian units of armed forces have, for the first time, taken part in military exercises in the State of Louisiana, USA, under NATO's Partnership for Peace programme. The military units from Kazakhstan, Kyrgyzstan and Uzbekistan's armed forces took part in the official opening of the exercises on August 8, 1995, alongside their counterparts from eleven other European countries and the USA, Germany, Great Britain and Canada.[59] Afterwards, a 60 men battalion of Central Asian peacekeepers made up of Uzbek, Kyrgyz and Kazakh soldiers, participated in the *Cooperative Osprey Exercise* in North Carolina, USA, in accordance with the NATO Partnership for Peace military exercise, on 16 August 1996.

Further to deepen cooperation with NATO, the Uzbek and the US military personnel held joint military manoeuvres on June 6-9, 1997, in the Ferghana Valley, in Eastern Uzbekistan. The *Ultra Balance* – 97 exercises were held in accordance with a 1995 bilateral agreement between the Uzbek Defence Ministry and the

US Defence Department. Uzbek Foreign Minister, Abdul Aziz Kamilov, held talks with US Secretary of State, Madeleine Albright, in Washington on June 12, 1997, and the two sides agreed to form a joint commission to expand cooperation in the areas of defence.[60]

The first stage of multi-national peacekeeping exercises under the NATO's Partnership for Peace programme, involving troops from three Central Asian Republics of Kazakhstan, Uzbekistan and Kyrgyzstan, which had agreed to create a Central Asian peacekeeping battalion under UN auspices, as well as troops from Russia, the USA, Turkey, Denmark, Ukraine, Georgia and the Baltic States, began in southern Kazakhstan on September 15-17, 1997.[61] The second stage of multi-national peacekeeping exercises with participation of a total of 1,400 troops from Uzbekistan, Kazakhstan, Kyrgyzstan, the USA, Russia, Turkey, Georgia and Latvia, began near the Uzbek capital, in the town of Chirchik, on September 18, 1997. It was organized within the framework of NATO's Partnership for Peace Programme. This special peacekeeping exercise ended on September 21, 1997.[62]

The second bilateral joint Kazakh-US military exercise – *the Balance-Kayak-98* began on June 6, and lasted until June 27, 1998, outside Alma-Aty. According to a senior Kazakh military spokesman, a Kazakh paratroopers brigade and members of a group of US special service troops participated in this military exercise.[63] A long peacekeeping exercise *The Centrasbat-98* was also held in Central Asia, near Tashkent on September 22, 1998. As a part of the NATO's Partnership for Peace programme, more than 700 servicemen from Uzbekistan, Kyrgyzstan, Kazakhstan, Russia, the United States, Turkey, Gorgia and Azerbaijan participated in this exercise.[64]

Besides military cooperation and peacekeeping exercises, under the Partnership for Peace Programme, Central Asian states have also established diplomatic relations with NATO by exchanging envoys mutually on regular basis. A US military delegation, on the diplomatic mission to the Central Asian states, led by the US permanent representative to NATO, Robert Hunter, visited Kazakh capital Alma-Aty on 3 April, 1996. He met the Kazakh Defence Minister Alibek Kasymov and First Deputy Foreign Minister Nurlan Danenov, and expressed deep concern over regional security. He conveyed the US willingness to assist financially in the creation of a battalion of peacekeeping forces of Central Asian states under UN auspices.[65]

To develop further military cooperation and transparency in relations with the newly independent Central Asian States, NATO Secretary-General Javier Solana, in his second visit to these Republics, arrived at Alma-Aty on March 11, 1997. Both Javier Solana and President Nazarbayev agreed to broaden co-operation with NATO within the framework of the Partnership for Peace programme. Solana expressed NATO's readiness to help in training of Kazakh's military officers.[66] Javier Solana also had talks with Uzbek Defence Minister Rustom Ahmedov and Foreign Minister Abdulaziz Komilov in Tashkent on March 13, 1997. Komilov clarified the stand of Uzbekistan to the visiting NATO Secretary General stating that Uzbekistan in accordance with its foreign policy principles would not join any military or military-political blocs.[6]

At present, the support rendered by the Central Asian states (Uzbekistan, Tajikistan, Kazakhstan, Tukmenistan) for America's coalition to fight terrorists based in neighbouring Afghanistan is, in fact, the realization of the NATO-Central Asian states' strategic partnership. In his well publicised tour concerning international security in the context of the current U.S. anti-terrorist campaign in Afghanistan, Donald Rumsfeld, the US Defence Secretary, visited Uzbekistan and Tajikistan. The Central Asian states of Uzbekistan, Tajikistan, Kazakhstan and Tukmenistan along with Russia have strongly supported the U.S. efforts to form an international anti-terrorist coalition, launched after September 11, 2001 attack on Washington and New York. The Central Asian States of Tajikistan, Uzbekistan and Kyrgyzstan have provided several strategically important military footholds and air bases to U.S. to launch military offensives against the *Taliban* in Afghanistan.

Conclusion

Russia's relations with the Trans-Caucasian and Central Asian region currently designated as "Near Abroad" in the lexicon of Russian diplomacy, have a history extending over a millennium. From the viewpoint of geography and history Russia and Central Asia constitute a common Eurasian geo-strategic security and economic space. This curious term "Near Abroad" implies that Russia has special interests in these Republics which are based on the historical background (they were part of the Tsarist empire and the Soviet Union), geographical factor of proximity and the presence of a multi-million ethnic Russian and Russian-speaking population in them. However, "Near Abroad" is not merely indicative of Moscow's imperial aspirations expressed in rhetoric terms, it is a grim reality of "propinquity and preponderance"[68] of Russian power notwithstanding the traumatic event of dissolution of the Soviet Union in December 1991. Central Asia, which adjoins Russia, is still ruled by Russified former Soviet elites. It is largely dependent on Russia not only for trade and energy supplies but also for arms, military training and security of the local regimes from threats both internal and external. From this it does not follow that in the post-Soviet period outside powers—the United States of America, Iran, Turkey, Japan, China, Israel, Saudi Arabia and international agencies, the United Nations, the Organization for Security and Cooperation in Europe (OSCE) and the North Atlantic Treaty Organization (NATO) have not stepped up their presence in Central Asia and the region has made no progress towards diversification of its relations. True, a wider option has been opened up before the newly independent Central Asian states. But in the short and medium term "no other state has the combination of interests, power and ease of access to serve as a counterweight to Russia there".[69]

Moreover, one need not take a too pessimistic view of Russia as a military and economic power in view of the rapid decline of the GNP and the falling morale of its ill-fate and ill-equipped military force. It would be a mistake to treat Russia as a "strategic paper tiger" with no capacity to influence developments in Central Asia. It very much remains a regional super power. No doubt there has been a steep decline of Russian economy since 1991, but Russia still has 26 times the GNP, four times as many soldiers, and a defence budget almost 40 times larger than the eight, Central Asian (5) and Trans-Caucasian states (3) combined.[70] The Central Asian states do not possess the capacity to create their own military power. Despite agreements for military training in Turkey and the United States of America and joint exercises under the Partnership for Peace Programme of the NATO, the Central Asian states remain overwhelmingly dependent on Russia for training and equipment and for spare parts for a force of Soviet vintage. Russian border troops patrol Kazakhstan's and Kyrgyzstan's border with China and Turkmenistan's border with Iran. The entire southern border of Tajikistan with Afghanistan is guarded by 201st Motorised Infantry Division of Russia.

However, efforts to associate the United Nations and the OSCE with the regional Collective Security System are obviously motivated by a desire to weaken Russian dominance. Such efforts may have the indirect support of the western powers but it would be difficult for them to justify before their public the conclusion of a military alliance with the Central Asian States. Western leaders still tend to view Central Asia as an area where Russia has special interest and can be entrusted the task of peace-keeping under broad international supervision. The United Nations and the OSCE did play an important role in the Tajik peace process but it was not designed to supplant Moscow.

The question of continuation of Russian preponderance in the security system of Central Asia in the long term, however, admits of no easy answer. There are several imponderables such as departure from the political scene of the present-day Soviet-era elite, the overwhelming domination of youth in the demographic composition of the Central Asian population, the economic recovery of Russia and the rising influence of Islam. All these factors are likely to pose a serious challenge to the geopolitical realities in Central Asia.

REFERENCES

1. Devendra Kaushik, (1970), *Central Asia in Modern Times: A History From the Early 19th Century,* Moscow, p. 6.
2. For detail views of these two schools of Russian Foreign Policy, see Alexander Rahr, (1992), "Atlanticists" versus "Eurasianists" in Russian Foreign Policy, *RFE/RL Research Report,* May, Vol. 1, No. 22, 29 p. 17-22.
3. *Summary of World Broadcast (B.B.C),* London, Part 1 (Former USSR), NO. SU/1524, P. A1/3-4, October 29, 1992.
4. Jed. C. Snyder (ed.), (1995), *After Empire: The Emerging Geopolitics of Central Asia,* Washington D.C., p. 54.
5. *Ibid.*, p. 56.
6. Amin Saikal, (1993), "The West and Post-Khomeni Iran", *The World Today,* October, Vol. 49, No. 10, p. 197-200.
7. Ronald Dannreuther, (1994), "Creating New State in Central Asia", *Adelphi Papers,* March, London, No. 288, p. 41.
8. *Narodnoya Slovo,* Tashkent, May 1994.
9. *Summary of World Broadcasts* B.B.C. London, Part 1 (Former USSR), No.SU/1262, P,C1/6, December 23, 1991.
10. *SWB*, SU/1383, p. P,C2/1, May 18, 1992.
11. *Kazakhstanskaya Pravda*, p. 2, May 23, 1992.
12. *Ibid.*
13. *Krasnaya Zvezda,* Moscow, pp. 11-12, July 3, 1992.
14. *FBIS – SOV,* 93-131, pp. 12-14, July 8, 1992.
15. *SWB,* SU/1594, p. C1/2, January 23, 1993.
16. *Ibid.*, p. C1/2-3.
17. *SWB,* SU/1665, p. B/5, April 1, 1993.
18. *SWB,* SU/1762, p. C2/7, August 9, 1993.
19. *Keesing's Record of World Events,* Vol. 40, No. 3, p. 39914, March 1994.
20. *SWB,* SU/2514, p. A/2, January 20, 1996.
21. *Ibid.*
22. *SWB*, SU/3118, p. G/1, January 7, 1998.
23. *Ibid.*
24. *Ibid.*
25. *Ibid.*, p. A/6.
26. *FBIS*-SOV 92-101, May 26, 1992, p. 14
27. *Ibid.*
28. *Keesing's Record of World Events,* Vol. 40, No. 7-8, August, 1992, p. 39054.

29. *SWB*, SU/1627, p. B/1, March 3, 1993.
30. *SWB*, SU/2521, p. G/1, January 29, 1996.
31. *Ibid.*
32. *SWB*, SU/3358, p. G/1, October 15, 1998.
33. *FBIS-SOV*, 92-107, June 3, 1992, p. 21.
34. *SWB*, SU/2369, p. G/4, July 30, 1995.
35. *SWB*, SU/3356, p. S2/1, October, 13, 1998.
36. *FBIS-SOV*, 92-114, June 11, 1992, p. 13.
37. *SWB*, SU/2553, p. G/1, March 8, 1996.
38. *SWB*, SU/2887, p. S1/4, April 7, 1997.
39. *FBIS-SOV*, 92-117, June 17, 1992, pp. 53-54.
40. *SWB*, SU/1788, September 8, 1993.
41. *FBIS* – Central Eurasia, January 23 1993, pp. 5-14.
42. *FBIS* – SOV, 92-150, August 4, 1992, p. 73.
43. *FBIS* – SOV, September 9, 1992, p. 11.
45. *SWB*, SU/2414, P.G/1, September 19, 1995.
46. *Ibid.*, P.G/2.
47. *SWB*, SU/2482, P.G/1, December 9, 1995.
48. *SWB*, SU/2530, P.G/3, February 8, 1996.
49. *Ibid.*,
50. Bruno Copieters and others, (1996), "The Central Asian Region in a new international environment" *NATO Review,* September, Vol. 44, No. 5, p. 29.
51. *SWB*, SU/2598, p. G/1, April 27, 1996.
52. *SWB*, SU/2787, p. G/4, December 5, 1996.
53. file://C:\MY%20Documents\OSCE%203.htm.
54. file://C:\MY%20Documents\OSCE%203.htm.
55. Cited by Oumirserik Kasenov "Central Asia: National, Regional and Global Aspects of Security (1997), "*Himalyan and Central Asian Studies*, April-June, Vol. 1, No. 1, p. 47.
56. Yongjin Zhang & Rouben Azizian (ed.), (1998), *Ethnic Challenges Beyond Borders: Chinese and Russian Perspectives of the Central Asian Conundrum,* New York, p. 216.
57. Bruno Copieters and others, (1996), "The Central Asian Region in a New International Environment" *NATO Review,* No. 5, September Vol. 44, p. 26.
59. *SWB,* SU/2379, P.S1/2, August 11, 1995.
60. *SWB,* SU/2942, P.S1/2, June 11, 1997.
61. *SWB,* SU/3026, P.S1/2, September 17, 1997.

62. *SWB,* SU/3028, P.S1/2, September 19, 1997.
63. *SWB,* SU/3247, P.S1/5, June 8, 1998.
64. *Kommersant Daily,* Moscow, September 23, 1998.
65. *SWB,* SU/2581, P.G/2, April 5, 1996.
66. *SWB,* SU/2867, P.G/1, March 15, 1997.
67. *Ibid.,*
68. See Rajan Menon's article, (1998), "After Empire: Russia and the Southern Near Abroad" in Michael Mandelbaum (ed.), *The New Russian Foreign Policy,* Council on Foreign Relations, New York, p. 100.
69. *Ibid.,* p. 101.
70. *Ibid.,* p. 105.

8

Afghanistan and Central Asian Republics 1991-1996

K. WARIKOO

Geographical contiguity, racial and religious affinity and long established border trade have provided a strong basis for cross-border fraternisation between the people of Central Asia and adjoining Afghanistan, particularly its northern part also known as Afghan Turkestan. Afghanistan not only shares its borders with the three Central Asian Republics of Tajikistan, Uzbekistan and Turkmenistan, but the majority of people settled in northern Afghanistan are also of the Central Asian stock. About 4.8 million Tajiks, 1.5 million Uzbeks and over half a million Turkmens live in Afghanistan. Besides, the Pamir Tajiks living in the Gorno Badakhshan Autonomous oblast of Tajikistan share their language and lifestyle with their counterparts in the Badakhshan region of Afghanistan.

AFGHANISTAN AND CENTRAL ASIA: TRANS-BORDER CONTACTS

Notwithstanding their intra-ethnic or intra-tribal diversities, this Central Asian population of northern Afghanistan has been quite conscious of its group identity as distinct from the Pashtun majority of Afghanistan. This was reflected from the political assertion by the Uzbek and Tajik factions led by General Dostam and Ahmad Shah Masood, respectively, in the post-Najib era in Afghanistan. For most part of its history, the influence of Pashtuns and the central government at Kabul over Afghan Turkestan including Badakhshan remained tenuous at least till Amir Abdur Rahman Khan subdued the area in 1884. And at about the same time, the northern boundary of Afghanistan was delineated and duly recognised by the Afghan, British and Russian authorities. Areas north of Oxus such as Shignan, Roshan, Pamirs etc. came under Russian control and the areas south of the Oxus including Wakhan were recognised as part of Afghanistan. But this did not mean the cessation of links between the two sides.

The traditional border trade and family ties between the people of this region developed over the years particularly after the improvement of communication facilities under the Soviet regime. The Soviets used the cultural similarities among people living in the north and south of the Oxus, to bolster the pro-Soviet regimes in Afghanistan. Closer interaction between Afghanistan and Tajikistan, particularly the exchange of students, academics, literatures, artists, media persons, cultural delegations etc. was encouraged. Mazar-i-Sharif became the main centre of economic exchanges between the two sides, as it was well connected by roads with Central Asia. Cotton produced in northern Afghanistan was trucked to Tashkent for processing. Movement of people and their goods increased. Afghanistan and Tajikistan signed agreements of technical, scientific, educational and cultural cooperation envisaging exchanges of scholars, scientists etc. A joint Afghan-Tajik enterprise *Intertrans* which was set up in southern Tajikistan' Kurgan Tyube oblast, engaged itself in the transport of textile and consumer goods from Afghanistan to Tajikistan.[1] In September 1992 Mayors of Dushanbe and Mazar-i-Sharif signed formal agreements on economic and social cooperation.[2] Similarly an Afghan firm concluded an agreement with the Central Samarkand Store undertaking to supply goods to Samarkand.[3] In southern Turkmenistan, a power line was laid upto Afghan border village of Mari Chaq to bring electricity to more than 1000 Turkmen families living in this village.[4] Soon after the independence of Central Asian Republics, Afghanistan joined the Iran sponsored Association of Persian Speaking Peoples. A joint meeting of its member countries—Iran, Tajikistan and Afghanistan was held in Teheran in February 1992 in which it was agreed to revive and spread the Persian language, traditions and customs of the three countries.[5] All these measures only helped in strengthening the bonds between the people and more so those of the Central Asian racial stock living on both sides of the Oxus.

RISE OF ISLAMIC MILITANCY IN TAJIKISTAN

The spectre of cross border movement, which was earlier limited to social and trade contacts, changed dramatically after the Soviet armed intervention in Afghanistan which was perceived as a direct Communist attack on Islam. The Soviets and those who represented the Soviet regimes came to be seen as the enemies of Islam. This was more so because most of the present settlers in northern Afghanistan had left Central Asia as refugees at the height of anti-Soviet Basmachi movement (1917-21) and the collectivisation campaigns in early 1930s. For instance, Azad Beg—the sixty year old leader of the Islamic Union of the Northern Provices of Afghanistan (*Ittihadiya-i-Islami-yi-vilayat-i-Shamil-i-Afghanistan*), who was responsible for numerous operations against the Soviet forces, was a relative of Ibrahim Beg, one of the leader of the Basmachi movement.[6] That this Islamic Union was founded in Peshawar in 1981 with the help of Pakistan government for "bringing together all the Turks (*az Nizhadi-Turk*) of Afghanistan and then to liberate Soviet Turkestan", was disclosed by Azad Beg himself in an interview to a French scholar, Olivier Roy.[7] Pakistan's Inter-Services Intelligence (ISI) provided Azad Beg "great deal of money and weapons to build an alternative framework for channelling Turkic nationalism against both the Soviet and Kabul regimes."[8] It is not a mere coincidence that Pakistan's forward policy in Afghanistan and trans-Oxiana was persued by Mirza Aslam Beg, former Chief of Pakistan's army, who himself is a descendant of a Central Asian *Muhajir* and is also related to Azad Beg.[9] Azad Beg did succeed in enlisting the support of some Uzbek, Tajik and even

Turkmen field commanders, notably Uzbek *Muhajirs* from former Soviet Central Asia like Khaluddin of Kunduz and Ait Murad from Burqa (Baghlan province).[10] Azad Beg who operated in Balkh, Djauzdjan, Farib, Sari Pul and Samangan areas, used to supply weapons to his Islamic supporters in Tajikistan.[11] That the Central Asian *Muhajirs* from Tajikistan who migrated to Afghanistan during the Bolshevik revolution, were in the forefront of what was described as *jehad* (Holy war), was confirmed by Mohammad Sharif Himatzade, Chief of Islamic Renaissance Party (IRP) who had set up his base in exile in Afghanistan.[12] Common ethnic and religious background of the people inhabiting this border region facilitated the cross-border smuggling of religious and subversive literature, arms and ammunition by the Afghan *Mujahideen* into Tajikistan.

The rapid politicisation of Islam and the emergence of a militant Islamic fundamentalist movement in Tajikistan took place after the Soviet intervention in Afghanistan. This coupled with the success of Khomeini revolution in Iran brought a new awakening among the Muslims of Central Asia.[13] The Central Asian clerics and Sufi brotherhoods which withstood the Soviet policies, now not only became stronger but came under the influence of *Wahabism*—the radical and politicised form of Islam. The Afghan *Mujahideen* established wide contacts with the Tajiks particularly after the Soviet troops most of whom were from Central Asia, landed in Afghanistan. They started crossing the border into Tajikistan where they were greeted by radical Islamic activists. Afghan *Mujahideen* leaders acknowledged that the 1979 Soviet military intervention in Afghanistan "helped re-establish links between the Tajiks and their Muslim brethren in Afghanistan, who have the same language, same culture, same religion and same ancestors in common."[14] Another *Mujahideen* leader Masood Khalili disclosed that Soviet soldiers conscripted from Tajikistan were not only reluctant to fire on Afghans but they even sold their rifles to purchase the Koran.[15] Two Afghan resistance parties, namely *Jamaat-i-Islami* led by Burhanuddin Rabbani and *Hizb-e-Islami* of Gulbadin Hikmatyar were particularly active enrolling members and distributing *shabnameh* (night letters) in Tajikistan and Uzbekistan.[16] These Afghan *Mujahideen* groups evoked maximum response from young Tajiks with high education, especially teachers and engineers.[17]

Reports about the active involvement of Afghan *Mujahideen* in propagating *jehad* in Tajikistan began to appear in the Soviet press since 1986, that is following Gorbachev's policy of *glasnost* (openness) in the media. K.M. Makhkamov, the then First Secretary of the Tajik Communist Party admitted at a party meeting held in Dushanbe on August 30, 1986 that young people and children were getting increasingly swayed by propaganda from across the border.[18] *Kommunist Tadjikistana* of December 30, 1987 published a statement of the then Tajik KGB Chief, Petkel confirming the existence of "hostile foreign ideological centres and organisations in Tajikistan." An article in the same paper of May 13, 1988 disclosed that Islamic revolutionary literature was being distributed in thousands, which was later confirmed by Afghan *Mujahideen* sources.[19] There was wide circulation of audio cassettes, video films etc. to spread radical Islam in Tajikistan. Works of Maududi—the founder of *Jamaat-i-Islami*, Said Kutab, Muhammed Kutab and Jamal Din Afghani, the noted Muslim revolutionaries were translated into Russian and printed at Peshawar and then smuggled across Afghanistan into Tajikistan for wide circulation. *Wahabism* gained roots in the rural areas of Tajikistan especially along the Tajik-Afghan border. The Wahabi literature that was smuggled via Afghanistan, laid emphasis on religious absolutism and was critical of Sufism and holy shrines which represent the traditional and tolerant trend in the Central Asian Islam. Tajijkistan's Wahabi leader Abdullo Saidov advocated the creation of an Islamic State[20] and called for *jehad* against the Soviets. This ideological onslaught was followed by the smuggling of arms and militant cadres across the Oxus. That the Soviet Border Guards under the authority of KGB failed to prevent illicit traffic on the Tajik-Afghan border was illustrated in March and April 1987 when Afghan *Mujahideen* staged two cross-border armed attacks in Kulyab and Kurgan Tyube regions of southern Tajikistan.[21] Apart from the surreptious trans-border movements and smuggling of arms and ammunition, Afghan *Mujahideen* leaders openly abetted rise of militancy among the Muslims of Tajikistan. For instance, Burhanuddin Rabbani and

Ahmed Shah Masood, both being Tajiks and belonging to *Jamaat-i-Islami* faction, reacted strongly to the Dushanbe disturbances of February 1990 (anti-Armenian riots). They characterised these disturbances as 'freedom movement' or 'internal revolt' against the 'Soviet subjugation'.[22] Stressing the linguistic, cultural, religious and racial affinity of Tajiks and Afghans, these leaders exhorted the Muslims in Central Asia to break away from Moscow.[23] Rabbani warned that "the Afghans living on this side could create complications for the Soviets."[24]

Obviously the Afghan *Mujahideen* groups with active guidance and assistance of Pakistan's Inter Services Intelligence (ISI) played a key role in fomenting the Islamic militancy in Tajikistan with a view to establish a friendly Islamic State there. The then Deputy Chairman of Tajikistan's KGB, Belousov openly accused Pakistan's intelligence services of carrying out a subversive programme code-named 'M' to destabilise the socio-political situation in Central Asia.[25] Belousov claimed that 150 groups of Afghan *Mujahideen* were operating near the Tajik border and training centres were set up to give religious and military training to young Tajiks.[26] And by the time the Soviet Union crumbled, an underground network of Islamic movements, arms dumps and trained Islamic militants had positioned themselves in Tajikistan for launching the offensive to oust the remnants of Communist system and establish an Islamic form of government. This has been borne out by the subsequent events in Tajikistan which witnessed the rise of Islamic fundamentalist political parties and proliferation of armed bands resulting in bloody armed clashes between rival groups.

CRISIS IN TAJIKISTAN

Soon after its independence in 1991, Tajikistan was engulfed by political conflict and violent inter-group clashes between pro-Communist and the Islamist forces and their supporters. Regional disparities both in terms of ethnic composition and economic-industrial base, further complicated the situation. Khodjend in the north and Kulyab in the south of Tajikistan, having a strong presence of Uzbek population and being the Communist strongholds, gave determined fight to the radical Islamic groups led by the *Islamic Renaissance Party* (IRP) and the *Rastokhez*, which draw support from majority of Tajiks living in Dushanbe and Kurgan Tyube and Gorno Badakhshan regions which are adjoining Afghanistan. Trans-border infiltration of armed bands and smuggling of arms was the main destabilising factor. Besides, Afghan *Mujahideen* controlling the Afghan border were actively involved in armed clashes with the Russian and Tajik border guards. About 500 Tajik transgressors were reported to have been detained at the Tajik-Afghan border in the first six months of 1992 alone.[27] 50 Afghans who were heading for Termez with drugs were also detained.[28] The establishment of Islamic government in Afghanistan led by the *Mujahideen* gave a boost to Islamic fundamentalist groups in Tajikistan. On May 10, 1992 the Chairman of Democratic Party of Tajikistan, Shodmon Yusufov issued a public appeal to Afghanistan asking for aid in the ongoing conflict between pro-Nabiyev and Islamic opposition forces and also against the "interference" of the CIS forces in "Tajikistan's internal crisis".[29] This statement only accentuated the crisis, as the incidence of cross-border infiltration and smuggling of arms from Afghanistan increased manifold. So much so, a civil war situation developed in some areas of Tajikistan resulting in bloodshed, killings and refugee problems. The then Deputy Commandant of the Central Asian Border District, Major General A. Martovitsky later confirmed that after Yusufov's statement there were increased attempts by groups to cross the Tajik-Afghan border and get weaponary for the opposition parties.[30]

The violent clashes in Kurgan Tyube between the rival parties and the victory of Islamic opposition parties over pro-Communists in May 1992 led to unprecedented exodus of Russians and Uzbeks from the region. In fact Shodmon Yusufov's public threat that they would seek aid from "Afghan brothers" and that "national minorities in Tajikistan could be used as hostages" created a panic reaction among the Uzbek and Russian minorities.[31] The situation on the Tajik-Afghan border became tense and all efforts by the local commander of CIS border forces to persuade the local Afghan *Mujahideen* leader belonging to *Hizb-e-Islami*, Abdul Latif Ibrahimi to prevent arms smuggling and infiltration of armed persons failed to yield any result.

Latif not only admitted the fact of illegal entry of Tajik groups into Afghan territory for arms, he also refused to hand over these people without authorisation by the Tajik opposition party which had sent these groups.[32] In Kulyab region too, otherwise the strong support base of Nabiyev, the members of opposition Democratic Party organised themselves with the active Afghan assistance. A number of groups from Kulyab came to Dushanbe and openly threatened to seek armed assistance from Afghans.

The spurt in incidents of border violations and armed clashes on the Tajik-Afghan border during July to September 1992 escalated the tension. In July alone more than 80 persons (both Tajiks and Afghans) were detained on the border and hundreds of automatic guns, grenade launchers, plastic mines and tens of thousands of ammunition pieces were confiscated. There were about 20 cases of firing on the border guards from the Afghan side. Over 150 border-crossers with arms and ammunition were reportedly captured by Russian border guards in September 1992 alone.[33] The situation became so tense that the Tajik government expressed concern over the continued and systematic violation of border and supply of Afghan weapons and drugs into Tajikistan. About 4,000 rifles were confiscated on the Tajik-Afghan border between May and December 1992, which was a meagre fraction of more than 20,000 weapons reported to be in illegal possession of armed groups in Tajikistan.[34] Fighting in Tajikistan which raged during this period involved regional, ethnic and clan disputes as well as differences in political and religious affiliations. By the end of 1992, about 50,000 were reported to have been killed in these armed clashes, whereas more than 600,000 became refugees.

Rakhmon Nabiyev, the former Communist who had been elected as the President of Tajikistan in November 1991, tried to buy peace by including members of the Islamist opposition groups in government and administration. But the IRP and its supporters were determined to wrest total political control. On September 7, 1992 Nabiyev's motorcade was attacked at Dushanbe airport and soon after his government was ousted by an alliance of Islamist forces comprising the *IRP, Rastokhez* and the *Democratic Party*, under the leadership of

A. Iskandrov. This was followed by violent clashes between Nabiyev's supporters and his opponents in Kurgan Tyube regions. Subsequently the anti-Islamists rallied their forces and formed regional government in Kulyab and Khodjend. Finally in December 1992, they stormed the capital and installed Imamali Rakhmanov as the new leader. Rakhmanov and his forces worked to rid Tajikistan of radical Islamic extremists, who retreated into the Gorno Badakhshan region and also sought refuge in Afghanistan. It was in January 1993 that the new government was able to strengthen its position in the eastern parts of Tajikistan. The Garmsky region, which had declared itself as an independent Islamic Republic was freed of Islamists' control in the last week of February 1993. On March 2, 1993 the Tajik Government announced the recapture of Tadjikabad. The then State Procurator General, Mukhamadnazar Sabikhov claimed that during the offensive over 100 tonnes of weapons and 20 tanks and armoured vehicles had been captured.[35] By March 1993, the Tajik government had consolidated its control over most of the country. Government sources claimed in early June 1993 that about 5,90,000 refugees had returned to their homes and the Tajik authorities had taken steps for guaranteeing their housing, employment and personal safety.[36] However, the Islamist radicals now concentrated in the southern mountainous province of Badakhshan, Tavildara, Komsomolabad, Kharog and other areas in the Pamirs, this vast and rugged terrain continued to pose problems for the Tajik government forces.

As long as the leaders of Tajik opposition groups and their Tajik supporters numbering about 90,000 remained in Afghanistan and with the active involvement of Afghan *Mujahideen* leaders in arming and training these Islamist radicals, peace and stability in Tajikistan remained elusive. Clashes between Islamist fighters and Russian/Tajik security forces continued along the Tajik-Afghan border. More than 50 militants were killed when some 200 to 300 Islamic radicals and Afghan *Mujahideen* intruded into Shurohabad around April 20, 1993.[37] Eruption of serious clashes on the Tajik-Afghan border on July 13, 1993 when at least 25 Russian border guards, 70 Islamic fighters and 200 civilians were reportedly killed,[38] highlighted the explosive nature of the situation. This incident sparked outrage in

Russia and Afghanistan was warned of punitive military action in the event of further trans-border raids into Tajikistan. Soon after, Russian forces launched artillery and air attacks on the bases of Tajik militant and Afghan *Mujahideen* in northern Afghanistan.[39] Tension on the border mounted again when 1 Kazakh and 4 Russian border guards were taken hostage to Afghanistan after their unit was ambushed by the Islamic militants on August 10, 1993.[40] Tajik opposition groups namely *Islamic Renaissance Party, Democratic Party* led by Shodmon Yusuf, *National Front* led by Abdul Jabbar Takir and *Lal-e-Badakhshan* of Atta Beg, joined hands and set up a Tajik Government-in-Exile in Taloqan, Afghanistan. Both the *Jamat-i-Islami* and *Hizb-e-Islami* led by Gulbadin Hikmatyar were "training and arming" Tajik militants in guerrilla warfare against the Tajik government.[41] A local *Hizb-e-Islami* commander, Mohammad Zaman claimed in an interview with *Washington Post* that his party had trained about 1,000 Tajiks most of whom "filtered back into Tajikistan".[42] An Islamic field commander in Gorno Badakhshan was quoted by *Interfax* as saying that 15,000 Afghan trained Tajik *Mujahideen* had infiltrated Tajikistan, which was in addition to several groups of 70 to 300 men undergoing training in Afghanistan.[43] In fact the fighting escalated in Pyandz in mid-September and Gorno-Badakhshan region in October 1993. The Tajik Islamist radicals even set up a new Radio Station "Voice of Free Tadjikistan" somewhere in Afghanistan, which started operating since mid-October, 1993. Encouraged by the active military support received from major political parties such as *Jamat-i-Islami* and *Hizb-e-Islami* of Afghanistan, the *IRP* leaders took a hardline posture declaring its opposition to any peace talks with the Tajik government. They also refused to accept Uzbekistan as a party in these negotiations.

Notwithstanding Rabbani's willingness to help in reconciliation between the Tajik government and Islamic opposition, the situation on the Tajik-Afghan border deteriorated. Russian Border Guards reported on 31 August 1994, that "some 3000 gunmen are currently being trained by instructors from Saudi Arabia, Pakistan and other states in several camps in Afghanistan's Samangan and Takhar provinces. Upto 550 Arab and Pakistani mercenaries and a detachment of Afghan *Mujahideen* have been brought upto the Tajik border."[44] On 18 August 2004 about 250 armed Tajik and Afghan mercenaries crossed the Tajik border to destroy the border posts.[45] Over 50 mercenaries were killed in the fighting. It was obvious that the Tajik opposition forces were trying to consolidate their position in Tajikistan before the ceasefire was enforced in the presence of UN observers. In view of these serious developments the Tajik leader Imamoli Rakhmanov in his address to the UN General Assembly in New York called for a special meeting of the UN Security Council to discuss the situation in Tajikistan.[46] He also demanded the status of UN peacekeeping forces for the CIS peacekeeping troops deployed on the Tajik-Afghan border. Rakhmanov accused the Tajik Islamic opposition of internationalising the conflict in Tajikistan by involving foreign mercenaries.[47] Warning that the ongoing conflict in Afghanistan posed serious threat to the Central Asian region, Rakhmanov urged the international community to work for settlement of the Afghan problem which in turn would resolve the Tajik problem.[48] Inspite of the continuing attacks by Islamist forces on the Tajik forces and Russian Border Guards using anti-tank, anti-aircraft guns and sophisticated weapons, Tajik government reiterated its commitment to continuing peace talks with the Tajik opposition.[49]

TAJIK-AFGHAN DIALOGUE

Occasional contacts were established between the Tajik/Russian Border Guards and the Afghan *Mujahideen* field commanders controlling the border on the Afghanistan side to resolve the recurrent problems of arms smuggling, infiltration of armed men or even to secure the release of captives. But these local contacts failed to bring the desired improvements in the border situation. The visit of high level Tajik delegation led by Prime Minister Akbar Mirzoyev to Kabul on July 14, 1992 to seek the help of new Islamic government of Afghanistan for stopping the *Mujahideen* field commanders from supplying arms and ammunition to Tajik militant groups also proved to be ineffective.[50] The Tajik delegation met the Afghan President, Burhanuddin Rabbani and other Afghan leaders including Ahmad Shah Masood.[51] Though the Afghan leaders shared Tajik concern over the increased border violations and smuggling of arms, they expressed their inability to exercise any control over General Latif Ibrahimi, the Afghan commander of rival *Hizb-e-Islami* group who was controlling the Pyandzh border stretch in Kunduz.[52] Similar opinion was later expressed by Rabbani during his visit to Tashkent in October 1992 when the Uzbek President raised the issue of Afghan interference in Tajikistan.[53]

It was in mid-August 1993 that the Afghan Foreign Minister visited Dushanbe at the invitation of his Tajik counterpart for talks to settle the vaxed border problem, to expedite the process of repatriation of Tajik refugees from Afghanistan and to prepare the ground for bilateral summit between the two heads of state of Tajikistan and Afghanistan. The Dushanbe meeting resulted in a joint communiqué (issued on August 15, 1993) which announced the setting up of a trilateral commission comprising representatives of Afghanistan, Tajikistan and office of the UN Chief Commissioner for Refugees to assist in the return of Tajik refugees from Afghanistan.[54] Both sides reposed faith in "principles of independence, sovereignty, territorial integrity and non-interference in each other's affairs."[55] But the Tajik-Afghan dialogue was made difficult by the kidnapping of 1 Kazakh and 5 Russian border Guards who were taken as hostages to Afghan territory on August 10, 1993.[56] It was no mere coincidence that the border incident occurred on the same day when Afghan Foreign Minister, H. Amin Arsala arrived at Dushanbe thereby assuming priority in the bilateral dialogue and pushing substantial issues to the backstage. Obviously the Tajik opposition groups and their Afghan supporters positioned in northern Afghanistan were seeking to disrupt the process of direct political dialogue between Tajikistan and Afghanistan. However, the Tajik government's unilateral decision to hand over 5 Afghan prisoners as a goodwill gesture to the Afghan authorities was calculated to pave way for the return of hostages.[57] Notwithstanding this gesture and the assurance by Afghan Foreign Minister to have the hostages released soon after his return to Kabul, the Russian and Kazakh Border Guards continued to be held captive by the Afghan authorities for about 20 days. On one occasion, Gulbadin Hekmatyar, the Prime Minister of

Afghanistan refused to free the CIS Border troops on the plea that the Russian guards were attacking Tajik refugees on the Afghan territory.[58] The hostages were finally released on August 31, 1993 when the Tajik Head of State, Rakhmanov arrived at Kabul to hold discussions with the President of Afghanistan, Rabbani.[59] Both sides discussed the border problem but had to content themselves with the ratification of earlier decision to create a trilateral commission for looking into the problems of Tajik refugees.[60] Later Rakhmanov conceded that release of CIS border guards was "the major result of his visit to Kabul."[61] However, this visit too was marred by renewed fighting on the border in which one Russian border guard was killed. This again reflected the rivalry between different factions of Afghan leadership. The problem was compounded by basic differences within the Afghanistan government as Hekmatyar was against the "deployment of Russian border guards along the Tajik-Afghan border."[62] To him the problem was the mutual concern of only two states-Afghanistan and Tajikistan.[63]

The peace process suffered setbacks due to the renewal of intense fighting in October 1993 on the border and in the Pamirs area and another kidnapping of 3 Russian and 3 Kazakh Border Guards by Tajik/Afghan militants. It was viewed as yet another attempt by the Tajik Islamic opposition groups and their Afghan *Mujahideen* supporters to disrupt the process of Tajik-Afghan dialogue and in particularly to sabotage the planned return visit of Afghan President, Rabbani to Tajikistan. However, Rabbani did visit Dushanbe on December 19, 1993 and held talks with Rakhmanov, the Tajik Head of State on issues of border security and repatriation of refugees. Both leaders signed a Friendship and Cooperation Treaty, economic and trade accords and an agreement on border security.[64] However, these conciliatory moves did not cut ice with the Tajik Islamist leaders, who dismissed it as meaningless. Tajik Islamic opposition leader, Haji Akbar Turajonzoda also discounted the possibility of Tajikistan conducting any trade with Afghanistan.[65] The Afghan Deputy Minister of Planning, D. Mahadi, who had earlier signed the trilateral agreement on the return of Tajik refugees with UNHCR and Tajikistan, also voiced his disapproval to the presence of CIS forces on the Tajik-Afghan border.[66] With the escalation of fighting between Hekmatyar and Rabbani factions in Afghanistan and due to persistent Tajik Islamists' opposition, the Tajik-Afghan peace moves initiated by Rabbani and Tajik government suffered setbacks.

Piqued by the recurrent attacks by the Islamic guerrillas of IRP on the Tajik government forces and Russian Border Guards,[67] Tajikistan Foreign Ministry sent a protest note to the Afghan Consul in Dushanbe on 22 February 1994 accusing the Afghan authorities of interference in the internal affairs of Tajikistan.[68] It accused Afghanistan of violating the December 1993 bilateral treaty on friendship, cooperation and good neighbourly relations. Tajikistan also reserved the right to strike and destroy the Tajik opposition bases on the Afghan border.[69] General Boris Pyankov, Commander of joint peace keeping forces in Tajikistan described the situation on the Tajik-Afghan border as very complex and tense.[70] On 10 March 1994 a group of 60 Tajik opposition fighters and Afghan Mujahideen were reported to have entered Tajikistan from Khorog.[71] Inspite of Tajikistan sending several protest notes to Afghan government about the continued intrusions on the Tajik-Afghan border, it did not receive any reply.

First round of talks between the Tajik government and Tajik opposition was held in Moscow in April 1994, which culminated on 19 April 1994 with both sides agreeing to work together for return of refugees.[72] A protocol was signed to set up a joint refugee commission.[73] Soon after Tajik Labour Minister S. Zahurov, who had led the Tajik government delegation to Moscow for talks, visited Tajik refugees living in Afghanistan on 28-30 April 1994.[74] He also met general Dostum, leader of the National Islamic Movement of Afghanistan to resolve issues concerning return of refugees residing in Mazar-e-Sharif.[75] And the Tajik Foreign Ministry confirmed on 26 May 1994 that over 35,000 out of the 60,000 UN registered Tajik refugees in Afghanistan had returned to their homes.[76] Another round of talks between the Tajik government and opposition was held in Teheran in June 1994, with both sides reiterating their commitment to the political resolution of the conflict and continuation of the dialogue.[77]

In fact Russia was in favour of defusing the crisis in Tajikistan through dialogue between the Tajik government and opposition. Even though the Russian military was against the proposal to disarm Tajik government forces and posting UN observers in Tajikistan, Russian Foreign Ministry was in favour of dialogue between the warring groups and promoting good neighbourly relations between Tajikistan and Afghanistan. Russian President Boris Yeltsin and the Chairman of the Tajik Parliament, Imamoli Rakhmanov issued a joint communiqué on 25 May 1993 expressing concern over the continuing tension on the Tajik-Afghan border.[78] Their joint statement called upon the Afghan military and political groups to strive for peace and cooperation and good neighbourly relations.[79] Soon after, the Russian Foreign ministry called upon both the Tajik opposition, armed and political groups in Afghanistan not to allow the situation on the Tajik-Afghan border to deteriorate.[80] However, the situation in Afghanistan was getting complicated due to exacerbation of conflict between Rabbani led government and his rival Hekmatyar. Afghanistan's Ambassador in Russia, Abdul Wahab Asefi in his press conference in Moscow on 9 August 1994 clarified that the "Islamic State of Afghanistan with President Burhanuddin Rabbani as its head is interested in untying the knotty problem prevailing currently on the Tajik-Afghan border and will make sincere efforts to normalise the situation in this region.[81]

Since Russia too was in favour of resolving the conflict through bilateral dialogue between the Tajik government and the opposition, it was reluctant to reinforce Russia's military presence in Tajikistan as was requested by the Tajikistan government in view of the latest attacks by the Tajik rebels on the Afghan border.[82] With the shifting of Shodmon Yusuf, leader of the Democratic Party of Tajikistan to Moscow, the prospects of peace process in Tajikistan increased, as he was critical of strident stand taken by Tajikistan's Islamic opposition.[83] In fact, representatives of the Tajik government and the armed opposition met in Moscow on 21 January 1995 to discuss the issues related to the implementation of ceasefire agreement which was signed earlier in September 1994.[84] Later, the Tajik opposition delegation held talks with the Russian political and military officials in Moscow on the Tajik peace process. However, the intensification of attacks by the Tajik rebels on the Russian border posts in the mountainous Pamir region, was met by aerial bombing by the Russian aircraft in Badakshan province in northern Afghanistan on the night of 11-12 April 1995.[85] Radio Afghanistan, Kabul claimed that over 100 people were killed and another 200 injured during the raids by Russian war planes on the town of Taloqan.[86] The Foreign Ministry of Afghanistan issued a statement on 12 April 1995 reaffirming its commitment to non-interference in the conflict between Tajik government and opposition forces.[87] Now Afghanistan replied to the protest notes of Russia, Tajikistan and Kazakhstan, reiterating its stand on non-interference in the internal affairs of other, principles of inviolability of borders, peaceful coexistence and strengthening neighbourly relations.[88] Claiming that the ongoing conflict on the Tajik-Afghan border stemmed from within Tajikistan, Afghanistan hoped that all issues would be resolved by the Tajik government and opposition forces through dialogue.[89] UN brokered talks between the Tajik government and opposition were resumed in Moscow on 24 April 1995.[90] both sides agreed on 26 April 1995 to extend the ceasefire by one month and to resume full talks in Almaty, the capital of Kazakhstan in May 1995.[91] Haji Akbar Turajonzoda, the Deputy leader of *Islamic Rennaissance Party* offered to set up the coalition government in Tajikistan, if the opposition would win in future elections.[92] The peace process moved further when the Tajik President, Imamoli Rakhmanov visited Afghanistan on 17 May 1995 and held talks with the Tajik opposition leader Syed Abdullo Nuri.[93] That this meeting took palce on the eve of fourth round of peace talks which were due to start in Almaty on 22 May 1995, reflected a step forward in the peace process towards reconciliation, stoppage of conflict, settling the problem on Tajik-Afghan border and return of refugees. This meeting had become possible only through the initiative of Afghan President, Rabbani who supported the political settlement of the Tajik conflict. Both Rakhmanov and Nuri signed an agreement at the Afghan Foreign Ministry, Kabul on 19 May 1995, to extend the ceasefire in Tajikistan for another three months, in presence of Afghan President, Rabbani.[94] Rabbani described the three day talks between the Tajik President and Tajik opposition leader as a major step towards resolving the conflict.[95] In their joint statement issued by Rakhmanov and Nuri on 19 May 1995 both sides agreed to continue peace talks and thanked Rabbani for his help in organising the meeting.[96] Simultaneously, Afghan President Rabbani and Tajik President, Rakhmanov signed a joint communiqué in Kabul on 19 May 1995, agreeing to setup a joint commission to improve relations between Tajikistan and Afghanistan.[97] Both sides reiterated their commitment to the independence, national sovereignty and territorial integrity of one another and non-interference in each other's internal affairs.[98] Both countries hoped that direct dialogue between Rakhmanov and Nuri would lead to national reconciliation and restore peace and stability in Tajikistan.[99] While the UN Security Council hailed these talks, the UN Special Envoy to Tajikistan, Ramiro Piriz Bellon visited Tajikistan and Kabul in early August 1995 to prepare the ground for forthcoming fifth round of peace talks. Afghan President, Rabbani held discussions with the visiting UN Envoy on the prospects of Tajik settlement.[100] Rabbani visited Dushanbe on 7 March 1996 to discuss the issues of border situation, return of refugees from Afghanistan and the relations between the Tajik government and opposition.[101] Following his talks with the visiting Afghan President, the Tajik President Rakhmanov expressed his readiness to meet the Islamic opposition leader Nuri "at any time and at any place".[102] He also extended an invitation to the representatives of Tajik opposition to a special session of the Parliament which was to be held on 11 March 1996.[103] On his part Rabbani conveyed his intention to meet the leaders of border districts of Afghanistan's Badakshan to work out measures for preventing attacks by the Tajik armed opposition from the territory of Afghanistan.[104] Rabbani regime in Kabul was clearly supporting the move for national reconciliation in Tajikistan through talks between the Tajik government and opposition. Rabbani even proposed to organise a meeting between Rakhmanov and Nuri to resolve the Tajik conflict.[105] He said, "peace in the entire region of Central Asia depends on the establishment of peace both in Afghanistan and Tajikistan."[106] Soon after in early May 1996, regional leaders from Tajikistan and

Afghanistan as well as the commander of Russian Border Guards in Tajikistan, Lt. Gen. Pavel Tarasenko met in Khorog, the city of Tajikistan's Badakshan region to discuss ways and means of curbing the border conflict in this region.[107] A senior Afghan military commander Gen. Najamuddin stated that he would take steps to remove the Tajik opposition fighters from the territory under his control.[108] In yet another confidence building measure, the Russian and Afghan commanders signed a local cooperation agreement in Khorog in Badakshan province of Tajikistan to establish a 25 kms. wide border exclusion zone in Afghanistan's Shighnan district, to prevent Tajik armed rebels from violating the border.[109] That the Russian Presidential Envoy to Tajikistan, Y. Mikhailov led a delegation to Kabul to discuss the security arrangements on the Tajik-Afghan border, reflects Russian earnest desire to have the situation stabilised in Tajikistan.[110] Moscow did not wish to be drawn into another Chechnya experience in Tajikistan. When Mikhailov met the Afghan Prime Minister, Gulbadin Hekmatyar in Kabul on 1 September 1996, he was impressed upon to make efforts for establishment of an interim government in Tajikistan, acceptable to all sides.[111]

But with the takeover of Kabul by the Taliban in September 1996 the rapprochement process between Afghanistan and Tajikistan received a blow. Tajikistan now appealed to the UN, USA, Russia and the international community to find a political settlement to the conflict in Afghanistan so that "there is peace and stability in Tajikistan and Central Asia as a whole." Leaders of the Central Asian Republics of Kazakhstan, Kyrgyzstan, Uzbekistan, Tajikistan and Russia met in Almaty, the capital of Kazakhstan, in early October 1991 to formulate a common approach and take necessary steps to defend the Tajik-Afghan border. The five leaders issued a joint communiqué expressing serious concern over the widening scale and intensification of armed confrontation in Afghanistan. It stated, "Executions and shooting and the brutal reprisal against the former President, Najibullah, have brought the situation in Afghanistan to the verge of disaster and the country to the verge of collapse. The flame of war is approaching the borders of the CIS states and this creates a direct threat to the national interests and security of these states and of the CIS in general and destabilizes the regional and international situation. We declare that any activity which undermines stability on the borders with Afghanistan, is unacceptable. Such activity will be regarded as a threat to our common interests and will meet with an appropriate response."[112]

UZBEKISTAN'S REACTION

Uzbekistan has been the foremost CIS state to take strong notice of the developments in Tajnikistan and the crisis situation on the Tajik-Afghan border. The Uzbek President, Islam Karimov was repeatedly warning against the "advance of Islamic fundamentalist and extremist forces from Afghanistan and Tajikistan". Karimov's fears were based on the belief that events in Tajikistan would not only consolidate the rapidly growing Islamic consciousness in Uzbekistan but also lead to its politicisation. The increasing clout of militant *Wahabi* radicals including the formation of armed bands in Ferghana valley and influx of Uzbek/Tajik refugees and even Afghan nationals into Uzbekistan further strengthened these fears. We have it on the authority of Tajik Islamist opposition leaders that Uzbek Islamic volunteers from Ferghana valley were participating in the ongoing *jehad* against pro-communist regime in Tajikistan.[113] It is also known that the Afghan General Abdul Latif, associated with the *Hizb-e-Islami* of Gulbadin Hekmatyar, is an ethnic Uzbek and he had been conducting fierce attacks on the Tajik government positions from his base in Imam Saheb area in northern Afghanistan.[114] Presence of a sizeable number of ethnic Tajiks who constitute about a quarter of Uzbekistan's population, has been yet another factor for the Uzbek concern over disorder in Tajikistan. Influx of refugees from Tajikistan, majority of them being Tajiks,[115] into the Samarkand and Bukhara regions of Uzbekistan was worrisome for Uzbekistan keeping in view Tajikistan's claims over these two cities.

Disquietened at these developments, President Karimov initiated a series of steps to meet the perceived security threat to Uzbekistan. During 1992 when the Islamic opposition groups were in control in Tajikistan, Karimov launched suppression of the Uzbek opposition groups like *Birlik* and the Islamic radicals in Ferghana. He sealed

Uzbekistan's borders with Tajikistan and Afghanistan and closed all traffic from that direction to prevent any influx of arms and men. More than 2000 foreigners[116] (mainly Tajiks and some Afghans[117]) were reported to have been expelled from Uzbekistan on charges of "illegal entry and for involvement in subversion in Ferghana valley." Uzbekistan's Security Chief, G. Aliyev claimed to have recovered arms, explosives and even drugs from the possession of some Tajiks who aimed at "sparking off Tajik style conflict in Uzbekistan and also foment Tajik-Uzbek clashes."[118]

At other level, Karimov kept channels of his friendly communication open with General Dostam, an ethnic Uzbek and the powerful military leader in Afghanistan with his stronghold in Mazar-i-Sharif. Dostam visited Tashkent several times and held discussions with the Uzbek authorities. In November 1992 Dostam's troops captured a key Amu Darya river crossing to Tajikistan at Sher Khan Bandar which was earlier used by Hikmatyar's *Hizb-e-Islami* as a staging point for cross-border forays.[119] Subsequently a network of border posts along the river supported by boat patrol was set up under the new Afghan Uzbek Commander incharge of border security, Maj. Gen. Abdul Hamid Aka.[120] This led to sealing of an important channel of supply of arms and support to Tajikistan's Islamic opposition. Besides, Dostam remained in close touch with General Nadiri, a leader of the Ismailis and some other important personalities in northern Afghanistan in order to influence the course of events there. That Dostam's family stayed in Tashkent on a long term basis is also cited as evidence of cooperation between Dostam and Uzbek authorities. There were reports that General Dostam and Uzbek President, Karimov even toyed with the idea of creating a "secular buffer state" in northern Afghanistan to cover the southern borders of Tajikistan and Uzbekistan which would act as a wedge against the spread of radical Islam from the direction of Iran from the west and from the side of Pashtuns under Hikmatyar from the south.[121] Thus there was a basic understanding between Dostam and the Uzbek leadership on the need to keep at bay the radical Islamist fighters.

The Uzbek President, Karimov took the initiative in mobilising regional response against external interference in Tajikistan. He called upon Russia to take into account the "powerful offensive of pan-Islamism" in the south and asked for continued presence of Russian forces in Tajikistan to control the Tajik-Afghan border.[122] Karimov explained that the "border between Tajikistan and Afghanistan is not only a border between these two states, it can turn into an open gate to all CIS countries from the point of view of arms smuggling, drug running etc." Karimov also initiated diplomatic moves to stop the situation on Tajik-Afghan border from spilling over into other Republics. He urged the leaders in Iran and Afghanistan to help in defusing the tension. Uzbek Foreign Minister was deputed to Teheran in October 1992 to seek Iran's cooperation for settling the issue peacefully.[123] Karimov pleaded with the CIS leadership particularly Russia and Kazakhstan to take note of the alarming situation. On March 14, 1993 Karimov appealed to the UN Secretary General seeking his help in "ensuring the security and inviolability of border between Tajikistan and Afghanistan."[124] He warned that the continuing conflict in Tajikistan could become a "powerful detonator of political and social upheavals in the region."[125] Karimov wanted the UN to take note of the "arms and ammunition being stockpiled and camps set up for terrorist groups in Afghanistan for sabotage and subversion."[126] Karimov's stand that the southern borders of Tajikistan are the southern boundary of all CIS countries, was finally accepted and endorsed by the CIS leaders in August 1993.

On its part Afghanistan raised the issue of Uzbekistan's financial and military support to General Dostam in his fight against the Islamic forces there. Afghan Foreign Minister Najibullah Lafrai led a high ranking delegation from Afghanistan to Tashkent which met the Uzbek Foreign Minister Kamilov on 23 November 1994.[127] Both sides discussed the existing problems between the two countries with a view to remove misunderstanding. However, the Uzbek President, Islam Karimov asserted Uzbekistan's right to defend its border abitting Afghanistan. Causing for an arms embargo on Afghanistan, Karimov discussed their issue with President Rabbani of Afghanistan.[128] On 3 August 1996, President Karimov sent a letter to the UN Security Council urging it to convene a meeting to discuss the draft resolution prepared by Uzbekistan for embargo on arms supplies to

Afghanistan.[129] The takeover of Kabul by the Taliban evoked strong reaction from Uzbekistan President Karimov held a meeting of Uzbekistan's National Security Council on 10 October 1996 which express concern over the escalation in terrorism and violations of human rights in Afghanistan.[130] This was followed by Uzbek Foreign Minister, Kamilov's assertion on 3 October 1996 that "Uzbekistan would not like to see the presence of the fundamentalist movement in Afghanistan."[131] He pointed out that Afghansitan "had become a hotbed of terrorism drug trafficking and a centre of illegal arms trade."[132] That President Karimov visited the town of Termez on Uzbek-Afghan border on 3 October 1996, to have a first hand feel of the situation and also to meet border guards and local leaders following the Taliban's seizure of Kabul, shows the serious concern in Uzbekistan over the issue.[133] Karimov declared his country's resolve "to prevent the Taliban from gaining a foothold in northern Afghanistan, which borders the three Central Asian Republics of Uzbekistan, Tajikistan and Turkmenistan".[134]

THREAT TO KYRGYZSTAN'S SECURITY

That the turbulence and strife in Tajikistan spilled over into the neighbouring state of Kyrgyzstan is evidenced by the influx of thousands of armed Tajik Islamic radicals into the Osh oblast.[135] The Kharogh Osh highway which provides direct access form Gorno-Badakhshan region of Tajikistan to the CIS was used as the channel of drug trafficking via Kyrgyzstan. The republican leadership got worried over the protracted civil war in Tajikistan and the possibility of Tajik armed groups supplying arms to Kyrgyz criminal bands.[136] The Kyrgyz President, Akayev publicly expressed his concern over the steep increase in the crime rate witnessed in Kyrgyzstan during 1992 (70 per cent in the whole country and 220 per cent in Osh oblast) and most of this crime was related to drugs.[137] To meet this new threat of illegal entry of narcotics and arms from Tajik territory into Osh through the Afghanistan-Pamirs route, the Kyrgyz army and milita units were transferred from Bishkek to Osh.[138]

Pan-Islamic Tajik radicals acquired some foothold in Osh. In early January 1993 reports came about the disruption of supplies to

Osh by the Tajik militants who also killed 3 local Kyrgyz and held 18 others hostages in the border area of Jergetal of Kyrgyzstan, for their refusal to join their pan-Islamic movement.[139] They were also reported to have hoisted the green Islamic flag on the building of regional administration.[140] These Tajik radicals were urging the local Kyrgyz populace, which is not so fervent in its Islamic zeal, to fight for the establishment of an Islamic state. The Islamic resurgence in Tajikistan and also in Ferghana region of Uzbekistan created a marked impact on the Uzbeks in the Osh oblast. This is reflected in a study conducted by the Bishkek Polytechnical Institute, which found that 25 per cent of Uzbeks in Osh oblast favoured the establishment of an Islamic state in Kyrgyzstan as against only 10 per cent of Kyrgyz there.[141] Bitter memories of the Uzbek-Kyrgyz riots that took place in 1990 and the border dispute between Tajikistan and Kyrgyzstan, which was the cause of Tajik-Kyrgyz clashes in 1989 in Batken region of Kyrgyzstan over division of land and water, remained the sources of social turmoil and political instability in the region.

Conscious of this uneasy situation, Kyrgyzstan pressed for the conclusion of a formal treaty with Tajikistan to confirm and consolidate the "inviolability of the existing borders."[142] At the same time, Kyrgyzstan in consonance with the CIS agreement on collective security of the Tajik-Afghan border, sent a battalion of Kyrgyz troops to take positions at the border posts of Ishkashim and Murghab in Tajikistan.[143] It signified an end to the earlier reluctance to commit Kyrgyz troops, which was essentially due to the local women's protest against sending their sons to what they viewed a second Afghanistan and in deference to the Parliament's decision against Kyrgyzstan's participation in defending the Tajik-Afghan border.[144] Due to the escalation of conflict on the Tajik-Afghan border, better understanding of the security threat to Kyrgyzstan from drugs and arms trafficking and influx of armed Tajik/Afghan militants dawned upon the political leadership. The need to take urgent preventive steps was felt more so because the Kharogh-Osh highway provides direct connection from the republic to the stronghold of Islamic radicals in Gorno Badakhshan region of Tajikistan.

The foreign ministers of Kyrgyzstan, Kazakhstan and

Uzbekistan met in Bishkek, the capital of Kyrgyzstan on 26 August 1996, to discuss a coordinated policy on the conflict in Tajikistan and the build up of Islamic forces on the Tajik-Afghan border.[145] Kyrgyz Foreign Minister, Roza Otunbayeva announced at the end of the Bishkek meeting that all the three countries agreed that Afghanistan "has become the main source of arms and drug supplies to Tajikistan, and through it to other Central Asian countries."[146] However, consequent upon the takeover of Kabul by the Taliban, Kyrgyzstan reinforced its southern border to prevent the possible infiltration of armed Afghan militants through Tajikistan into the Republic. Kyrgyz President, Askar Akayev visited southern Kyrgyzstan on 6 October 1996 to take stock of the situation. Kyrgyzstan, which was opposed to the official recognition of Taliban government, called upon the UN to hold an international conference to be attended by different afghan warring groups, to work out a peaceful resolution of the problem offering to host such a conference in Bishkek.

KAZAKHSTAN

Even though Kazakhstan did not share its borders with Afghanistan and Tajikistan, it remained concerned over the conflict in these countries. Kazakhstan also contributed its forces for the joint CIS peace-keeping troops to guard the Tajik-Afghan border. When in April 1995 the Tajik Islamic rebels attacked and killed the Russian and Kazakh border guards the Foreign Ministry of Kazakhstan lodged a strong protest with Afghanistan on 9 April 1995.[147] Kazakhstan even offered to the Tajik government and opposition groups to hold peace talks in Almaty. Kazakhstan joined Uzbekistan and Kyrgyzstan calling upon the warring groups to find a peaceful solution to the conflict. However, Kazakshtan reaffirmed its support to the view that Tajik-Afghan border was a common CIS border.[148] Kazakh President, Nazarbayev evenoffered to mediate between the Tajik government and the Islamic opposition, when he met the visiting Tajik President Rakhmanov in Almaty on 23 August 1996.[149] Nazarbayev even sent a message to the Afghan President Rabbani and Tajik opposition leader, Mullah Ahmed Nuri stressing the need for national reconciliation in Tajikistan.[150] However, soon after the takeover of Kabul by the Taliban, Kazakhstan urged the UN Security Council to call on urgent meeting to discuss the conflict in Afghanistan.[151] Kazakh President, Nazarbayev warned that "CIS countries will take commensurate measures if the crisis in Afghanistan over to Kazakhstan."[152]

CONCLUSION

The crisis in Afghanistan has had a direct impact on the situation in Tajikistan due to supply of arms and ammunition and training imparted by the Afghan *Mujahideen* to Tajik Islamic extremists. After the demise of Soviet Union narcotics trade in the Golden Crescent found yet another lucrative supply route via Pamirs-Tajikistan to the Commonwealth of Independent States and European countries. The Afghan *Mujahideen* played an overt role in subverting the socio-political situation in Tajikistan to establish an Islamic regime there. The situation was further complicated by different Afghan *Mujahideen* groups exercising control over different areas in northern Afghanistan who kept on pressing ahead on the Tajik border regardless of what happened in Kabul.

The civil war in Tajikistan took a heavy toll of over one lakh killed and injured and more than seven lakhs rendered homeless. The belligerent Tajik Islamist radicals even set up a "Tajik Government in Exile" in Afghanistan. Interestingly Tajik opposition groups used to intensify their attacks on the eve of or during the peace talks with a view to secure physical control over more areas in Tajikistan, so that it got enough bargaining position in the negotiations. The Tajik-Afghan peace process was marred by Hekmatyar's continued support to Tajik Islamist extremists and his opposition to the presence of CIS troops on the border. The intensification of bloody fighting between rival groups led by Rabbani and Hekmatyar turned the situation murkier. The trans-border movement of armed Tajik and Afghan Islamist extremists and smuggling of drugs and arms remained the main source of destabilisation for the entire Central Asian region. Even though two tonnes of drugs were seized on the Tajik-Afghan border during the year 1995, and even more quantity was seized in

1996, this region became the leading route for drug trafficking to CIS and Europe.

External factor in Tajikistan's crisis, particularly the trans-border export of Islamic extremism and terrorism from the direction of Afghanistan evoked strong reaction from the adjoining Central Asian States and Russia. Whereas Uzbekistan played a key role in galvanising opinion against "the advance of Islamic fundamentalists and extremists forces", Russia was concerned over the security of ethnic Russian minorities and the defence of Tajik-Afghanistan border. Conscious of the highly destabilising potential of the situation and the efforts made at redrawing of borders in this region, Russia and the adjoining Central Asian states of Uzbekistan, Kazakhstan, Kyrgyzstan and Tajikistan declared their firm commitment to the "Inviolability of State Borders." Not only that, Russian jet fighters on several occasions bombed the bases of hostile Tajik and Afghan militants in northern Afghanistan, thereby following the policy of hot pursuit. The CIS peace-keeping forces defended the Tajik-Afghan border, which was treated as part of the CIS border.

Advance of the Taliban and its seizure of Kabul in September 1996 escalated the conflict situation and reinforced the threat perceptions of Russia and the Central Asian Republics. However, Turkmenistan being keen to push its gas pipeline project via Afghanistan and Pakistan, tried to steer clear of any active involvement in the Tajik-Afghan border. Turkmenistan remained engaged with both the Taliban and Pakistan, at the same time hosting a few rounds of peace talks on Afghanistan as well as intra-Tajik talks. Uzbekistan being concerned over the rise of Islamic fundamentalism and the Taliban in its direct neighbourhood maintained its policy of general embargo on arms supplies to Afghanistan. However, in its earnestness to secure the overland access via Afghanistan to warm waters, Uzbekistan wanted to have the situation stabilised there. The Afghan conflict was seen as a major constraint in developing the overland road and rail communications and pipelines through Afghanistan and Pakistan. As such the belligerence of Taliban and rise of Islamic extremism in Afghanistan, Tajikistan, Uzbekistan and in adjoining areas remained the main cause of concern for the Central Asian Republics.

REFERENCES

1. *Summary of World Broadcasts* SU/W 0208 December 6, 1991.
2. *Ibid.*, SU/W 1490 September 19, 1992.
3. *Ibid.*, SU/W 0208 December 6, 1991.
4. *Ibid.*, SU/W 0209 December 13, 1991.
5. *Ibid.*, ME/1310 February 21, 1992.
6. *Far Eastern Economic Review* October 25, 1990. Naseeruddin, the last Amir of Kokand was Azad Beg's maternal great grandfather
7. See, Olivier Roy, Ethnic Identity and Political Expression in Northern Afghanistan. In *Muslims in Soviet Central Asia*. Edited by Io Ann Cross. Duke University Press, 1992. pp. 79-81.
8. *Ibid.*
9. This information was provided to this author by Abdul Zahir Khan Noori, Former Judge, High Court, Kabul, presently staying in Delhi.
10. Olivier Roy, *op. cit.*
11. *Newsweek*, February 3, 1992.
12. See his interviews in *News*, Islamabad July 28, 1993.
13. K. Warikoo, Soviet Central Asia in Ferment. In *Ethnicity and Politics in Central Asia*. Edited by K. Warikoo and Dawa Narbu. New Delhi, 1992. p. 67.
14. See Interview of Rabbani, Masood and Khalik with AFP dated February 15, 1990.
15. *Ibid.*
16. See *Central Asian Newsletter* Vol.7, No.3, July 1987, p. 3.
17. Five Tajiks stood trial in Dushanbe in the summer of 1982 for distributing leaflets against the war in Afghanistan. See *Central Asian Newsletter*, July 1987, p. 3.
18. K. Warikoo, *op.cit.*, pp. 68-69.
19. For their interview with AFP (Agence France Presse) see *AFP Report*, February 15, 1990.
20. Muriel Atkin, *The Subtlest Battle: Islam in Soviet Tajikistan*. Philadelphia, 1989. pp. 34-35. Saidov's arrest in 1987 provoked a big demonstration.
21. *Washington Post* April 13 and 19, 1987.
22. *AFP Report* February 15, 1990.

23. *Ibid.*
24. *Ibid.*
25. *Summary of World Broadcasts* SU/1141 August 3, 1991.
26. *Ibid.*
27. *Ibid.*, SU/1928 July 9, 1992.
28. *Ibid.*, SU/1377 May 11, 1992.
29. *Ibid.*, SU/1379 May 13, 1992.
30. *Ibid.*
31. *Ibid.*, SU/1405 June 12, 1992.
32. *Ibid.*, SU/1381 May 15, 1992.
33. *Ibid.*, SU/1507 October 9, 1992.
34. *Ibid.*, SU/1572 December 24, 1992.
35. *Central Asia Newsfile*, London No.5, March 1993.
36. *Itar Tass*, Moscow June 4, 1993.
37. *FBIS-SOV-93-140* July 7, 1993.
38. *Hindustan Times* May 4, 1993.
39. *Ibid.*, July, 1993. *Navoya Yezhednevnaya Gazeta*, Moscow July 23, 1992. *Hindustan Times* August 1, 1993.
40. *Ibid.*, August 12, 1993. The hostages were released on August 31, 1993.
41. *Washington Post* April 27, 1993.
42. *Ibid.*
43. *Interfax* September 27, 1993.
44. *Komsomolskaya Pravda*, Moscow 1 September 1994, pp. 1-2.
45. *Itar-Tass*, Moscow 19 August 1994 *SWB/SU/2084, G/6* dated 26 August 1994.
46. *Itar-Tass*, Moscow 29 September 1994 *SWB/SU/2116, G/2* dated 3 October 1994.
47. *Ibid.*
48. *Ibid.*
49. *Itar-Tass*, Moscow 4 January 1995 *SWB/SU/2194, G/3* dated 6 January 1995.
50. *SWB SU/1435* July 17, 1992.
51. *SWB SU/1440* July 23, 1992.
52. *SWB SU/1468* August 25, 1992.
53. *SWB SU/1512* October 15, 1992.
54. *FBIS-SOV-93-156* August 16, 1993.
55. *Ibid.*
56. *FBIS-SOV-93-153* August 11, 1993.

57. *FBIS-SOV-93-155* August 13, 1993.
58. *FBIS-SOV-93-161* August 23, 1993.
59. *Pravda*, Moscow September 1, 1993.
60. *FBIS-SOV-93-168* September 1, 1993.
61. *Ibid.*
62. *FBIS-SOV-93-173* September 9, 1993.
63. *Itar-Tass* September 8, 1993.
64. *SWB SU/1882* December 30, 1993.
65. *Voice of Free Tajikistan* December 22, 1993.
66. *Afghan Radio*, Kabul December 24, 1993.
67. The Commander of Russian Border Guards, Maj. Gen. Anetholy Chechulin stated in a TV interview that cross-border firing was a daily occurrence on the Tajik-Afghan border. *SWB/SU 1917, G1* dated 9 February 1994.
68. *Itar Tass*, Moscow 22 February 1994 cited in *SWB/SU 1930, G/2* dated 24 February 2004.
69. *Ibid.*
70. *Ibid.*
71. *Russia's Radio*, Moscow 29 March 1994 *SWB/SU 1963, G/1* dated 5 April 1994.
72. *Tajik Radio*, Dushanbe 20 April 1994 *SWB/SU/1979, G1* dated 23 April 1994.
73. *Ibid.*
74. *Tajik Radio*, Dushanbe 2 May 1994. *SWB/SU/1989, G3* dated 5 May 1994.
75. *Ibid.*
76. *Itar Tass*, Moscow 8 July 1994 *SWB/SU/2045, G/9* dated 12 July 1994.
77. *SWB/SU/2039, G/2* dated 5 July 1994.
78. *Russia's Radio*, Moscow 6 May 1994 *SWB/SU/1993, G/3* dated 10 May 1994.
79. *Ibid.*
80. *Itar-Tass*, Moscow, 12 May 1994, *SWB/SU/1994, G/4*, dated 14 May 1994.
81. *Itar-Tass*, Moscow, 9 August 1994, *SWB/SU/2071, G/4*, dated 11 August 1994.
82. *Itar-Tass*, Moscow 11 April 1995 *SWB/SU/2277, G/2* dated 13 April 1995.
83. *Itar-Tass*, Moscow 24 January 1995 *SWB/SU/2215, G/2* dated 31 January 1995.

84. *Itar-Tass*, Moscow 22 January 1995 *SWB/SU/2210, G/3* dated 25 January 1995.
85. *Radio Afghanistan*, Kabul 10-11 April 1995 *SWB/SU/2278*, G/1 dated 14 April 1995.
86. *Radio Afghanistan*, Kabul 13 April 1995, *SWB/SU/2279, G/3* dated 17 April 1995.
87. *Radio Afghanistan*, Kabul 12 April 1995, *SWB/SU/2278, G/2* dated 14 April 1995.
88. *Radio Afghanistan*, Kabul 13 April 1995, *SWB/SU/2279, G/3* dated 17 April 1995.
89. *Ibid.*
90. *SWB/SU/2286, G/2* dated 25 April 1995.
91. *Itar-Tass*, Moscow 22 April 1995 *SWB/SU/2290, G/4* dated 29 April 1995.
92. *Ibid.*
93. *Itar-Tass*, Moscow 17 May 1995 *SWB/SU/2307, G/1* dated 19 May 1995.
94. *Radio Afghanistan*, Kabul 19 May 1995, *SWB/SU/2310, G/1* dated 23 May 1995.
95. *Itar-Tass*, Moscow 20 May 1995 *SWB/SU/2310, G/1* dated 23 May 1995.
96. *Tajik Radio*, Dushanbe 20 May 1995 *SWB/SU/2310, G/2* dated 23 May 1995.
97. *Radio Afghanistan*, Kabul 20 May 1995, *SWB/SU/2310, G/3*, dated 23 May 1995.
98. *Ibid.*
99. *Ibid.*
100. *Radio Afghanistan*, Kabul 12 August 1995, *SWB/SU/2381, G/1*, dated 14 August 1995.
101. *Interfax News Agency*, Moscow 7 March 1996, *SWB/SU/2555, G/3*, dated 8 March 1996.
102. *Interfax News Agency*, Moscow 7 March 1996, *SWB/SU/2556, G/1*, dated 9 March 1996.
103. *Ibid.*
104. *Ibid.*
105. *Ibid.*
106. *Ibid.*
107. *Interfax News Agency*, Moscow 30 April 1996, *SWB/SU/2602, G/1*, dated 3 May 1996.

108. *Ibid.*
109. *Itar-Tass News Agency*, Moscow 23 August 1996 *SWB/SU/2700, G/3* dated 26 August 1996.
110. *Interfax NewsAgency*, Moscow 27 August 1996 *SWB/SU/2703, G/1* dated 29 August 1996.
111. *Radio Afghanistan*, Kabul *SWB/SU/2707, G/7* dated 3 September 1996.
112. *Khovar News Agency*, Dushanbe 5 October 1996 *SWB/SU/2736, g/1* DATED 7 October 1996.
113. See interview of Tajik Chief Qazi, Turajonzoda in *Al-Hayah*, London (in Arabic) March 3, 1993.
114. See Interview of General Latif in *Nezavisimaya Gazeta*, Moscow March 31, 1993.
115. A report puts their number at 2 lakhs. See G.L. Bondarevsky, Tajikistan-Afghanistan: two hot beds of war. *World Affairs* June 1993, p. 51.
116. *SWB SU/1824* October 20, 1993.
117. A group of Afghans was deported on September 8, 1992 from Uzbek territory. See *Nezavisimaya Gazeta*, Moscow September 17, 1992.
118. *SWB SU/1814* October 8, 1993.
119. *Asiaweek* November 27, 1992.
120. *Ibid.*
121. *Yezhednevnaya Gazeta*, Moscow 14-20 May 1993. Salamat Ali and Ahmed Rashid, Afghanistan: separate ways. *Far Eastern Economic Review* September 24, 1992.
122. *SWB SU/1508* October 10, 1992.
123. *SWB SU/1516* October 20, 1992.
124. *SWB SU/1642* March 20, 1993. For full text of Karimov's letter see Appendix I.
125. *Ibid.*
126. *Ibid.*
127. *Radio Afghanistan*, Kabul 23 November 1994.
128. *Interfax News Agency*, Moscow 15 July 1996 *SWB/SU/2666, g/4* dated 17 July 1996.
129. *Itar-Tass News Agency*, Moscow 3 August 1996 *SWB/SU/2682, G/1* dated 5 August 1996.
130. *Interfax News Agency*, Moscow 2 October 1996 *SWB/SU/2734, g/3* dated 4 October 1996.
131. *Interfax News Agency*, Moscow 3 October 1996 *SWB/SU/2734, G/2* dated 4 October 1996.
132. *Ibid.*

133. *Ibid.*
134. *Interfax News Agency*, Moscow 5 October 1996 *SWB/SU/2736, G/3* dated 7 October 1996.
35. *Pravda*, Moscow January 10, 1993. *Nezavisimaya Gazeta*, Moscow January 13, 1993. Incidentally Tajik Muslim leader and chief cleric Turajonzoda claimed to have escaped from Tajikistan via Kyrgyzstan. See his interview in *Al-Hayah*, London (in Arabic) March 3, 1993.
136. See Kyrgyzstan's Prime Minister T. Chyngyshev's statement in *SWB SU/1493* September 23, 1992.
137. See his interview published in *Rossiyskaya Gazeta*, Moscow December 30, 1992.
138. *SWB SU/1630* March 6, 1993.
139. Kyrgyzstan's Radio quoted by *Itar-Tass*, Moscow January 11, 1993. See *FBIS-SOV-93-006* January 11, 1993.
140. *Ibid.*
141. *Nezavisimaya Gazeta*, Moscow January 13, 1993.
142. *FBIS-SOV-93-012* January 21, 1993.
143. *FBIS-SOV-93-142* July 27, 1993.
144. Kyrgyzstan's Parliament had voted on August 14, 1992 against sending troops into Tajikistan. See *SWB SU/1513* 16 October 1993.
145. *Interfax News Agency*, Moscow 26 August 1996 *SWB/SU/2707, G/1* dated 28 August 1996.
146. *Ibid.*
147. *Itar-Tass*, Moscow 9 April 1995 *SWB/SU/2275, G/2* dated 11 April 1995.
148. *Inter Fax News Agency*, Moscow 14 April 1995 *SWB/SU/2279, G/2* dated 17 April 1995.
149. *Inter Fax News Agency*, Moscow *SWB/SU/2700, G/5* dated 26 August 1996.
150. *Inter Fax News Agency*, Moscow *SWB/SU/2702, G/2* dated 28 August 1996.
151. *Itar-Tass*, Moscow 30 September 1996 *SWB/SU/2732, G/2* dated 2 October 1996.
152. *Itar-Tass*, Moscow 4 October 1996 *SWB/SU/2736, G/2* dated 7 October 1996.

9

Uzbek–Indian Relations

Fatih Teshabaev

Relations between Uzbekistan and India have a continuous history, spanning through several thousands years. One can see the evidence of it in all spheres of life of the two countries. Having such deep rooted and vast relationship both countries can and should think about how this relationship could be developed further as they could play a vital role in shaping the future of their cooperation in the 21st century.

Much before the independence of India, its national leaders like Mahatma Gandhi, Jawaharlal Nehru, Rabindranath Tagore, Maulana Abul Kalam Azad and others started to pay their attention to the social and political transformations which were taking place in the post-second world war Uzbekistan. In mid-fifties when Jawaharlal Nehru visited Uzbekistan he was very much impressed by the life, he saw there. Then started an era of new mutual re-discovery in the Uzbek-India relations.

Though ten years of Uzbekistan's independence may seem historically a short span of time, these were the years of historic changes that shape the future of the dynamically emerging nations.

When the totalitarian system collapsed and the cold war came to an end, the Republic of Uzbekistan—the young and consolidating nation striving for the great future—was born in the land of ancient history. The path for the future chosen by Uzbekistan was the path of democratic polity through the introduction of a Constitution, which embodied modern ideas of governance and the rights and liberties of the people, blended with strong social policy for support of specific sections of the society. The dual process of nation-building and cultural revival, which have started after the proclamation of independence was yet another unique feature of the last ten years.

Within ten years Uzbekistan has achieved very tangible and undeniable results in the process of implementing political and social reforms and advancing on the path of modernization. Ten years ago its economy was primarily based on raw material source, but now Uzbekistan is rapidly becoming a country of industrial and agricultural production. From total dependency it became a self-reliant economy so much so that it is gradually integrating itself into the global economic space. Foreign currency reserves of Uzbekistan are steadily increasing and there is a stable annual increase in GDP (around 4%). Uzbekistan is among leading cotton producing and exporting countries. The country's gold production is growing to achieve planned targets and energy sector has become one of the leading spheres of the economy.

While the changes were taking place everywhere with some concepts of change becoming more popular than the others, Uzbekistan followed its own way, which later came to be known as the "Uzbek model" that was based on the concept of relying upon the strength of country rather than on that of IMF and other international bodies. All these factors coupled with many strategic and economic factors, make Uzbek-Indian relations important and relevant. Geo-strategic location of Uzbekistan, its rich natural resources, secular state policy, considerable market potential are the key factors which make this country extraordinarily important. Uzbekistan as the most populous country in the region constituting the largest powerhouse of the region.

It should be noted that the first official visit of the President of Uzbekistan to India took place on 17-19 August 1991, just two weeks before Uzbekistan's independence, i.e., when Uzbekistan had declared its sovereignty. During this visit the foundations of independent Uzbekistan's cooperation with India in the fields of economy, science, technology, culture and politics were laid down. India was among the first countries to recognize Independence of Uzbekistan, which was declared on 31 August 1991. Further the visit of the head of State of Uzbekistan to India in May 2001 and the negotiations which took place between the President of Uzbekistan and Prime Minister of India opened the new level of cooperation. Wide range of issues concerning bilateral relations were discussed, which once again provided the evidence for mutual understanding and closeness between the two sides on a number of issues including regional security. Agreement was also reached to widen cooperation on tackling the problems of regional security, particularly in areas such as the struggle against international terrorism, religious extremism, drug trafficking and illegal sale of arms.

The legal basis of Uzbek-Indian relations has been strengthened throughout the years of independence. In the year 2000 itself, 10 inter-governmental and inter-departmental agreements were signed. The total number of agreements signed between the two countries was 44 as on the beginning of 2001. They provide solid basis for furthering the relations in all fields of political, trade, economic and cultural relations.

Trade and Economic Relations

From the first years of independence Uzbekistan paid special attention to the development of mutually beneficial and fruitful cooperation with India in the field of trade and economic relations. In 1992, a Joint Uzbek-Indian governmental Commission on trade, economic, scientific and technological cooperation was established which held its meetings in Tashkent and Delhi. In 1999, an Uzbek delegation visiting India and FICCI signed an agreement on the establishment of joint business committee between the Chamber of Entrepreneurs of Uzbekistan and FICCI. In 2000, Ministry for Foreign Economic Relations of Uzbekistan and Confederation of Indian Chambers of Commerce signed the Memorandum of Understanding on cooperation between the two sides. According to another Agreement on trade and economic cooperation signed in 1993 both countries provide each other the status of most favoured nation in trade and economic relations. The statistics show that trade turn over between Uzbekistan and India in previous years has had the tendency of stable growth. In 2000 it was 12 times more than what was recorded in 1992, amounting to a total turn over of $ 25.3 million. Further growth was registered in the first six months of 2001 which already reached $ 15.61million.

Structure of the exports includes: industrial goods, non-ferrous metals, semi-precious metals, vegetables, finishing items, chemical fiber, services etc. Imports are also growing. These include paper, carton paper, pharmaceutical products, organic chemical compounds, glass and glass products, tobacco, chemical products, mechanical equipment, instrumentation and optical devices, coffee, tea, spices, plastics and plastic goods, sugar and confectionery, and different types of services.

Four Indian companies and organizations have been accredited and Indian investors are involved in 70 Uzbek enterprises and projects that include 47 joint ventures and 24 Indian owned enterprises with 100 per cent investment. Main activities of these enterprises include production of consumer goods, reprocessing of agricultural products, manufacturing of pharmaceuticals, assembly of computers and the supply of computer software etc.

Indian Investments in Uzbekistan

Cooperation in the field of investments started when on 24 May 1993 an agreement was signed in Tashkent between the two countries by which India granted a $ 10 million credit for financing the projects on Uzbek import of equipment, goods and services from India. This first credit was utilized for financing the supply of equipment for tea packing and modernizing the tea factory in Samarkand, for the production of tomato ketchup in nearby Tashkent factory, and for the production of medicine by Surhan-Ajanta joint venture as well as for the production of kitchenware by Uzbek-Indian joint venture "East butterfly". In 1994, second Indian credit of $ 10 million reached Uzbekistan, out of which $ 2.8 million was financed for the furnishing work of a hotel in Bukara. On 2 May 2000, third credit of another $ 10 million was given which is being used for the financing of modernization project of the Buvaida yarn spinning factory in Uzbekistan.

Conclusion

The general view is that Indo-Uzbek cooperation has shown an enormous potential of growth and progress. But at the same time it is to be noted that this potential has not been used to its full extent. India has not yet made a stronghold in Uzbek market so far as its strategic and advantageous goods are concerned. Figures for trade turnover do not put India in leading place in the list of trade partners of Uzbekistan. Both sides, therefore, can take coordinated steps to unfold enormous potential of the two countries and increase trade and economic cooperation to their maximum level.

Since the two countries have expressed their willingness to work for the promotion of peace and prosperity in the 21st century, it is necessary to take a number of steps to intensify their cooperation and do the following:

(*a*) To maintain high level of contacts and bilateral summits,
(*b*) To institutionalize consultations on foreign policy issues,
(*c*) To continue bilateral efforts for strengthening regional security,
(*d*) To cooperate closely by starting initiatives like multi-literal forums etc. so as to contribute to the stability in the culturally diverse and rapidly transforming Asia vis-a-vis the world globalization process.

As the two countries see an enormous potential for the enhancement of economic and business relations, the development of trade and business relations should be top priority for both sides.

It is necessary to create supportive structures for both private as well as public business to utilize existing credit lines more efficiently and to provide the capacity to cope with existing financial and investment realities. Besides, Uzbek-Indian cultural relations are very strong and have deep roots in their history constituting the basis of common civilization, which must be one of the core elements of Uzbek-Indian relations in future. Similarly, Science and technology are considered to provide the path for the future and Uzbekistan and India have much to share with each other in this field.

Tenth years of independence is an appropriate occasion not only to look back but to look with confidence at the future, which is going to be full of challenges. There should be no doubt that these challenges will be met with the full commitment of the people and government to the path chosen by them. The peoples and governments of both countries have on several occasions expressed their full commitment to the cause of the development of mutually beneficial cooperation. Uzbekistan and India can boldly develop their relationship on the basis of ideals and values, which they commonly share and cherish.

Uzbekistan and India—the cradles of ancient civilization—are eager to build great future for their peoples. In the 21st century and beyond Uzbekistan and India should maintain the heritage of their traditional ties as the core of their relations. It is heartening that the two countries are slowly being integrated into the process of globalization. It is, therefore, in their interest to cooperate more with each other, which in turn would contribute to regional and international development, security cooperation and prosperity.

10

India-Uzbekistan Relations during the 1990s and Future Prospects

SHRI PRAKASH

It is a truism to say that due to India's policy and practice of Non-alignment as one of the central principles in the conduct of its ties with other countries, Indian diplomacy has found it relatively easy to build good all round relations with the newly emerging nation-states of Central Asia. The fact that in 1991 the Soviet Union was dissolved voluntarily and unilaterally, that the largest constituent unit to emerge from it—the Russian Federation, *ipso facto* recognized all the other 14 Republics, which were the political successors to the former Soviet Union; and that shortly after being born as independent entities 11 of these states reconstituted their co-existence in a new form—the Commonwealth of Independent States (CIS), formed between 8-21 December 1991[1]—promising to consult and help each other in preserving their mutual sovereignty and territorial integrity, made their recognition by India a straightforward matter.

Uzbekistan with a population of 24.6 million in 2000 A.D. is the most populous state of the Central Asian region which also consists of Kazakhstan, Kyrgyzstan, Turkmenistan and Tajikistan. Under the guidance of its President Islam Karimov, it was indeed Uzbekistan which shortly after becoming independent took the first steps in establishing direct and cordial relations with India as one of its most prominent neighbours. The Uzbek President visited India in August 1991 and signed a number of agreements on economic and cultural cooperation. His visit was followed by a delegation of Uzbekistan Parliamentarians led by the Speaker Yuldashev who reiterated his country's stand that "Kashmir was an internal matter of India and any dispute with Pakistan should be resolved on a bilateral basis under the Shimla Agreement."[2]

These visits were soon reciprocated by the highly placed Indian leaders and officials. R.L. Bhatia, the then Minister of State for External Affairs, was the first high level Indian dignitary to visit Uzbekistan in October 1992. His visit followed India's formal recognition of Russia and other Republics of the former Soviet Union on 26 December 1991[3]. During his visit, India and Uzbekistan signed an agreement to establish a Joint Commission for technical and economic cooperation, which would meet once in two years alternately in New Delhi and Tashkent, the capital cities of India and Uzbekistan. As the Uzbek Foreign Minister, Abdur Razakov stated on this occasion, "it was the first such agreement signed by Uzbekistan since its independence in 1991 and would serve as a model for Uzbek cooperation with other countries".[4] The two sides also signed protocols on culture and arts, higher education, mass media and sports to give shape to the earlier agreement signed at the time of the Uzbek President's visit to India in August 1991. At this time, the Indian Government offered to extend the Indian Technical Exchange and Cooperation Programme to Uzbekistan for training Uzbek nationals in trade and banking.

The establishment of new and direct relations between India and Uzbekistan has taken place in the context of regional approach adopted by both countries in Central Asia. It is due to the regional approach that Uzbekistan joined hands together with other members of the Commonwealth of Independent States. However, the Uzbek President Islam Karimov in his book *Uzbekistan on the Threshold of the Twenty First Century* strongly argued for "the integration of the nations of Central Asia" as well. According to him, "Central Asian integration is an objective necessity, conditioned by a common means of communication, the basic and leading branches of their economies, a need for joint exploitation of water and energy objects and the provision of energy resources – to say nothing about our common culture, language and spiritual values, about our deep, penetrating intertwining roots and the general threats to the security of all the nations that inhabit this region, viz., the drying up of the Aral Sea, drugs and arms smuggling, emerging terrorism and religious fundamentalism and the threat of the escalation of tension and instability that comes from Afghanistan."[5] He further states that "there are grounds to look forward optimistically to the future of the Central Asian Commonwealth. The necessary legal and organizational base has been laid down by the Tashkent summit of January 1993 summoned by Uzbekistan: the Inter-state Council, the Executive Committee on Commonwealth Programmes Implementation, the Central Asian Bank for Cooperation and Development have been set up. The programme for the year 2000, has been worked out to lay down the foundations of a unified economic area. We are very close now to the coordination of defence policies: the Charter of the Council of Defence Ministers of member-states of the Agreement has been approved".[6]

Sensing that the effort to build independent nation states in Central Asia was occurring in the context of an existing and growing regional inter-dependence, India too sought to build a broad based relationship with all the Central Asian states. In November 1991, the Indian Prime Minister, Narasimha Rao wrote to the Presidents of Republic of Russia, Turkmenistan, Kazashstan and Kyrgyzstan inviting them to visit India in order to pave the way for establishing direct relations. In October 1992 Salman Khurshid, the Deputy Minister of Commerce led a multi-disciplinary delegation including businessmen to Central Asia and visited Turkmenistan, Kazakhstan, Kyrgyzstan and Uzbekistan from 27 October to 10 November 1992. The delegation had wide ranging discussions on expanding trade and economic cooperation with these countries. Preliminary discussions were also held on establishing joint ventures in various sectors. The Indian side also announced credits of US Dollars 10 million each to Kazakhstan and Uzbekistan and US Dollars 5 million each to Kyrgyzstan and Turkmenistan.[7] The first ever Indian Prime Ministerial visit to Central Asia took place when Narasimha Rao visited Uzbekistan and Kazakhstan in May 1993, and promised to upgrade the Indian consulate in Tashkent to a full scale embassy which was done in September 1994. During Narasimha Rao's visit India and Uzbekistan vowed to jointly fight the menace of "externally supported terrorism and religious fundamentalism" and agreed to expand their "commercial, trade and investment ties." To this effect five agreements were signed relating to political relations, trade, civil aviation and tourism.[8] In 1995 Uzbekistan joined the Non-Aligned Movement.

It is worthwhile at this point to recollect some aspects of the historical perception India has had about the Central Asian region since the nineteenth century. These perceptions are additional factors in explaining why India took immediate steps to establish direct relations with its newly independent neighbours, the Central Asian states, when they became free from the Soviet Union in 1991.

India and Uzbekistan have shared a geo-cultural affinity and a long tradition of historical contacts which date back to antiquity. Notwithstanding the great mountain barriers of the Karokoram and the Hindukush, there is a history of close economic, cultural and diplomatic contacts between the two regions. These similarities are easily discernible from the type of habitat, foot and drinking habits, ornaments, arts and crafts prevalent in this region. The archaeological findings in Northern India and Uzbekistan reveal remarkable parallels in stone and bone tools, pot forms and other artifacts which suggest a rare intensity of communication across the Himalayas since prehistoric times.

Whereas the sculptures excavated at Khalchayan and Dalverzin-Tepe in Uzbekistan depict the influence of Indo-Buddhist traditions, the discovery of a Buddhist monastery at Kara Tepe and the existence of Brahmi/Kharoshthi inscriptions on the artifacts clearly demonstrate Indian cultural influences in this area. Frescoes found in Panjikent and Varakhsha also bear testimony to this effect. For instance, a painting depicting a blue dancer with a trident and body draped in tiger skin is linked to the legend of the blue necked Shiva Nilkantha. Another painting shows a king hunting a tiger on elephant back, which is obviously based on Indian experience.

Indo-Uzbek contacts developed further during Uzbek times. The Khawarezmian scholars, Al Beruni and Abdur Razak Samarkandi not only visited India but their writings also helped in projecting India back home.

Three hundred years of Mughal rule—established by Babar of Andijan in the Ferghana valley the better part of which is in Uzbekistan—changed the social complexion on India and led to further growth of Indo-Islamic culture. Due to its central position on the Silk Route, Uzbekistan with its famous cities of Bukhara, Samarkand and Tashkent became important cultural and trading centres of Asia. Traders, travellers and pilgrims from Uzbekistan and adjoining areas preferred to follow the Bukhara-Kabul-Peshawar-Punjab route or the route that traversed through Ferghana, Kashgar, Yarkand, Ladakh, Kashmir and Punjab, as they were shorter and more established routes. It has been established that hundreds of Indian traders hailing from different parts of India stayed for several years in Bukhara, Karshi, Samarkand, Tashkent and other Uzbek towns for trading purposes even as late as the nineteenth century.

Indian exports to Uzbekistan included shawls, books (printed as well as calligraphed), tea, muslin, brocades, spices, herbal medicine, indigo and the. Indian imports from that quarter comprised mainly of Bukharan and Kokandi gold coins (*tillas*), silks, carpets and coarse cotton goods. However, the incorporation of Uzbekistan and India into the Russian and British empires respectively restricted the trade and cultural movements between the two regions.[9]

By the time the Indian National Congress came into existence in 1885, Russia had already established its control over Central Asia. After conquering and annexing the Emirates of Bukhara in 1868, the Khanate of Khiva in 1873, the Khanate of Kokand in 1876, the Turkmen region of Merv in 1885 and Pandjeh in 1886, it was ready to knock at the doors of Afghanistan. While at the beginning of the

19th century more than 3,000 kms. separated the Russian Empire form the British Empire, by the end of the century this distance shrunk to a few hundred and even as little as about 30 kms in parts of the Wakhan ridge. In order to preempt any chance of conflict breaking out, an Anglo-Russian Convention was signed in 1907, delimiting their respective spheres of influence and consequently relegating the London-Moscow rivalry over Central Asia to a secondary position.

Once the Soviet Union recoganized the Central Asian region into administrative zones conforming more or less to the boundaries of the present five countries of Uzbekistan, Kazakhstan, Kyrgyzstan, Tajikistan and Turkmenistan during the 1920s and the 1930s, there were rapid social and economic changes. Jawaharlal Nehru was impressed and influenced by the nature of rapid changes taking place in the Central Asian region. In his famous *Glimpses of World History,* in September 1933 Nehru cited the example of Central Asia where "a dozen years ago this part of the world was perhaps the most backward and superstitious. Women there were kept in a hopeless state of subjection. Today the country has progressed amazingly. Women are not only free but are taking great part in education, in medical and sanitary work as well as in other occupations. There are innumerable schools and colleges, hospitals and dental clinics all of them manned largely by the people of the country themselves."[10] During the days of the Soviet Union, India used to maintain a Consulate in Tashkent, which was also selected as the venue for the famous Indo-Pakistan summit of 1965 and the signing of the Tashkent Agreement thus concluding the Indo-Pak war of 1965.

Links between India and Uzbekistan are many and varied. What is most appreciated in Uzbekistan are Hindi films. The songs of Hindi films can be heard over cassette players in taxis and restaurants throughout Uzbekistan and even Doordarshan TV which has special slots for the Uzbek people relays programmes based on Hindi film songs. There is a Lal Bahadur Shastri square in Tashkent which was created in memory of the late Prime Minister who died there in 1965. A school is also named after Lal Bahadur Shastri, where besides an elaborate curriculum, Hindi is taught which accounts for people who speak 'shudh' Hindi.[11]

Considering the significant degree of mutual appreciation which exists between India and Uzbekistan, the leaders of the two countries have made consistent efforts to further develop their relations in the post-Soviet period. Following the Indian Prime Minister Narasimha Rao's visit to Uzbekistan in May 1993, the Uzbek President Islam Karimov made a three-day visit to India in January 1994. It was during this visit that the two countries signed six agreements for cooperation in various areas including one on comprehensive economic tie up.[12] The next year saw the second meeting of the Indo-Uzbek Joint Commission which followed the start of the Indian Cultural Centre in May 1994, relaying of Doordarshan programmes on Uzbek Television, and the establishment of an India Chair at the World University of Economics and Diplomacy. Subsequently, the then External Affairs Minister, Pranab Mukherjee made a three-day visit to Uzbekistan in April 1996. He met a number of Uzbek leaders including President Islam Karimov, Prime Minister U. Sultanov and Foreign Minister A. Kamilov. He also co-chaired the third meeting of the Indo-Uzbek joint ventures in fields like pharmaceuticals, tea packaging and stainless steel. It was also decided that cooperation in science and technology will further be strengthened. On the Afghanistan issue both sides stressed that its territorial integrity should be maintained and all external interference be ended.[13]

Mutual exchanges and interactions at the highest level further continued between India and Uzbekistan. During 19-23 January 1994, the Uzbek Foreign Minister Kamilov paid a visit to India and signed a new agreement for imparting training to 25 Uzbek diplomats. There were several exchanges of visits by scientists as well. Besides, an Indian cultural group participated in the international music festival held at Samarkand in August 1997 and won the first prize in the music competition.[14] In December 1997, the India Business Centre was started in Tashkent which is being run jointly by the Confederation of Indian Industry and the Ministry of Commerce.

Changes in governments in India have not affected the ongoing interaction between India and the Central Asian Republics. K. Ramamurthy, Minister for Petroleum and Natural Gas headed a delegation to Uzbekistan in October 1998. In May 1999, Jaswant Singh, the Minister for External Affairs visited Uzbekistan and signed the bilateral investment protection agreement. Both sides promised each other to share intelligence with regards to counter insurgency operations against terrorism. Uzbekistan has welcomed India's proposal seeking its participation in a cargo transfer arrangement along a land corridor through Iran via the rail route which terminates at the Iranian port of Bandar Abbas. During Jaswant Singh's visit to Uzbekistan India agreed to extend another 10 million US dollars credit to Uzbekistan. On its part in September 1999, Uzbekistan gifted India with a 1.5 Kilowatt solar furnace.

India has been making determined efforts to promote Indian products in Uzbekistan. It is evidenced by the fact that India Trade Promotion Organization held an Indian Trade Exhibition in Tashkent from 14 to 20 September 1995. Over 84 leading companies from India displayed a diverse range of products covering engineering equipment, machinery and accessories, electrical and electronic equipment, automobiles, kitchen equipment, hospital equipment, petrol pumps, stainless steel castings, cables, pipes, welding electrodes, telecommunication equipment, chemicals, pharmaceuticals, bicycles and bicycle parts, sanitary fittings, household appliances, electrical appliances including batteries, rubber products, leather board sheets, leather garments, textiles, woolens, fabrics, footwear, handicrafts, medicines, stationary, TV cabinets, non-ferrous metal articles, plywood, wood enamels, paper and paper boards, coolers, cosmetics, toiletries, consumer goods, home furnishings, toys, lenses, sports goods, spirits and beer. Leading corporate giants like TATA Exports Ltd., Maruti Udyog, Avon Cycles, US Global Corpn. Ltd., Usha International Ltd., Malhotra Global Eximp. Ltd., Kirlosker Bros. Ltd. and several other companies together with a few state organizations participated at this exhibition with favourable results. It was estimated that they generated business worth Rs. 106 crores.[15]

Tables I and II present an empirical profile of trade between India and Uzbekistan for the period between April 1994 and March 2000. As can be seen from Table I that total value of the trade between India and Uzbekistan has doubled from 48.32 crores in 1994-95 to 99.9 crores in 1999-2000. After Kazakhstan, this is the second largest total trade value for India among the Central Asian Republics. This in itself is a noticeable feature because access to Uzbekistan from India is not easy at present. The shortest and the most direct route through Pakistan and Afghanistan is not usable due to turbulence in Afghanistan and the state of adversarial relations between India and Pakistan. Hence the cost of transportation is high as are the tariffs at several points which have to be paid when goods cross from one country to another. These tariffs need to be reduced by introducing a phased transition to what may be envisaged as the North Asian Free Trade Area. India can also seek the support of Uzbekistan in joining the Economic Cooperation Orgnanization (ECO), a regional grouping of Pakistan, Afghanistan, Turkey and Iran founded in 1985 to which the Central Asian countries were admitted in February 1992.

Table 10.1 and 10.2 indicates that the principal commodities being exported from India such as tea, coffee, Basmati rice, drugs and pharmaceuticals, plastic products, transport equipment, electronic goods, handicrafts and ready made garments have a lot of potential for future expansion. Similarly, imports form Uzbekistan such as raw silk, wool and cotton will also be needed in greater quantities with the growth of demand for textiles in India.

While the potential for India-Uzbekistan trade in the future seems to be very high, it has been realized that India's share in the total value of Uzbekistan's trade at present is miniscule. In 2000, the total trade value of Uzbekistan was 6,157 million US dollars. The main destinations for its exports were Russia (13%), Switzerland (9.8%), UK (10.1%), Belgium (3%), Kazakhstan (4%) and Tajikistan (4%). The imports were mainly from Russia (13.8%), South Korea (13.6%), Germany (1.3%), USA (7.7%), Turkey (3.9%) and Kazakhstan (4.1%).

Table 10.1: Total Trade Values between India and Central Asian Countries including Uzbekistan (Values in Rupees laksh)

Period April 1994 – March 95	*Kazakhstan*	*Kyrgyzstan*	*Tajikistan*	*Turkmenistan*	*Uzbekistan*	*World*
Imports from	1,261.96	NA	648.51	3,344.26	2,617.37	89,97,069.65
Export to	2,561.77	NA	31.78	166.25	2,213.31	82,67,339.98
Total Trade Value	3,823.73 (100)		670.29 (100)	3,510.51 (100)	4,831.68 (100)	1,72,64,408 (100)
April 1995-March 96						
Imports form	2,656.97	8.33	1,115.13	919.86	3,590.63	1,21,64,659.00
Exports to	2,986.99	13.55	1,631.8	391.64	2,502.50	1,06,46,486.00
Total trade Value	5,643.66 (148)	21.88 (100)	2,746.93 (143)	1,311.50 (1,430)	6,093.13 (126)	2,28,11,145 (132)
April 1996-March 97						
Imports from	4,461.18	406.07	285.57	94.63	923.94	1,38,91,987.96
Exports to	1,558.73	346.21	257.52	490.26	2,888.32	1,18,81,731.53
Total Trade Value	6,019.95 (158)	752.28 (344)	543.09 (80)	584.89 (17)	31,812.26 (79)	25,57,73,718 (149)
April 1997-March 98						
Imports from	15,685.4	32.35	65.57	13.38	1,006.42	1,78,33,169.38
Exports to	5,623.61	4,008.41	415.21	632.23	6,538.31	1,39,75,177.25
Total Trade Value	2,160.01 (557)	4,040.76 (1,847)	480.78 (71)	645.61 (18)	7,544.73 (210)	3,18,08,346 (184)
April 1998-March 99						
Imports from	5,229.28	42.60	1,064.62	44.50	701.28	1,78,33,169.38
Export to	15,986.31	3,652.19	213.68	810.61	5,399.71	1,69,75,177.25
Total Trade Value	21,216 (555)	3,704.79 (16,932)	1,278.30 (188)	855.11 (132)	6,100.99 (129)	3,18,08,346 (184)
April 1999-March 00						
Imports from	4,670.30	857.20	1,017.84	169.65	5,535.93	2,04,58,265.55
Export to	12,119.23	6,215.0	1,375.21	2,683.14	4,445.5	1,62,92,491.73
Total Trade Value	16,786.53 (439)	7,072.2 (32,322)	2,393.05 (352)	2,852.79 (81)	9,981.88 (207)	3,67,50,756 (213)

Source: *Foreign Trade Statistics of India*

Table 10.2: Commodity Composition of Trade between India and Uzbekistan
A Imports into India from Uzbekistan

Sr. No.	Item	Unit	Period April 1998 – March 1999		April 1999 – March 2000	
			Qty.	Value in Rs. lakhs	Qty.	Value
1.	Pulses	ton	17	2.23	194	26.09
2.	Silk Raw	ton	21	141.06	10	68.05
3.	Raw Wool	ton	62	15.27	179	25.73
4.	Raw Cotton	ton	945	519.74	1,136	4,876.98
5.	Non–Electric Machinery	–	–	–	–	139.78
6.	Electronic Goods	–	–	–	–	12.04
7.	Other Commodities	–	–	0.02	–	261.80
B. Exports from India to Uzbekistan						
1.	Tea	Kg.	17,32,788	1,578.13	1,92,042	155.49
2.	Coffee	Kg.	54,888	81.37	2,520	1.04
3.	Rice Basmati	ton	17	4.29	17	4,029
4.	Floriculture	Kg.	1,60,000	152.47	12,400	12.31
5.	Tabacco Unmanufactured	Kg.	7,762	10.58	18,000	14.69
6.	Drugs Pharmaceuticals	–	–	791.85	–	1,895.28
7.	Inorganic Drugs Chemicals	Kg.	1,02,160	40.86	20415	145.03
8.	Paper Wood Products	–	–	169.47	–	239.30
9.	Plastic Products	–	–	252.69	–	139.57
10.	Manufacture of Metals	–	–	1,111.01	–	106.00
11.	Transport Equipment	–	–	8.54	–	30.15
12.	Electronic Goods	–	–	100.83	–	55.69
13.	Cotton Yorn Fabrics	–	–	170.15	–	89.10
14.	Handicrafts	–	–	2.8	–	241.32
15.	Ready made Garments (wool)	–	–	15.85	–	400.04
16.	Other Commodities	–	–	483.22	–	282.50

Source: Foreign Trade Statistics of India

As regards maintenance of peace and stability, Uzbekistan's membership of the CIS may enable it to get Russian support if it faces trouble in the neighbourhood. It is also evidenced by the fact that since 1994 Uzbekistan's membership of NATO's partnership for Peace has enlarged the sphere of support it can call for when in trouble. India can help to enlarge this network still further by offering to sign a new agreement with Uzbekistan along the lines of the earlier Indo-Soviet Pact for Peace and Friendship promising to help to preserve mutual territorial integrity. It can also offer to provide training for Uzbek officers. In this respect preservation of political stability in Central Asia is in the interest of both Russia and India who can hope to cooperate on this issue in the future.

REFERENCES

1. N.M. Khilnani, (1992) "Indian diplomacy and CIS", *National Herald*, 2 June.
2. "Indo-Uzbek Panel to Boost Trade Ties," *Times of India*, 14 October 1992.
3. *Annual Report of the Ministry of External Affairs (MEA), Government of India (GOI), 1991/92*, pp. vi/vii.
4. Report on "Indo-Uzbek Panel——," *loc. cit.*
5. Islam Karimov, *Uzbekistan On the Threshold of the Twenty-First Century*", Curzon Press survey, U.K. 1997 pp. 192-193.
6. *Ibid.*
7. *Annual Report of MEA, GOI, 1992-93*, p. 42.
8. Jyoti Malhotra, (1993), "Uzbekistan, India, now to fight Terrorism," *Times of India*, 24 May.
9. K. Warikoo, Retracing Samarkand, *The Telegraph*, Calcutta, 9 January 1995.
10. Jawaharlal Nehru, (1982), *Glimpses of World History*, New Delhi, Oxford University Press, Reprint, p. 850.
11. "Along the Silk Route again," *The Patriot*, New Delhi, 29 October 1995.
12. "Indo-Uzbek ties get a boost," *The Pioneer*, New Delhi 14 October 1992.
13. *Indian Recorder*, April 22-28, 1996, pp. 1925-1941.
14. *Annual Report of Ministry of External Affairs, Government of India, 1997-98*, p. 43
15. Uzbekistan, *EIU Country Report*, December 2000, p. 5.

11

Central Asia-Iran Relations

S.P. Singh

The Historical Perspective

For thousands of years in the ancient and meaiaeval periods, the Central Asian region was within the domain of the Iranian civilisation and Persian was its *lingua-franca*. This area was ruled by the Samanids, who hailed from Iran and were the cultural ancestors of the Uzbeks. Cyrus the Great, the founder of the Persian Empire and Darius, his enterprising successor, ruled this region for a long period in the sixth century BC. They left indelible imprint on the Central Asian culture. The Samanids considered themselves as Iranians and descendants of Baharam Chubin, the celebrated general of the Sassanian king of this region. He belonged to the Arsacid dynasty of ancient Persia, which ruled Iran from 129BC to AD226, and had direct access to this vast region[1].

The Arabs no doubt introduced Islam to Central Asia in the seventh century, but the people of this region preferred to adopt the Persian model of Islamic culture. Though, Arabic was the language of the Koran, Persian became fully established as the language of science and literature until the occupation of the area by the Russians. Central Asia was subsequently conquered by the Turks, who also patronised the great Persian literary and artistic traditions. There was sufficient cultural intercourse between Iran and Central Asia even during the subsequent period. The Iranians had stretched all the way into the Xinjiang province all along this period. For the last two centuries, Iran's involvement with Central Asia has been tightly circumscribed due to the Czarist occupation of this area and the advent of the Soviet rule, which barred interaction between Iran and its northern neighbours.

The Beginning

Teheran's attitude towards Central Asia, however, underwent a sea-change in the wake of the dismantling of the former Soviet Union (FSU). Akbar Ali Velayti, the Foreign Minister of Iran, visited all Central Asian countries where he made commitments of economic assistance, worked out details of direct air and railroad links as well as communication network with this region. He offered to sponsor membership of the Organization of Islamic Countries (OIC) for the Central Asian Republics (CARs).[2]

Following the Alma Ata resolution, which was passed on 21 December 1991, the dissolution of the former Soviet Union and the formation of the Commonwealth of Independent States (CIS) were announced. Just after it, the Supreme National Security Council of Iran recognised the independence of the CARs. The Iranian *Majlis* later endorsed this decision.[3] The Iranian Foreign Minister declared that his country did not nourish any design of exporting Islamic fundamentalism to that area. The promises of the Iranian Foreign Minister notwithstanding, Iran made available huge donations to the mosques and the political parties of amiable disposition. The Revolutionary Guards of Iran lent support to some of the fundamentalist groups in the CARs. A faction within the Iranian leadership sought to export radical Islam to the CARs. While allocating US$1 30 million for the CARs, Teheran sent several hundred *mullahs* to this region for propagating radical Islam.[4]

In the initial stages, Radio Teheran maintained that "the existence of potential Islamic sentiment and tendencies among the peoples of these republics was the most significant aspect of Iran's relations with the CARs". Iran took the onus of defending the rights of the Muslims of this area. While reminding the listeners of the ever-growing influence of the USA and Israel in this area, it demanded self-determination for the Muslims of this region and a socio-political as well as economic system for them based on the Islamic tenets[5]. The Iranian Foreign Minister observed that both the friends and foes of Iran liked to see the emergence of this country as the "Mecca of the aspirations of all the Muslims", and "a model for the fifty Islamic countries[6]. Radio Teheran started broadcasting Islamic programmes in eighteen different languages of the area. Iran organised cultural and trade exhibitions in the CAR for countering the increasing influence of the Western media and Turkey.[7]

Multi-Lateral Linkages with the CARs

Iran has maintained multi-lateral linkages with the CARs through the common membership and collaborative efforts in the two regional groupings; the ECO and the Caspian States Cooperation Organization (CASCO). It has played a leading role in reviving the former and in founding the latter. The Teheran summit of the ECO, which was held in February 1992, was aimed at the evaluation of the new political geography in Central Asia. The ECO conceived of several path-breaking initiatives such as the establishment of an investment and a development bank to facilitate joint projects in crucial areas. In order to achieve the long-term goal of creating a viable trading block for the easy mobility of goods, it was envisaged to eliminate all trade barriers and reduce custom tariffs. Iran looked at this organization as the means to end its isolation, to turn its economy and to safeguard its security. The ECO, however, has been impacted enormously by the rivalry between Iran and Turkey as well as its projection as a "fundamentalist block" due to the exclusive grouping of the Muslim states.

So far as the CASCO is concerned, it was formed in 1992 with headquarters in Teheran. Iran played a leading role in establishing this organization. It is aimed at facilitating cooperation among the riparian states on issues such as environmental dangers to the Caspian Sea and the exploitation of its resources like gas and oil. Iran has fully tried to exploit its geographical location on the Caspian Sea. The institutional approach of Teheran to regional economic cooperation is aimed at the opening of its economy and serving the common objectives of all the member-states. Certainly political concerns have also prompted Iran to participate in these two institutions through which Iran tries to discourage the CARs from excessive reliance on the west and its multi-national corporations. Teheran has also worked hard to counter-balance the US policy to isolate in the comity of nations. But the US sanctions on Iran and its open patronage to the establishment of the multiple energy export pipelines on the Caspian Sea region with support from Turkey and the other riparian countries have seriously affected the working of CASCO.

Interplay of Domestic Roots, the Regional Context and International Factors

Iran's Central Asia policy is the result of an inter-play of domestic, regional and international factors.

Domestic Roots

Iran's policy towards the CARs is a natural outcome of the contentious but ongoing reform process in the country. The domestic roots of Iran's recent foreign policy orientation and its close linkages with the economic reforms of the country should not be overlooked. The change in Iran's foreign policy posture under the Rafsanjani-Khameini coalition which took over the charge of the Islamic Republic of Iran after the death of Ayatollah Khomeini in June 1989, was the result of the interaction of the policy of domestic economic reforms and the consequent shifts in foreign policy. Iran's Central Asia policy under the new dispensation is its by-product.

It is worth mentioning here that from the beginning of the Islamic revolution in Iran in February 1979 under Khomeini up to his death in June 1989, Teheran Radio maintained an intensive propaganda programme for the CARs. Throughout this period some of the highly inflammatory speeches of the Ayatollah were regularly broadcast in the Central Asian languages. Cassettes in the Turkmen, Azeri and Russian languages, which contained revolutionary Islamic songs, were in wide circulation in the CARs. They were used even at the weddings and at the religious festivals.[8]

Iran set up several broadcasting stations along its borders with the FSU. Regular Iranian telecasts were beamed in the Turkmen language from the middle of 1986. It was in June1987 that an Iranian newspaper laid wild claims on the territories ofTajikistan, Uzbekistan and Turkmenistan. The Iranian radio stations of Gorgan and Bandar-e-Turkman used to beam highly religious broadcasts to the Muslims of this area.[9] In 1989, about 50 million copies of the holy Koran were reportedly printed for free supply in the CARs.

There is no denying the fact that for a whole decade the Ayatollah harboured the ambition of becoming the ecclesiastical chief of the Muslim world and thereby replacing the Saudi domination. He preached the pristine glory of Islam and profusely contributed to the foundation of the Islamic resurgence in Soviet Central Asia. So strong was his impact in neighbouring Tajikistan that several parents in this republic named their new born babies as Ayatollah.

With the death of the Ayatollah, however, the previous thrust in Iran's policy towards the CARs was gradually changed. The Rafsanjani – Khamenei leadership coalition entered office with a mandate to make economic reforms their highest priority. The two leaders held dramatically opposite viewpoints. Ali Akbar Hashemi Rafsanjani represented the pragmatists, who sought reconciliation with the West. He wanted to enhance Iran's economic position and neutralize religious extremism. Ayatollah Khameni represented the more ideological faction of the ruling clique in Iran which believed in the export of Islamic revolution beyond the country's borders and opposed any type of reconciliation with the West. Differences between the two leaders, however, did not persist for long because the main problems within Iran were having a direct impact on the conduct of external affairs. They sank their differences and set in motion the new orientation in Teheran's foreign policy in general and its attitude towards Central Asia in particular. The pragmatists won over the revolutionary zealots who had stood under the banner of the *Mujaheddin-e-Khalq*. While seeking simultaneously to protect the gains of the Islamic revolution, the new dispensation worked hard to devise means to pursue these two ends.[10] Iran's policy towards the CARs is the natural outcome of the integration of the two approaches. Hanna Yusif Freij rightly holds that Iran's foreign policy towards Central Asia is driven by three factors—security, economic objectives and messianic.[11] Similar views have been expressed by Javed Moinaddini.[12]

There has been little political opposition to the expansion of the multi-faceted ties with the CARs, which have evoked wide appeal at the societal and state levels. The outlays of Iran's first and second Five Year Plan bear testimony to the fact as to how foreign economic cooperation based on oil-led industrialization is expected to assist in national reconstruction and development. These two plans have incorporated measures to attract external assistance and foreign markets. They laid stress on the expansion of the transportation infrastructure and the establishment of free economic zones.[13] Teheran's Central Asian policy is aimed at fulfilling the goals of its foreign policy objectives, which are deeply enmeshed in the domestic roots.

Regional Context

Along with the common historical experiences and the millenia-old cultural ties, the geographical proximity between Iran and Central Asia suggests that their relationship is quite natural. Iran shares land border with Turkmenistan north of which are situated the three landlocked republics of Uzbekistan, Tajikistan and Kyrgyzstan. The Caspian Sea connects it with Kazakhstan. Iran alone provides a territorial connection to the CARs with the Middle East and by sea with the rest of the world.[14] Iran's policy towards Central Asia has stemmed from its geographical location, which has made it a natural player in this region. Right after the disintegration of the FSU, Teheran perceived itself as a natural geo-political power in Central Asia and ever since it has been insisting on this status.[15]

The overtures of Shia Iran to the CARs have been prompted by a deep rooted sense of regional competition with secular Turkey and also Sunni Saudi Arabia. Right from the beginning, Teheran projected itself as a natural geo-political player in this area, whereas these two competitors have tried to outflank it. Ankara plays upon the fact that Turkish people are ethnically closer to their brothers in Central Asia. The Saudis feel religious proximity with the Central Asians due to their common Sunni faith. Iran has had to compete with two other regional actors in the area – the Islamic republic of Pakistan and its protégé—Taliban in Afghanistan.

While referring to the regional context of the Central Asian politics, Parson argues that on the face of it Turkey has the upper hand since all the people of the five CARs are Turkish in origin and they speak languages, which are akin to the Turkish. "Turkey has vigorously presented the attraction of its democratic political system with its separation of state from religion and its close ties with the United States and Western Europe", the author maintains. He adds that the Turkish model has evoked a positive response from the Central Asian leaders as evidenced by public statements following the "epidemic of VIP visitors and their missions in both directions…."[16]

Another regional rival of Iran in Central Asia is Saudi Arabia, which has invariably branded Iran as a dangerous and a revisionist power. It maintains that Iran espouses anti-Western values and threatens the Gulf countries by pursuing the re-armament programme.

In addition to competition from the two rivals like Turkey and Saudi Arabia in this area, Iran has been enormously affected by the Afghan imbroglio, the Tajik civil war and the consequent exodus of refugees. Teheran remained in constant touch with the rival factions in Kabul and Dushanbe. It goes without saying that the efforts of the various regional actors have reinforced Iranian presence in this area.

International Factors

The US and the Russian attitudes towards Iran have also been quite instrumental in shaping Teheran's perception of the CARs and its consequent policy. Right since the emergence of the CARs on the world scene as distinct political entities, the containment of Iran in this area has been the primary objective of the US administration. In January 1992, James Baker, the Secretary of State, tried to convey this impression to his Central Asian hosts. He alleged that Iran was nourishing regional and hegemonistic ambitions in. In an effort to limit or counterbalance the influence of Iran in this area[17], Washington declared it as a "rogue" state and enlisted the support of Turkey, Saudi Arabia and Egypt in this area. Pakistan and Israel were also encouraged to play against Iran.

During the Kazakh President's visit to Washington in February 1992, he was persuaded by the US President not to export the Kazakh oil through Iran. The US administration felt deeply concerned about Iran's re-armament plan, its civil nuclear programme, its opposition to the Middle East peace process, its initial religious activities and long time support to the terrorist groups. The Clinton administration imposed sanctions on Iran in 1995 and discouraged major pipe-line projects with international funding.[18] The US sanctions immeasurably hurt Iran's global interests in general and in Central Asia in particular. Washington's pressures have prevented several affluent countries from making investments in the Iranian oil and the gas industries having connections with Central Asia. The USA successfully excluded Iran from a number of lucrative Caspian Sea gas pipeline deals giving preference to Turkey, which has now entered in a big way. It opposed the construction of the Turkmen and the Kazakh pipe-line to Europe, whereas these two countries consider this route as the cheapest. As a result of the Iran-American tension, Iran's huge assets have been frozen, its efforts to secure western investments have encountered obstruction and many of its schemes have been put on the backburner.

There is thus no denying the fact that the US reaction to Iran's policy towards Central Asia adversely affected the desired development of Teheran's relations with this area. But there was thaw in relations between these two countries, particularly after the bombing of the US embassies in Kenya and Tanzania by the Taliban, its role in the execution of 11 Iranian diplomats, the massacre of thousands of ethnic Shiite Hazaras and its take-over of the Mazar-e-Sharif near the Uzbek border, which bridged the differences with both Washington and Tashkent. The common threat of the Taliban diluted the mutual animosities of USA, Iran and Uzbekistan which are now co-operating in the "Six-plus Two" forum.

While addressing the "great American people" in an interview with the CNN in January 1998, President Muhammad Khatani of Iran launched a "thoughtful dialogue" with the US administration. This development could end up the diplomatic estrangement between the two countries and even lead to direct negotiations between these two countries.

It is no doubt true that the revolutionary guards, the paramilitary forces, the powerful security agencies, the conservative clerics and their fundamentalist followers will not like the normalisation of US-Iran relations. But the Iranian President's America initiative has been popular with Iran's large middle class. After the victory of the reformists in the parliamentary elections, the issue of Iran-US relations came to be at the core of the reassessment of Iran's foreign policy. Its outcome would influence the future course of Iran's relations with Central Asia. An improvement in US-Iran relations could remove the misgivings of the CARs towards Iran.

Teheran knows it well that any breakthrough in Central Asia is bound to go along with an improvement in relations with Washington. It has, therefore, been changing its foreign policy behaviour. The recent improvement in Iran's relations with Israel, Turkey and the conservative Arab states, its role during the Gulf War and its renunciation of the Islamic ideology could help in graduate dilution of US antagonism.

Teheran's priority has remained to secure the cancellation of the US sanctions on Iran. It prodded big western companies to exercise their pressure on Washington, asking them to make investments in the construction of the gas and oil pipeline from Turkmenistan to Turkey. Several US multi-nationals have criticized the Clinton administration for preventing the newly independent States from becoming fully independent by pushing them into the Russian fold. Iran's assistance contributes to the economic development of the CARs and the US sanctions are obviously aimed at restraining Iran from completing its various pipeline schemes in this area. It is no doubt true that due to its designation as a "rogue State" by the USA, Iran has suffered due to isolation and dependency. The prospects of lifting of the US sanctions on Iran have thus become intertwined with the successful operation of Teheran's foreign policy towards the CARs.

If the US administration tried to restrain Iran from playing an active role in the Central Asia, the Russian policy helped it attain certain successes in this area. It is no doubt true that in the initial phase, Moscow did not approve of an active role for Teheran in this region due to its partnership with the West and doubts regarding Iran's championship of radical Islam. Kozyrev's agenda had chartered a course for the extension of Russo-Western partnership in Central Asia. As such, Turkey was preferred to play an active role. But factors such as Turkey's credentials as a frontline supporter of the West and the subsequent shift in Moscow's foreign policy orientation cleared the deck for Iran's penetration into Central Asia.

In fact, the June 1989 visit of President Rafsanjani had already opened up the door of Central Asia for economic interaction with Iran. The bilateral Soviet- Iranian agreement which was signed during Rafsanjani's visit, covered the period up to 2000 AD. It made provisions for huge institutional framework of Iran's economic penetration into the CARs. In the wake of the Soviet collapse in December 1991, Iran re-negotiated the terms of its economic cooperation with all the CARs in order to meet the challenges coming from the regional players and some outside actors in this area. In recent years, Russia's significance did go up for Teheran due to the US-inspired boycott of arms supplies to Iran from the West. Moscow turned into Iran's principal supplier of military hardware, nuclear reactors and relevant technology. Their economic relations have enormously expanded. This factor has impacted upon Iran's activities in Central Asia, in which Russia continues to be the chief outside actor.

Tajikistan-Iran Relations

Iran was the first country to establish an embassy in Dushanbe on the renamed Teheran Street. Of all the Central Asian countries Iran shares the closest historical, cultural and religious heritage including the Persian language with Tajikistan. In the initial phase of the post–Soviet period, both countries tried to strengthen their ties for the assertion of their common historical identity and Persian heritage[19]. In the wake of the victory of the *Mujaheddin* in Afghanistan in April 1992, when Tajikistan was enveloped into the throes of the civil strife, Iran became quite active in this tiny republic.

Iranian clerics arrived in Tajikistan in large numbers and worked hard to bridge the gap between Iranian Shia and Tajikistani Sunni faiths.[20] The Islamic Republic of Iran tried to rehabilitate Persian culture and language. It freely supplied Persian language text books. The Iranian Ministry of Guidance opened bookshops in Dushanbe, which sold both classical Persian books and works of the well known political authors of Iran. The satellite system of Iran helped Tajikistan in the introduction of modern communication system.[21] Several mosques and Islamic educational institutions in Tajikistan were financed by Iran, which was projected by some of the Tajik intelligentsia as the model Muslim nation.[22]

Role during Civil War

Iran funded several political parties and militias in Tajikistan including the *Islamic Renaissance Party* (IRP). But all of them were defeated by the neo-communists[23]. It gave political asylum to some of the leaders such as Qazi Akbar Turjanzade of the IRP and Yusuf Shademon of the Democratic Party. The Iranian Embassy was opened in the thick of the ongoing strife in October 1992. While supporting the Islamic opposition during the civil war, it tried to maintain relations with the neo-communist faction also. Iran was one of the few countries, which provided humanitarian aid to the people of Tajikistan throughout the civil war. In October 1992 itself when Tajikistan called for the dispatch of troops from the CIS to restore law and order,

Radio Teheran expressed concern over the ongoing violence in the trouble-torn country. It warned that the intricate situation would provide an excuse for foreign intervention in this Republic.[24] Later on, when Imomali Rakhmanov took charge of the Presidency, his government was recognised by Teheran. On 9 December 1992, however, the Foreign Ministry of Iran issued a statement expressing Iran's deep concern over the situation in Tajikistan. Demanding a neutral stance from the CIS troops, it expressed the hope that serious steps should be taken to alleviate the anxiety of the Muslim world.[25]

The state-to-state relations between the two countries began with the visit of the Tajik Foreign Minister to Teheran in February 1992. During this visit, the Iranian President offered to give "special priority" to Dushanbe in the political, cultural and other fields.[26] In June 1992, the Tajik President Abdur Rakhman Nabiyev visited Iran as the first head of the republic. The Iranian President offered to help Tajikistan resume its normal life. He addressed it as the "Muslim and Persian speaking republic"[27] . A Memorandum of Understanding (MoU) was signed between the two countries, which envisaged an agreement to set up a body to deal with the issues of political crisis in the region and problems around the world. Provision was made for periodic exchange of visits of the Foreign Ministers of the two countries and the establishment of a joint economic commission. According to the joint communiqué, the two sides agreed not to take resort to force or threat for the settlement of possible disputes. They offered to observe human rights, political freedom and international commitments. They agreed to have bilateral cooperation in the fields of trade and finance, oil, gas, banking, industry and other areas. While standing against the installation of nuclear and chemical weapons in the region, both sides expressed their keen desires to augment their contacts in the field of science, religious affairs, art, literature, medicine and health, mass communications as well as tourism. Subsequently, several agreements were signed between Dushanbe and Teheran during the Tajik President's visit to the Iranian capital in June 1995.

Throughout the Tajik peace talks on the Tajik situation, Iran advocated a political solution, based on a coalition between the communist Kulyabis and the Islamic Gharmis. The first peace negotiation between the Tajik Government and the United Tajik Opposition (UTO) was held in Teheran. Several subsequent rounds of negotiations were held under the aegis of the United Nations in Moscow and Teheran for a peaceful solution of the Tajik issue. The Iranian President visited Dushanbe in April 1997 to alleviate its misgivings about Iran's role in the ongoing peace talks. In December 1997, the agreement on Tajikistan was signed in Moscow. Under pressure from Teheran, Turjanzade joined the coalition government.

Turkmenistan-Iran Relations

Of all the Central Asian Republics, Turkmenistan has maintained a high profile in its relations with Teheran. It has the record for the highest number of bilateral meetings with Iran at the topmost level. Barely two months before the disintegration of the FSU, Turkmen President Sapr Murad Niyazov paid a visit to Teheran. It was again in February 1992 that he visited the Iranian capital to attend the first summit meeting of the Economic Cooperation Organisation (ECO). He signed the agreement for the establishment of the diplomatic relations between the two countries. The Turkmen President paid a second visit to Teheran in August 1992.[28]

The Iranian President visited Ashgabat in October 1993. While making a pointed reference to the ongoing ethnic conflict in Tajikistan, he laid stress on the need to maintain stability in the region and offered full co-operation in this direction[29]. It was in his presence that the common border between the two countries was opened on 22 October 1993. Iran and Turkmenistan signed a document facilitating consumer cooperation, border protection and free movement of nationals of the two countries. Iran and Turkmenistan agreed to set up nine committees to explore the possibilities of expanding mutual co-operation in various fields such as political affairs, transport, oil and gas, culture, science and technology, education, industry, mining, communications and energy.[30] The joint communiqué issued at the end of the visit maintained that peace and national reconciliation in Tajikistan should be facilitated through constructive dialogue with the opposition groups in accordance with the wishes of the people of Tajikistan.[31] Niyazov paid a return visit to Teheran in January 1994 during which the two countries reached an agreement on the study of the technical feasibility of the construction of pipelines between them for the export of Turkmen gas to Iran.[32]

Economic Co-operation

The Iran-Turkmen relations have been shaped by pragmatism and are based on economic co-operation in the energy and transportation sector. Iran has tried its best to link up with Central Asia through a network of road and railway systems. The opening of the Ashgabat-Mashad-Teheran highway marked the beginning of this process. It has enormously contributed to the completion of the Sarakhs-Mashad railway link, which connects the Central Asian network with the Persian Gulf. This much delayed rail link was opened with great fanfare in the presence of many regional heads of the states in May 1996.[33] This railway system has given Turkmenistan access to the ports of Bandar Abbas and Bandar Imam Khomeni in the Persian Gulf.[34] It links up the Iranian railway network with that of Turkey and through Julfa to the railway system of Azerbaijan and other Transcaucasian states. The completion of this railroad has provided direct connection from Urumchi in western China across Central Asia and Iran to Istanbul and further beyond in Europe. Several deals have been signed between Teheran and Ashgabat for the exploitation and production of oil and natural gas in Turkmenistan and their export through the Iranian seaports. Ashgabat is following Iran's advice not to allow the Western countries to plunder and pillage its gas reserves.[35] Iran has agreed to finance part of the cost of the pipeline from Turkmenistan to Europe through Iran and Turkey.[36]

Elements of Pragmatism

Both the countries have displayed pragmatism in their relations. Iran is an Islamic country, whereas the Turkmen constitution conceives of a *dunyavi* (secular) state. Ashgabat maintains close relations with the secular government of Turkey, Islamic Republic of Iran and Jewish State of Israel. Teheran has preferred to remain silent on Turkmenistan's close relations with Israel following Niyazov's visit to Tel Aviv in May 1995, whereas it has been critical of Kyrgyzstan's ties with Israel. Ashgabat has granted the contract for the management of the Turkmenbashi Oil Refinery to an Israeli company. Turkmenistan has an agreement with the US company, called UNOCAL, which was close to the Taliban.[37] Iran favours relations with Turkmenistan. Due to the concentration of sizeable Turkmen minority on its territory known as Turkmen Sahra, Iran has been keeping good ties with Ashgabat. It has economic advantages of cooperation with this republic for which Iran is the only shortest as well as the cheapest outlet to the world.

Uzbekistan-Iran Relations

State-to-state Relations

With the visit of the head of the Economic Reforms Committee of Uzbekistan's parliament to Teheran in February 1992, relations between the two countries began on the state-to-state level. In September 1992, the Uzbek Foreign Minister visited Teheran and in the last week of that month, the Iranian Embassy was opened in Tashkent. Islam Karimov, the Uzbek President, visited the Iranian capital in November. The two countries laid stress on the need to respect the sovereignty and territorial integrity of Afghanistan and to prevent interference in the internal affairs of this country. They expressed their willingness to help put an end to the Tajik conflict and to lend assistance in its reconstruction.[38]

Despite various types of diplomatic activities, initial relations between Iran and Uzbekistan were marred by suspicion. Towards the end of December 1992 Islam Karimov reportedly observed that Iran was helping the United Tajik Opposition.[39] He alleged that Iran was largely instrumental in the Tajik civil war and by exporting Islamic Revolution to Tajikistan which contributed to political instability in this region[40]. With a view to diminishing the growing Iranian influence, the government of Uzbekistan switched to Uzbek, Turkish and Russian as the contemporary lingua franca.[41] Tashkent apprehended that Iran's influence would soon grow in the Persian-speaking population of Samarkand and Bukhara. Hence it did not allow Iran to open its cultural centre in the heart of the capital city. The security agents of Uzbekistan delayed the commencement of the Iranian cultural week by thoroughly checking all the materials, which were brought from Iran for display. The exhibition of religious books and the display of the Koran was not allowed.[42]

The visit of the Iranian President to Tashkent in October 1993 also did not go well because Uzbekistan had some inhibitions about Iran's role in the spread of Islamic fundamentalism in the area and in the revival of Tajik nationalism. The Uzbek President openly criticized Niyazov for promoting Iran in various ways and thereby allowing "fundamentalism" a foothold in the region[43]. Islam Karimov was the only leader apart from the Israeli Prime Minister to applaud the US embargo against Iran, which was imposed in May 1995. In December 1997, he did not attend the highly successful meeting of the OIC simply because it was hosted by Teheran.

The entire Irano Uzbek relations, however, were overhauled with the occupation of all the Northern Afghan Territory bordering Uzbekistan by the Taliban and the take-over of the Mazar-e-Sharif by it in August 1998. It was the day after the bombing of the US embassies in Kenya and Tanzania that the Taliban had marched on this shrine. In its killing spree, it had executed eleven Iranian diplomats. Iran was equally seized of the massacre of thousands of ethnic Shiite Hazaras. Thus hard pressed by the aforesaid circumstances, Washington, Tashkent and Teheran came to realize that the common threat to them was posed by the militant brand of the ultra-revolutionary and spurious faith of the Taliban. This reactionary force has been linked to the Saudi-Sunni Wahabism and the military oligarchy of Pakistan as well as some other disgruntled elements of the area. This realization augurs well for the recent warming of Iran's relations with both the USA and Uzbekistan.

The "Six-Plus Two" Forum gave both Uzbekistan and Iran enough scope to expand bilateral cooperation over the myriad of problems presented by the Taliban with sufficient backing from both the USA and Russia. This UN-based forum brought together all of Afghanistan's six neighbours—China, Iran, Pakistan, Uzbekistan, Tajikistan and Turkmenistan—with the USA and the Russian Federation. In recent years, Iran shared Uzbekistan's grievances against the Taliban, as Uzbekistan felt threatened by military advances.

Kazakhstan-Iran Relations

Relations between Iran and Kazakhstan have not been so close. They are rooted in their common energy concerns and based on a number of trade as well as transportation agreements. The Kazakh President paid a visit to Iran in November 1992 during which both countries displayed identity of views. They expressed the desire to use peaceful means to resolve regional as well as bilateral disputes. They demanded an immediate end to the clashes in Tajikistan. The Iranian President supported the Kazakh proposal of the convening of the meeting on promoting co-operation and mutual confidence in Asia.

The President of Iran visited Kazakhstan in October 1993 and signed nine agreements with President Nazarbaev. These accords provided the framework for bilateral cooperation in the field of transport, communication, agriculture, banking, energy, trade and industry, customs and consular affairs. The Iranian President thanked his Kazakh counterpart for having repatriated the Kazakhs living in Iran. Nazarbaev expressed his appreciation for the Iranian President's contribution to the cause of peace and stability in Asia.

The two countries expressed the desire to observe the principle of non-interference in the affairs of others and agreed to cooperate for ending the conflict in Bosnia, the Nagorno-Karabach crisis and the civil war in Tajikistan.[44] The Kazakh embassy in Iran was opened in January 1994. In May 1994, the Kazakh Premier visited Teheran and signed several agreements related to visa arrangements, formation of joint chambers of trade and industry, banking cooperation and free-trade zones.

Like Turkmenistan, Kazakhstan also sought cooperation from

Iran for an alternate shipping route through which it could export its oil and gas. It signed an agreement with Iran to promote international and bilateral shipping of goods and passengers.[45] Iran also agreed to buy five million tons of Kazakh oil per year to transport it to the Gulf for export. These two countries have undertaken several schemes of cooperation in the Caspian Sea region.[46] Hundreds of Iranian companies have been registered in Astana, the Kazakh capital. Direct air links were also established between the two countries in the spring of 1993.

Recently China has played an important role in establishing closer links between Iran and Kazakhistan. According to their bilateral agreement signed in the summer of 1997, China proposed to spend US$ 9 billion for the construction of the pipelines from western Kazakh fields to the Pacific Rim through Xinjiang whereas the Uzen-Iran connection via Turkmenistan would provide a sea outlet in the Persian Gulf.

There has been controversy between Iran and Kazakhstan regarding the alleged clandestine procurement of nuclear weapons and some vital components by Teheran from the military stores in this Republic.

Kyrgyzstan-Iran Relations

Of the five Central Asian Republics, Kyrgyzstan has the weakest relations with Iran. On 24 August 1992, Iran and Kyrgyzstan signed an agreement on air and road links between them. In October 1993, the Iranian President visited Bishkek and signed 12 agreements as well as a MoU, which provided the framework for future co-operation. These agreements were related to the formation of joint economic, technical and cultural commission, banking and transport.

In May 1994, the Speaker of the Kyrgyz Parliament visited Iran. He discussed the prospects of parliamentary cooperation between the two countries, as well as expansion of collaboration in economic and technical fields within the framework of the Economic Co-operation Organization (ECO).

Relations between Iran and Kyrgyzstan were largely strained due to the expansion of the latter's ties with Israel, opening of the Kyrgyz embassy in Jerusalem and the visit of President Askar Akaev to Israel in 1993. Ties were further affected by the statement of Kyrgyz Security Minister, who alleged that the Wahabi activists in the city of Osh were trained in Iran. This sounds ironical as Iran is a Shia country. The Kyrgyz President, however, has taken personal care to assuage the Iranian feelings. He reportedly told the visiting Iranian Foreign Minister about his childhood years spent in a house where he found books of Persian literature such as the *Shahnamah* of Firdausi and the *Gulistan of* Sheikh Saadi.

Conclusions

Our foregoing discussion on Iran's multi-faceted relations with the CARs makes it evident that in the wake of the dismantling of the former Soviet Union, the western media in general and the USA in particular widely propagated the view that the Central Asia would be a fertile area for the Islamic Republic of Iran where it would engage in proselytising with a view to bringing about an Islamic order. Unprecedented opportunity was indeed available to this country for the export of radical Islam into this area. Such a policy could have no doubt easily reduced the huge internal pressure from the revolutionary zealots in the country and, on the other hand, it would have given incalculable opportunities to Iran for its deep economic penetration into the neighbouring CARs. Iran's activities, however, were marred by serious lack of resources and its image as an exporter of Islamic revolution as well as a sponsor of terrorism. Iran's population is overwhelmingly Shiite whereas the majority of Central Asian Muslims is Sunni. This factor also limited Teheran's adventures in this sprawling area. The Shia-dominated Islamic Republic of Iran was enormously rebuffed by the secular leaders of the CARs for the alleged attempt at the export of its theocratic model as well as ideological penetration.

Iran's policy towards the CARs stemmed from its international isolation and also from the fact that it is a natural player in this region due to its geopolitical location. Compounded further by ideology and the mixture of cultural, confessional as well as strategic elements, Iran's orientation towards the CARs is based on realistic considerations which are predominantly economic in nature. The ardent clerics of revolutionary Iran also fervently subscribed to economic interaction with this region because they were seized of the utter failures of the various reform programmes at home. It was complimentary to religious-cultural ties on the one hand, and on the other hand it was bound to enliven the economies of all the participating countries.

With the passage of time, Iran proved to be less of a player in the new "Great Game" for some regional and international factors. Iran's moves are limited by the strategic depth of Pakistan and Turkey in this area, which further shot up in view of the deepening of their ties with the USA. This, however, cannot be denied that Iran's credentials in the CARs have largely improved in view of its large capacities for the expansion of rail, road and energy transportation linkages which neither Turkey nor even Russia can offer. Furthermore, Teheran's agreement to provide convenient access to the Persian Gulf for oil and gas pipelines has enormously increased its status throughout the area.

Despite various handicaps and its inability to be a major donor and a source of technological assistance to the CARs, Iran's multi-faceted ties with Russia have also added to its ever-increasing relations with them.

The foreign policy orientation of Iran towards this region has been quite cooperative and constructive. Teheran has showed calculated restraint and respect for the territorial integrity of the newly independent status of Central Asia Republic. In view of its role as a communication hub, its proximity with Afghanistan, its energy resources, its access to high technology and its balanced foreign policy postures with most of the important powers, Teheran is confident of further improving its position in Central Asia. Coupled with the mix of the domestic, regional and international factors, security as well as economic dimensions of Iran's relations with the CARs will also augment its clout in this vast region.

REFERENCES

1. See Shireen Hunter, (1992), *Central Asia and the Middle East*, Central Asia Monitor, Vermont, No. 6.
2. *Izvestia*, 10 December 1991.
3. *Link*, New Delhi, 13 December 1992, p. 34.
4. *Wall Street Journal*, New York, 17 December 1991.
5. *SWB – ME*, 27 August 1992.
6. *FBIS – NES*, 16 February 1993.
7. *Ibid*, 6 October 1993.
8. *Turkmenskaya Iskra*, 14 October 1984.
9. *Ibid.*, 22 July 1987.
10. Iran: Reconstruction and Economic Growth, World Bank Report (Washington), 1991, pp. 1-15. See also Reconstruction and Regional Diplomacy in the Persian Gulf, London, 1992, pp. 84-96.
11. Freij, Hanna Yusif, State Interests Vs. The Umma: Iranian Policy in Central Asia, Middle East Journal, London, Vol. 50, N1, 1996, p. 72.
12. Javel Moinaddini, Iran and Central Asia Republics: Opportunities and Challenges, *Pakistan Horizon*, Karachi, N1, January 1995, p. 51.
13. *Middle East Economic Survey*, 7 September 1992. See also *MEED*, 30 October and *FBIS-NES*, 18 February 1993.
14. *SWB-ME*, 9 January 1993.
15. *Middle East*, London, March 1992, p. 33.
16. Anthony Parsons, *Central Asia: The Last Decolonization*, London, 1993, p. 8.
17. *SWB-ME*, 11 February 1992.
18. *NATO Review*, Brussels, 1996, p. 30.
19. *Middle East Economic Digest (MEED)*, 6 November 1992.
20. *Sunday Times*, London, 2 August 1992.
21. *FBIS-NES*, 26 May 1994.
22. Theodore Karasik, (1993), *Azerbaijan, Central Asia, and the Future of Persian Gulf Security*, Santa Monica, CA, p. 31.
23. Ahmed Rashid, (1994), *Islam or Nationalism*, Karachi, p. 214.
24. *FBIS – NES*, 21 October 1992.
25. *Ibid*, 9 December 1992.
26. *SWB – ME*, 20 February 1992.
27. *Ibid*, 2 July 1992.
28. *Ibid*, 27 August 1992.
29. *Ibid*, 25 October 1992.

30. *Ibid.*
31. *Ibid,* 27 October 1992.
32. *Ibid,* 11 January 1994.
33. *The Independent,* London, 14 May 1996.
34. *FBIS-NES,* 12 November 1993.
35. *NEED,* 4 February 1994.
36. *Ibid,* 6 May 1994.
37. Oliver Roy, The Iranian Foreign Policy Towards Central Asia. See his book *The New Central Asia,* or *The Fabrication of Nations,* Tauris, 1999.
38. *SWB – ME,* 26 November 1992.
39. Bruce Pannier, Turkey and Iran in Former Soviet Central Asia and Azerbaijan, (1998), *Perspectives on Central Asia,* Washington, April, Vol. 2, No. 13.
40. *Middle East,* London, February 1993, p. 36.
41. *Ibid.*
42. *FBIS – NES,* 20 May 1993.
43. *Segodnya,* 1 July 1994.
44. *SWB – ME,* 27 October 1993.
45. *FBIS-NES,* 13 May 1993.
46. *MEED,* 4 December 1994.

12

Tajikistan and the Afghan Cauldron

Sheel K. Asopa

Tajikistan shares with Afghanistan a 1,300 kms. long border and has centuries old ethno-cultural, religious and linguistic ties with the people of Afghanistan. As a political entity, Afghanistan is much older than Tajikistan although existence of Tajikistan as an ethno-cultural entity dates back to ancient times.

During the 19th century Tajikistan had been a part of the Russian Empire. In 1918, northern Tajikistan was conquered by the Bolsheviks and its territory was incorporated into the Turkestan Autonomous Soviet Socialist Republic (TASSR). The southern part of Tajikistan which had been under the control of Emir of Bukhara also fell pray to Bolshevik onslaughts in 1921. Regardless of organized resistance given by the *Basmachis* the Bolsheviks went ahead with the formation of an Autonomous Republic of Tajikistan under the Union Republic of Uzbekistan in 1924. The Pamirian region in the southern Tajikistan was made a part of the Autonomous Republic of Tajikistan and was renamed as Gorny Badakashan. Tajikistan became a full-fledged Union Republic of the USSR in 1929.

In 1895, Abdur Rehman, the Amir of Kabul was made to concede the right bank of the river *Panj* (the area later came to be known as Gorny Badakshan) to the Amir of Bukhara, keeping the left bank as part of Afghanistan. The *Darya-ye-Panj* thus became a state border for the first time between Tajikistan and Afghanistan. The population of the north-east of Afghanistan and south of Tajikistan can, therefore, be considered as one large group which has evolved differently on either side of the border because of different ethnic policies and socio-economic development.

Until the dismemberment of the Soviet Union in 1991, Tajikistan's borders were guarded by Moscow as international borders of the USSR. The disintegration of the Soviet Union and emergence of Tajikistan as an independent sovereign state created the problem of management of the safety of Tajikistan's borders with Afghanistan although a substantial number of Russian troops remained stationed on the Tajik-Afghan border even after the breakdown of the Soviet Union.

The closing decade of the 20th century has been a period of trials and turbulations for the countries of the post-Soviet political space. The Soviet forces withdrew from Afghanistan in 1989 without leaving any stable government behind. The warring factions threw the country into civil war. The US-Pak supported Islamic militants (*Mujahideen*) had already been active during the Soviet era in Afghanistan. In the post-Soviet period they became ruthless and brutally massacred the supporters of the communist regime in Afghanistan. The Pushtun population organized under Gulbuddin Hekmatyar, planted and promoted by Pakistan, emerged as a major aspirant for power. His rivals General Rashid Dostum (Uzbek) and Ahmad Shah Masood (Tajik) also organized the respective ethnic groups under their control and a bloody civil war crept up in Afghanistan.

During the civil war in Tajikistan in 1991-92, the *Mujahideen* of Afghanistan established close relations with the Islamists of Tajikistan. They made a common cause against the government in Dushanbe and the security forces of the CIS on the Tajik-Afghan border. The external interference in Tajik affairs created a problem of internal and external security and integrity of the newly emerged State of

Tajikistan. Tajikistan was seen by the Islamic militants as a bridge-head for the extension of Islam into Central Asia and from there into Russia's autonomous Muslim republics. The drug mafia had also been active behind the Islamists as they wanted to create a safe supply route for drug traffickers to Europe via Tajikistan and Russia. However, the termination of the civil war in favour of secular forces made the Islamists run away from the country to Afghanistan. In the course of time these Tajik refugees became an instrument in the hands of *Mujahideen* to harass the government in Dushanbe and the forces of the CIS on the Tajik-Afghan border.

The infighting between the *Mujahideen* and their divided loyalties towards the leaders of various factions kept the civil strife smouldering – getting wild off and on, the Pakistan-run *Madrasas* trained more disciplined and strongly ideologised Taliban to replace the *Mujahideen*. The Taliban captured Kabul in 1996 and through a reign of terror, mass killings and brutal and inhuman acts of vindictiveness almost paralyzed the nation. Taliban rule in Afghanistan had been highly nerve-taxing not only for Afghans but also for its neighbours in the north. Pakistan and the Western media gave credit to Taliban for providing a stable government and bringing major part of the country under the control of the central government. But stability at what cost? It is also an important question. Through naked force, violence and reign of terror they kept the people crippled, hidden in their houses and silent for fear of getting subjected to inhuman laws of Taliban. The stability was a farce. They did not enjoy the voluntary support of the people. Taliban were not real muslims either. Their brand of Islam and Islamic laws are of their own creation to keep the nation crippled, backwards and totally prostrated to perpetuate their power and run the *jihadi* movement from Kabul. The Taliban have no *locus standi* to claim a share in the management of post-Taliban Afghanistan.

The seeming elimination of Taliban has rekindled the hopes of all the ethnic units to share power. This, if not restrained through their leaders and the United Nation's representatives, may lead to another bout of internal fighting, divisions and dissensions making the political settlement difficult. The Central Asian states, Russia and India need to play a major role in the emerging political scenario in Afghanistan because a stable, strong, secular, united and democratic Afghanistan alone can provide security and peace to the Central and South Asian states bordering Afghanistan and liberate the world from fear of terrorism.

Islam as a faith is sublime but Islamic militancy, Islamic fundamentalism and crude and illogical interpretations of the religion are facets of political Islam invented to serve the political interests of its exponents. It is a foremost responsibility of the coalition forces and the UN to see that perverted Islam has no place in the post-Taliban Afghanistan and even Pakistan is cleansed of such detestable elements.

The coalition partners are not able to arrive at a commonly approved model for future government of Afghanistan as they have their own stakes in Afghanistan. The US-UK-Pakistan group would like to plant a government loyal to them and that can also be under the influence of Pakistan. Islamabad's insistence on giving the largest share to Pushtuns is not motivated by the desire to give justice to the Pushtuns but it sees in Pushtun government security of its own interests. A huge segment of Pushtuns having lived as refugees in Pakistan for a long time have come under the influence of the ISI and the Islamic groups active in Pakistan. Their government might ensure the continuity of old patterns and policies in Afghanistan. The drug mafia is also likely to support this line.

The coalition forces' unthoughtful dependence on Pakistan may undo whatever has been attained by this war. Pakistan may relish another civil war which might bring back Taliban in the run once again and throw the country in a political whirlpool. Afghanistan's integrity, stability and survival as a secular democratic republic is of vital interest to the Central Asian states, Russia and India. They are required to assert their opinion in the US-led anti-terrorist coalition.

The interim government may be formed under Burhanudin Rabbani, President of the Northern Alliance or under the former King Zahir Shah because it will be for a short period. A new constitution can be drafted and elections can be held after the war-torn country returns to normalcy. However, thinking of making a broad based government through consultations with *loya jirga* is not an easy exercise. It would require a prolonged process that can be pursued under the care of the UN representatives or peace keeping forces. Looking at Afghanistan as a conglomeration of tribes, clàns, sub-clans, ethnic communities and religious factions is not a correct approach. Only the well identified ethno-cultural and political units should be taken into consideration for the purpose of elections. Pushtuns (the majority group), Tajiks (second in terms of majority), Uzbeks and Hazaras are the prominent groups. Ismailis, Nuristani, Turkmen, Kyrgyz and Baluchis are smaller groups but they should also be brought in the mainstream of national life through elections. The constituencies can also be made on this basis only. The main spokespersons on behalf of the groups that have been fighting against the *Mujahideen* and later against the Taliban like General Rashid Dostum, General Mohammad Fahim Khan (he took over the command of Tajik group after the assassination of General Ahmad Shah Masood by the Taliban) should be brought in interim government. In addition to these, representatives of small ethno-religious and tribal groups should also be included in the government as a confidence building measure.

Pushtuns are a major problem. A large number of Pushtuns have been living in Pakistan as refugees from 1979. They have been trained in Pakistan-run Islamic *madrasas* and given training to fight as Islamic millitants with the special purpose of wiping out the 'Russian influence' from Afghanistan and coverting the people to fundamentalist Talibani Islamic regime. It is very difficult to de-ideologise them. Transforming them into secular-nationalists is going to be a tedious exercise. How easy it is to trust them (as many of them may be Talibani themselves) is another significant question.

In this context it may be suggested: why not create a Pushtunistan by incorporating the territory on both sides of the Durand Line and make it an autonomous self-govern region initially under the patronage of the United Nations. Pushtuns have been demanding a state of their own all through the 20th century and the government in Afghanistan has never recognized the Durand Line as an international boundary between Afghanistan and Pakistan. Border across the Durand Line has always remained open for the Pushtuns of both sides. This would make the formation of government in Afghanistan comparatively easy. The representatives of Pushtuns may be included in the interim government but a difference should be made between the Pushtuns who have been residing in Afghanistan till the outbreak of the anti-terrorist war and having fled for security are living in the refugee camps on the border of Pakistan and Afghanistan set up by the United Nations Humanitarian Assistance groups.

The Central Asian States, Russia and India have to make the coalition partners realize the need to ensure the safety of Afghans against any future re-appearance of Taliban elements from Pakistan. De-ideologization and political re-orientation of the Pushtun community living as refugees in Pakistan for almost a decade or more is not an impossible task although it is a tedious exercise which may take a long time. Yet, it is worth attempting in the interest of unity, integrity and stability in Afghanistan.

13

Politics and Society in Tajikistan in the Aftermath of the Civil War

SUCHANDANA CHATTERJEE

The present study deals with recent writings on the post-Civil War situation in Tajikistan. The purpose is to show how these writings reflect firstly on the conflictual relationship between the Tajik government and the opposition, secondly on post-1997 reconciliatory gestures that has led to the accommodation of the opposition in government structures and thirdly, there is a focus on regions unaffected by mainstream Tajik politics. While dealing with the first and second aspects, the paper takes into account the contesting rhetoric of the government and the opposition in the aftermath of the Civil War. It indicates the paradoxical situation that has emerged in the post-Civil War situation. The paradox lies in the fragile nature of all peace arrangements culminating in the Moscow Accord of 1997 that have not been able to submerge the differences between the two sides. In most of the writings, attention tends to revolve round prime zones of conflict (the Karategin valley) where there has hardly been any appreciation of the Accord. A mood of estrangement prevails among rebels in this valley who are totally disillusioned with governmental rhetoric about 'peace' and 'unity'. Some articles indicate that such rhetoric, relying mostly on the sentiments of the people, is not very effective in binding together various political groups whose interests are very disparate in nature.

The third aspect, however, focusses on regions that have remained outside the whirlwind of politics in Tajikistan. One striking example is the Pamir region where sentimentalities of the people are sometimes grossly misrepresented as expressions of localism or *mahalgaroi.* It should be borne in mind that their expressions are very subtle and, therefore, dissimilar to the terror and violence that has been seen in other parts of the republic. Gorno-Badakhshan, compared to Garm, has not experienced any act of violence in the post-Civil War period. According to an observer, Pamir region suffered from economic isolation in the period following the war but was spared the direct effects of warfare.[1] The people of this region have been able to survive the shocks of the war through the organizational abilities of the Aga Khan Foundation. It has provided them the means of sustenance and has managed to bring into effect some kind of harmony with the Tajik people of Gorno-Badakhshan. The growing awareness among academicians about undertaking a mountain-development strategy keeping in mind the behaviour of nature, socio-demographic potentials of the mountain regions of Tajikistan is an appreciable development.[2]

However, the Pamirian example is an exception. The general impression is that there is a total lack of social security in the urban and rural locales, particularly in regions that have been directly affected by unequal social relationship in the aftermath of the war. Here, the people's (the Garmis' for instance) experiences do not match with the Pamiri experience. The former struggles for survival while the latter looks for spiritual contentment. The contrasting pictures are taken up to show the anomalous situation that has emerged in the wake of the Civil War.

The Rhetoric

In order to rally public opinion and to legitimize their respective stand in the power struggle, both the government and the opposition have been engaged in a battle of words. It is interesting to examine the ways in which the Presidency of Emomali Rakhmanov tried to legitimise its control *vis-à-vis* an opposition that comprised of various political groups or people of various convictions. These groups included a nationalist-democratic combine that allied with liberal Islamic resurgence movement of the early 1990s guided by spiritual leaders and Islamic theologians who also transformed themselves into a somewhat beleaguered opposition called the United Tajik Opposition (UTO). However, the most recent threat to the Tajik Presidency comes from a motley of subgroups identified and called *boeviki* (fighters) *modzhakhedi* (mujahids) and terrorists. It will perhaps be interesting to examine the ways in which the Tajik presidency counteracted various segments of the opposition by popularising notions of unity, stability and, more recently, the 'other'. He used these notions to denounce the opposition. The purpose, therefore, is to focus on the rhetoric of the government through which it has by and large tried to generate confidence among the people. The rhetoric has also tried to identify the opposition as comprising of various groups who did not share the people's interests or to put it in more idealist terms, the interests of the 'nation'. These two become fairly clear in a book that has been written by the President himself and has been published very recently. [3] Written during the difficult phase of peace talks and inter-Tajik negotiations, the book portrays Rakhmanov as a pragmatist who is solely interested to legitimize his stand in the international scene. Amidst the twist and turn of events of the post-1992 situation, Rakhmanov with his political training of the Soviet era, has managed to survive.

In the first part of this book, the Tajik President appeals to the sentiment of the Tajik people by repeatedly drawing attention to the role of the Tajiks in Central Asian history. He repeatedly delves into pre-1917 history to show how individuals, people's organizations and publications left indelible mark on Tajik history and culture. By citing instances from pre-1917 history where Tajik language acquired significance among Central Asia's literary circles, Rakhmanov tries to instil awareness about Tajik national identity. His 'nationalism' is strictly bound by a Tajik identity.

Rakhmanov's 'nationalist' bent of mind comes to sharp focus vis-à-vis the argument of the Islamic-democratic opposition which is pro-Iran. Rakhmanov's book appreciates the works of the pre-Iranian era. Rakhmanov quotes incessantly from the Avesta, which shows his familiarity with the works of 'Avestologues' to indicate how places of Zoroastrian learning developed in Tajik lands (*Vakhsh*) under the Bactrians. The way the argument develops to show how culture flourished in the land of Tajikistan even prior to the advent of Islam is something that is very striking. There is emphasis on the historical value of particular regions like *Vakhsh* which otherwise tends to get lost in the motley of writings that focus only on hotspots of conflict. While owing his knowledge to earlier depictions of Tajik history (that of Bobojan Gafurov), Rakhmanov does not fail to attribute greater significance to his native place, Kulyab that fell within the *Vakhsh* region. Also, by stressing on the significance of pre-Islamic culture situated in the lands adjoining the Amu Darya, Rakhmanov depicts the inter-relationship between regional histories. The subtle intention behind such portrayal is to downplay the presence of Islamic religious sentiments that are concentrated in eastern and south-eastern region.

However, Rakhmanov's historical position differs considerably from that of the opposition. He does not share the democrats' sense of belonging to Persian and the uniqueness of Persian linguistic traditions among the Tajiks. Rakhmanov defines the Tajiks as the descendants of the Soghdians who were formerly the masters of Central Asia and were later conquered by the Arabs, Persianised and Turkified. This delinking of the Tajiki identity from the Persian identity is fairly clear in Rakhmanov's book. His book offers fresh insight by establishing cultural contacts with pre-Iranian traditions of Soghdian and Zoroastrian culture. This approach is very different to the democrats' indebtedness to Iran emanating from linguistic and historical affinities between the Iranians and the Tajiks that has resulted in sensitiveness towards each other.[4]

There are also two very recent articles by Franz Wennberg that focus on other aspects of the government's rhetoric in Tajikistan in the wake of the Civil War. The author draws attention to how concept of the 'other' gained ground in Tajik political discourse since the outbreak of the Civil War. Wennberg shows how at different times, politicians denounced their political enemies as national enemies. Right from the time of the Civil War till the presidential elections of 1999, politicians of various convictions (Islamic democrats or the communists) raised allegations of treachery, foreign interference and sabotage. During the presidential elections of 1999, other presidential nominees were denounced as people who lacked morality. This psychological dissociation from one's rivals became more apparent in one of Rakhmanov's speeches in which he not only stressed that they lacked any social basis but also accused them of denigrating the authority of the motherland and the nation.[5]

The appeal to *watan* or motherland was very strong immediately after the Civil War. The vexed issue at that point of time was refugee crisis. The influx of 60,000 Tajik refugees who had fled Tajikistan at the high point of the Civil War and their repatriation were the most daunting tasks of the Rakhmanov government. At that time, it was more crucial to attract people's attention to the cause of motherland. Instilling nostalgia in the minds of the people was the best way to attract popular sentiment. Rakhmanov's emotional appeal lay with the Tajik people (*khalqi Tojikiston*) who due to the war were either 'internally displaced' or evacuated their homes and hearth for being united with their Tajik bretheren in Afghanistan. The Tajik government's appeal to 'refugees' to return from their exile to their motherland could not have come at a more opportune moment. The idea of sharing common bonds with their motherland (*watan*) was immensely appealing to those who were struggling for survival and were desperately in need of refuge. A verse published in the Tajik daily *Sadoi Mardum* (1996) is illustrative of the political rhetoric of the post 1993 period:

> *Bi watan nist qaribe kyi kunad*
> *yaad-e-watan*
> *Dar watan bude-i yaad-e-watan*
> *bi watan ast.*

(It is not the exile who dreams
of his country, has no country
He who is at home and doesn't think
of his country, has no country).

The sentimental rhetoric was used as an antidote to regionalism and regional factions in the republic. It is to be borne in mind that the Kulyabi faction of the government was under severe pressure from the Uzbek-dominated Khojent lobby and Garmis and Pamiris who increasingly demanded positions of importance in the republic. The rhetoric of unity implied that it was impossible to have different political opinions as the people of Tajikistan had one common interest and the representatives of this common interest were the only legal actors in the political arena. Such open verbal attacks against the opposition were carried out by the state media through government publications from Dushanbe like *Sadoi Mardum* and *Tojikistani Soveti* and the Khorog based government-sponsored regional publication *Khatlan*. The 'denunciation', i.e., the propaganda against the opposition, characterizing them as enemies of the people began immediately after 1993 and continued even after 1995.[6] In 1993, the murder of Popular Front leaders Sangak Safarov and Faizali Saidov was criticized as acts by the enemies of the people (*millat*), a concept that is indistinguishable from the 'people'.[7] Another newspaper *Jamhuriyat* also denounced the Tajik opposition as enemies of the people particularly after the murder of Muhammad Asimi, the Tajik Head of the Academy of Sciences. [8]

The mood of denunciation somewhat changed after the signing of the peace accord in June 1997. As would appear from government-backed publications, a political rhetoric was constructed through notions that were appealing not only to the society at large but also sought to attract several disparate elements within the Tajik republic. In a period when 'national reconciliation' (i.e., integration) of the opposition was the most sought-after goal, this rhetoric was very useful in improving the President's image in the political scene. Rakhmanov revised his earlier strategy of taking a tough line vis-à-vis the opposition represented by the nationalists (*Rastakhez* and the

Democratic Party) and the Islamic bloc represented by the Islamic Renaissance Party. In the post-1996 period, his attempts to conciliate the opposition by inducting few recalcitrant elements (notably Qazi Qalon Akbar Turadzhonzoda) in his government sought to improve his image as the arbiter of disputes in faction-ridden politics of Tajikistan. The improvement of his image is evident in the mood of the people of the republic. According to a report in *Nezavisimaya Gazeta*, local Karateginis, tired of war, recognized Rakhmanov as the leader of the country. According to a local Karategini, "for us it is not important to know which region the Tajik President Rakhmanov belongs to. In this district, we feel relatively secure. Our lives are improving, and if Rakhmanov succeeds in preserving peace, then may Allah give him long years!"[9]

In the wake of the aborted military coup of the Leninabadi general Khudoberdiyev in 1998, governmental rhetoric tended to revolve round the third enemy— Uzbekistan. It is interesting to note that most of the Uzbeki loyalists of the regime belonged to Leninabad (Khojent) and most of them were employed in the security services of the country. Given the uncomfortable nature of power-sharing arrangements between Uzbek and Tajik lobbies, and in the context of the Khudoberdiyev revolt, the denunciation of unreliable partners was a foregone conclusion. The Tajik security agencies were in the forefront in identifying what they considered to be a challenge to their security interests. In their opinion, certain ousted military and political figures with the connivance of Uzbekistan's security agencies wanted to destabilize the Tajik republic by supporting terrorist activities across the porous Tajik-Afghan border. The Tajik Minister of Security was particularly critical of Uzbek "interference" in Tajikistan's internal affairs and of elements conspiring against the Rakhmanov regime.[10] There was a lot of speculation about armed bands receiving training from Uzbek militia and experienced military commanders (General Dostum) who were part of the unstable Northern Alliance fighting the Taliban in Afghanistan. Thus, the Rakhmanov government tried to enunciate a programme of action that was directly related to the country's regional interests. Currently, Rakhmanov is very firm in his conviction about the 'other'—to him

Uzbek interference has cast a deep shadow on almost every aspect of Tajik life and politics. Such interference has percolated largely through terrorist activities of splinter groups. The ideal of the 'nation' or '*watan*' is being projected as having no meaning to such people or groups who are interested in derailing the government in Tajikistan by promoting or supporting acts of violence. These to him are foreign elements that ought to be crushed.

The Alternatives

The above discussion indicates that the government's stand on the opposition changed in the aftermath of the Civil War. The conflictual relationship was transformed into an integrative one, particularly during the phase of national reconciliation. It is this factor of integration that gave a definitive legitimacy to the Islamist movement. This is evident in a series of articles written by specialists of the Carnegie International Centre, Moscow. According to one opinion, from the 1920s, political Islam in the Central Asiatic region in general and Tajikistan in particular has been recognised and accommodated by the state. In the post-Soviet period, its importance in the individual's social life has increased substantially. Therefore, the accommodation of political Islam is a desired objective in the whole of post-Soviet Central Asia. In Tajikistan, such accommodation was noted in the case of Haji Damullo (1892-1989), the leader of the Islamic Party of Resurgence (IRP) who worked in the Tajik Academy of Sciences and gathered round him a band of followers, mostly researchers belonging to Dushanbe.[11]

The reconciliation may have legitimized the role of the Islamist movement in the national political scene, but failed to generate confidence among the local Tajiks. This lack of trust indirectly led to the failure of the Islamist movement in Tajikistan. Its adaptation to notions of democracy accounted for its inability to become an alternative to Sovietism, localism and nationalism.[12] These twin aspects of conflict and integration in politics are measured in terms of the opposition's viewpoints.

At the initial stage, the Islamic-democratic experiments

represented an alternative to the government model. The government's stand on *watanniyat* may be compared and contrasted with the Islamic-democratic stand on cultural heritage. The latter, also relying on popular opinion, focussed their argument round the people's culture, beliefs and religiosity. Their views appear to be very similar in tone and spirit of the government. The only difference is that these leaders tried to instil awareness among the people (particularly the younger generation) about past religious and cultural heritage. This, they felt, was suppressed by the advocates of communism. Here, one notices their scepticism about revolutionary concepts that ran contrary to the spirit of the Islamic tradition. As successors of the Soviet regime, the Tajik government continues to be critical of the practice of Islamic faith. On the contrary, the Tajik Islamic leaders, most of whom are people of strong religious convictions, often try to inculcate faith as the driving force of the Tajik nation.[13] The recent view of the UTO leader, Said Abdullo Nuri in a pamphlet that is addressed to the people of Tajikistan is a pointer to this direction. From the very outset the UTO leader makes a distinction between the Communist advocates (whom he calls the Bolsheviks) and the nationalists. He denounces the former as enemies of the Tajiks and the latter as victims of their misdeeds.[14]

The members of the Democratic Party and the *Rastakhez* were votaries of similar denunciation of the Soviet regime. The *Rastakhez*, dominated mainly by the Pamiri intelligentsia, upheld cultural and political revival and questioned Soviet style functioning. The coming into prominence of provinces like Kurgan Teppe or Gorno-Badakhshan was something that was unthinkable in the Soviet period. The wresting of power from the Khojenti power bloc and the introduction of a Tajiki identity were in the *Rastakhez* agenda. This in a way also questioned the legitimacy of all those in power, centred in Dushanbe and having close links with Moscow. The Democratic Party of Tajikistan, established in August 1990, also dominated by the Pamiris, was articulate in expressing similar voices of dissent. The ipso-facto analysis of the Civil War period by Shodmon Yusuf, the leader of Tajikistan's Democratic Party is available in his book that has been published in Teheran. The account, published in 1994 is a telling account of a man who was trained in Soviet milieu and served important positions in academics and administration, He was thoroughly disillusioned with the system that he lived and worked in. Communist Party membership, the criterion for political ascendancy during Soviet days, was totally meaningless to him. He was extremely critical of the Communists who disregarded the fact that Tajik heritage evolved and grew essentially out of the linguistic connection between Farsi and Tajik. His contention about Tajik being a dialect of Farsi was not common to the argument of Bobojan Gafurov. The latter like Rakhmanov of today, believed that Tajik was a different and independent language. On the other hand, Shodmon Yusuf articulated the beliefs of the Tajik youth by trying to emphasize the connection between Farsi and Tajik. He supported the argument that the knowledge of Tajik culture could only come through Farsi writing and reading. In other words, the leaders of the democratic bloc stood for close contacts between Tajikistan and Iran. An overall Islamo-Persian identity was sought to be maintained by the national-democratic and Islamist groups.[15] The common denominator here was the Islamic-Persian synthesis in its Sunni form. Tajik nationalism crystallized around language in affirming its Persian-ness, and called for a return to the Arabic-Persian alphabet. The inclinations of Yusuf are fair and clear: 'he tends to be quite enamored with the people of Iranian stock, Iranian metaphysics, philosophy, religion, culture, history and especially the Iranian language.'[16] Despite the excitement raised by the argument (that there should be a return to Persian), it could not be embodied as part of a nationalist project.[17] As a movement they failed and could not be integrated into the process of reconciliation that encompassed the Islamic leaders of the opposition.

The integrative approach was upheld by Qazi Akbar Turadzhonzoda, the spiritual head of the Tajiks, living in exile in Takhor in northern Afghanistan. He was aware of the differences within various fractions of the Islamic Movement of Resurgence in Tajikistan. Tajikistan's democratic-Islamic components represented only a minority in such a hybrid mix. Given such differences, the head of the Qaziyat realized in 1995 that a long-term political solution to the Tajik tangle without regional cooperation was impossible. At that stage, he was supportive of Russian, Uzbek and Iranian help for the realization of peace in Tajikistan. He understood that it was important to win political recognition for the Islamist movement and hence it was not wise to take a very tough stand on religion.[18] His proposition was that the Tajik people had to be spiritually revived. Given the wariness of the government about the rise of Islamic radicalism in Tajikistan, such an argument revealed the opposition's softened stand. In that particular context, the latter's reciprocal gestures during peace-building became understandable. The government too reciprocated by accepting Turadzhonzoda as the Deputy Premier of Tajikistan in 1999.

It is interesting to observe how in the political discourse of the opposition, the image of the enemy underwent change. At the time of the disintegration of the Soviet Union, the Communist state and its functionaries represented by President Nabiev and his entourage were denounced. The Islamic opposition also denounced the artificiality of all arrangements created and recreated by the Soviets. In the changed situation where Tajikistan enjoys the status of independent statehood, the opposition considers Rakhmanov as a viable alternative. The reasons are not difficult to seek. First, he belongs to a different region (Kulyab) that contested the hegemony of the Khojenti *nomenklatura*. To the Islamist opposition craving for political legitimacy, Rakhmanov's presidency offered them a chance to succeed. Secondly, Rakhmanov heads a political system that recognizes the opposition leaders as representatives of the Tajik people who need to be resurrected and revived. This recognition has bolstered their image and is something that has not happened in the past. Therefore, a changed mood was noted among the Islamic leaders.

Such reconsideration was lacking among the less prominent members of a fractured Tajik Opposition (UTO) who stepped in after 1997 to fill what might be regarded as a vacuum in the ranks of the opposition. They disapproved the 1997 Accord primarily because they were asked to disband. Consequently, there was growing suspicion among field commanders that they would lose their local spheres of influence. According to specialists, the lack of popularity about the ideal of national reconciliation in Badakhshan and

Garm-Karategin sectors set off counteractive trends. In these two regions, there were (*a*) Badakhshani wing of the opposition that operated as Self-defence forces of Badakhshan and looked for support from the world leader of the Ismaili sect Aga Khan and (*b*) *Mujahids* of Garm and Karategin who were not willing to accept the clauses of what has been called 'command peace'.[19] Given the motley of solidarity networks in Tajikistan, individuals both within the government and the UTO strongly opposed power-sharing when it threatened their control of a geographic area or function (e.g. drug trafficking).[20] It so happened that the government had to negotiate directly with field commanders and other strong men in retaining what they called their pockets of influence.

Reportage from Theatres of Conflict

In recent times, the rebels' local centres of control have generated curiosity among journalists. Media reports, given their instantaneous communicative capacity, have sometimes proved to be extremely valuable in indeterminable and unexpected situations. Sometimes, however, they tend to be more imaginative. Sensational reports by UN agencies, Russian and Tajik freelance reporters associated with *Nezavisimaya Gazeta*, Radio Free Liberty, the Eurasia Foundation, Asia Plus give the impression that there was a total lack of government control in the Garm-Karategin sector.[21] Here is a report that spread terror in human mind about rebel activities in the capital and its neighbourhood.

In 1998, in the city of Dushanbe, streets close to the Presidential palace and government departments were being besieged by attackers coming from areas that were supposed to be strongholds of the opposition. One such region was Kofarnikhon where opposition fighters, originally based in Karategin, assembled to take up arms against the government in Dushanbe. Their armed attacks against the 25th Batallion in May 1998 were intended to disrupt normal life in the area where the roads connecting Kofarnikhon and Dushanbe lay. Here was a country which was breaking up into several 'zones of influence'. Independent political units, supported by their respective private military and political networks became influential. This phenomenon is indicated in a report:

> 'like the entire republic, the city of Dushanbe is divided into zones of influence controlled by Gafur Mirzoyev, commander of the Presidential Guard, Sukhrob Kasymov, commander of a special forces brigade of the Tajik Interior Affairs Ministry and Cholov brothers, Kurban and Sultan, who previously fought in People's Front detachments. [22]

The terror-filled atmosphere is also evident in the people's responses in Dushanbe. Here, according to another report, peace is maintained through government regulations. According to reporter Arman Dzhilavyan, the city of Dushanbe is safe only during curfew hours that extend from dawn to dusk. When asked about their city centres, the Tajiks say 'normalno'. This remark expresses the uncomfortable bent of mind of the people who hardly dare say anything more than that. After 7 p.m., the streets of Dushanbe turn desolate and an atmosphere of fear engulfs the city. Civilians are still wary of their experiences during the civil war when about 3,000 people were killed. People who risked going out on the streets were shot at almost for no reason at all. Unemployed, poor and shaken by the permanent threat of violence, most of the residents' minds are marred by the terror of reminiscences of the civil war. There was not a single day that was uncertain and people did not know whether their next day would bring in tragic memories. This account depicts a post-war situation that was unbearable to the civilians living in the capital. Peace hardly could give them the guarantee of their lives. [23]

Often confusion is generated when other reports, particularly the OSCE news releases report on the interaction between the OSCE Head of Mission and various social categories (women's groups, local authorities called *hukumats*, militia, judicial head) which suggest slow but steady return to normalcy in the Karategin valley.[24]

Very often the nature of dissemination becomes clear from on-the-spot reports of Russian correspondents. Igor Rotar recalls an incident in 1995 when he was witness to the beating of a Karategini by a Kulyabi militiaman with the butt of a gun for the simple reason that the latter was not offered a particular brand of cigarette. This is an example of how rumours, without any substance, affected the mood of the people in this region.[25] Such accounts also depict the sentiments of *modzhakhedi* or *boeviki* (fighters). In the Russian journalist usage, the term denotes self-acclaimed religious chiefs and local Tajik commanders who are young, illiterate, born and brought up in rural milieu that is dominated largely by traditions of ancestor worship, and who have not quite identified themselves with the history of the making of a Tajik nation.

Two different images emerge from such a description. On the one hand, people have been represented as victims of the civil war. On the other hand, a valorized identity of the martyrs of the civil war emerges; this is a new aspect of the recent literature on Tajikistan. Such imageries have rendered new dimensions to the aspect of Islamic radicalism in Tajikistan. An article in the Russian journal *Vostok* deals with obituaries of Islamic fighters of the Karategin and Kurgan Tyube oblasts who were members of the Islamic Party of Resurgence that was banned by the Tajik government in 1994. According to this article, the IRP weekly publication *Nahjot*, immortalized their leaders as *shahids* or martyrs fighting the Russian troops and the National Front (Tajik army) in the autumn of 1992. The *shahids* were Mahmud Kozikoda Yavoni, Namatolla Kulabi, Ismatullah Kofarnikhoni, Dadarbek Shahid, Simuddin Shahid and Bakhtiyar Shahid. The author, D.V. Mikulsky, indicates how through archaic practices as the worship of cult figures and deities, their memories were revived. In a region where traditional practices are a way of life, such obituaries tended to popularize martyrdom among the Tajiks of Garm, Karategin and Kurgan Tyube. The general message is that memories of local heroes should be revived, just as in the case of worship of deities and cult figures. [26] The purpose of these depictions is to show divergences in the Islamic movement. The spread of Islamic radicalism and its manifestations, largely dissociated from mainstream movement for Islamic resurgence/revival in Tajikistan, is a post-1997 development. Reportage on this development is fairly scattered. In more recent times, there are indications that such radicalism has disturbed the social fabric and has brought into being social anomalies.

Social Anomalies

The conflictual relationship between the government and the disparate elements in the opposition and the contentious issue of Islamic radicalism gave birth to social anomalies. In the aftermath of the civil war, social fragmentation is witnessed not only among the top echelons or those vying for power, but also among the common people who are badly affected by drug abuse, ill health and social inequalities. Inequitable relationships seem to have affected the capital Dushanbe as well as the regions in the south, particularly Kurgan Tyube and Khatlon. A sociological survey conducted by the Open Society Institute indicates that the deterioration of socio-economic standards of living and the prevalence of porous Tajik-Afghan borders have resulted in a secret inflow of drugs and contraband items into the country through channels and networks that have become extremely difficult for the Russian border guards to control. The following features emerge from the study: (*a*) Women are worst affected by drug abuse; (*b*) People belonging to power structures and the service sector are principally lured by drugs; (*c*) Dushanbe is the hardest hit by drug abuse (*d*) maximum consumption of heroin is among youth.[27] These features point to the lack of urban security in Tajikistan.

Thus, sufferings of the social strata do not seem to have ended even nine years after the civil war. The trauma of the war and the fear of being victimized by fellow Tajiks from rival regions or representing rival clans have now been replaced with the fear of internal displacement. Women belong to a particular social category that has constantly faced such fears. Their traditional roles in their families have undergone major transformation. How this happened and how it affected the social rubric in Tajikistan is discussed quite often.

In 1994 a Tajik specialist spoke about the ways in which women became victims of war. [28] At that time there were pictures of grieving mothers, wives and sisters. There were also nation-wide surveys that reported on war-induced stress among mothers. There was widespread documentation by Human Rights Watch and Helsinki Watch about human rights violations committed against women in Tajikistan. The rape of unmarried women in villages was a devastating blow to the *Nomusi Tajik* (chastity of the Tajiks). Women as refugees also became the theme of *Sadoi Mardum*. There were spouses of the Democratic Party who had to endure the fate that befell them and their children following their husbands' denouncement. There were others who were less compliant and voiced opinions and became noted dissidents (Gawhar Juraeva, Sofia Hakimova and others). This was the time when these women were criticized for not fulfilling their traditional roles in the society. These are descriptions of women victims at the time of conflict.

During the period of national reconciliation, the image of women as victims no longer worked. At that time, the establishment was trying to manufacture consent by laying importance on the traditional role of mothers as wives and mothers. This was done to legitimize the so-called concerns about reconciliation and unity.

The argument runs further to show how politicians among the opposition too popularized images to legitimize their struggle against the government. There was extreme use of emotional language in the Moscow-based opposition newspaper *Charogi Ruz*. The point this analyst tried to make is that women's roles after the civil war were transformed both by the establishment and the opposition in order to suit their political interests. The purpose of sentimental rhetoric in the pre-1997 period was to seek legitimacy in politics. Even in the post-1997 scenario, the women's subverted status in Tajik society has not ended.

Studies about Tajik family's difficulties and the transformed role of young wives offering support to elder members of the family as their husbands migrate to distant lands in search of livelihood are available. This is particularly witnessed among Garmi women who stayed back in their village locales. The risk of staying alone or even supporting a family on their own was the hardest task that these women faced in the aftermath of the war. Nutrition and health of women were badly affected due to their greatest exposure in the poorest of circumstances. The bottom line of such arguments, therefore, is coping with life in post-Soviet Tajikistan has been far from easy.[29]

Identities Redefined

Reports on rebel territories as theatres of war and being shrouded in obscurity and mystery are fairly substantial. However, there is hardly any historical appreciation of these very regions. Nor there is any interest in the region's long-forgotten histories. I will take up the case of Garm-Karategin sector. Its significance as a region of mixed sub-regional identities—the Karateginis, Darwazis, Yazgulemis, which were groups that were constituted within Eastern Bukharan *viloyats* (provinces) under the control of Uzbek *beks,* who owed allegiance to the Manghyt sovereign, the Emir of Bukhara in the 19th century. This is seldom taken into account. What is also not considered is the fact that these local chiefs virtually turned them into spheres of influence which, according to archival records, grew apathetic to central control, manoeuvred from Bukhara. Now this mood of estrangement gave them an exclusive identity which they seem to have retained till the present times. Community patterns and social behaviour point to a traditional mode of living that is very different from urban patterns of living of the Tajiks living in the plains. Their isolation from the Tajik ethos continued during the Soviet period. In the post-Soviet situation, particularly after the civil war, these groups tended to become more resilient, trying to preserve characteristics of communities with strictly radical Islamic sentiments.

Sometimes, scholars have studied other regions where community traditions prevail and solidarity networks thrive on an unprecedented scale. Regional case studies have become a very exciting subject in recent years particularly due to the scholarship of Sergei Andreyev, Hafizullah Emadi and Nejima Susumu who have done useful studies about the Ismaili communities in the Pamir borderlands in Badakhshan (Tajik and Afghan) and Northern Pakistan respectively.

The Pamiri literati in Badakhshan has identified itself more as a social community of the Ismaili faith. Cultural revivalism to the community of believers in Badakhshan did not imply power sharing in Dushanbe. On the other hand, through cultural clubs (Nasr Khusrau cultural club and Lal-i-Badakhshan), the scattered linguistic sub-groups in Badakhshan have demanded recognition in terms of autonomy. Today, they represent themselves as members of a significant minority (Gorno Badakhshan Autonomous Council) in the *Majlis-i-Oli* (Tajik National Parliament) with aims of cultural revival. By undertaking sociological surveys in the Pamirs dealing with forgotten identities in Tajikistan, Hafizullah Emadi and Sergei Andreyev have described in their own characteristic ways the scattered communities like that of the Badakhshanis. First and foremost, it is interesting to note how Andreyev distinguishes mountain Pamiris (Badakhshanis) from plain Pamiris. The Badakhshanis' apolitical views derive strength from the humanistic principles of the Ismaili creed, and these have hardly anything to do with the political aspirations of the plain Tajiks. They depend exclusively on Aga Khan Foundation for material, spiritual and cultural support.[30] The European Community too is sympathetic to the community of Ismailis at large. Andreyev's argument attacks the view that the Ismailis in Afghanistan and Tajikistan are held together by a chord of unity in "local power struggles". The implication of his argument is that none of the Ismaili political and cultural groups in Badakhshan-Lal-i-Badakhshan or Nasr-i-Khusrau Cultural Club have embroiled themselves in *mahalgaroi* as the Kulyabis and the Khojentis. The Ismailis' search for social distinction is researched upon by Hafizullah Emadi. He describes how the Ismaili community, traditionally known for its association with the *pirs* and *khalifas*, adopted a more human stance and became apathetic to the 'politicization' of Islam by fellow countrymen. During the Soviet period, particularly during the 60s and the 70s, this community of Ismaili elite found socialism to be a better choice. This sense of distinction further continued to prevail and even enabled the Gorno-Badakhshanis to re-assert themselves as a brotherhood and not as a faith. The Ismailis in Gorno-Badakhshan became well settled compared to other Ismaili settlements in the Pamirs (scattered in Afghanistan and Sinkiang in China). With their well-entrenched administrative infrastructure, educational institutions like the University of Khorog, the Badakhshani community today promises to develop into a leading centre of Ismaili authority in the region.[31] They seek to preserve their social identity as followers of Nasr Khusrau (11th century), safeguard the interests of their community through enviable support of the Aga Khan Foundation. In a hostile environment that has taken shape since the Tajik civil war, this community has appreciably maintained its non-partisan stand towards *mahalgaroi*.

Nejima Susumu's research establishes a chord of unity between various Ismaili groups spread across the Indian subcontinent, Central Asia and East Africa. Some of these groups have established themselves fairly well because of their trade contacts. Others are situated in the border region of Central Asia and South Asia along the mountain regions and valleys of the Hindukush and the Karakoram and speak various Persian dialects (*Khowar, Shina, Burshaki* and *Wakhi*). The author indicates the predominance of the *pirs* and their unchallenged local authority in this region since the late 19th century. The evolution of their authority through organizations and *tariqas*, local councils and religious education boards has been analyzed. The institutional structures of the Ismaili community in the border regions of northern Pakistan and the pockets of Ismaili communities in Tajikistan, Afghanistan and China indicate interaction and integration. They have evolved as an autonomous social community which though not hostile to the state, are extremely influential because of the preponderance of their leaders (*pir, waiz* and *imam*). The result, according to Susumu, is a construction of an autonomous space that cannot be wholly disregarded.[32] Such a view tends to contest the view that Tajikistan's Pamiri enclave is a region of extreme religiosity. Therefore, such redefined identities point to regions that are removed from the theatre of conflict.

Conclusion

In the light of post-civil war writings, this paper has attempted to analyze politics and society in Tajikistan. The presence of contradictory images is the dominant theme in all these writings. The symbiotic relationship among identities seldom exists in this war-ravaged country. Yet, some surveys indicate the possibilities of survival. It is this instinct of survival that makes scattered identities in Tajikistan an interesting area of study.

REFERENCES

1 John S Schoberlein Engel, (1997), "Overcoming the Ravages of the Civil War", in Michael M. Curnea and Ayse Kudats (eds) *Social Assessments for Better Development: Case Studies in Russia and Central Asia*, The World Bank, Washington, pp. 206.

2 Khojamakhmad Umarov, (1998), "The Demographic Boom and its impact on the Mountain Regions of Tajikistan", *in* Shirin Akiner et al (ed) *Sustainable Development in Central Asia*, Curzon, pp. 186-194.

3 Emomali Rakhmanov, (2001), *Tadzhiki v Zerkale Istorii, Kniga Pervaya, Ot Arieitsev do Samanidov*, London: London and Flint River Editions.

4 Mohammad Reza Djalili, (1997), "In search of New Friends: Iran and Central Asia", *World Affairs*, January-March, Vol. I, No. 1, p. 111. Mohammad Reza Djalili, Frederic Grare, Shirin Akiner et al., (1998), *Tajikistan: The Trials of Independence*, Surrey: Curzon, p. 127.

5 Quoted in *Narodnaya Gazeta*, 12 November 1999. Franz Wennberg, The Configuration of the Other in Tajik Political Discourse, *Central Asia Monitor*, No. 3, 2001, p. 7.

6 Franz Wennberg, (2000), "Two Central Political Concepts in Tajik Political Discourse", *Central Asia Monitor*, No. 6, pp. 7-10.

7 *Sadoi Mardum*, 2 May 1993, cited by Wennberg, *op. cit.*

8 *Jumhuriyat*, 3 September 1996, cited by Wennberg, *op. cit.*

9 Igor Rotar, "V Kraiyu Modzhakhedov", *Nezavisimaya Gazeta*, November 16 2000.

10 Najam Abbas, (1998), "Tajik Fingers pointing North-Rakhmanov's rare display of resentment over Uzbek interference", *Eurasianews*, November 13.

11 Muzaffar Olimov, Saidat Olimova, (2001), "Politicheski Islam v Sovremennom Tadzhikistane' *Islam na Postsovietskom Prostrantsve: vzglyad Iznutri*, Carnegie Endowment Centre.

12 Olivier Roy, *The New Central Asia: The Creation of Nations*, I.B. Tauris, London, 2000, p. 157.

13 Abdullah Saidov, better known today as Sayyid Abdullah Nuri came from a traditional family. His radicalism evolved from his links with traditional Islam. At the same time he was educated in the Soviet system of secular education. This symbiosis enables him to establish a network across ex-USSR, India and Africa and with future founding-members of the Islamic Renaissance Party (IRP) like Himmatzade.
In Qazi Akbar Turadzhonzoda, there is a combination of conservatism

of the ulemas, Sufism and political radicalism of the IRP. He is the son of a respected Qaderi *murid.* There are indications about sufi solidarity in Tajikistan. This has enabled the Qazi to command a great deal of respect as the spiritual leader. Compiled from Olivier Roy, *op. cit*, chapter on *Islam*, pp. 143-157.

14 Sayyid Abdullah Nuri, *Imruzu Fardoi Tochikiston*, Dushanbe, 2000.

15 Roy, *op. cit*, p. 123.

16 *The Iranian Journal of International Affairs*, Vol. VI, Nos 3-4, Fall/Winter 1994-95, p. 595.

17 The groups survive today through individual initiatives of intellectuals and their *fonds* (inventories) run parallelly from Moscow and Dushanbe. One of these fonds is *Umed/Nadezhda* in Russian (Hope), established to help Tajik refugees. Another group *Sedat-I-Nejat-I-Vatan* in Dushanbe is run by Shodmon Yusuf based in Teheran.

18 Interview with Qazi Akbar Turadzhonzoda, (1995), *Central Asia Monitor*, Issue No. 2.

19 Shahrbanou Tadjbaksh, (1996), "National Reconciliation: The Imperfect Whim", *Central Asian Survey*, 15 (3/4), p. 329.

20 R. Grant Smith, (1999), "Tajikistan: The rocky road to peace", *Central Asian Survey*, 18 (2), p. 247.

21 Konstantin Parshin, (2001), "Four Years After End in of Civil War, peace remains tenuous in Tajikistan', *Eurasia Insight*, June 27; Iskander Aliev, (2001), "Namangani Presence in Tajikistan, even if IMU can't be seen", *Eurasia Insight,* June 4;

22 Sanobar Shermatova, (1998), "Operation Fishing Trip' thwarted-Struggle for Spheres of Influence Leads to New Bloody Clashes in Tajik Capital", *Moskovskiye Novosti*, No. 17, May 3-10. Condensed text cited in *Current Digest of the Post-Soviet Press*, Vol. 50, No. 18, 1998, pp. 19-20.

23 Arman Dzhilavyan, "Gorod Nenastupayushevo Ponedel'nika: Tadzhiki v poiskakh Samoidentifikatsii", *Nezavisimaya Gazeta*, 11 November 2000.

24 Head of mission visits Karotegyn Valley, Tajikistan, *OSCE Latest News Releases*, 30 March 2001.

25 Igor Rotar, "V Kraiyu Modzhakhedov", *Nezavisimaya Gazeta*, 16 November 2000.

26 D.V. Mikulsky, "Opyt Analiza Nekotorov Chlenov Islamskoi Partii Vozrozhdeniya Tajikistana: Traditsionnoe I Sovremennoe", *Vostok*, No. 1, 1996, pp. 56-64.

The existence of a local subculture in Garm-Karategin, Darvaz, Gissar and Kulyab has also been indicated by a Tajik scholar, A. Sh. Niyazi. The differences of food, dress, rituals and dialects distinguished one group from the other. They were all Pamiris, but were distinct in terms of their identities-Kulyabskaya, Vancho-Darvazskaya, Garmi-Karategini, Karatagskaya etc. Aziz Sh. Niyazi, 'Tadzhikistan: Konflikt Regionov', *Vostok*, No. 2, 1997, pp. 94-107.

27 Survey by Tatiana Borzikova between February 1 to May 1 2000. Survey supported by Open Society Institute Assistance Foundation-Tajikistan, *Eurasia Policy Forum*, 13.6. 2001.

28 Shahrbanou Tadjbaksh, (1994), "Women and War in Tajikistan", *The Iranian Journal of International Affairs*, Spring/Summer, N. 1 & 2, pp. 207-217.

29 Colette Harris, "Coping with daily life in post-Soviet Tajikistan: the Gharmi villages of Khatlon province", *Central Asian Survey*, Vol. 17, No. 4, December 1998, pp. 655-669.
Yokubjon Abdukholikov, (2000), "The Social Condition of Rural Women in Tajikistan", *Central Asia Monitor*, No. 2, pp. 13-17.
Gulbakhor Makhamova, (2001), "Primary Indiactors of Women's Health in the Republic of Tajikistan: Social Aspects", *Central Asia Monitor*, No. 3, pp. 10-11.

30 Sergei Andreyev, "Ismaili Traditions-Central Asia", Forthcoming in *Encyclopedia of Asia*, 2000. His paper 'The Shaping of the Ismaili Community in Badakhshan', *ESCAS VII Conference*, Vienna, 27-30 September 2000 provides interesting data on the Ismaili consciousness in Badakhshan.

31 Hafizullah Emadi, (1998), "The End of *Taqiyya*: Reaffirming the Religious Identity of Ismailis in Shughnan, Badakhshan-Political Implications for Afghanistan", *Middle Eastern Studies*, July, Vol. 34, No. 3, pp. 106-119.

32 Nejima Susumu, Pir, Waiz and Imam: The Transformation of Socio-Religious Leadership among the Ismailis in Northern Pakistan, (2001), *Islamic Area Studies Working Paper Series*, Tokyo, No. 23, p. 26.

14

Regional Cooperation in Central Asia

Some Perspectives

M.N. Sabirov

Soon after the disintegration of the former Soviet Union, absence of any effective forms of cooperation among the newly independent republics and also in view of the need to resolve the regional problems within the framework of inter-state associations with objective expediency, began the foundation of the regional organization in Central Asia.

The necessity of resolving the regional problems jointly and making coordinated efforts for ensuring effective socio-economic development of the independent countries of Central Asia motivated the political leaders for setting up a regional association in Central Asia. As such, on 30 April 1994, a Treaty on creating a single united economic space was signed by the Republics of Kazakhstan, Kyrgyzstan and Uzbekistan, to which, on 26 March 1998, joined the Republic of Tajikistan. On 17 July 1998, the Inter-State Council approved the name of the regional association functioning on the

* Translated from original Russian into English by Sushmita Bhattacharya.

basis of the aforesaid Treaty as "The Central Asian Economic Association (CAEA)." At present the CAEA enjoys quite a high international prestige. This, side by side with other constituents, confirms the fact of assigning the CAEA of the status of an observer to the Inter-State Council and its institutions of Russian Federation, Georgia, Turkey Republic, Ukraine, and also the availability/ presence of declarations about assigning such status from a number of States.

The Treaty on creating a single united economic space points out the political and economic terms which condition the opportunity and expediency of economic integration process in the Central Asian region. These conditions are:

1. bilateral treaties signed between States on friendship, cooperation and mutual assistance;
2. historical common character of the peoples of Central Asia;
3. desire of the people and leaders of the States to comprehensively develop and extend good neighbourly relations;
4. possibility of coordinated execution of economic reforms and development of market relations;
5. feasibility of building mutually beneficial trade and economic relations;
6. opportunity of creating favourable legal, organizational and economic conditions for realization of joint programmes on developing integrated processes;
7. advantage of joint utilization of economic potential of the countries of Central Asia.

These terms together with the present objective factors of the integration of economy of the Central Asian states create the real perspectives of expediting socio-economic development of the subjects of the CAEA. The basic factors for the development of economic integration process within the framework of the CAEA, are extension of international division of labour, rise in the level of openness in the national economy, internationalization of economic activities, speeding up the science and technological progress and others. Extension of international division of labour and on the basis of it internationalizing the economy is the important factor that widens the possibility of increasing the efficiency of national economy. For, running a secluded national economy and carrying out reproduction process within the national boundaries limit the efficiency and rate of economic development.

Division of labour among the states of the region, building stable economic relations among them, maintaining the openness of national economy and on the basis of it mutually beneficial utilization of productive forces of each of the countries of the region at present wholly correspond to the regional interests of the CAEA member-states. In fact, these conditions predetermine the feasibility of integration process and long-term task of the CAEA, i.e., creating a single economic space. However, as indicated by the practical activities of the CAEA and other regional associations, it is first of all necessary to resolve various grassroot level problems and overcome impediments so as to achieve this long-term goal.

Developing relations on the basis of mutual cooperation and consequently raising the level of mutually beneficial national economy are the essential factors in establishing and expanding integrated relations among the states in the CAEA. Earlier, the absence of these aspects of cooperation within the framework of an association was "the weak point" for any kind of integrated development. The countries of Central Asian region before gaining independence were part of the USSR system, the economy of which represented a single national economic complex. The economic mechanism laid down in the planned economy enabled the countries of Central Asia to have a high rate of socio-economic development. At the same time, the Central Asian countries to a great extent were assigned the task of providing raw materials to the industrially developed regions of the former Soviet Union. In fact, initially a highly raw materials oriented economy of the Central Asian Republics and the long-term division of labour among them was one of the motivating causes behind their struggle for getting national independence. But still they have not become the subject of purposeful study and examination. As a result there has been a lack of motivating factors in the integration process in of the countries of the Association. A study carried out on the integration process of the CAEA States during 1990s shows that in these countries deformation of industrial structure continued which indicates a substantial increase in the resources producing sectors (electro-energy, fuel industry, ferrous and non-ferrous metals) and corresponding decrease in the proportion for the resource-consuming industry. During the period 1990-1999, in the whole industrial structure the share of the resource-producing sectors of Kazakhstan increased by 1.9 times, while that of Kyrgyzstan increased by 6.1 times, Tajikistan by 3.6 and Uzbekistan by 3.0 times. These changes in the industrial structure of the countries reduce the motivating incentives for economically viable relations in the framework of the CAEA. It is more so because only the development of resource consuming sectors can generate the mutually beneficial economy in the integrating countries.

The theory of international economic relations determines the conditions and pre-requisites of national integration, which in turn depends on the extent and pattern of integrated targets to be achieved. These conditions and pre-requisites are as follows:

(*a*) approximate equality in the level of economic development of the member countries of the integrated association;
(*b*) the economy of the integrating countries to be in a developmental stage;
(*c*) territorial proximity of the countries;
(*d*) agreement on the political will of the leaders of the countries on the issue of integration;
(*e*) willingness of the countries to delegate their separate individual powers to jointly established structures; and
(*f*) formation of an initiating centre in one of the states.

These conditions are not outlined in accordance with their increasing or diminishing significance. Each of them has its specific impact on the process of integration and has also its own graphic meaning in the concerned matter under review. What is now required to be done is to examine the extent of existence and realization of these pre-requisites in the case of the CAEA. While establishing the CAEA on the basis of above mentioned conditions, particular role has been played by the two key components: territorial proximity and unity of political will of the Central Asian leaders on the issue of regional integration.

Situated at the centre of Asia, the CAEA states are neighbouring countries and have centuries-old experience of good neighbourly trade and economic relations. They are directly connected by transport and communication network, but remain located at a remote distance from other economic regions of the world. These conditions are positive factors for regional integration in the CAEA.

The decisive condition for the formation and functioning of the CAEA has been the common realization of the political leaders of the Central Asian States about the need for developing integration process in the region. Since concluding the Treaty on creating a single united economic space, the heads of the member States have repeatedly issued joint declarations which in clear terms pointed to the necessity of subsequent development of integrated relations in the region.

However, at the same time, practical realization of this pre-requisite in the framework of CAEA has not been carried out to its full extent. The directions for developing integration process, which were outlined in various documents, have been sufficiently worked out and expanded by the institutions of the Inter-State Council of CAEA governmental body, ministries and department as well as the national groups of experts, sometimes on various pretexts they are even blocked. Therefore, in the framework of the Association an effective mechanism is needed in accordance with the conformity of each State on the activities of the executive bodies and other structures for implementation of the decisions taken in collaboration with the head of the State.

For example, one may cite the implementation of the treaty concluded on creating a single united economic space on the basis of declaration made by the heads of the States and resolutions of the Inter-State Council particularly on the formation of the free-trade zones within the framework of the Association. The thesis on the advisability and necessity of creating such zones has been steadily functioning since the CAEO came into existence. But in order to take a concrete decision on realizing this issue, various "grounds" will have to be considered. By this it is not meant that the above cited "arguments" on reasoning and deferring the process of implementation of the resolutions of the executives of an individual state contradicts the documents signed by the head of this State along with that of the others. Thus, elimination of lacuna in understanding the urgency of the problems that exist among the heads and executives of the States is a significant direction to maintain purposeful development of integration processes in the CAEA. In this connection we consider it advisable to introduce an agreed procedure, in conformity with each state, within a certain period of time after the adoption of a document by the heads of States.

As mentioned above, one of the conditions for inter-state integration is that the level of economic development of the integrating countries should more or less be equal. However, it is impossible to give a simple answer to the question on the presence of this condition in the CAEA. In 2002, by the volume of manufactured gross domestic product the difference recorded in the CAEA countries was more than 18 times. By this index per capita population was calculated and the difference was recorded as 7 times, while the difference in the average monthly salary was found to be 11 times.

The other pre-requisite of inter-state integration is that the economy of the countries becoming member of regional association should be of a developing nature. The economic trend in the CAEA countries throughout the entire period of its functioning has a multi-directional tendency. During the period 1994-2000, for instance, the gross domestic product steadily increased in Uzbekistan, while in the rest of the three States there were fluctuating changes. At the same time an analysis of the socio-economic development of the CAEA States for the last three years shows that several macro-economic indices of development have not only been improving, but have also gained momentum towards stability.

The above stated pre-requisite also demands considerable development in the economic reform process. Economic reform is being carried out in all countries, though by paces and outcomes it differs considerably. The initial years of independence for the countries of Central Asia were highly difficult. The economic crisis and slump in production that had started during the last years of Soviet rule continued and further aggravated inflation processes as well as depreciated working capital of enterprises. Besides, after gaining national independence the Republics were not fully prepared for its fast and efficient realization. The newly sovereign States had to determine and legalize their political, economic and social structures. As a result, aggravating economic problems to a large extent remained unresolved.

In such conditions several financial institutions offered their help to the Central Asian States. These institutions offered credits for economic reform provided that the latter strictly fulfilled their recommendations. The Central Asian States to a large extent agreed to the terms and conditions with regard to the rate of interest for the credits given to them. Depending on the domestic potentialities of the independent states to solve the economic problems, and also owing to the fact that irrespective of many common features of the people and States of Central Asia, the financial institutions recommended different terms and conditions for carrying out economic reforms.

However, the onward development of the Central Asian Association in terms of economic integration can not overlook the shortcomings present in the functioning of the above mentioned pre-requisites. Yet another pre-requisite of international economic integration is the willingness of the member countries of a regional association to delegate individual powers to the jointly formed Inter-State Council, the higher governing body which has been set up in the CAEA consisting of the Presidents and Prime Ministers of all the member states. Within the Inter State Council there are Council of Prime Ministers and Council of Foreign Affairs Ministers. It also has a working body known as the Executive Committee which carries out coordination and consultative/advisory tasks as well as brings out the resolution of the Inter State Council and its institutions. At the same time in the process of preparing a draft to determine the CAEA structures a decentralized approach is taken which in many cases keeps track towards maximum realization of national interests of the member States.

In the decentralised approach the contradiction between national and regional interests becomes glaringly exposed. This in the CAEA framework becomes apparent while working out common economic module of integration. In this connection, the experts of individual CAEA States when coming to an agreement about the drafts of many common economic decisions substantiate the inexpediency to adopt them by the national legislation. Such an approach as indicated by the world-wide practice of regional associations does not yield optimum benefits. Failure to carry out many tasks in the framework of CAEA for creating a single economic space also confirms the need to alter the approach towards preparing the drafts on common economic agenda and their fulfilment. Thus, in my opinion, the CAEA agenda must include the question of setting up an institution accountable to the Inter-State Council having specific powers and authority for centralised guidance to the integration process as well as creation of a single economic space. Of course, the power to exercise certain sovereign rights by such an institution will have to be handed over by the individual States.

The Treaty on Creating a Single Economic Space was primarily signed on 10 January 1994 by the developed and highly potential States of Central Asia—Republic of Kazakhstan and Republic of Uzbekistan. The initiating role taken by these States during the initial years of the formation contributed much to the expansion of the Association. Formation of an initiating centre in one of these two States will be a significant positive step towards the development of the CAEA.

This thesis, of course, does not intend to limit the scope of the necessity and significance of the initiative displayed by other states of the Association. On the other hand, it should in no way be linked with display of "hegemonism" in the CAEA. The fact is that for performing the role of a "hegemony" (predominant force), not a single subject of the Central Asian regional association has the suitable conditions at its disposal. For such a role to play in the association or in the region, a country must possess the potentials to have the following: It should be a market for procuring and selling raw materials that are in demand in the countries of the region; flow of its capitals in the region; it should serve as the largest market of the region as well as the centre of manufacturing highly scientific technological products used in the region.

During the period of existence of the Central Asian regional association the member states of the CAEA have adopted 215 documents, of which 107 have been adopted by the Inter-State Council, and 108 by the Council of Prime Ministers. Out of 107 documents of the Inter-State Council 3 are treaties, 10 agreements, 3 declarations, memorandum and communiqué, 8 appeals and statements, 75 resolutions and 8 protocol resolutions. The heads of the governments have signed 32 agreements, 68 resolutions, and 8 protocol resolutions.

In order to resolve the issues on regional association, the functioning of the CAEA can conditionally be divided into following states:

1. **Formation Period of Regional Association** (1984-1995): During this period the treaty on creating a single economy was concluded among the Republics of Kazakhstan, Kyrgyzstan and Uzbekistan. The setting up of the Inter-State Council consisting of the Presidents and Prime Ministers of the above-mentioned three States and the establishment within the structures of the Inter-State Council of the Council of Prime Ministers, Council of Foreign Affairs Ministers and the Council of Defence Ministers laid the organizational foundations for the management of the regional association. With the establishment of a working body in the Inter-State Council – the Executive Committee, the organizational base for working out drafts and documents of conceptual and strategic nature, and carrying out coordination job in the regional association was completed. The establishment of Central Asian Bank of cooperation and development provided relief to manage certain monetary resources of the States which were part of the regional association for financing the regional projects. During this period, basic documents concerning all activities of regional association were worked out and approved, and also procedural aspects to solve the organizational problems were determined. The entire organisational work that had been done helped to start intensive work for working out and implementing the first programme oriented measures to realise

the treaty on creating a single economy. At the first stage, the programme on Economic Integration up to year 2000 and the list of top priority investment projects were approved. Besides, the documents on cooperation in military and technical fields, as well as provision for Inter-State treaties and agreements concerning pharamaceutical industry and health protection, research on earthquake and prognostication of seismic danger and others were also approved.

2. **Development Period of Regional Association (1996-1998)**: This period is characterized by intensive and purposeful work on development of inter-state integration and implementation of steps towards forming a single economy. During this period several decisions were made including the adoption of a two-year programme on activities of the member-states in forming a single economy, as well as resolutions on developing production cooperative system, on special economic zones, on Special Programme of the UNO for the economy of Central Asia (SPECA), on principles to form international consortiums, on setting up international water energy consortiums, on principles to build a market of securities etc. A number of agreements on cooperation in the sphere of utilization of water energy resources, anticipation and elimination of emergency situation, utilization of thermal-energy and water resources, pursuing the agreed policy in the sphere of transport and communications, setting up joint enterprises, regulation for migration of population, health protection and medical science, development of tourism, conservation of environment and rational use of nature, intensification of fight against illegal turnover of narcotics and psychotropic drugs. Several key decisions aimed at forming a single economy included the agreements on creating legal, economic and organizational conditions for free movement of labour force, and discarding the anti-monopoly policy, on principles to draw closer the basic orientations of national legislations which regulate the economic activities on crating a common science and technology, as well as on tariff policy for railway transport.

During this period particular attention was paid to the military and technical cooperation particularly regulating the activities of the peace-making battalion. At this stage expansion of members within the regional association also took place. As a result, Republic of Tajikistan became the full fledged member of the Treaty on creating a single economy. The Central Asian regional association functioning on the basis of the Treaty after deciding to create a single economy was named as "Central Asian Economic Association (CAEA)".

3. **Abatement Period in the Intensity of CAEA Activities (1999-2001)**: During this period the strategy for integrated development of the CAEA for the period until 2005 and a three-year programme on top priority actions to be taken by the member-states for building a single economy were approved. A resolution on the formation of the Economic Forum of the CAEA was also adopted. Besides, the agreements were reached on the parallel work on the energy sector and on cooperation in the field of hydro-meteorology, quarantine of plants, veterinary science and medicine, development of sanatoria and health resorts, sanitary and tourist organizations. Moreover, resolutions on top-priority investment projects were also adopted. However, at the same time, opportunities for developing regional association were not fully utilized. A large number of prepared draft resolutions aiming at the formation of a single economy and development of integration process were not considered viable by the group of experts of individual states on various "grounds". As such lack of consensus did not permit to adopt important resolutions. The intensity of meetings among the heads of the States and heads of the governments during this period considerably declined. Whereas during 1994-1998 the Inter-State council sessions were held two to four times a year, during 1999-2001 these sessions took place just once a year.

In terms of abatement of intensity in the integration process, which in my opinion, was caused due to the desire of individual member states to play a leading role in the Association, there came up a suggestion to re-organize the CAEA into the Central-Asian

Forum. But it may be assumed that in the Forum framework each State would independently determine its priority of cooperation and would undertake only those commitments which would satisfy its interests. Such a form of cooperation, on the face of it, seems to be attractive for the sovereign States. But on the regional scale these are the problems common to all the States, which would pave the way for various kinds of conflict with the clash of interests of the individual subjects. In such cases the proposed form of organizing inter-State mutual relations is simply incapable of resolving these questions.

In the current situation the prospects of integrated relations in the Central Asian region are seen in the following two variants:

(*a*) restrained and differentiated formation of integration process based on bilateral inter-State relations;
(*b*) progressive formation of a single economy and advancement of integration process based on multilateral inter-State cooperation.

The variant "a" for developing integration process in Central Asia assuming that it would give this process a spontaneous nature, becomes real provided the Central Asian Economic Association is transformed into Central Asian Forum, for it means that:

- the member-states of the CAEA roll up their activities for purposefully formed single economy;
- the transformation is a veiled form of discontinuance of the process by multi-planned and multi-state integration in Central Asia as well as the activities of its regional association;
- the priority form of inter-State cooperation would turn into bilateral relations.

The transformation of a regulated regional association into a deliberative and consultative body has a number of negative consequences. Such a step creates a notion about the absence of readiness on the part of the CAEA member-States to reach an agreement on major strategic questions, and consequently about the presence of vital differences in the approaches to the development of economy within the framework of regional association which may lead to stackening of security and making the destructive internal forces, particularly with extremist and religious orientation more active. The proposed reorganization may also substantially worsen the investment attraction of all the countries of the region since the foreign investors are interested in developing the entire market of Central Asia, and not the small markets of the individual countries of the region.

At the same time, the creation of the Central Asian Forum within the structure of Inter-State Council of CAEA would be fully justified. By this the Forum would ensure wide consultations within the CAEA for establishing its inverse relations with the civil society, the social organizations and representatives of science and business circles, the experts of the member-countries and foreign states, and the representatives of international organizations. Thus the re-organization proposal in no way aims at developing integration process in our region, rather it seems to be an expression of its initiators' desire to complete the process of the multilateral cooperation in the region.[1]

The variant "b" for developing integration process in Central Asia—the progressive formation of a single economy and advancement of integration process on the basis of the development of multilateral inter-state cooperation—aims at utmost realization of the tasks reflected in the Treaty on creating a single economy by means of making the CAEA activities perfect. In the current scenario of globalization of the world economy the urgency to intensify the regional integration process has increased even greater, for in the new condition of the activities of the world economy and increase in competition at the macro level not a single State is able to maintain its high socio-economic development. It is worth mentioning that the high significance of regional economic associations including the CAEA, which are functioning in the post-Soviet space, in pursuit of developing integration process was particularly emphasized at an informal summit of the heads of the CIS States held from 1 to 3 August 2001 in the city of Sochi.

For implementing this variant it is necessary to retain the CAEA to continue its activities that would enable the member-states to consistently carry out the joint measures in accomplishing the tasks

Table 1: Common Characteristic of the CAEA States

	Kazakhstan	*Kyrgyzstan*	*Tajikistan*	*Uzbekistan*
1. Political System	Unitary State with Presidential form of government	Sovereign, Unitary, Democratic Republic	Sovereign Democratic Lawful Secular United Republic	Sovereign Democratic Republic
2. Presidents	Nazarbaev Nurzultan Abishevich (6.7.1940)	Akaev Askar Akaevich (10.11.1994)	Rakhmonov Emomali Sharipovich (5.10.1952)	Karimov Islam Abduganievich (30.10.1938)
3. Legislative Power	Bi-cameral Parliament: (Senate (47) and Majilis (67) (on permanent basis)	Bi-cameral Jogorku Kenesh: Legislative Assembly (35: permanent) and Council of People's Representatives (70: sessional)	Bi-cameral Parliament Majlisi Oli: Majlisi Milli (sessional) and Majlisi Namoyandagon (Parmanent)	Unicameral Parliament Olii Majlis (250)
4. Executive Power	Government and the ministries and departments accountable to it	Government and the ministries and departments accountable to it	President is the head of the state and the executive authority (the government)	President simultaneously performing the functions of the Chairman of the cabinet of ministers
5. Judicial Power	Supreme Court, Military Court and Local Courts	Constitutional, Supreme, Highest Court and Arbitration and Local Courts	Constitutional, Supreme, Highest Court for Economy and Local Courts	Constitutional Supreme Highest Court for Economy and Local Courts
6. Territory	2,724.9 thousand sq. km.	199 thousand sq. km.	143.1 thousand sq. km. (43% mountains)	447.4 thousand sq. km
7. Administrative-Territorial Division	14 provinces	7 provinces	2 provinces and Gorno-Badakhshan Autonomous Republic	12 provinces, 1 Autonomous Republic of Karakalpakstan

(*Contd.*)

(Contd.)

	Kazakhstan	Kyrgyzstan	Tajikistan	Uzbekistan
8. Population	15.6 m. people	4.6 m. people	6.1 m. people	23.9 m. people
9. Composition of National of the Population	Kazakh–52% Russian–31.4% Ukrainian–44% Uzbek–2.2% Tatar–1.7% German–1.5%	Kyrgyz–60.8% Russian–15.3% Uzbek–14.3% Kazakh–2% Ukranian–1.5%	Tajik–62% Uzbek–28% Russian–8%	Uzbek–71.4% Russian–8.3% Tajik–4.7% Kazakh–4.1% Tatar–2.4% Karakalpak–2.1%
10. Main religions	Islam of Sunni Persuasion and orthodox Christianity	Islam of Sunni Persuasion and orthodox Christianity	Islam of Sunni Persuasion and Ismaili	Islam of Sunni Persuasion
11. Holidays	January 1-2 – New Year March-8 International Women's Day March-22 Nauryz of Meirama May-1 Festival of Unity of the people of Kazakhstan May-9 Victory Day August-30 Constitution Day October-25 Republic Day November-16 Independence Day of the Republic	January-1 New Year January-7 Christmas March-21 Nauroz May-1 Day of International Solidarity May-5 Constitution Day August-31 National Independence Day According to Orozo ait, according to Kurman calendars.	January-1 New Year March-8 International Women's day May-1 Day of solidarity of the working people May-9 Victory Day September-5 Independence Day November-6 Constitution Day According to Idi Ramazon According to Idi Kurbon Calendars	January-1 New Year March-8 Women's Holiday March-21 Navruz May-9 Victory Day September-1 Independence Day October-1 Teacher's and Preceptorship's Day December-8 Constitution Day According to Ramzan Hait According to Kurban Hait Calendars

Table 2: Common Characteristics of the CAEA States and Basic Economic Indexes in the Year 2000

	Kazakhstan	*Kyrgyzstan*	*Tajikistan*	*Uzbekistan*	*CAEA*
Territory (thousand sq. m.)	2,724.9	199.0	143.1	447.4	3,514.4
Population (million people)	14.9	4.6	6.1	23.9	49.5
Density of Population (person/sq. km.)	5.7	23.1	42.6	50.4	14.3
Gross Domestic Product					
billion/milliards in individual national currency (INC)	1,893.5	48.3	1,345.0	2,048.4	
milliards (billions US dollars)	15.8	1.2	1.1	16.4	34.5
GDP per head (US dollars)	1,049.5	245.0	178.3	672.1	697.0
Volume of industrial products					
milliards/billion (INC)	1,112.7	34.1	852.1	833.0	
millions US dollars	8.0	0.8	0.5	6.7	16.0
Gross Agricultural Product					
milliards (INC)	329.6	31.3	412.9	833.0	
Milliards US dollars	2.4	0.8	0.3	6.7	10.2
Capital investments milliards (INC)	276.9	5.4	102.9	503.2	--
Goods dispatched by all th means of transport (million ton)	1,049.4	36.1	7.2	812.5	1905.2

Bottom Reference: Average rate of Information exchange:

Kazakh Tenge 1$	=	45 T
Kyrgyz Som 1$	=	47.72
Tajik Soman1$	=	1.833 S
Uzbek Sum 1$	=	330 S

Table 3: Density of Population in the Ferghana Valley[2] (According to the position by the end of 1999)

Name	*Number of Population (in thousand)*	*Territory (th. sq. km.)*	*Density (person per sq. km.)*
Republic of Uzbekistan	24,406	447.4	54.6
Including the provinces:			
(*a*) Andijan	2,177.3	4.2	518.4
(*b*) Namangan	1,714.3	7.9	242.3
(*c*) Ferghana	2,657.4	7.1	374.3
Altogether from three province	6,749.0	19.2	351.5
Republic of Kyrgyz	4,895.2	199.945	24.5
Including the Provinces:			
Batkenstan	385.5	17.0	22.7
Djalalabad/Jalalabad	881.0	33.648	26.2
Osh	1,193.3	29.189	40.9
Altogether in three provinces	2,459.8	79.837	30.8
Ferghana Valley	9,208.8	99.2	92.8
Taking Leninabad Province of Tajikistan into account	10,708.8	–	–

contained in the Treaty on Creating a Single Economy. With this at present it is of particular significance to concentrate on the potential of the State for realizing the Strategy of Integrated Development of CAEA throughout the period till the year 2005 and the Programme of the top priority jobs of the States in the CAEA for building a single economy during the period till 2002, which were approved by the Inter-State Council of the CAEA on 14 June 2000.

It should be mentioned here that this variant is fully in line with the accomplishment of tasks stated in all joint declarations by the heads of the States and adopted within the framework of the CAEA. Proceeding from this in my opinion, the realization of the second variant for developing the integrated process seems to be prospective for the States in Central Asia and that is the progressive formation of a single economy and advancement of integrated process on the basis of development of multilateral inter-state cooperation.

REFERENCES

1. The history of integration in Europe gives evidence of the complications of this process. In the formation of EC also there were periods of stagnation and slump. For instance, at the beginning of 60s during De Gaul's government because of "on Principle" position of France on separate issues and policy of employ chair followed by it the process of integration in the EC was held up for some years. However, the resolution to break up the EC was not adopted and the present level of integration in Europe testifies to the expediency of the faresighted approach while examining the question about the prospects of inter-state integration.
2 The basic totals of the first national census of KR 1999/National Statistics Committee KR-Bishkek, 2000.
Uzbekistan in the figures of 1998, Statistical Data/State Department of Statistics under the Ministry of Macro Economy and Statistics, RU, Tashkent, 2000.

15

Region, Regionalization, Regionalism

The "Myth" of *Tsentralnaya Aziia* Revisited

Anita Sengupta

There are grounds to look forward with optimism to the future of the Central Asian Commonwealth.[1]

Regions and Regionalism

Writing in 1994 and echoing many others, Martha Brill Olcott had pointed out that the disincentive for regional integration in the Central Asian region was such as to ascribe to the eventuality of such an integration the possibility of a myth.[2] The argument for this ran as follows: Rivalries within the region coupled with the fact that independence had been embraced with enthusiasm by each of the states, which also immediately began exploring independent developmental and economic relations with other international bodies, would effectively ensure that attempts to create any organization designed to treat Central Asia as a single unit would remain a "specter conjured to ward off specific threats or problems".[3] The "weak state" structure argument was also put forward to point out that the Central Asian states, confronted as they were with the necessity of national consolidation, would be unable to take any action towards regional integration.[4] Otherwise, according to Olcott, regional integration and cooperation would only prove to be workable in such minor incentives as educational and scientific policy, a regional commission on the media and in commissions to address ecological conditions as the Aral Sea or the disappearing caviar yields of the Caspian. While the author also noted that the less than three years that had passed were insufficient to correctly indicate the complete failure of efforts at integration, yet she was of the opinion that the five states were being increasingly drawn apart rather than being pulled together. The completion of ten years of independence of the Central Asian states is the juncture at which such predictions can be fruitfully re-explored.

Prior to an examination of the Central Asian experience at integration and cooperation it is necessary to take into account debates centered around regions and regionalism and the sharpened awareness of the possibilities of regional cooperation and institution building that emerged in the post-Cold War era. Three central elements were identified by analysts as constituting the core elements of regionalism. First, a common historical experience and a sense of shared problems among a geographically distinct group of countries or societies which constituted a *region*. Second, close linkages of a distinct kind between those countries and societies, in other words recognition of a boundary to the region within which interactions would be more intense than those with the outside world, in other words, *regionalization*. Finally, the emergence of organization giving shape to the region in a legal and institutional sense and providing some rules of the game within the region, the element of conscious policy which is central to *regionalism*.[5]

In the Central Asian case, it is pointed out, the identification of what could be termed as *Tsentralnaya Aziia*, has itself eluded precise definition particularly since the people of the region never thought of themselves as "Central Asians". Geographically the region has been identified as the vast space between China and the Black Sea, in socio-cultural terms it has been used to define the lands that lay beyond the borders of the great sedentary civilizations. There are, however, continuing debates on the validity of both positions.[6] In more recent times the five SSR's of the region were known by the Soviet era term *Srednaya Aziia i Kazakhstan*. The emergence of a region, known as *Tsentralnaya Aziia*, has been identified in a meeting held in Tashkent in January 1993. Here the Presidents of Uzbekistan, Kazakhstan, Turkmenistan, Kyrgyzstan and the Chairman of Tajikistan's Parliament, concluded their discussion of common concerns with the decision that they would now be known as *Tsentralnaya Aziia*.[7] The element of construction that is pointed to is evident. This creation of a region however, is neither new nor unique.[8] Every region and sub-region, indeed Europe itself, first had to be conceptualized in its current form before European institutions meant to tackle the problems of Europe as a region could come into existence. And the numerous concepts, alliances and ententes that finally resulted in the creation of Europe as the "common homeland" of Europeans took nearly a century to evolve.

A broader though more ambiguous definition of the region identifies it as a geographical area with limited scope, constituted out of at least three actors, which are objectively recognized by other actors as constituting a distinctive community, and whose members identify themselves as such. That *Tsentralnaya Aziia* constitutes a region in this sense is defined in the following words by of President Karimov, when he notes that the region is

> ....conditioned by common territory, common communication means, basic and leading branches of economy, by need for joint exploitation of water and energy objects, provision of energy resources. To say nothing about common culture, language and spiritual values of our nations that have deep penetrating common roots. This region has always been integrated in this or that form. The nations of Central Asia comprehended the need to rebuild their future with joint efforts after they gained their independence.[9]

The necessity of integration and regionalization is also well defined by President Karimov when he notes:

> In fact there is a series of initial conditions and pre-requisites for the integration of the Central Asian republics. They imply an equal starting level of economic development, similarity of social and economic problems, unified transport and energy supply, communications and water resources. Apart from this, there exist general threats to security of all the regions that inhabit this region. Among them are the drying of the Aral, drugs and arms smuggling, emerging terrorism and religious fundamentalism, threats to escalation of tension and instability that comes from Afghanistan and a number of other factors. Such threats despite their apparat disparity are unifying factors, because none of these threats may be surmounted autonomously, relying on one's own forces.[10]

Similarly, the development differential between the states is narrow and this is seen as a significant advantage for regionalization.[11]

While the existence of the region and the need for regionalization are unquestionable whether regionalism will succeed remains to be examined. It should also be recognized at the onset that the level of enthusiasm towards cooperation and integration among the former Soviet states varies.[12] While Kazakhstan is an enthusiastic supporter of both integration with Russia and Central Asian regional integration and does not view that the two are separate processes, Turkmenistan has on the whole preferred to keep away from both the CIS and Central Asian multilateral cooperation frameworks. The other states have adopted postures in between the two extreme positions. The situation is of course fluid and subtle changes in the position of particular states are not uncommon. In the aftermath of the September 11 events, Uzbekistan for instance, assumed an independent stance and extended its air space and other facilities to the US, whereas Tajikistan, along whose borders with Afghanistan Russian troops are stationed was more cautious.

In dealing with regionalism three elements emerge as important. The first element relates to the spatial dimension of regionalism, i.e, how large is the area covered and how is the area defined or redefined as conditions change. The second element relates to its scope, in other words the tasks or areas of interaction covered by the region or by regional organization. And the third feature is the level and extent of the organization.[13] These three are useful since they indicate the variety and unevenness of regionalism that is crucial for a correct understanding of its success or failure. This paper argues that just as there is no single model for nations and nationalism, no "fixed" model of regions and regionalism is likely to survive transplantation and to a great extent the success or failure of a particular variant would have to be premised on an understanding of the characteristics of the region. This is particularly significant in Central Asia and for that matter any non-western situation. Besides, any advocacy of regionalism would have to take into account the fact that regionalism per say could be a force of integration as well as disintegration, since like forces of nationalism it expresses a desire for both common action and unity as a desire for distinctiveness and difference.

Also situated as it is at the intersection of the national and the global systems, regionalism has implications for statehood that are difficult to reconcile with the new face of nationalism in the Central Asian region. Regionalism, therefore, expresses a constant tension between the demands of statehood and adjustments to regional realities. In fact a correct balance between regional and state interest is what makes a regional organization viable. Indeed, Central Asian analysts have noted this duality with which all regional organizations have to deal:

> ....Central Asian integration is vital for the regions' countries. The economic integration of Central Asian states opens up vast opportunities to solve socio-political, economic and environmental problems. Integration can benefit all the countries of the Central Asian region and accelerate their socio economic development, allowing them to find their respective niches in the world economy.[14]

It is possibly this "finding of respective" niches while keeping regional requirements in view that will determine the direction of integration. In fact it is pointed out that the region has three options in terms of regional integration. The first is in terms of reinforcement of relationships with the CIS countries on a new economic and institutional basis, the second is the formation of a community of Central Asian states and the third is in terms of integration with her immediate neighbouring states.

A large part of the debate on the viability or otherwise of regionalism in the Central Asian region rests on a comparison of Central Asian initiatives with the most formal and wide ranging expression of regional interaction, the European Union, which represents not just a highly developed set of institutions expressing economic but also increasingly the political integration of Western Europe. It has been argued that the final aim of the European Union is the construction of a kind of "regional state" in which the traditional roles of national state authorities are transferred to the European level. It is generally assumed today that following the example of the European Community, the world order will be reworked around a combination of regional associations. Since globalization had made states obsolete and a single world order is still a utopian dream, the obvious solution seems to lie in the creation of regional groupings. However, such regional efforts imbibe numerous complexities.

With the disintegration of the Soviet Union, when the Central Asian states emerged as independent republics, a similar examination of prospects of regional cooperation began. Indeed, one of the first, proposed by President Nazarbaev, was inspired by this European vision, and envisaged the formation of a Eurasian Union. This was visualized as a multinational model that would aim at creating a unified state through various stages of confederation and finally arriving at a union. A major problem with this vision of a union lay in the way the idea of the union was interpreted. Keeping the European example in view it was possibly envisaged as an economically focussed, monolithic and invasive model of integration, demanding a high level of market sophistication, openness and readiness to compromise on sovereignty. Like the European Union it was envisaged to address political relations only as an implicit function and through weaker mechanisms keeping internal conflict off the agenda.[15] However, the EU type integration was unattainable for these states at their current levels of economic development and also irrelevant for their political ills.

The Eurasian Union initiative did not really take off and this was one possible reason why integrative efforts on a regional level were generally assumed to be unworkable in Central Asia. What remained un-emphasized was that most regional organizations, including the European one, gradually developed over the years through a number of initiatives and still remain beset with numerous problems, not the least of which is the reconciliation of state with regional interests. The more modest achievements of regional cooperation were ignored as the focus was on a more comprehensive EU type integration "or nothing". This was all the more so since Russia claimed to be pursuing CIS integration on the model of the EU political union. It has also to be recognized that the success of the EU has largely been based on the principle of parity between states, an unsustainable assumption in the CIS conditions. Similarly significant relational dyads run through the EU's membership whereas the only relationships that mattered for the now sovereign states of the former Soviet Union were aligned to Moscow. Intra-regional dyads and triads are more recent developments in the Central Asian region which are yet to prove their viability. Also, realistic models of integration would be ones where the states had significant leverage and influence within the structures that would enable them to maintain the image of their newly attained sovereignty.

It is undeniable that any prospect of regional integration in the Central Asian region would have to begin by taking note of Russian interests in the region as also how Russia perceives regional integrative efforts and the involvement of other states in these regional organizations. Similarly, a major debate in all efforts at intra-regional integration remains the level of Russian involvement in each of the states and in any regional effort. And a movement away from the Russian sphere of influence is seen as a positive signal for regional integration. In any case all the states are members of a larger regional organization, the CIS, where Moscow remains, at the very least "first among equals". Whether *Tsentralnaya Aziia* remains a "myth" or emerges as a reality, therefore, remains premised on a recognition of this relationship. Thus the complexities involved in this relationship need to be examined.

Russia and *Tsentralnaya Aziia*

Towards the latter half of the 1980s, the regional balance of power in the then Soviet Union began to acquire important political meaning in the fight for succession within the hierarchy. It is important to remember that at this stage Mikhail Gorbachev could rely on the almost total support of a "monolithic block" of Central Asian deputies in the then Supreme Soviet of the USSR in his fight against internal opposition that since 1989 was being identified with Boris Yeltsin. The Central Asian Republics were staunch supporters of Gorbachev's 9+1 proposal for ensuring the survival of the USSR. When this plan was abruptly brought to an end with the Minsk Agreement, which excluded these Republics, the Central Asian Republics reacted by attempting to create the "Turkestan Confederation". Therefore, it is noted that regionalism in Central Asia actually emerged in opposition to Slavic efforts at integration. Open confrontation between the Slavic and the Turkic republics of the former Soviet Union could only be averted by efforts at conciliation by leaders like Nursultan Nazarbaev who helped to negotiate the Central Asian membership in the CIS in Almaty in December 1991.[16] However, the early years of the decade were marked by steps taken by the new Russian state that demonstrated her independent status and her separateness from the former Central Asian Republics.

However, this position changed with the emergence of a coalition who spoke in favour of restoring Russian-Central Asian "special relations". It included influential industrial groups who were dependent on Central Asian raw materials and semi-finished products and on Central Asian markets for their finished products. Some communist factions were also to be found in this coalition who stood for preserving ties with Central Asia as a means for restoring the Soviet legacy. There were also groups of Russian nationalists who considered Russian-Central Asian relations as a prerequisite for "Eurasian unity". They were joined by parts of the Russian military-industrial complex that perceived the disintegration of the Soviet strategic space as a threat to Russian security interests. Support for this "re-integrationist" approach came from the Russian National

Security Council as also the Russian Supreme Soviet and the ministries like the Ministry of Defence, Interior and Counter-intelligence.

As Russian perspective on its relations with the West changed, so did its approach to third party involvement in Central Asian politics and economics. It was suddenly recognized that by "abandoning" Central Asia and reducing its presence in the region, Russia left vacuums that had begun to be filled up by others, particularly western countries, including Turkey as a NATO member, as well as China, Iran, Saudi Arabia and Pakistan. Turkey was recognized as a particularly alarming case because of its cultural proximity to the republics and its political backing from the West. Examples of this concern abounded. In May 1993, a quasi official article by the Ministry for Foreign Economic Relations was published in the *Nezavisimaya Gazeta* that lashed out against the decision adopted by the five Central Asian states to create the Central Asian Regional Council, which was intended to exclude the Russian Federation. It was asserted that this intra-regional integration was hostile to Russian interests and that it undermined the previous agreements on a single CIS military-strategic space. It was also claimed that these integratory attempts were being orchestrated by Turkey and other Western powers.[17] Similarly, when in the summer of 1993, the majority of the Central Asian states supported the Turkish idea for the creation of a custom and tariff union, the then First Deputy Prime Minister of Russia, A. Shokhin, declared that Central Asian regimes had to make the choice between integration with Turkey or with Russia, Ukraine and Belarus. Central Asia could not be involved in both communities.

Concurrently, Russia became more perceptive about what could be considered as "positive" tendencies and moves in the Central Asian states. As ideas about the Eurasian school of thought began to take root in official Russian thinking, compatible ideas began to be felt in the Central Asian context, especially in Kazakhstan. It was under such conditions that the proposal on creation of a "confederate union" between Kazakhstan and Russia was put forward at a Congress of the Socialist Party of Kazakhstan that took place on March 14, 1992. At a later stage some other Kazakh political groups notably the Peoples'

Congress Party headed by O. Suleimenov, supported the idea of a Russia-Kazakhstan Confederation, although other such groupings of nationalist orientation rejected the idea, fearful of the eventual degradation of such a confederation into a federation and the re-establishment of total Russian control over Kazakh independence and sovereignty.[18] In the winter of 1995, Moscow took a number of steps for the re-integration of the post-Soviet space, in the wake of the crisis in Chechnya and the threat of NATO expansion to the east. It included the signing of a customs and free trade agreement with Belarus and Kazakhstan and the call for an active re-integration policy.

However, under Kozyrev's guidance it was decided that a separate ministry to deal with these newly independent states would not be formed. Since Russia had entered the CIS on the principle of full equality with the other independent states, the creation of separate ministries may suggest that they were being treated as less sovereign than other foreign countries. As a result management of relations with the states was assigned to different directorates of the Foreign Ministry. [19] In the two years with Yeltsin and Kozyrev in charge, Russia is noted to have moved towards "re-gathering" into the CIS the lands of the Russians. Re-integration could mean a *federation*, a *confederation* or a *union of the CIS countries* with the Russian Federation. A course towards re-integration was made into law by a decree of September 1995 and received further impetus with the departure of Kozyrev and the appointment of Yevgeni Primakov. Primakov advocated not only economic but also political and military re-integration of the former Soviet republics. With Primakov's appointment, the CIS headquarters was moved to Moscow. Also the Foreign Affairs Ministry was given a coordinating role in the implementation of Russian foreign policy.

The endorsement of Vladimir Putin by Russian voters is said to have marked a new, dynamic and active phase in the relationship between Russia and Central Asia. It has been noted that Putin's past experience is likely to guide his policies, particularly, his "near abroad" ones. Putin's focus on Central Asia is being pointed as relatively new in the post- Kozyrev period. While under Primakov, a Eurasianist stand did enter post-Soviet Russian policy in the mid 1990s, it was the NATO intervention into the Balkans and its encroachment into the former Soviet bloc that turned Russia's focus to Central Asia. In the Russian assessment of 1999, Moscow viewed Central Asia as the key component of Moscow's economic future. In the year 2000, President Putin spent the weekend of May 19-21, in Ashkabad where he reached an agreement in principle to increase gas purchase from Turkmenistan. Beyond natural gas talks, Russia and Turkmenistan have established an inter-governmental commission for general economic cooperation and agreed to enhance bilateral relations. Russia has also agreed to take over Kazakhstani energy operations from the Belgian company Tractebel. Moscow has also increased its concerns about militancy in the Central Asian region with Putin indicating that the recent fighting in the Central Asian region would be a priority topic at the Yalta CIS summit. [20]

On the other hand, over time, the response of the Central Asian states has varied and an interesting example of this would be the way Russo-Uzbek relations have evolved. In the immediate post-independence days, the requirement for strengthening its security in the south induced Uzbekistan to enter into a military alliance with Russia. However, while collaborating militarily, reservations were expressed about Russia's June 1994 draft mutual security pact for the CIS and also about Russia's proposals for dual citizenship. Uzbekistan also criticized Yeltsin's attempts to centralize the CIS around Moscow. President Karimov made energy independence a priority and laid more than 600 miles of pipelines a year to lessen dependence on Russia. Steps were also initiated to use the natural gas from Bukhara for local needs rather than pipe it to Russia.[21]

It is also significant to note that the projection of Uzbek policy towards Russia has also been modified over the past decade. It is interesting that writing in 1993, President Islam Karimov had begun his foreign policy initiatives by pointing to the importance of the "... development of direct and multilateral relations with the signatories of the CIS" and the "...development and consolidation of equitable relations with Russia and reliance on its potential".[22] By 1997, this priority had been vastly reduced. Here, President Karimov begins by pointing to the significance of participation in the UNO, then the international financial and economic organizations, like the IMF and the World Bank, the European Union, the OSCE, NATO, close cooperation with other international organizations primarily from the Asian region bilateral contacts with the United States of America, relations with other European countries, and finally relations that are shaped between the countries of the former Soviet Union. [23]

President Karimov had also voiced his dissatisfaction about comments regarding revision in the status of the post-Soviet independent states in certain sections of the Russian press. He also criticized the projection of intra-regional integration within the Central Asian states as a possible "threat from the south" for Russia. Karimov has quoted Yeltsin's position that "the restoration of the former Union will turn out to be a tragedy" as correct and noted that equal relations between the CIS states should be the foundation of inter-relations between Russia and Uzbekistan. He notes

> Criticizing the great power chauvinism and aggressive nationalism, we, here in Uzbekistan, stand for the development of qualitatively new relations on the territory of the former Soviet Union and first and foremost with Russia. We have centuries old links of friendship, brotherhood and mutual assistance with that country and its great people.[24]

The Uzbek state declared in February 1999 that it would not renew its membership in the Commonwealth of Independent States Collective Security Treaty. However, it also declared that this would not in any way affect the bilateral arrangements with countries of the CIS. Moscow reacted to this by pointing out that it was the sovereign right of every nation to decide whether it wanted to be a part of any collective treaty. And this was projected as a signal reflecting a more independent stance of politics in the Eurasian region.

However, Putin's support of Karimov's hard line policies has recently led to an increase in Russo-Uzbek relations. President Karimov's hardline anti-militant policies have been endorsed by Putin, who has himself assumed such an approach towards Chechnya.[25] The meeting between Putin and Karimov towards the end of

December 1999 made this clear. Karimov publicly stated that he "recognized Russia's interests in Uzbekistan".[26] However, more recently the Uzbek government has denied having requested for a common security pact with Russia. And Russia on her part has denied that any firm agreement on such an arrangement was reached.

Despite such variations in policy statements it is, perhaps, significant to take note of numerous continuing invisible connections that till date remain significant in an examination of Russo-Central Asian relations. All across the territory of the former Soviet Union, for instance, there is still a single Russian speaking elite which shares a common set of old political ties and connections. This is an objective reality and remains an important factor in cementing relations between segments of the population in Russia and Central Asia. At an informal CIS summit at the Russian resort of Sochi in early August 2001, the Kyrgyz President made the point that the Kyrgyz Constitution would soon be amended to include Russian as an official language. In fact a nuanced reading of the way relations between the two regions will develop would have to take note of this and other such social patterns that are located below the political surface but which nonetheless shape the institutional functioning of a society. Any movement towards a Central Asian regional organization would have to take all of this into account. Recently President Putin described the CIS as a "regional organization".[27] The projection of the CIS as a regional organization and the more active role that Russia intends to play in it calls for a reassessment of the interplay between CIS integration and any regional integration within Central Asia.

Four possible scenarios have been envisaged as far as regional integration in Central Asia is concerned.

1. Regional integration is performed according to the will of the leaders.
2. Regional integration is executed under influence of big partner countries that have more developed market institutions (China, Russia, USA).
3. Development of sub-regional integration. The states become integrated not at once, but in pairs with the help of third forces, under the effect of internal political forces.

4. Break up of relations and disintegration.[28]

While the last one has not actually occurred what is taking place in the region today is possibly a combination of the first three.

Forming *Tsentralnaya Aziia*: Efforts at Regional Cooperation

The basis on which a Central Asian Union could emerge is indicated in this passage by President Karimov:

> As far as integration on the level of the Central Asian countries is concerned, it has its own specific features. This integration has always been and remains to be public in its essence. During all its history the nations of this region shoulder to shoulder struggled against the domination of foreign conquerors. Representatives of these nations had always been guided by the ideas of independence and creation of independent states. These nations have been living on a vast territory called Turkeston during centuries.

First of all it is necessary to note that integration of the nations of Central Asia is not a dream or a project for the future, it is a reality which needs only organizational, legal and political forms.[29]

The collapse of the Soviet empire brought to the forefront the idea of creating a Central Asian regional union. Almost immediately, it was pointed out that the five states that were being brought together were anything but homogeneous. It was also noted that the construction of five separate republics in the course of national territorial delimitation and the identification of five separate groups of people meant that "national" identities could no longer be denied. Interestingly, however, while identities and histories were separated, in economic terms Uzbekistan, Tajikistan, Turkmenistan and Kyrgyzstan were combined into a single economic region and a number of specialized organs were put into place to achieve economic integration.[30] More importantly, infrastructural investments were made to the region as a whole which meant that the region inherited an integrated infrastructure on achieving independence. This imposed a certain level of continuity.

Another element that ensures continuity is the emphasis that the problems of development must first be addressed on a regional level before being taken up on a global level.[31] The linkages that had been established in vital spheres would thus necessarily be maintained in order to ensure that the period of transition is smooth. As President Karimov points out:

> The Republic's economy emerged and developed within the constraints of the former Union. A single transport and power system bound it to other regions by a tightly knit economic network....[32]

This necessarily induced a certain level of enthusiasm about establishing regional economic links and a common economic forum among the Central Asian states. Unfortunately in most cases the economic requirements of the Central Asian states overlap, for instance, oil and gas are the principal items for Kazakhstan, Turkmenistan and also Uzbekistan while cotton is a common item for Uzbekistan, Turkmenistan and Tajikistan. As a result there is very little enthusiasm for integration on an economic level and there is an element of competition rather than complimentarily.

In fact it should be noted that steps towards the creation of a single Central Asian economic space was underway even prior to the disintegration of the Soviet Union when prospects for integration were discussed in the 1990 during a conference in Almaty. In the subsequent years a number of measures were undertaken and agreements were signed to coordinate economic reforms and create multilateral institutions.[33] In addition, even today a differentiation is recognized between the countries of the former Soviet Union and those outside it. For instance there is a difference between taxation of imports and exports to the ruble zone and that outside it. Most exports of key commodities outside the former Soviet Union countries are strictly controlled through export registration and licensing requirements and monopoly on trading rights for certain product lines held by state foreign trade organizations.[34] However, this limited export base proved problematic. Uzbekistan, for instance, has huge reserves of natural gas. The inability to export it to hard currency markets due to unavailability of transport lines may lead to limitation of economic gains. Economic union thus proved difficult to put into practice. Similarly, it was noted that cultural bonds could hardly become the basis of regional union.

Yet despite these predictions a number of measures towards integration were undertaken and a number of agreements were signed. In 1991, an agreement to form an Inter-Republican Council of Central Asian Republics and Kazakhstan was signed. This initiative was never realized, however, due to the disintegration of the Soviet Union and the formation of the Commonwealth of Independent States. In order to accelerate the integration process in Central Asia and fulfil previously achieved agreements, the Presidents of Kazakhstan, Kyrgyzstan and Uzbekistan signed the Treaty on the Formation of Unified Economic Space in 1994. The document laid a firm foundation for economic cooperation based on principles of friendship and neighbourly relations, equal rights and non-interference in domestic affairs, consistent implementation of mutual agreements and generally recognized norms of international law.

On 8 July 1994 in Almaty, the leaders of three countries signed a number of basic documents including the Appeal to the People of the Three Republics, the Memorandum on Migration Agreement, the Agreement on Military and Technological Cooperation, the Agreement on the Informational Support of International Treaties and Agreements, the Agreement on the Foundation of the Central Asian Bank for Cooperation and Development, and other documents providing for vital interests of the three states. At the meeting, the International Council and its administrative body as well as the Executive Committee, were founded as were the Prime Ministers' Council of Member Countries and the Foreign Ministers' and Defence Ministers' Councils. In 1995, the Executive Committee held five leadership meetings, while three meetings of the Prime Ministers' Council were also convened. As a result of these meetings, important steps towards further economic integration was adopted.

The Executive Committee prepares and adopts multilateral and bilateral agreements on trade, fuel, energy supply, and the shared costs of electricity produced at the Naryn power stations. The Committee issued a number of documents facilitating the creation of unified economic space such as the free trade agreement between Kazakhstan and Kyrgyzstan and the protocol approving Kazakhstan's participation in the customs' union of Belarus, Kazakhstan and Russia. A committee composed of representatives of each country's health ministry began implementing the mutual agreements on pharmaceutical production and health protection. At the Executive Committee's initiative the First International Central Asian Forecasting and Statistical methods, Main Trends in the Economic Development of Member Countries Conference was held in Tashkent in July 1995. Leading scientists, economists and the heads of ministries and government institutions participated in the conference. The participants worked out uniform approaches to development forecasting and highlighted the leading trends in industrial integration in the conferences' final document, the Tashkent Declaration.

The Central Asian Regional Cooperation Conference held in Kyrgyzstan in June 1995, formulated cooperative solutions to the areas' political, social, environmental, demographic and economic problems. The Conference resulted in the Issyk-Kul Regional Cooperation Declaration. Kazakhstan, Kyrgyzstan and Uzbekistan have developed the Economic Integration 2000 Programme, which was adopted at the Bishkek meeting of the Council of Prime Ministers. In addition, a Kazakhstan-Uzbekistan Science and Technology programme consisting of 107 projects in 16 fields has been developed. The International council and the Prime Ministers of the member countries have chosen priority projects for financing by the Central Asian Bank for Cooperation and Development. These include electric and gas meter production by the Saiman and Zhanar corporations and electric engine production by Kyrgyzstan Electric Plants. As a whole the integration programme includes important industries related to fuel and energy production, iron and steel, chemicals, machinery, geological prospecting, light manufacturing, communications, construction materials and agriculture. The Uzbekistani-Kyrgyzstani New Technologies Centre has also been founded. The exchange of information and analytical materials and preparation for proposals to exchange data bases and data banks have created a largely unified domain of science, technology and information between these two countries. Discussions were also held on trilateral military cooperation between Kyrgyzstan, Uzbekistan and Kazakhstan. In 1995, Turkmenistan, Tajikistan and Azerbaijan were invited to join. Similarly, political rhetoric reflected a commonness that had resulted out of centuries of existence as one people. Speaking at the inauguration of the Kazakh day in Uzbekistan, President Karimov said that "We are well aware that in the past our states were not divided. We hope that in the future also it will not be so."[35]

Yet, despite this, recent reports note that "integration exists on paper" and that neither Collective Security Arrangements nor economic integrative bodies have been successful.[36] Most writings also note that imperatives for regionalization in order to deal with what are identified as the myriad problems that the states face today cannot, equally, be denied. [37] On 11 October 2000, the Presidents of Kazakhstan, Kyrgyzstan, Tajikistan, Belarus and Armenia met at the Kyrgyz capital Bishkek to sign an agreement on Collective Security to combat aggression and carry out anti-terrorist operations. The absence of Uzbekistan from the Agreement however reduces its effectiveness. Similarly, on 10 October 2000, the Presidents of Kazakhstan, Russia, Belarus, Tajikistan and Kyrgyzstan met in the new Kazakh capital Astana and signed an agreement to set up a new economic body called Eurasian Economic Union. The Eurasian Union aims to harmonize the tax and customs law of the member states, a goal that the customs union had failed to achieve. In fact Kazakhstan has introduced a 200 per cent tariff on imports from Kyrgyzstan.[38]

Another level on which integration has been attempted is through the integration of the Central Asian economy with extra-regional states. The Economic Cooperation Organization has considered the Central Asian region as a sub-system and in 1992 Azerbaijan, Turkmenistan, Uzbekistan, Tajikistan, Kyrgyzstan, Kazakhstan and Afghanistan were incorporated as members. The ECO was organized as a forum for the discussion of regional disputes and peaceful cooperation between the original members (Iran, Pakistan, Turkey) and the newly independent member countries. The ECO's current plans of action underline the need for mobilizing the region's natural and human resource base on a market oriented economy. While there has been a certain amount of expansion of trade among the ECO members, it has been constrained by the limited nature of the agreement on preferential tariffs, the lack of transportation networks in the region as also competition among the member states on a number of issues.[39] It has also been observed that the basic minimum level of economic, cultural and political common ground that is required for the successful working of a regional organization does not exist among the states.[40] Similarly, the Organization of the Caspian Sea States (CASCO) for development of cooperation between the littoral countries of the Caspian Sea (Russia, Iran, Azerbaijan, Kazakhstan, and Turkmenistan) has been faced with similar dilemmas.

It is necessary to take into account that as primary providers of security, regional organization at the Central Asian level may not be workable. It would be unable to convey hard defence guarantees, create joint military units, negotiate arms reductions or enforce the end of overt conflicts. Its impact on security would have to be more oblique and subtle and start with existential significance as groups of states that recognize themselves as sharing some elements of community and can define their national identity as complementary rather than adversarial to their neighbours. Regular meetings and the creation of personal ties encourage *esprit de corps* and may help to defuse crisis. Non traditional security issues like environment, defence against pollution, water management, drug smuggling, organized crime, migration and refugees provide more useful areas for regional discourse.

Similarly, given the economic structures of the states and the fact that they do not sufficiently complement each other the creation of a single economic territory becomes questionable. A number of questions remain unresolved in terms of trade policy. Immediate establishment of a free trade area or a common market may be overly ambitious steps at this juncture. The creation of smaller cooperative ventures may actually be more fruitful. The tangible activities of a regional organization could be focussed on economic development, transnational planning for infrastructure and transport, environmental problems and natural resource management and human contacts especially in the fields of tourism, culture and education.

The Central Asian summit held in Bishkek in June 1999 was a step in this direction. It recommended the adoption of effective measures for creating a free trade zone which would function as a mechanism of the stage by stage formation of a single economic space in the region. The summit emphasized the need to first create conditions for effective multilateral trade and economic cooperation by means of preliminary agreements on measures for regulating bilateral and multilateral relations. This was to be done in particular in the spheres of regional transport and communication, water, fuel, and investment resources, creation of favourable conditions for reciprocal and joint investments, free passage of goods, capital and man power, guarantee of ecological safety and attraction of investments for the member states of the community and further development of production cooperation on the basis of long term programmes for developing the main sectors of economy.

The recently formed Central Asian Battalion composed of forces from Kazakhstan, Kyrgyzstan and Uzbekistan, for increasing and coordinating local peace keeping endeavours is another example in this direction. Similarly, the Eurasian Transport Corridor (Transeca) has increased trade among Kazakhstan, Uzbekistan, Azerbaijan, Georgia and Turkey. The symbolism of keeping borders robust but permeable for trade could be another achievable target. For any such organization to be viable, each government must feel that it has more to gain from such a collective restructuring of the local environment than unbridled power play. Also identification of fields that afford the maximum potential for cooperation would also be useful.

There have also been moves to set up regimes for controlling organized crime, drug trafficking, terrorism and illegal migration and supporting environmental protection. There have for instance been a series of Central Asian summits on water management and the Aral Sea crisis leading to an agreement by which each state pledged 0.3 per cent of its GNP to an environmental fund supporting the resolution. The very fact that the four states have reached an agreement with Moscow for the creation of a common market indicates a new stage in Eurasian union. Not a small part has been played in this process by the eastward extension of the NATO and the increasing influence of the Taliban. However, complexities remain in the process of integration and cooperation. The complexities involved in the process of regional integration is perhaps best demonstrated by the case of water and energy swaps within the region.

Water and Energy Swaps

Until recently, in Central Asia, a unified system of water and energy resources had existed. In the course of the last decade the countries of the region have had to work details for sharing these resources, while keeping their "national interests" in mind. Here the approach of the countries are varied. The upper riparian states, who have control over the water resources in the region, like Kyrgyzstan, prefer the policy of "user pays", whereas lower riparians, like Uzbekistan have put forward the idea of the development of cooperation based on joint regional utilization of water resources.

Uzbekistan's approach of cooperation is based on a number of significant factors. First, all the water management bodies in the upper riparians are built within one large and unified country, i.e., the former Soviet Union. This is not the optimum arrangement for maintenance and operation in these systems by individual countries. Secondly, there is no single and unified system of calculating the price of water and there are no parallels in the world that could be applied in Central Asia. In the international practice of the use of water resources from across borders, payment for the use of water is not involved in a number of cases. Thirdly, the schedule of release of water from the main water reservoirs in the upper riparian is not always rational. For example, an increase in the release of water and power generation during the winter months becomes the cause of water shortage during summer when more water is required for agriculture. Fourthly, joint effective use of water resources in the region, requires the development of an integrated programme of rational water use within the country.[41]

The differences in the two approaches necessitated prolonged negotiations to reach a compromise solution. In March 1998, Kyrgyzstan, Kazakhstan and Uzbekistan had signed an agreement on the joint use of water resources as well as payment of equivalent compensation for water generation losses by countries receiving the water. However, recently there have been conflicts about the amount of water released by Kyrgyzstan for downstream-users Uzbekistan and Kazakhstan. Since independence Kyrgyzstan has been faced with economic problems because of shortage of energy supply which previously used to come from Russia and other republics. In order to make up for this shortfall, it has attempted to take advantage of its abundant water resources. The primacy of energy production over the needs of irrigation in the middle and lower courses of the river has created discord between Uzbekistan and Kyrgyzstan.

Needs for irrigation often do not correspond to needs for maximum utilization for energy use. In summer when demands for irrigation is high, water is sought to be stored in the reservoirs for winter when demands for energy is at a maximum. In the summer of 1993, for instance, Kyrgyzstan retained about 50 per cent of the water allocation granted to Uzbekistan in the Toktogul dam. Since the introduction of the national currency in Kyrgyzstan, Uzbekistan raised the prices of oil and gas for its neighbours. Kyrgyzstan in its turn tried to prevail on Uzbekistan to purchase hydro-energy as a recompense for the usually free amount of water flowing into Uzbekistan. Since Uzbekistan has sufficient fossil fuel resources of its own, it accused Kyrgyzstan of intending to sell water to its neighbours. In the winter of 1993, Kyrgyzstan was accused of dumping too much of water from the Toktogul dam down the Syr Darya. The extra water could not reach the Aral due to freezing of the lower Syr Darya but flowed into the Aydarkul depression. On the other hand Kyrgyzstan has complained of delays in compensation payment.

It has been predicted that Uzbekistan and Kazakhstan, who as downstream states are dependent on Kyrgyzstan and Tajikistan for water, will be faced with problems in order to ensure adequate supplies for the growing season. Earlier in winter Uzbekistan had imposed an embargo on Kyrgyzstan in an attempt to force Bishkek into settling a territorial dispute raised by Tashkent and to exert pressure on Kyrgyzstan to pay off the $ 1.35 million in debts. This hard line practice may end up backfiring for Uzbekistan and implicating the entire region. To compensate for gas shortages, Kyrgyzstan diverted water resources into hydroelectric power and the resulting depletion in the reservoirs has raised the spectre of crop failure. Hot and dry summers, further pose a threat to Uzbekistan's cotton crop and Kazakhstan's rice crop.

This is reflective of a growing tension between upstream and downstream countries who are locked in relationships of mutual dependence. Kyrgyzstan and Tajikistan, the upstream countries possess more water than they need for domestic use and consume more power than they can produce themselves. The downstream states, Kazakhstan, Uzbekistan and Turkmenistan, lack water but have abundant supplies of natural gas and oil. This should have ideally produced mutually beneficial arrangements but has actually given rise to discord. This problem is reflective of a disjunction between physical infrastructure and the desire of the states to foster economic self-sufficiency. Natural resources were, till very recently, centralized.

Having suffered severely during the winter months because of Tashkent's gas cut off, Kyrgyzstan now appears less inclined to honour its irrigation commitments to Uzbekistan. During the energy blockade, Kyrgyz Prime Minister Kurmanbek Baikov, had warned his Uzbek counterpart several times that Uzbekistan's hardline stance on the gas cut off could force a large discharge of water from the Toktogul reservoir, with potential harmful consequences for Uzbek cotton. Since independence, Uzbekistan and Kyrgyzstan have often clashed over water. Uzbekistan, whose irrigation systems are totally dependent on water flows from Tajikistan and Kyrgyzstan has suggested that water resources in the region be dealt with as a "common wealth". However, Kyrgyzstan, like every other newly independent state is now conscious of preserving its natural resources, and has not responded positively.

In the Uzbek-Kyrgyz case, authorities in Bishkek would prefer to utilize the water during the peak periods to satisfy local demands for heat. Meanwhile, Uzbekistan depends on a uniform supply of water for cotton cultivation. To reach an accommodation between the competing uses of water and power the countries have developed an elaborate system of swaps.[42] In the Uzbek-Tajik case also, similarly there exists some tension. Tajikistan has two electricity grids. One in northern Leninabad and the other in the southern part of the country. Tajikistan has only limited natural gas and relies heavily on Turkmenistan and Uzbekistan for supplies. Tajikistan and Uzbekistan have been exchanging gas and electricity under terms of a barter arrangement that also sets a monetary value for the use of rail transport. The irony of the Tajik position is that it is a leader in world per capita production of hydropower and yet it must purchase electricity at international prices. Tajik officials are working to alter existing arrangements. Officials of the state-owned electricity corporation Barqi Tajik are seeking developmental funds to bring into production the Sangtuda station, the fourth dam on the Vakhsh cascade.

The General Director of *Kyrgyzenergo*, Bakirdin Sartkaziev, has revealed that Kyrgyzstan is only willing to provide 750 million cubic meters of water instead of the agreed 2.3 billion cubic meters.[43] Kazakhstan which is also dependent on Kyrgyz reservoirs has taken steps to avert a shortfall. Both the Kazakh and Kyrgyz authorities have signed a protocol under which Kazakh side agreed to settle a $ 21.5 million debt in order to facilitate negotiations on water supply. Kazakhstan has also promised to supply Kyrgyzstan with fuel and coal.

However, despite the problems with implementing the Bishkek Agreement a number of positive factors are evident. One of these is the functioning of the United Energy System of Central Asia (UESCA) which has ensured parallel functioning of the energy system that had been created as one single system. With the transition of the energy sector to a market economy the issue of parallel functioning of the UESCA with the energy system of Northern Kazakhstan and the united energy system of Russia has become crucial once again. Such approaches in coordination with national programmes of rational water use would increase the efficiency of hydrotechnical facilities of the upstream countries as well as provide for agreed irrigation schedules, coordination of decisions on water releases, power generation and transfers and compensation of energy losses on an equivalent basis.

In August 2001, this was achieved when the Central Asian states signed a treaty forming a regional energy grid.[44] The system derives its strength from the fact that it not only combines the national grids in Kazakhstan, Kyrgyzstan, Tajikistan, Turkmenistan and Uzbekistan but also links with an energy network across Eurasia through Kazakhstan's connection with Russia's Unified Energy System. This new system will use public tradeable prices. Energy ministers have pledged to account for power costs as a function of supply and demand rather than political priorities. Each system carries a monetary value, which changes with demand for power and available resources. This would allow a more efficient production and distribution of power throughout the region.

A unified grid should foster efficient trading among the five states. In June just prior to the treaty signing Kyrgyzstan, Kazakhstan and Uzbekistan agreed to settle their inter-state energy accounts through commodity swaps rather than cash payments. Under the agreement, in the year ahead, Kyrgyzstan will supply Kazakhstan and Uzbekistan with electricity. Uzbekistan will repay the debt with natural gas, fuel, turbine and transformer lubricants and fuel; Kazakhstan will provide coal and fuel oil. While this will ensure a more efficient system of distribution of energy, the other equally scarce resource, water, is not a part of the agreement.

Conclusions

It is generally accepted that the purpose for any regional organization is two fold—the acceleration of economic development and the reinforcement of regional stability. Evaluated on these two criteria it may well be said that regional integration in the Central Asian region has, till date, not proved to be very successful. It is equally undeniable that compared to the more successful of regional efforts, a great deal remains to be achieved. However, before any evaluation of these efforts it is crucial to keep in mind that ten years is insufficient to judge the failure or success of any such regional endeavour. Also in a number of indirect ways both development and stability have been contributed to by regional processes. Representative of this are the numerous agreements that have been made regarding environmental degradation. This is a case that in the Central Asian region could lead to regional instability and also affect economic development. Many analysts have argued that the fact that environmental degradation can lead to serious conflict is doubtful and that it is difficult to identify specific links between environmental problems and major threats to security.[45] Skeptics include those who are concerned with more "traditional" issues like territorial disputes and balance of power as threatening to regional security. In the Central Asian region, for instance, problems associated with "nation-building" in the background of artificially drawn borders and the existence of numerous ethnic groups within each of the states, has been identified by analysts as the focus of future flashpoints. What is largely ignored in the course of such analysis is that environmental problems are rapidly reaching a stage where they will threaten regional security. Threats to stability posed by disputes over pollution, food, water and energy resources bring to the forefront questions about the extent to which environmental issues shape the security agenda.

This is particularly so since the ecological crisis in the Central Asian region overlays and aggravates a structural, economic and social crisis. Central Asia is a developing region, characterized by a high share in agricultural production, low industrialization, mass unemployment and a high population growth. With the standard of living considerably below the Soviet average it was very dependent on the subsidies from the centre. The disintegration of the Soviet Union meant the beginning of a new process of nation-building in the region and the redefinition of political and cultural identities. It also saw the emergence of a new international water basin, the Aral, with all consequent consequences for the political, ethnic and economic relations between the states. The entire political geography changed and once shared natural resources that were controlled by central directions became the "national wealth" of the newly independent states. Rivers became national borders and the division into up and down stream riparians became politically relevant.

While it is accepted that environmental issues are unlikely to be the primary cause of conflict, it is also argued that they play a complex role in shaping relations among states. And here the success of regional cooperation in the Central Asian region cannot be denied. While skepticism continues about the prospects of regionalism in Central Asia one should not lose sight of such initiatives which could develop as alternative mechanisms for integration in the region.

REFERENCES

1. Islam Karimov, (1997), *Uzbekistan on the Threshold of the Twenty-First Century: Threats to security, Conditions of Stability and Guarantees for Progress*, Tashkent, p. 275.
2. Martha Brill Olcott, "The Myth ofTsentralnaia Aziia", *Orbis*, Fall 1994, pp. 549-565. Similar ideas were expressed by others who pointed to economic, political and social reasons of discord. See for instance, Anatoly Khazanov, *After the USSR: Ethnicity, Nationalism and Politics in the Commonwealth of Independent States*, London: The University of Wisconsin Press, 1995.
3. *Ibid*, p. 554.
4. See for instance Paul Kubicek, (1997), "Regionalism, Nationalism and Realpolitik in Central Asia", *Europe-Asia Studies*, Vol. 49, No. 4.
5. See R Stubbs and G Underhill (eds) , (1994), *Political Economy and the Changing Global Order*, London: Macmillan.
6. For a detailed discussion on definitions, see Andre Gunder Frank, (1992), *The Centrality of Central Asia* .
7. Olcott, *op. cit.*
8. For a detailed discussion on the construction of a region see Ranabir Samaddar, (1996), *Whose Asia Is It Anyway: Region and the Nation in South Asia*, Calcutta: Pearl Publishers for Maulana Abul Kalam Azad Institute of Asian Studies.
9. Karimov, 1997, *op. cit.*
10. Karimov, 1997, *op. cit.*
11. For details of the relative homogeneity of the Central Asian economic region see Heribert Dieter, 1996, "Regional Integration in Central Asia: Current Economic Position and Prospects", *Central Asian Survey*, Vol. 15, No. 3/4.
12. The CIS states have been divided into three broad groups according to

their level of enthusiasm for cooperation. For details see Devendra Kaushik, "Regionalization as a Peace Instrument: Central Asia", in Ranabir Samaddar and Helmut Reifeld (eds) *Peace As Process: Reconciliation and Conflict Resolution in South Asia*, New Delhi: Manohar, 2001.

13. Brian White, Richard Little and Michael Smith (eds) *Issues in World Politics*, London: Macmillan, 1997.
14. Serik Primbetov, (1996), "Central Asia: Prospects for Regional Integration", in Bartlomiej Kaminski (ed) *Economic Transition in Russia and the New States of Eurasia*, Armonk and London: M. E. Sharpe, p. 167.
15. See Ian Bremmer and Alyson Bailes, (1998), "Sub-Regionalism in the Newly Independent States", *International Affairs*, January, Vol. 74, No. 1, for a detailed discussion.
16. For details on why the Central Asian leaders decided to join the CIS see, Bakhtior A. Islamov," Post Soviet Central Asia and the Commonwealth of Independent States", in Beatrice Manz (ed) *Central Asia in Historical Perspective*, Westview Press: Boulder, 1994. Here it is pointed out that the primary reason for this was economic and the result of the administrative command integration set up in the Soviet period.
17. *See Nezavisimaya Gazeta*, 13 May, 1993.
18. *See Argumenty and Fakty*, 26 June, 1993.
19. Sergei Gretsky, (1997), *Russia's Policy Towards Central Asia*, Washington D.C.: Carnegie Moscow Centre.
20. "Russia Frets Over Islamic Militants", *Asia Times Online*, August 29, 2000.
21. For details see, S. Frederick Starr, "Making Eurasia Stable", *Foreign Affairs*, January/February Vol. 75, No. 1, 1996.
22. I.A. Karimov, (1993), *Uzbekistan: The Road of Independence and Progress*, Published in New Delhi, India for the Publishing House of Uzbekistan.
23. Karimov, 1997, *op. cit.*
24. *Ibid.*
25. Birgit Brauer, "Central Asia Readjusting to Life in Putin's Orbit", *Central Asia and Caucasus Analyst*, March 29, 2000; also see Sophie Lambroschini, "Central Asia: Russia Sanctioning Anti-Islamic Crackdown" RFE/RL Report, Moscow, 2 August, 2000.
26. See Robert M. Cutler, (2000), "Russia Slouches Towards Central Asia" *Central Asia and Caucasus Analyst*, April 12.
27. *NIS Observer*, Vol. VI, No. 13, August 2001.

28. *Vecherni Bishkek*, March 15, 2001.
29. Karimov, 1997, *op. cit.*
30. For details see Boris Rumer, (1996), *Central Asia in Transition: Dilemmas of Political and Economic Development*, Armonk and London: M.E. Sharpe.
31. G. Karimova, (1995), *Politico Aakonomichyeskoiye Reforme v Uzbekistane, Realii i Perspektivi*, Tashkent: "Uzbekiston".
32. Karimov, 1993, *op. cit.*
33. For details including the joining of the states with the ECO, creation of the Central Asian economic cooperation area in 1993, common economic space between Kazakhstan and Kyrgyzstan in 1994, single economic space between Kazakhstan and Uzbekistan in 1994, see Kaushik, *op. cit.*
34. See *Studies of Economies in Transition: Statistical Handbook 1996; States of the Former USSR*, Washington D.C., World Bank, 1996, pp 522-523 where the difference in the volume of trade between the CIS countries and others is clearly evident from the geographical distribution of foreign trade.
35. Islam Karimov, "Yedinstvo, Proshlovo i Budusheyevo", Rech na Torzhestvennom Otkritii Dnei Kazakhstana v Uzbekistane, 23 may, 1994, *in Turkestan Nash Obshii* Dom, Tashkent: Uzbekiston, 1995. Similar ideas are found in "Solnitse Drushbe Nashei Svetit iz Glubin Tesyacheletii", *Rech na Torzheshtvennom Otkritii Dnei Uzbekistana v kazakhstane*, 20 May 1995, in *Turkestan Nash Obshii Dom.*
36. Sergei Blagov, (2000), "Mostly Integration Exists on Paper", *IPS*, October 13.
37. Kaushik, *op. cit.*
38. Blagov, *op. cit.*
39. For details of this regional initiative and the drawbacks of the organization see Erhan Buyukakinci, (2000), "Patterns of Integration in Central Asia", *Perceptions*, March-May, Vol. V No. I.
40. Dieter, *op. cit.*
41. Yulia Petrenko, "Water and Energy Security in Central Asia", in Jasjit Singh (ed) *Peace and Security in Central Asia*, Occasional Paper Series, New Delhi:Institute of Defence Studies and Analysis, September 2000.
42. Gregory Gleason, "Upstream-Downstream: The Difficulties of Central Asia's Water and Energy Swaps", *Eurasianet*,
43. Arslan Koichiev, "Water Games Could Leave Central Asia High and Dry this Summer", *Eurasianet.*

44. Gregory Gleason, (2001), "Mixing Oil and Water: Central Asia's Emerging Energy Market", *Eurasianet,* August 27.
45. Daniel Deudney, (1990) "The Case Against Linking Environmental Degradation and National Security", *Millennium: Journal of International Studies*, Vol. 19, No. 1.

16

Economic Integration in Central Asia

Problems and Prospects

LEILA MUZAPAROVA

Kazakhstan as well as other newly independent states of Central Asia have only two options for their future formation in the contemporary conditions:

(*i*) To decide independently the tasks of socio-economic development by relying exclusively on themselves. In this regard, they constantly appear to be under the influence of stronger neighbouring states (which is obviously an unsuccessful option).

(*ii*) To develop mutually advantageous ties with neighbouring states and make joint efforts to strengthen their national economies.

A whole range of urgent economic problems, which cannot be decided by the countries of Central Asia separately, nowadays underlines the need for integration. Increasing globalization and internationalization of economies as well as deepening international division of labour make traditional style of support to free competition by one particular country ineffective. Not a single country today can resist rigid competition in the world market alone. This has led to a search for new forms of international interaction, which could pave the way for sustainable development of each country within the system of world economy. One such form is an integration of countries into various kinds of inter-state unions, including large scale regional economic complexes with common territory, devices of management, financial system, economy, citizenship and foreign policy.

At the same time, regional economic integration is not only a way of protection from global competition but also protection against economic expansion supported by globalization. It is a way of maintenance of sustainable and independent development of each country. In general, globalization and integration are objective and inter-connected processes which will define global economic development in the coming decades. Thus, if regional economic integration for the leading developed states is a way of bringing together and uniting their efforts with the aim of preserving imposed order in the world economy, then regional integration for developing countries is actually the only opportunity to resist the negative consequences of globalization and the dominance of developed countries.

Regional integration is, therefore, the only way out for the newly independent states of Central Asia, whose economies were structured within the powerful uniform economic complex of the former USSR, to find their worthy place in the world economic community. The economic integration of Central Asian states is an objective and a natural process conditioned by the national interests of the countries of the region. In many respects, the necessity of economic integration in the region is based on deep-rooted interdependence and mutual economic benefit of the countries of the region. Besides, the integration process gets major importance nowadays for the maintenance of both the regional and national security of Central Asian states.

Economic Integration of Central Asian Countries: Basic Directions

Economic cooperation in the region is possible in the following basic spheres: (*a*) utilization of rich natural resources of the region as well as energy and water usage; (*b*) transport, communications and construction of gas and oil pipelines; (*c*) industrial cooperation and development of a network of joint ventures on the basis of an inter-state division of labour; and (*d*) in the ecological sphere as all Central Asian countries are interested today in solving common ecological problems.

However, in order to achieve positive economic integration in the region it is necessary to concentrate all efforts on the priority directions. Following can be four such directions:

Rational Use of Water and Power Resources

Cooperation in this priority direction is explained by the fact that the Central Asian states are connected by common river pools of Syr Darya and Amu Darya, uniform ecological system and common gas pipelines (Gazli-Bukhara-Tashkent-Chymkent-Almaty).

In the hydro-economic sphere of the region today there are following problems: (*a*) general deficiency in water resources; (*b*) absence of uniform legal base; (*c*) frequent ignorance of interests of the neighbouring countries; (*d*) infringement of available principles of water distribution from trans-border rivers; and (*e*) default in compensatory deliveries (i.e., compensation to Kyrgyzstan for water taken from Toktaghul reservoir was made through supply of heating and power resources in the winter). All these problems can be solved by having political will on the part of Central Asian states, and that too through constructive negotiations. It is important not to turn water into the instrument of political and economic pressure. It is also necessary to give water the status of a common wealth so that it could become a uniting force. The interaction between the regional states in this direction should be carried out by pursuing standard principles such as respect for sovereignty, equal partnership, accountability in the national interests and diligent fulfilment of mutual obligations.

The main tasks to be accomplished with efforts by all countries of the region include (*a*) development of a new strategy for rational use of water resources, and (*b*) defining principles for exploitation of inter-state water bodies located in the territory of neighbouring states. With the aim of more effective utilisation of water and power resources in the region it is also necessary to develop a joint strategy for Kazakhstan, Kyrgyzstan, Uzbekistan and Tajikistan. A large hope in realization of common water and power policy of Central Asian countries is also connected with the Inter-state Water & Power Consortium.

Beginning of Trade-Economic Cooperation

Today, there are a plenty of barriers in carrying out of mutual trade relations between the countries of the region. As a result, smuggling has prospered causing direct damage to the economies of the region. An analysis of dynamics of trade among the Central Asian countries in the last few years shows that the overall volume of mutual trade tends to decrease despite some revival in particular years. For instance, the trade between Kazakhstan and Uzbekistan in the year 2000 declined by almost two times in comparison with the 1995 figure (from 422 to 212 million US dollars). The trade between Kyrgyzstan and Kazakhstan also decreased by more than two times in 2000 in comparison with the 1996 figure (from 202 to 90 million US dollars).

Such a situation has developed not because the states have nothing to trade among themselves but, on the contrary, Central Asian economies have problems in many ways. The reduction in trade evidently points to the existence of unsolved problems in this sphere. These problems can also be solved by taking into account interests of the parties concerned. Moreover, following measures can be adopted to sort out problems in the sphere of trade-economic cooperation: (*a*) harmonization of customs and tax laws in volume is necessary for effective functioning of a free trade regime; (*b*) unification of customs rules and procedures, and (*c*) prevention of unilateral action to restrict the import of goods from the countries of Central Asia.

Cooperation in Transport and Communication Sphere

Today, due to numerous customs taxes, insurance payments and other payments the transit of oversized transport across the region has become very expensive. Therefore, in transport and communication sphere a favourable legal, economic and organizational condition has a vital importance for transportation of cargo and passengers by transit through the territories of the states of the region. The efficiency of economic integration in the region depends on decisions taken in this direction. Besides, Central Asian countries must (*a*) pull together to have a legal base in the field of transport; and (*b*) coordinate and carry out uniform tariff policy on all types of transport and transportation of cargo and passengers.

If we achieve certain results on the above three mentioned directions required for economic integration, it is possible to shift to the next level of cooperation, i.e., investment cooperation.

Strengthening of Industrial Cooperation and Development of Economic Ties

Realization of this direction needs to have (*a*) rapprochement of national legislations which regulate an economic activity; (*b*) maintenance of uniform organizational/economic activities of companies and enterprises in the regional states; (*c*) realization of coordinated policies in the field of specialization of industrial manufacturing; (*d*) support of highly effective manufactures who represent interest of the states in the region; (*e*) development of scientific/technical and industrial cooperation at the level of enterprises; and (*f*) formation of joint programs and investment projects on a number of the inter-connected directions.

On the whole, economic integration in Central Asia calls for a step by step movement from a free trade zone to a common market of goods, services and capitals. Customs union and currency union have significant roles to play. Besides, economic integration in the region will also be promoted by rapprochement of the national legislation and normative acts, maintenance of harmonization of the customs legislation and other measures.

Regional Integration in Central Asia

Ten years of independent development after the disintegration of the former USSR witnessed the creation of many regional and inter-state organizations such as the CIS, the Central Asian Economic Community, the Customs Union, and many others.

Being a pragmatic leader the President of Kazakhstan Nazarbaev appeared among few politicians who offered to keep the existing economic connection to achieve maximum benefit and to use industrial potential rationally in order to promote contacts with the people occupying the sixth part of the planet. It is to be remembered that establishment of the CIS in Almaty, or ideas of formation of the Eurasian Union, the Customs Union, Central Asian Economic Community, Shanghai Cooperation Organisation are the results of his pragmatic approach. All these initiatives show the adherence of Kazakh leader to the development of integration process in the Eurasian space.

Among these organizations, the Eurasian Economic Community (EAEC) officially came into existence in April 2001 which was formed on the basis of the Customs Union incorporating Kazakhstan, Kyrgyzstan, Russia, Belarus and Tajikistan. In the opinion of many Kazakh politicians, the EAEC is the most advanced model of economic community in the CIS region today. This organization, which united the countries having population over 180 millions people apart from extensive territory, rich natural resources and advanced industrial infrastructure, has a real chance to become the self-sufficient partner in the world market. To achieve this purpose, the community has the status of an international organization with precise structure and mechanism of performance of accepted decisions (that was not the case with the Customs Union). It is important to note that the EAEC countries are obliged to ensure continuity in agreements concluded earlier. The uniform economic space of the Customs Union was created in 2000. At that moment, interaction in legal and cultural/educational spheres was also extended. It, therefore, became possible to simplify some customs procedures in order to coordinate the uniform approaches of the ministries concerned to take decisions on financial and economic matters particularly in transport and power sectors. Cancellation of several customs duties and restrictions paved the way for an increase in trade between Kazakhstan and its partners, which recorded a 44 per cent increase in 1995. This indicator further grew annually, except during the crisis period of 1999. For example, in 1996 it exceeded the previous parameter to register a growth of 82 per cent, in 1997—53 per cent, in 1998—24 per cent, and in 2000—57 per cent.

What are the distinctive features of the EAEC? First of all, all countries of the EAEC believe that at the first stage of preparation of documents of the organization they will not delegate the powers to supra-national structures, thus ensuring their independence and sovereignty. However, in the process of consolidation of community the preconditions for transition from inter-state to supra-national bodies like the European Union will be created. The organizational/legal form outlined at this moment allows negotiations for entry into the World Trade Organization by a uniform team on acceptable terms so as to protect their interests in the world markets.

Another distinctive feature of the EAEC is the system of accepting decisions by vote. The countries will vote and finance the activities of the Integration Committee, in accordance with their economic potential. The payment by Kazakhstan to the community budget is 20 per cent. For other states the payments have been distributed as follows: Russian Federation—40 per cent, Belarus—20 per cent, Kyrgyzstan and Tajikistan each—10 per cent. The acceptance of decision needs a majority of 2/3 votes that brings to an end the monopoly of one state. However, to ensure a balance of interests in the supreme body of the EAEC (the Inter state Council, which takes place annually with participation of the leaders of member states and twice a year with participation of the Prime Ministers) each country has one vote and the decisions are accepted by consensus.

Besides, the EAEC differs from other regional organizations in terms of concrete purposes and their achievement. At present a strategy has been planned for the development of EAEC till 2015. The uniform methodology of foreign trade of the member countries will come into force in the next two years. During the same period rules for both the procedures of customs registration and customs control of the goods and vehicles imported and exported from one country of the EAEC to another will also be unified.

By early 2004, EAEC is supposed to proceed to the coordinated system of measures ensuring economic security of the member countries. By 2005 the general approaches to the coordinated boundary policy will be introduced and multilateral boundary cooperation will be advanced. While by 2006 it is planned to finish arrangement for license units on external borders, by 2010 task for coordinated protection of external borders of the EAEC countries will be completed. Further. By 2010 it is also planned to create a uniform control system of customs services and to cancel the customs control on borders between the EAEC states. By 2015 the uniform control system of boundary services for the member states will also be created.

The Integration Committee and Commissions of the constant representatives were generated at the first session of the EAEC Inter-state Council held on September 14, 2001, in Almaty. Grigory Rapota, former first Vice-Minister of Industry and New Technologies of Russian Federation was elected as the first General Secretary of the EAEC. Besides, the structure of Secretariat of the EAEC Integration Committee was formalised along with the approval of the budget of the community for 2002. As a whole, it seems that the coordinated action of all five member countries of the EAEC is going ahead towards real economic integration in the region.

Another regional organization having good scope of real economic integration is the Shanghai Cooperation Organization (SCO), which is considered today as one of the most effective regional organizations on security and cooperation in the world. In June 2001, "the Shanghai Five", which was initially aimed at combating terrorism and extremism, has undergone serious transformation. It is more so not only because of joining of Uzbekistan, but also because the leaders agreed to expand their interaction in military, political and economic areas.

The concrete mechanisms and directions of economic cooperation were discussed at the first meeting of the Prime Ministers of the SCO countries, which was held in September 2001 in Almaty. During this meeting areas of future interaction were identified as transport infrastructure and telecommunications, fuel and energy sector, agriculture, tourism, bank sphere, water and nature protection area.

The Memorandum of Understanding on basic purposes and directions towards regional economic cooperation and beginning of process on creating favourable conditions in the field of trade and investments was signed at the first session. This memorandum became the basis for development of long-term program on economic cooperation. The basic objectives of development of the SCO include, overall development of economies, assistance to development of joint enterprises and trade-economic activity, harmonization of national legislations regulating trade activities, etc. The creation of the Shanghai Cooperation Organization takes the relations between the countries of the region on a new height and simultaneously strengthens security and stability in the region and the world over.

The deepening of integration process and expansion of regional cooperation in Central Asia will promote not only socio-economic ties of the countries of the region to make a joint entry to the world market, but also create conditions for security, stability and sustainable development of the region.

17

USA—Caspian-Central Asian Region

New Realities

LAURA YEREKESHEVA

Caspian-Central Asian region is a sphere of interest for different powers—USA, Russia, China, EC and India. It is mainly due to its geographical location that the region serves as a convenient communication outlet along the "west-east" and "north-south", routes. There are other reasons as well, such as availability of energy resources to meet the increasing world-wide demand, besides being a strategically important region especially when a war against international terrorism is being conducted by the coalition of different countries. In the light of such realities there are several factors which are turning the region into a very attractive place for mighty powers, mainly USA.

Security Factor

This factor has recently gained a new ground for the US. Within the framework of the declared war against terrorism the Caspian-Central Asian region is of great importance due to having common borders with Afghanistan. This implies the concentration of resources (human, humanitarian, military) therein, conducting anti-terrorism war including intelligence activity from outside Afghanistan. The US considers the region as a deterrent buffer in the fight against the spread of radical ideas—both of religious and political character.

However, in the new realities one could trace some changes in the priorities in the US policy towards this region. In the middle and even end of the 1990s, the main US interest concentrated upon filling the gap of the geopolitical vacuum, by trying to loosen the ties between the countries of the region and their powerful neighbours—Russia, China and partially Iran—through various means including the tools of economic pressure.

But nowadays in cooperation with the countries of the region the US is trying to tackle one of their most priority tasks—fight against international terrorism. Along with it the necessity of developing energy resources potential of the region, for their maximum use mainly in Kazakhstan and Azerbaijan, the US considers the entire region as a rear backyard, which means that the present and future US policy is characterized by the high degree of pragmatism both in political as well as economic fields.

This postulate becomes apparent today, particularly due to the fact that after the decision made by one of the Central Asian states, Uzbekistani to provide its air corridor and military base at Khanagat near Tashkent to American troops (about 2,000 soldiers),[1] the US has stopped criticizing the policy of Uzbek leadership with regard to the democratic development and human rights situation in that country.

Another example of the new policy line of Washington is the decision of the Bush administration to lift its Article 907 of the Freedom Support Act adopted earlier against Azerbaijan (at least to suspend it till 31 January 2002). The step to lift this ban undertaken by the White House administration came as need was felt to combat effectively international terrorism and radical religious fundamentalism. Moreover, it is noteworthy that along with this decision the US administration also took another important and counterbalancing step of increasing the scales of the military-technical assistance to Armenia by allocating a supplementary amount of 4.6

billion dollars. This step could also be considered at the same time as Washington's answer to Moscow as the latter was striving for strengthening its own influence in the Caucasus region (it is known that for the past one and half years there was intensive cooperation, including in the military sphere, between Russia and Armenia).

Economic Factor

On 17 May 2001, the White House administration unveiled its report on National Energy Policy highlighting the situation in energy sector and main trends of its development. The report, in particular, stated that the biggest hydrocarbon consumer of the world was the United States, followed by China at the second place and India at the sixth place. Obviously, this situation shows the importance of discovering other regions having energy resources, which are not connected with Persian Gulf or South America.

According to the US Energy Information Administration, the demand of the developing Asian countries would increase by 129 per cent over the next 20 years.[2] Moreover, recent trend shows that the biggest consumers are expected to be India and China. If we take into account the existence of large oil and gas reserves in the Caspian region, the possibility of shifting to gas consumption by Asian economies (but not necessarily restricted by it) and the fact that the proven and potential gas resources in this region alone form 2/3rd of all gas resources in the world, it becomes clear that several countries may show their unfeigned interest towards the region.

On the question of developing energy resources potential of the region, the USA follows their traditional line, i.e., to carry out oil and gas production by American companies without any hindrance and at the same time to deter attempts by Russia and Iran to strengthen their economic influence in Kazakhstan, Turkmenistan and Azerbaijan. Such policy has become vividly apparent particularly with the US lobbying for the hydrocarbon routes to be built outside Russia and Iran.

However, nowadays, Washington will have to take into account the objective factors as well. Due to their increasing oil and gas consumption, India and China may pose a challenge to US energy security, besides becoming main competitors in the region's market. Taking into account the already existing competition with Russia and Iran (the sanctions against Iran annually cost the American exchequer $ 15-19 billion), it seems that in future the countries of the region will be brought under the influence of Washington diplomacy particularly during the process of choosing the most beneficial transport routes for USA. This could imply the development of negotiation process with Russia and Iran (which is not surprising due to the character of relations under the current war against terrorism) and a possibility of the intensification of the dialogue with each of the countries separately.

Geopolitical Factor

It seems that among the powers showing their interest in the region, USA, China and India will pursue an active policy. Taking into consideration the role of littoral states—Russia and Iran—in the Caspian-Central Asian region, it can be presumed that there may be possible collisions among various countries around the region due to their competing geopolitical interests.

For China and India it is mainly due to their increasing demand for energy resources and also due to the relative closeness of their borders to the region. Being close to the borders would make the cooperation more effective and low cost (although China as a border state considers the region as a sphere of its national interest). As far as USA is concerned, this factor is connected with the necessity of strengthening the geopolitical presence as one of the means to tackle its own problems in the region that emerge due to its common borders with Russia, Iran, China, Afghanistan and South Asia. It is known that American interest in this part of the world developed largely due to concerns for their defence and so US is pursuing its foreign policy interests effectively in this region. The vivid sample of such policy is Baku-Ceiyhan route which was chosen as a most representative and defined route not in terms of economic but mainly due to political expediency.

It is important for the USA to concentrate its sphere of their interest on the Caspian hydrocarbon reserves; firstly, in the landlocked states of Azerbaijan, Kazakhstan and Turkmenistan. Which would help counter the influence of littoral states. The spread of American influence in the Central Asian states is very important considering the ties between these regional states and Russia, although these ties have not been openly expressed. Besides, the Caspian resources are important for USA also because of the possibility of future oil and gas transportation along the so called 'Asian route' to India and China, whose rapidly developing economies could compete with the American one within ten to fifteen years.

The transportation routes to China could be extended from western Kazakhstan to India through two possible ways: (*a*) from Turkmenistan via Afghanistan and Pakistan; and (*b*) from Iran via Pakistan or bypassing Pakistan, through the deep water pipeline or importing liquified natural gas (LNG) by tankers. The Indo-Iranian relations are now on the high level of strategic partnership which influences the US administration policy. In early 2001, the US policy still continued to follow the policy of sanctions towards Iran according to the 1995 Iran-Libya Sanctions Act. For USA the so-called "Asian route" could also mean more dependence of such countries as Kazakhstan and Turkmenistan on the policy of consumer countries of Asia. Besides, bearing in mind the Russian tendency of strengthening its position in the region and also growing Russian-Iranian cooperation, all these factors could imply certain "geopolitical loss" for Washington. The Caspian energy resources are vital for Washington, more so because of the political instability and explosiveness of the Middle East region in terms of war against terrorism and the more rapid division along the lines of "Islam– west, personified by USA".

In conclusion it can be said that today the economic and security factors have become more inter-dependent. One of the methods of lessening tension and possible negative consequences of war against terrorism can be economic and political integration of the Central Asian countries. Referring to history one could see the crucial role played by the post-war Germany by involving itself into the orbit of regional and European cooperation within the Marshall Plan scheme. Such involvement allowed Germany to decrease the threats of the post-war negative rehabilitation. This postulate stresses the importance and necessity of the regional integration factor in Central Asia as an inevitable factor for maintaining security in the region as well as in the surrounding countries. That is why it seems that USA having been objectively interested in strengthening regional stability and security particularly in those countries that share border with Afghanistan, will now no more stand up against this factor (every attempt of regional cooperation till now has been considered by Washington as being pro-Russian), and may also use it conceptually or partially while conducting its middle-term foreign policy in the Caspian-Central Asian region.

REFERENCES

1. *The Economist*, (2001), October 27–November 2, p. 62.
2. Hill, F., Spector, R., (2001), The Caspian Basin and Asian Energy Markets, In: *Brookings Institution Conference Report # 8,* September, p. 1.

18

Caspian Region
The Unending Conflicts

R.G. GIDADHUBLI

Caspian is an inland sea without any great maritime significance. Yet it has become a scene of international conflict in the post-Soviet era. It will be worthwhile to understand as to what are the sources of conflict, how serious are the conflicts and what are the prospects of the solution of the conflicts. These are some of the questions and issues that need to be addressed. An effort has been made in this paper to examine these and related issues.

Source of Conflict

The main source of conflict in Caspian is the energy resource namely, oil and natural gas. Oil is the essential energy requirement in the world, which is scarce and is considered as liquid gold. Hence those countries which possess this resource have an important role to play in the world economy. The Caspian region (comprising the Caspian sea and immediate surrounding territory) is rich in oil and natural gas. In a detailed study conducted in 1997-98, Rajan Menon has opined that the Caspian region has total reserves of 180-200 bln. barrels of oil (comprising proven reserves of 17-30 bln. barrels and possible reserves of 152 bln.) and about 328 trillion cubic feet of natural gas. While it was well known even in the past that this region had oil resources and that during the Soviet era oil and gas was extracted, since the Soviet break-up in 1992 there has been a great euphoria about energy resources of this region. It was contended by some analysts that the energy resources of Caspian would rival those of the Middle East. Turkmenistan was called 'Kuwait of the 21st Century'. With this hype several international oil giants entered the scene with vigorous exploratory activities. But in several cases actual situation did not correspond to the expectations. Even as efforts are going on, as per the estimate made in 2000 by the Energy Information Administration of the USA, the Caspian region has about 270 bln. barrels of oil comprising 35 bln. barrel of proven and 235 bln. barrel of potential oil resources. This is a much higher estimate than the earlier estimates. Thus whether or not reserves in the Caspian region will equal those in the Gulf, there is no doubt that it is one of the major energy zones of the world.

The Caspian sea, which is about 700 miles long, contains six separate hydrocarbon basins, and most of the oil and gas reserves in the Caspian sea region have not been developed yet. Although the littoral states of the Caspian sea already are major energy producers, many areas of the sea and the surrounding area remain unexplored.

What has added to the conflict in the Caspian region is the fact that while before the Soviet break-up the Caspian sea was shared by only two countries namely the USSR and Iran, after the disintegration three more countries have been added. They are—Azerbaijan, Kazakhstan and Turkmenistan. Thus energy resource is to be shared not by two but by five countries. This increase in the number of littoral states of the Caspian sea is adding a new dimension to the conflict. What is important to note here is that the new sovereign and independent littoral states of Caspian do not want to be bound by the agreements entered into by the former USSR and Iran in the past on the question of sharing the resources of the sea.

Resource Potentialities

Even as it is known that the Caspian sea is rich in energy resources, there are several specific aspects of resource potentialities which deserve consideration. It is important to note that energy resources are unevenly distributed among the five states which share the Caspian sea. Table 1 gives an idea about the countrywise distribution of oil resources in the Caspian Region.

Table 1: Oil Resources of the Caspian Region (billion barrels)

Country	*Proved resources*	*Potential resources*	*Total resources*
Azerbaijan	12.5	32	45
Iran	0.1	15	15
Kazakhstan	17.6	92	110
Russia	2.7	14	17
Turkmenistan	1.7	80	82
Uzbekistan	0.3	2	2
Total	34.9	235	270

Source: Energy Information Administration of the USA.

From the above data available at present it appears that so far as oil is concerned about 88 per cent of total reserves are located in three states namely, Azerbaijan, Kazakhstan and Turkmenistan (Uzbekistan is not a littoral state of Caspian but is generally considered to belong to the Caspian Region). Hence the share of Russia and Iran in the Caspian is relatively modest although they have vast energy resources in other parts of their territory. The situation with regard to geographical distribution of natural gas is also the same. This uneven nature of the distribution of energy resources seems to have contributed to occasional conflicting situations in the Caspian region, particularly because both Russia and Iran which are the original partners for several decisions taken in the past concerning the energy resource development often make efforts to retain their position and influence in the Caspian Region.

Another specific aspect which deserves attention is that the information available indicates that collective effort seems to be lacking for exploring resource potentialities and it is done mainly by individual countries. According to some Central Asian analysts, only three out of five Caspian Sea States (CSS) are actively engaged in intensively exploring and developing energy resources in their respective shelves. For instance, during the last few years Kazakhstan intensified the exploration of oil and gas. Since August 2001 the Offshore Kazakhstan International Operating Company (OKIOC) which is being renamed as AGIPKCO (Agip Kazakstan North Caspian Operating Company), began its appraisal programme by drilling a third test well not far from the site in East Kashagan where the Consortium first struck oil in July 2000. OKIOC plans to drill up to five test wells while simultaneously conducting seismic surveys over a 1,600 sq. km. area. This appraisal will help the Consortium members to get a more precise estimate of the size of Kashagan. This has become necessary possibly because the estimates of reserves at the field have ranged from 8 bln. to 50 bln. barrels of oil as reported by the Golden Eagle Services in May 2001.

Similarly, Azerbaijan is active in exploration work with the participation of several international oil firms. So far as Turkmenistan is concerned, by August 2001, 6 onshore and 2 offshore oil-gas fields have been under intensive development programmes in various parts of the country. One of the most perspective onshore sites is the southern part of Turkmenistan in the Caspian sea. According to Turkmen sources, reserves here equal 2 billion tons of oil and 2 trillion cubic meters of natural gas. Total space of the area is 40,000 sq. kms. Another big offshore oil-gas region is the central part in Turkmen sector of Caspian sea where oil reserves equal 1 billion tons and gas reserves some 2.8 trillion cubic meters. Total space of the area is 30,000 sq. kms, with 23 explored structures. The most perspective onshore zone is Amoodarya (eastern Turkmenistan). Prospective resources of this region are estimated at about 1.1 billion tons of oil and 1.765 trillion cubic meters of gas. There are 74 prospective structures here with total area equalling 16,000 sq. kms.

So far as natural gas is concerned, based upon proven reserves, Kazakhstan, Turkmenistan and Uzbekistan each rank among the world's 20 largest natural gas countries. Overall proven gas reserves in the Caspian Region are estimated at 243-248 Tcf, which is comparable to North American reserves of 300 Tcf.

Production

In the year 2000, overall oil production in the Caspian sea region totaled 1.3 million bbl/d. Production in the region is projected to increase several fold, led by three major projects currently under development in

Azerbaijan and Kazakhstan—Tengiz (6-9 billion barrels of recoverable oil) and Kashgan oil fields in Kazakhstan (10 billion barrels of recoverable oil) and Azeri, Chirag and Gunashli oil fields in Azerbaijan (3-5 billion barrels of recoverable oil). (*Economic Intelligence Unit: Country Reports*, Second Quarter, 2001; *Caspian Business Reports*, 2000 and *BISNISS USA*).

Overall, natural gas production in the Caspian sea region (including Uzbekistan) reached 4.3 Tcf in 2000. Projects currently underway could help boost Caspian sea region production to over 8 Tcf by 2010, and it is hoped that the enactment of laws barring the flaring of gas may increase the region's total gas production.

Kazakhstan has opened its resources to development by foreign companies. International oil projects in Kazakhstan have taken various forms—joint ventures, production-sharing agreements, and exploration field concessions and so on. After Russia, Kazakhstan was the largest oil-producing republic in the former Soviet Union, but after independence, Kazakhstan's oil production dropped more than 115,000 bbl/d to just 414,000 bbl/d in 1995. Boosted by foreign investment in its oil sector, Kazakhstan's oil production has increased steadily since then, with output of 693,000 bbl/d in 2000, almost half of which came from three large onshore fields (Tengiz, Uzen, and Karachaganak). In addition, preliminary drilling in Kazakhstan's offshore sector of the Caspian has turned up spectacular results, raising hopes that Kazakhstan may become one of the world's largest oil producers.

There are a few proposed projects underway with some international oil firms. These projects, along with others currently underway, could help boost Caspian sea region production to almost 4 million bbl/d by 2010. By 2020, production could increase by another 2 million bbl/d. Although not "another Middle East," as some analysts have claimed, the Caspian Sea region certainly is comparable to the North Sea in its hydrocarbon potential. (BISNIS USA).

Status Issue

A major source of conflict among the Caspian Sea States (CSS) is their inability to arrive at a consensus about the 'Status of Caspian'. There are persisting differences among the CSS over the last decade on the legal status of the Caspian sea. As observed earlier it was contended that the Russo-Iranian treaty of 1921 and 1940 be considered as valid and that the resources of the Caspian sea be exploited with the agreement of all littoral states without dividing the sea into national sectors. Initially there was convergence of opinion between Russia and Iran in this regard which in effect meant that both the bottom of the sea and surface water of the sea were to be utilized equally by all the Caspian Sea States. Subsequently, Iran insisted that the Caspian sea be divided into 5 equal zones which, according to some experts, would increase Iran's share of the sea from 14 per to 20 per cent. The Central Asian States have not agreed with this position. While initially in 1992-93 Russia was in agreement with the position of Iran, it has shifted its position and has come closer to the Azeri view. The view that Caspian be divided into equal sectors was not shared by other three states Azerbaijan, Kazakhstan and Turkmenistan since, as observed earlier, over 80 per cent of energy resources of Caspian are located in their national sectors. Even as a common general consensus on the issue of status of Caspian among all the CSS has eluded over the last decade, differences among them have persisted and in fact intensified.

For instance, Azerbaijan has advocated a phased approach to the division of the Caspian sea. In this context, during talks in Baku on 31 August 2001 with visting Russian Deputy Foreign Minister Viktor Kalyuzhnii, the Azerbaijani President Heidar Aliev suggested that the five Caspian littoral states should first reach an agreement among themselves on dividing the sea bed into national sectors, and only then proceed to discussion of whether and how to divide the waters and surface (*Turan* and *Interfax* report). Kalyuzhnii expressed regret at the delay in reaching an agreement on the legal status of the sea, and hinted that Azerbaijan should attempt to "meet Tehran halfway," a suggestion that Aliev rejected. The crux of the matter is that Iran's claims on several oil deposits in what are currently regarded as Azerbaijan's sector of the Caspian sea are on the agenda of the proposed visit of Aliev to Tehran. Russian leaders hope that such a visit will prove crucial to resolving the disagreements between Azerbaijan and Iran and will help all littoral states.

Similarly, there are differences between Turkmenistan and Azerbaijan. The Turkmen President has stated that Azerbaijan has decided unilaterally many issues pertaining to the development of Caspian energy resources. According to him "Unilateral proposals that have not been agreed with partners and which are dictated by short-term priorities and sometimes by private ambitions... do not facilitate achieving a reasonable compromise." He has not only approached the Russian President, Vladimir Putin in this regard but has tried to involve the USA. The Turkmen President while discussing the Caspian issue with the U.S. Charge d'affaires in Ashgabat, Eric Schultz, on 20 August 2001 opined that there were problems arising from the absence of a formal agreement among Caspian littoral states on the legal status of that body of water. (*Turan Report*, 21 August 2001). Differences between Turkmenistan and Azerbaijan have been persisting because Turkmenistan claims ownership of several oilfields that Azerbaijan is already exploiting.

Russia has been playing a more active role in the Caspian Region during the last few years. In January 2001 during the visit of the Russian President Vladimir Putin to Azerbaijan, a joint declaration was signed. The text of the joint declaration included a procedure of sea bed division "based on the method of Middle Line drawn according to equal remoteness of the points and modified on the parties agreement, as well as, according to universally recognized principles of international law and practice used in Caspian sea". It seems that this is a modification since, earlier, Azerbaijan insisted that Caspian sea bed be divided as per national sectors. It is opined that this is the first consensus arrived at among Russia, Azerbaijan and Kazakhstan based on the principle of 'modified middle line' concerning the division of the sea bed and the resources.

Conflicting Economic Interests and Foreign Investment:

Be that as it may, even as the legal status of Caspian has been discussed and debated since 1992 at political levels, the economic interests of the states have forced some of them to swing into action. For instance, in 1992-93, Azerbaijan, Kazakhstan and Turkmenistan exercising their sovereign rights formed international consortia and even called for tenders for the exploration and exploitation of oil and natural gas. Azerbaijan formed the Azerbaijani International Oil Consortium (AIOC) which included British Petroleum, AMOCO, Penzoil, Unocol, Exxon, Lukoil (of Russia), Turkish Petroleum and the Azerbaijani State Oil Company (SOCAR). Similarly, Kazakhstan formed the Caspian sea Pipeline Consortium (CPC) which includes Chevron, Rossneft of Russia and Kazak Oil Company. The Russian government, however, had reservations about these international consortia initially on the ground that it was not represented in their formation even as Russia's privatized energy firms such as Rossneft and Lukoil were members of these consortia. From this it was evident that political interests and economic interests were operating at different levels often leading to conflicting situations among the Caspian Sea States.

Differences on the status issue of Caspian have affected foreign investment climate. There are disputes among the Caspian states on some oil deposits which are located on the border. For instance, what Azerbaijan claims as Kyapaz oil feild, Turkmenistan calls it Serdar oil field. As stated by a Turkmen commentator, "During presentations in Ashgabad and also in London, Turkmenistan has included Serdar (Kyapaz) in the list of perspective fields many times. Moreover, the government of this country signed agreement with Mobil company for the development of Serdar field in 1998. However, one of the clauses of the agreement reads that Mobil will not carry out oil-gas operations in the field until legal status of Caspian sea is determined". It is, therefore, opined by some specialists that persisting ambiguities about the status of Caspian hamper the plans to pursue balanced investment policy in the Caspian shelf, because any big international company can not afford working in such a risky region closed both legally and geographically.

Even as Kazakhstan has been able to attract some foreign investment in its oil-gas sector, President Nursultan Nazarbaev has urged that the domestic oil firms should become "socially active" participants in major economic projects, including the development of the country's oil resources. He reminded that while in the years immediately following independence in 1991 there was no alternative to inviting foreign companies to exploit major oil and gas fields, Kazakhstan's business community has now accumulated the capital required to do so. He noted that out of some 200 blocks on the Caspian sea shelf, only 18 are being developed by international consortia. Similarly, although Turkmenistan has large reserves, the country is not able to attract foreign investment to the extent desirable due to the fact that foreign investors seem to consider that there are risks of investment because the states concerned have not solved the status issue.

Pipeline Issues

One of the principal sources of conflict in the Caspian Region relates to the network of pipelines for exporting oil to the western markets. During the Soviet era, pipelines were passing through the Soviet territory or through Iran and each had its own pipeline routes and hence there was hardly any conflict. In the past oil and natural gas produced by the Soviet Union in the Caspian Region including production from Azerbaijan, Kazakhstan and Turkmenistan was transported by pipelines passing through Russia, known as the 'Northern Route'. All decisions were taken in Moscow and as such the Central Asian states did not have much say in the matter, more so as it concerned exports. After the Soviet break-up, a new set of situation has emerged so far as exports of oil and gas from the Caspian region is concerned.

Some argue that Russia would like to give preference to Russian firms exporting from their oil-gas fields thus trying to protect the interests of its domestic producers as against other CIS members. Besides this political factor, it appears that there is a technical aspect since, as per some reports, there is capacity constraint on this pipeline as export demand has increased in the 1990's. Due possibly to these politico-technical factors, the Central Asian states were often at a disadvantage in exporting oil-gas produced in the Caspian region. Hence not to depend entirely upon the export outlet through the 'Northern Route', the Central Asian states expressed their desire to diversify their export options. And this suited the western countries also which wanted to contain the influence of Russia in the Caspian Region. Even more importantly, some western powers and in particular the USA want to avoid Iran which is considered to be politically sensitive and unpredictable. All these factors taken together gave rise to the concept of developing 'multiple pipeline' routes from the

Caspian Region. In this new scenario, Turkey and Georgia have become important players. Thus, during the last decade, two new pipeline routes have emerged. They are Baku-Ceyhan pipeline (western route) linking Azerbaijan and Turkey via Georgia and Baku-Supsa pipeline route passing through Georgia.

There has been considerable debate and discussion about the economic viability and technical feasibility about these new pipeline routes. Both Russia and Iran have expressed their reservations about these routes from time to time as they affect their interests, while Azerbaijan, Central Asian countries and the Western countries besides Georgia and Turkey have been trying to justify them. During the last few years Russia has been making efforts to attract the Caspian Sea States to export more oil and gas through Russian pipelines by offering various incentives. Needless to say that by this policy Russia would like to increase its role and significance in the region. For instance, Russia is keen that Azerbaijan should double its oil exports through its pipelines so that its pipeline facilities for export of Azeri oil are being utilized more intensively and with that in view attractive terms are being offered. This is evident from the fact that during a press conference in Moscow on 1 August 2001, the Russian Deputy Prime Minister Viktor Khristenko urged Azerbaijan to increase oil exports via the Baku-Novorossisk pipeline from the current 2.5 million tons to 5 million tons in 2002 and that the two countries should sign a long-term agreement on the volume of future exports. In this context Transneft President Semen Vainshtok offered to cut transport tariffs for SOCAR crude exported via the Baku-Novorossiisk pipeline if Azerbaijan guaranteed the export of a minimum of 5 million tons per year. This shows how the Russian state and the Russian oil giants work in tandem to achieve their political and economic objectives in the Caspian region.

Even as Russia is keen to attract the Caspian Sea States to use its pipeline route, Kazakhstan has often been experiencing difficulties in exporting oil through Russia. To solve its own problem, the Caspian Petroleum Consortium (CPC) has been formed in which besides oil firms such as Chevron and a few other oil firms, Russian, Oman and Kazak states themselves are members of the Consortium. Russia has 24 per cent share and Kazakhstan has 19 per cent share in the CPC. Further it appears that in May 2001 issues regarding customs were solved with the Russian Prime Minister Kasyanov. Hence there was a lot of fanfare about the ceremony to be held in July 2001 for transporting oil by pipelines of CPC. The Caspian Pipeline Consortium (CPC) announced on 4 August 2001 that a meeting of its shareholders endorsed an oil transportation treaty removing the last obstacles to inaugurate the 1,700-kilometer pipeline 'Tengiz-Novorossiisk,' (Report by *RIA-Novosti* on 4 August 2001). The CPC's initial capacity through that route will be 28 million tons and will gradually grow to 67 million tons over the next 10 to 15 years. The capacity of all Russian pipelines currently in operation is about 130-140 million tons. According to some experts, this pipeline is seen by the Kremlin as a resolution of the dispute between the 'southern' (via the Transcaucasus) and 'northern' routes for Caspian oil in favour of Russia. Inspite of all this even in early September, the ceremony was not held and it was getting postponed and Kazhkastan was not able to export oil through the pipelines of the CPC which was to be loaded in tankers at Novorussisk port for export purpose. While there were no technical problems involved, Kazakhstan felt that Russia was having 'negative attitude' on the issue. But as per some reports there were differences among the consortium members on the terms of the use of the pipeline. Moreover, a new dimension has been added to the problem as there is resentment and protest by some people in the coastal town of Gelenjik and Novorussisk region about the ecological impact of the pipeline handling such huge quantity of oil for export purposes. In this regard Turkey has also expressed its environmental concerns about a possible collision (and ensuing oil spill) in the Bosporus Straits as a result of increased tanker traffic from the launch of the Caspian Pipeline Consortium's (CPC) Tengiz-Novorossisk pipeline which was scheduled in March 2001.

In addition, most of the existing Russian oil export pipelines terminate at the Russian Black Sea port of Novorussisk, requiring tankers to transit the Black Sea and pass through the Bosporus Straits in order to gain access to the Mediterranean and world markets. Turkey has raised concerns about the ability of the Bosporus Straits, already a major chokepoint for oil tankers, to handle additional tanker traffic. In order to reduce pressure on the Novorussisk port as also presumably to address the ecological issue, Russia is making its own efforts to take certain measures. On 18 September 2001, Russia's First Deputy Transportation Minister Vyacheslav Ruksha told an international conference in Moscow that his agency has worked plans to develop the port of Makhachkala in Daghestan for export of oil and natural gas from the Caspian region. While stating that Russia's port capacity is inadequate to meet the task at present, he emphasized that this proposed scheme will ensure better transportation for oil from Kazakhstan and Turkmenistan to the West (*RIA-Novosti Report*). It is worthwhile to examine issues concerning alternative pipeline routes being developed in the Caspian region.

In August 2001, Azerbaijan and Georgia were in the process of entering into an agreement for the construction of a gas pipeline to export natural gas to Turkey via Georgia from Azerbaijan's offshore Shah-Deniz Caspian field. The President of Georgia, Shevernadze stated that his country "may" sign an agreement on purchasing Shah-Deniz gas for its own energy need to lessen its dependence on Russia. It was suggested that the two countries had to finalize agreement on the terms of those sales. There could be several issues involved in this, such as who will invest in pipeline construction, payment in hard currency, rates for the delivery of gas etc. There are also differences between the two countries on the issue of tariffs for transiting oil through Georgia. While details about actual rates are not known, according to Azeri sources, Georgian government is urging Azerbaijan authorities for the enhancement of tariffs. It is reported that the World Bank has advised the Georgian government to seek a negotiated settlement with the Azeri government for the enhancement of tariffs for transiting oil and gas through Georgia. It is hoped that the two countries would find a solution to these issues as they would like to enter into a bilateral agreement on wider economic cooperation.

Conflict between Azerbaijan and Iran

Azerbaijan has certain differences with Iran arising out of the energy resources in the Caspian, which have taken a serious turn. According to Azeri reports, on 23 July 2001, Iran used its warship to force Azerbaijani vessels out of a disputed section in the Caspian sea. This issue was further aggravated by the fact that on 29 July 2001, an Iranian military aircraft overflew the disputed Araz-Alov-Sharg Caspian oil field where two survey ships leased by BP to the Azeri firm had conducted geological surveys. While the Azeri government has tried to downplay this incident contending that Iran is not a hostile country, opposition parties in Azerbaijan raised the issue. Moreover, there were also reports that about 1.5 bln. tonnes of oil was 'illegally' exported through Iranian pipeline due to which Azerbaijan had incurred loss of revenue. What has added to the seriousness of the matter is that the son of the Azerbaijan President, Ilham Aliev who is the first Vice President of the state oil company SOCAR, said that "Baku will have to take similar measures if the threat of force is made" in the ongoing stand off with Iran. This issue has assumed international significance by virtue of the fact that with growing cordial relations between Azerbaijan and the USA, the latter has expressed its support to Azerbijan should there be any dispute with Iran. In this context, while the Turkmen President was reported to have criticized the Azeri President, Turkey which is another actor in Caspian has called for dialogue to defuse the dispute because Turkey has fundamental interest in the export of Azerbaijan's Caspian oil via its territory. In a statement released on 9 August 2001, the Turkish Foreign Ministry spokesman Husein Dirioz called on Azerbaijan and Iran to resolve their differences over the Caspian through peaceful dialogue, noting that neither the use nor the threat of force is compatible with the fundamental principles of international law. An idea about the growing complexities of differences in the region can be had from the fact that according to some reports Armenia which is another Caucasian state has been drawn into the picture. According to an article in a Russian paper *Ekho* on 25 August 2001, "any escalation in either the Caspian or Karabakh disputes" could trigger a "domino effect," with Armenia seeking to work with Iran against Azerbaijan. If Azerbaijan gets locked in a conflict with Iran, Armenia might take advantage of that by taking some action in Karabakh; while if the Nagorno-Karabakh conflict resumes, Iran may play a spoiler role.

Trans-Caspian Pipeline

Both Kazhkhstan and Azerbaijan are keenly interested in the proposed 'Trans-Caspian' pipeline which is to be laid along the sea-bed and it would be linked to Baku-Ceyhan project. Kazakhstan is extremely interested in this proposal as it would help the export of huge oil resources of Kashagham oil deposit directly to the western markets bypassing Russia and hence it has decided to join the international Baku-Ceyhan project. But it appears that Russia and Iran have voiced their open disagreement on this issue. It is contended that the proposed construction of "any environmentally hazardous oil and gas pipelines under hyperactive geo-dynamic conditions" on the Caspian sea is not desirable. This view was expressed in the Russian-Iranian memorandum. Disagreeing with this contention, political analysts of both Azerbaijan and Kazakhastan opine that there is vested interest of both Russia and Iran that oil from Caspian should be exported through their own established pipelines. This issue is critical because even when the proposed summit meeting takes place and a decision is taken by the five countries concerning the 'middle line division of the seabed' to get closer, a number of anti-pipeline amendments might be adopted, that would infringes upon the interests of Azerbaijan and Kazakhstan.

It appears that the original proposal of the Trans-Caspian pipeline was to be extended which would help Turkmenistan as well. But differences have cropped up between Azerbaijan and Turkmenistan. According to Natik Aliev, the President of Azerbaijan's state oil company SOCAR, the proposed Trans-Caspian pipeline to export gas from Turkmenistan via the South Caucasus will not be built (*Interfax Report*, 8 October 2001). Although Azerbaijan, Georgia, Turkmenistan, and Turkey signed a letter of intent on that project in Istanbul in November 1999, Azerbaijan subsequently pegged its consent to implement the project to Ashgabat's willingness to place half the planned pipeline's throughput capacity at its disposal to export gas from Azerbaijan's offshore Shah Deniz field. Turkmenistan has rejected that condition, which is again an indication of the ongoing conflict of interests among the Caspian countries.

Conclusion

In the years to come as demand for oil and natural gas increases the world over and the needy countries will search for new sources of supplies, the significance of the Caspian Region will increase particularly because of its high quality and export potentiality. In the opinion of energy experts, exports from the Caspian Region which was about 8 lakh bbl/d in 2000 (accounting for 60 pc of production), could increase to 3 million bbl/d, i.e., by four-fold by 2010 and 5 million bbl/d, i.e., six-fold by 2020. Similarly, the export of natural gas can increase from the level of 1.3 Tcf (out of total output of 4.3 Tcf) in 2000, to about 3 Tcf by 2020.

Notwithstanding great prospects of export of energy products from the Caspian, what affects the Caspian Region at present is the situation of unending conflicts among the Caspian Sea States on several issues as discussed above. In view of this, in the near future the Caspian Region may not be a serious competitor to the Gulf Region. But if the conflicts affecting this region are resolved and consensus is arrived at by the concerned states on various issues, efforts for which are also in progress, then in the medium term, the Caspian Region along with the non-OPEC output may threaten the predominant position of the Gulf region in the world energy sector.

REFERENCES

1. Ariel Cohen, The New Great Game: Oil Politics, In *The Caucasus and Central Asia Backgrounder*, The Heritage Foundation, Washington, 25 January 1996.
2. Rajan Menon, Trecherous Terrain. The Political and Security Dimensions of Energy Development in The Caspian Sea Zone, *NBR. ANALYSIS USA,* Vol. 9, No. 1.
3. Caspian Pipelines: The Key to the New Oil Rush, *Russia Business Watch*, Washington, Fall 1997.
4. Gidadhubli, R.G., Oil Politics In Central Asia, *Economic and Political Weekly,* Mumbai, 30 January, 1999.
5. *Economic Intelligence Unit,* Country Reports: Russia And Central Asia, Third Quarter, 2000.
6. "*Summary of World Broadcast* (BBC), Former USSR, 1998 and 2000.
7. "Radio Free Europe and Radio Liberty Reports", *Newsline on Websites.*

19

Steady Socio-Economic Growth in Uzbekistan

A. GAFUROV AND A. URINOV

For a State with transitional economy more important task is to secure a steady socio-economic growth which is the base for solving top priority social and structural problems. As per data for the year 2000 majority of the independent States of Central Asia have achieved a growth in the Gross Domestic Product (GDP). However, questions may be raised whether the dynamics of GDP reflects the real situation of the economy and also does the growth achieved in the year 2000 really mean the completion of the phase of crisis development and transition to a steady economic development?

These questions are conditioned by the fact that during transitional period measuring GDP becomes complicated by high level of inflation, slump in the traditional planned regime of production and inadequate scope of the market forces of non-government sector of the economy. Besides, an appraisal of the extent of stability of one or another trend in the dynamics of macro-

* Translated from original Russian into English by Sushmita Bhattacharya.

economic indicators need to be analysed on long-term basis keeping in view total period of market reforms in these independent States of Central Asia.

However, the above-stated circumstances do not permit to draw simple conclusions concerning the presence (or absence) of steady socio-economic growth on the basis of dynamics of one index of GDP. Application of other alternative indicators is also required. They include combined indices of physical dynamics of production of important kinds of goods and services, the level of production efficiency, disposable income of the population, dynamics of export and import and a number of other things. The major trend by analyzing the socio-economic stability seems to determine such correlations between macro-economic indicators and parameters of economic environment in which a steady growth is most likely.

The alternative theoretical conceptions and approaches to the condition of economic growth discussed above enable us to draw the following conclusions:

(*a*) Complexity of problems of the socio-economic growth, diversity and specific character of concrete conditions of its manifestation do not permit to simply attribute top priority or another model of economic development, particularly in the States with transitional economy and that too of raw material orientation.

(*b*) While determining the conditions of economic activation one should refrain from extreme appraisal and simplification of complex economic phenomena (inflation, money issue, repression of rise in prices etc.).

(*c*) Formal and logical analysis of statistics of socio-economic development of different States around the world should be taken into consideration in order to mark the sphere of change in macro-economic indicators within which economic activities are expected to reach the highest level.

(*d*) While applying such schemes it is necessary to ensure the methodical correctness of approaches used by selecting the objects of observation and circle of indicators analyzed in such a way that they most perfectly meet the aims and purposes of the analysis.

From these conclusions we can determine the sequence of stages in research and substantiation of conditions for steady economic and social development in Uzbekistan. First of all, it is necessary to determine the enumeration of the States that can serve as the model in the comparative analysis of macro-economic and social environment. These States must meet a number of requirements such as,

(*a*) they must have a high steady rate of socio-economic development during the last 10-15 years with low starting level, which they had 30-40 years ago;
(*b*) they must be comparable to Uzbekistan in terms of number of population, mentality of people and a number of other parameters (natural and climatic);
(*c*) they must have spiritual, historical and cultural bases similar to that of Uzbekistan.

It seems that in the first place South Korea, Malaysia, Turkey and Saudi Arabia can be ascribed to such countries. Taking into account the aforesaid requirements we can now proceed to examine the results of socio-economic development of Uzbekistan in the last ten years of independence.

In the beginning of economic reform process, Uzbekistan lagged behind other countries of the Commonwealth of Independent States (CIS). In terms of drop in real volume of production Uzbekistan was one of the lowest among other republics of the former Soviet Union. Thus in the year 2000 as far as Gross Domestic Product was concerned Uzbekistan practically restored the pre-reformed level of production as was the case in Russia and other States. In 1990 in Russia it was recorded as 62 per cent, in Ukraine-44 per cent, in Kazakhstan-67 per cent and in Kyrgyzstan-66 per cent.

The process of economic reforms in Uzbekistan has been carried out in two stages. During the first stage (1991-1995) several measures were taken for denationalization and privatization of State property. Besides, permission for entrepreneurial activities was given as well as towards policy establishing open economic relations with all the countries of the world was pursued. Stabilization and growth of production during this period was combined with the improvement of other macro-economic indicators. But the splash of inflation in 1992 caused by tempering of prices and breakdown of single rouble clearance, reduced the growth of consumption prices to 25 per cent in 1993 and 23 per cent in 1995. However, due to active economic policies of the Government the level of price rise began to reduce by an average 6 per cent per month in 1995 and 2.1 per cent in 1997. During the second stage that started in 1996, the economic reforms in Uzbekistan yielded positive results in many direction. Thus the inflation came down further to 1.9 per cent in 1999-2000. During 1998-2000, there was no problem in Uzbekistan as regards timely payment of salary, allowances and pensions to the workers in different organizations.

The last 10 years witnessed the setting up of a new banking sector with a network of banks, insurance and leasing companies apart from funding institutions. A normal base regulating the banking activities has been worked out by the Central Bank in collaboration with commercial banks in accordance with the demands in the market. The main aim was to ensure the stability of the national currency. The remarkable role in achieving the macro-economic stability has been played by the new budgetary and taxation system set up during the years that followed the independence. It has ensured building up financial resources needed for rapid growth of priority fields especially oil and gas, power engineering, petro-chemical, non-ferrous, machine-building, textile, food-producing sectors as well as for social protection of the people. Besides, it also helped securing defence, law and order of the country, maintaining government bodies, carrying out the State obligations toward external and internal duty. Simultaneously, budgetary taxation, credit and monetary policies have been used for implementing the policy of macro-economic stabilization which further enabled the State budget deficit to remain within 2.5 per cent to 3 per cent of GDP in order to bring down the level of inflation to 2.3 per cent a month.

Uzbekistan's economy has been gearing up in line with generally accepted procedures in the world economy. The focus has been kept on developing property relations, by means of forming a class of proprietors, as well as denationalization and privatization of State monopoly in the property by forming and developing small and medium business (MSB/SMB). The individual, small and medium business has become one of the factors for a steady economic growth of the country. The main strategic goals include the formation of a real class of proprietors, a balanced growth of economy, steady growth of MSB/SMB share in the GDP structure, organization of production in processing industry and in the sphere of services.

The institutions set up in a comparatively short span of time to support the business undertakings have favoured not only the involvement of a considerable section of the population into individual entrepreneurial activities but also rapid increase in the number of private microfirms, small and medium enterprises. As a result of government support the subjects of small and medium as well as individual business undertakings are augmenting the volumes of production year by year. In the year 2000 they produced 31.6 per cent of Republic's GDP as against 1 per cent in the year 1991. In the same year, 44,627 thousand people or 49.7 per cent of the total number of people engaged in the country's economy were found to be involved in the MSB/SMB sector. The structure of MSB/SMB in the year 2000 produced 11.3 per cent of industrial output and in agriculture it contributed 724 per cent output of total volume of commodity production of the country.

Since the first year of independence a structural planned policy has been implemented aiming at strengthening economic and political independence, ensuring power and food production and utmost utilization of rich natural and mineral raw material resources. Its basic purposes seem to have been making a radical change in the economic structure, technological and economic modernization, transition from raw material orientation to production of ready material and bringing its quality to the world standard. One of the most important outcomes of the reforms has been the positive improvement at the institutional structure. In the year 2000, 65.4 per cent of the industrial and 99 per cent of the agricultural production fell to the share of non-government sector while in 1990 the entire production was carried out by the government. At present a full fledged private sector is being set up and multi-structural economy is taking shape in the republic. The share of government sector has decreased in a number of enterprises so much so that it was recorded a merely 10.4 per cent of the overall number of enterprises in 2000.

The activization in the business of middling secured strategy of entrepreneurs at present is paramount in terms of importance at the evolutionary stage towards developed market. This target can be achieved by active implementation of legal methods. Significant measures are being taken to improve and increase the efficacy of incentives and deterrents as well as consolidate normative legal acts. For this purpose unnecessary bureaucratic impediments are being removed as far as business undertakings are concerned. Further, at the primary stage, self-developing market is being strengthened through the supportive role played by State organs.

The above analysis shows that a well developed personal legislation in Uzbekistan without having either effective mechanism or full fledged experience for law making activities is one of the impressive outcomes of the last decade. At the same time the normative-legal base of private business undertakings that took shape in the process of reforms today needs a systematic unification so as to be more consistent in acquiring positive experience. President Karimov has emphasized that "we must inculcate interests and impel people first of all the youth, to get involved in the entrepreneurial activities to create economic and legal conditions for organizing their own affairs and own business by themselves."

It, therefore, must be emphasized that in Uzbekistan no entrepreneur with all his heart and soul would ever want to strive for a cut in number rather they would try to secure uniformity in demands, thereby bringing the demands in a system more simple to understand and learn. One of the most important pre-conditions for the growth of MSB/SMB is to create in the society an environment of respect for inviolability of ownership. The constitutional right to private ownership seems to be an absolute right. And it means that only the proprietor is the sole master of his property. Therefore, some of the most significant outcomes of the economic reforms can be seen through positive progress in creating MSB/SMB institutions within the system of the Chamber of commodity producers and supporting the business undertakings. A full fledged private non-government sector of economy is being set up and extended. At present 203.3 thousand subjects managing the economy including 183 thousand medium, small and micro firms have been registered in the Republic. The share of the subjects of MSB has been recorded as 31 per cent of overall volume of construction works throughout the country, while of the 45.3 per cent of total retail commodity turnover, roughly 38 per cent of all the paid services rendered to the population. However, the quantity and volume of jobs and services of MSB are still not enough for 25 million people of Uzbekistan.

The multiform and multiplayer economy of Uzbekistan shows that the proportion of enterprises in forms of ownership at the end of the year 2000 consisted of 46 per cent private enterprises, 14 per cent farming industry, 6 per cent enterprises of joint and collective ownership, 2 per cent enterprises of mahalla ownership, 2 per cent cooperative, 2 per cent joint and foreign establishment, 2 per cent Government undertakings, 5 per cent joint-stock companies and 2 per cent limited companies. Considering the data it can be concluded that in the socio-economic life the private undertakings and farming (60%) predominate the overall numbers of undertakings in the Republic. If the enterprises of joint-stock company, under mahalla ownership, joint and collective ownership and cooperative ownership (15%) are added, it may be concluded that in Uzbekistan the market relations are taking shape.

The mining industry production is of great significance as it has increased from 72 per cent to 77 per cent, while mining has been reduced from 27.8 per cent to 23 per cent. The priority directions include the development of establishments having both productive and non-productive infrastructures. Since 1999 the financing on construction of transportation and telecommunication system has been increasing in the country and in 2000 up to 15.2 per cent of the total capital investments was allocated in this sector alone. The volumes of international traffic and national sector of the transit Asia-Europe optical-fibre line of connection have been widened considerably. The Tashkent-Andyan-Osh-Irkitash (China) motarable roads are also being constructed. The tourism sector has been given priority for development. During 1993-2000 the flow of over all tourists increased by 3 times and that of the foreigners by 5.5 times.

Structural improvement in the industry played a determinant role in the socio-economic growth of the country. The reforms enabled to enhance the proportion of metallurgical (including non-ferrous metallurgy) and petrochemical products as well as flour-grinding, cereals, and mixed-fodder branches. A marked structural improvement has occurred in machine-building, electrical engineering and micro-biological industry. During the period that followed independence the industry maintained pace of development and by the year 2000 the increase in industrial volume totalled almost 5 per cent. The chemical and petro-chemical branches may be marked out amongst the most developing ones, in which average annual rate of increase in the volume of production is mounted to more than 10 per cent.

The development in fuel and energy sector as well as automobile, aviation, tractor and other branches of machine-building sector is considered to be a stable factor influencing the economic condition of the basic branches. The share of fuel and energy sector in the year 2000 amounted to almost 25 per cent of the volume of total industrial production. It has been achieved due to the development in operational drilling of oil and gas, thereby giving boost to the Bukhara Oil Refining Port. The fuel branch alone has exceeded the level 1994 and makes 2.3 per cent of average annual rate of growth. The "Uzbek (Oil and Gas) Neftegas" has contributed much to the stabilisation and growth of production due to realization of investment projects involving foreign capital. The increase in extraction of oil and natural gas owes much to the steady provision with regards to light oil products and other kinds of fuel in all branches of real sector of economy.

In terms of production the percentage share of different branches in the entire industry in the year 2000 was recorded as, the fuel: 16.7 per cent, electrical engineering: 9.3 per cent, ferrous metallurgy: 1.4 per cent, non-ferrous metallurgy: 11.3 per cent, chemical and petrochemical-5.9 per cent, machine building and metal processing: 9.0 per cent, light industry: 20.1 per cent, food industry: 11.8 per cent, building materials: 4.2 per cent, timber woodworking: 0.9 per cent and other branches: 9.2 per cent. All these indexes in comparison to that of the year 1991 show a trend towards growth. A stable annual growth in metallurgical production has been secured from 1996 owing to substantial increase in gold mining at the joint undertakings "zarafshon-N'mont" and "Amantaimau–Goldfilds/Goldfields", where modern technology of mining and dressing gold-containing has been applied. It enabled to raise the share of non-ferous metallurgy in industrial output. In the ferrous metallurgy, during the years of independence, there has been an appreciable expansion in the range of products which are being sold by the Bekabad Plant for the domestic market.

The machine building sector possesses strong industrial potential and, therefore, it is the foundation for successful development of the entire economy of Uzbekistan. As a result of active investment policy a modern automobile industry has now been set up with outlet of its product for the domestic market. The joint Uzbek-Turkish undertaking "CAMKOCHAVTO" and joint Uzbek-Korean undertaking "UZDAWOOAVTO" are picking up strength. The production of oil-field equipment and also the equipment for light, food and cattle breeding industry has been re-animated. The farm-machinery building industry has been manufacturing equipment in collaboration with the foreign firm "Keis".

Putting personal resources of raw materials into production of building materials helped the development of cement industry, production of non-metallic wall materials, prefabricated ferro-concrete, ceremics and decoration materials made of natural stones. The capacities for producing granite decorative slabs have been introduced at the AO Gazalkent "KOK" and imported diamond-rope installation for extracting stone have started operating in AO "Samarkand Mramor (marble)", the products of which go for export. Besides, glass industry too has been developed, which produces multi-coloured construction and domestic glasses.

The volumes of production of the light industry have also shown a trend towards growth. In the year 2000 this branch recorded the highest rate of growth, i.e., 20.8 per cent. The state support and liberalization of external economic activities as well as involvement and protection of interests of foreign investors helped develop new establishments, technical re-equipment of the operating undertakings, and also increase in production of export oriented commodities. The volume of cotton fibre processing has increased cotton fabric and yarn which have been competing with other products in the foreign markets. It, therefore, determines the profitability of export and sets the base for positive external financial turnover.

The problem of providing people of the country with sufficient food stuffs still remains the most important concern. Steady rise in the volume of production of foodstuff including grain is under intense observation of the government. The increase in processing of local agricultural raw materials and expansion of the processing branch have distinguished the food industry as one of the most important priorities, which enabled to expand the range of foodstuffs. During the years of independence more than 900 new varieties of food stuffs have been produced.

Since independence the strategy to develop the rural economy has been witnessing positive results which enabled the diversification of branch, departure from mono-culture of cotton plant, self-provision for foodstuffs and development of production in the processing of agro-products. In the sown areas there has been progress towards crop culture. In the year 1991 crops occupied just 25.7 per cent area, while in 2000 they have been spread over 42.7 per cent of the overall sown area. Owing to this policy the grain production in the year 2000 increased by more than twice in comparison to the year 1991 and amounted to 4.1 million tonnes. Today 99.4 per cent of the agricultural commodities are being produced in the non-governmental sector, particularly in the villages managed by shirkats' farmer's or dekhkans farm. However, the prevalent is dekhkan's farm, which occupies more than 1,540.4 thousand hectares of land, and produces 66 per cent of the gross output of agriculture, including 89 per cent of cattle breeding. The state prohibition on all kinds of agriculture products except cotton and grain has been abolished. The cattle breeding farms have been privatized. Denationalized gardens and vineyards have been transferred to individual sector and state prohibition on their product has also been abolished. It led to the expansion of private business undertakings in the village and rise in the number of small commodity products. In all categories of farming the production includes 841.1 thousand tonnes of meat, 3,636.9 thousand tonnes of milk and 1,252.9 million eggs. These indices are slightly higher than what were in the year 1991. Thus the share of household farmings in the total production of above mentioned items amounts to 91.1 per cent, 90.2 and 60 per cent respectively as against 59 per cent, 71 per cent and 37 per cent of the year 1991. Besides, more than 5,246.7 thousand tonnes of fruit and vegetable products, grapes and potatoes are also produced.

The reconstruction of economy during 1991-1994 created conditions for the flow of investment resources. Owing to the consistent economic policy and creation of favourable climate for foreign investors, a constant growth of investment activity has been observed since 1996. Moreover, the main positive factor has been the increase in the share of capital expenditure in the GDP. During the last two years investment has increased in the social sphere as well, particularly in the education related to training programme for national specialists.

One of the key principles for reformation of economy of Uzbekistan is the adherence to a strong social policy. In ten years 22,000 kms. of water supply line and 54,000 kms. of gas line have been laid down. New hospitals with 19,000 beds, polyclinics, schools providing general education with 8,05,100 learning places and 69.9 million sq.m. dwelling places have also been established. More than 95 per cent of financing from the State budget has been made in the government sector for carrying out the investment projects through strategically important establishments. Up to 57.3 per cent of expenditure of the state budget has been spent on realization of national programmes like training of specialists and development of infrastructure in villages. The growth of such accumulation like public savings further enabled to cut down external borrowings. The positive dynamics of these savings is an evidence of economic stabilization due to the reform policy. Thus, a trend of substantial increase in the volume of foreign investments has been observed. While in the year

1993 their proportion in the overall volume of capital investments amounted to only 0.1 per cent, in the year 2000 it went up to 24 per cent. The foreign investors spent their money mainly in such branches which are having export-oriented trend.

In the ten years of Uzbekistan's independence there has been marked changes in the external economic activities. The State monopoly in foreign trade under which export and import used to be planned in a centralized way has been abolished. The external economic policy of Uzbekistan is now directed towards integration into the world economic systems, international commodity and finance markets. For this purpose the main task of reforming the external economic activities has become a key gradual liberalization policy.

The role of indirect State regulation of tax, customs and foreign exchange control has been widened. The protective, compensating and anti-dumping measures, as well as technical, phytosanitory, ecological and other standards requirements for the imported commodities accepted in the world trade are now legally stipulated for protecting the country's manufactures and consumers.

All this and other changes have resulted in a steep rise in the foreign trade turnover, which in comparison, to 1991 figure has increased by almost three times. Unlike other countries of CIA, in Uzbekistan it is characteristic to have a balanced correlation between export and import. Besides, traditional commodities (fibre, non-ferrous metals and chemical fertilizers) the export items also include oil-refining products, light motorcars, manufactured goods of assembled domestic appliances. In these items the share of raw materials like cotton and fibre has come down from 60 per cent in 1991 to 27.5 per cent in 2000. The trend of raw material's export has reduced to 1.8 times during 1994-2000, the share in the import of power-bearers has come down by 6.7 times and of provisions by 3 times. At the same time import of modern equipment for reequipping production has increased by more than 1.5 times.

Thus, the economic growth seems to be the best means to fight inflation. Since there are rich natural, mineral and raw materials and labour resources available in Uzbekistan, a healthy and steady economic growth can be achieved by considering the following:

(*a*) The maximum improvement of business investment climate is important, which needs strengthening the right to property; raising the level of corporate management and contracts culture; securing law and order; deregularization of economy, restricting the influence of bureaucracy; setting up active competitive environment, lowering taxes. All this is stipulated in the programme of the Government of Republic of Uzbekistan.

(*b*) Levelling the conditions of competition, curtailing subsidy, liquidating the structural deformations and narrowing down the non-market sector will be accompanied by widening the level of economic materialization. The measures through securing formation of structures and institutions of free market economy will obviously favour the economic growth, but not immediately. However, they are necessary so that effective mechanisms and stimuli of growth start operating in the future economy.

(*c*) The development of banking system and stock markets ahead of schedule is required. If the lag in this sphere persists then the mechanisms of transforming savings into investment will be carried out by different ways, less effective risky manner in the socio-economic context. Therefore, it is necessary to expand the extent of credit mechanisms for mobilization and effective distribution of financial resources and increasing government investments, which might play a positive role for improving the structure of economy. All this will create conditions for accomplishing the task of socio-economic development.

20

Structural Changes in the Economy and Policy of Uzbekistan

A. Gafurov, D. Hakimov and A. Urinov

In the Republic of Uzbekistan, building open economy, integration in the world economy and utilization of advantages of international division of labour have been the main priority tasks of the economic reforms. For this purpose, structural improvements in the economy through investment including the foreign one, have played an important role not only in the development of export potential of the Republic but also in bringing into domestic market good quality commodities.

Of late, in Uzbekistan, particular attention has been paid to the activization of investment activities. The investment programme of the government has been implemented which took several measures for stimulating investment including mobilization and effective utilization of investment resources for overall economic growth. As it is generally known, making investment in the condition of transitional economy has its own special feature. It is connected in the first place with the necessity of redistribution of human and

* Translated form the original Russian into English by Sushmita Bhattacharya.

physical capitals accumulated in the old system, i.e., with the necessity of adopting a structure conducive to the demands of market economy. Simultaneously, carrying out structural reconstruction of economy may face problems related to macro-economic instability. Besides, lack of development of financial system which is typical of a country having transitional economy, does not permit to utilize the available resources effectively. In this situation the economic policy should be balanced and aimed first of all at creating conditions for taking effective decisions on investment.

The terms, "structural changes in the economy" and "structural policy of the government" have yet not been settled in the literature on economics and, therefore, they have often been interpreted in various semantic senses. In a narrow sense structural changes denote changes in the structure of branches of economy, and structural policy is interpreted as conscious activity of the government aimed at bringing above mentioned changes. The structural changes in a broad sense imply techno-economic modernization and revival that include:

(*a*) reorganization of structures of the branches of economy (it might happen either in the course of natural development of economic system or under the influence of proper economic policy);
(*b*) improvement in the territorial structures of the economy (development of structural improvements in the region);
(*c*) renewal of fixed capitals;
(*d*) introduction of achievements of science and technology policy (NTP), as well as technological requirement of production (it might be favoured by the government policy on science and technology);
(*e*) improvement in human capital;
(*f*) improvement in production and market infrastructure, and institutional reformation;
(*g*) creation and upgradation of mechanism to stimulate and support the economic growth (it can be both in raising the effectiveness of operation of market mechanism and in improving the government's structural policy); and
(*h*) improvement in the ecological viability of producible product and its economic capability.

The structural policy is usually pursued with the purpose of creating conditions for steady economic growth. In the Western literature on economics two basic approaches have been made towards structural policy of a government.

Firstly, the Keynesian approach propounds that market economy does not guarantee the optimum distribution and utilisation of resources and therefore, does not provide a stable economic growth. It is all the more correct as far as the economy of Uzbekistan is concerned. The markets in Uzbekistan are undeveloped and so the government must actively intervene not only in the process of resources distribution but also stimulate investment activities in every possible way.

Secondly, the neo-liberal approach considers that the government participation in the distribution of resources of investment activity is ineffective, and, therefore, this sphere must be regulated by market mechanism.

The structural policy of Uzbekistan seeks to redistribute material, labour and financial resources among various sectors of the economy. The sources of means for its implementation are:

1. National savings and investment.
2. Private (non-government) savings and investment, public savings.
3. Direct foreign investments and establishment of joint ventures.
4. Portfolio foreign investments and short-term loans (credits).

However, while carrying out rapid reforms the government often prefers administrative methods of resource redistribution and Uzbekistan has been pursuing exactly the same policy towards improving structural reorganization in the national economy.

It should be emphasised that market reforms and structural policy during the transitional period supplement each other to a considerable extent, since the latter under the condition of its successful realization helps the undertakings to get adapted to the new economic environment. At the same time it is necessary to keep in mind that there is contradiction among these two goals. And particularly, as the practice during the past years in Uzbekistan shows, the more active the government's structural policy, the slower the pace of market reforms. This must be taken into account while pursuing structural policy in the condition of transitional economy. That is why considering the circumstances, the President of Uzbekistan at the 14th session of the *Olii Majlis* put forward the thesis on "liberalization of economy in the beginning of the 21st century".

The necessity of structural changes in the process of transformation of the Republic's economic system is connected, first of all, with disproportions and backwardness of the technological base inherited from the planned economy. On the other hand, the main objective of the State is aimed at creating effective working institutions and mechanism of market economy. Without realising this objective it is impossible to attain a steady economic growth.

In all the countries having transitional economy the rate of investments in the initial period of market reforms started coming down. For example, in the countries of East Europe the share of investments in the Gross Domestic Product dropped from 21 per cent in 1989 to 17.3 per cent in 1993. The decline in the CIS and Baltic countries was more substantial. The average slump of the proportion of investments in GDP was recorded as roughly 9 to 10 per cent. During 1992-2000 the investment process in the national economy of Uzbekistan was determined by the dynamics of internal and external savings. As a result a trend toward growth was observed. The process of accumulation and investment activity in Uzbekistan can be divided into three periods.

The First Period (1992 to 1994)

During this period there was a substantial slump in the volume of savings and as a consequence in the scale of investment too. The rate of slump in the total volume of investments from all financial sources was so high that various forms of proprietorship opened up by the enterprises topped the rate of overall economic recession by 1.8 times. The main cause behind this phenomenon was the sharp decline in the volume of internal savings, primarily of the State during 1992-1993. The entire sphere of the economy, especially the major construction work having high capital-intensiveness and fund-intensiveness, reacted badly to the ongoing economic process. The deterioration in the conditions was aggravated by intensification of macro-economic instability manifested in high level of inflation. It was also due to lack of balance between budget and balance of payment as well as high rate of interest in both the debit and credit. All this led to the decline in the volume of internal savings.

The Second Period (1995)

It was the period when a trend towards macro-economic stabilization was noticed in Uzbekistan. This was evidenced by the introduction of national currency, slowing down of inflation rate and cessation of economic slump due to reactivation of certain business activities. All this resulted in creating conditions for overall economic growth and also reduced the budget deficit. As the investment sphere got enlivened, there was growth in the total volume of real capital investment. As per the World Bank estimate the real capital investment in 1995 amounted to 7.4 milliard of sum (in value of 1991) which in comparison to the 1991 figure increased by 1.2 times and 6 times while compared to the 1994 figure. In 1995 the volume of State savings achieved favourable results. The share of State savings in the GDP was recorded as 3.3 per cent. The share of non-government savings increased by 2 times totalling 18.4 per cent. Thus the year 1995 can be regarded as the year of re-animation of investment activity as well as the foundation for the economy of Uzbekistan.

The Third Period (1996 to 2000)

It was the period when growth in savings and investment in comparison to that of the preceding periods was observed. While analysing the sources of investment in the national economy during 1992-2000, not only internal ones, but also external savings and sources (foreign investments) has been taken into account. The share of the latter was substantial except for the years 1994 and 1995. Thus the experience of reforms carried out by Uzbekistan during the transitional period concerning structural policy and structural changes, was not an exception to the general rule of the developing countries, i.e., attracting foreign investment for "catching up" the national economy. Through foreign investment the growth in real investment in 1995 resulted in the growth of real GDP in the year

1996. The country made much effort to achieve the real increase in GDP which amounted to 1.6 per cent and this was mainly due to 25 per cent increase in the real capital investment. During the year 1996, substantial investments were injected into country's economy which further increased the real GDP in 1997 by 5.1 per cent. This growth trend continued during 1998-1999 as well, which to a considerable degree was favoured by the structural policy of the government, aiming at modernization and technical refurbishing of production.

The structural policy concerning different economic branches was carried out simultaneously with solving the problems of macro-economic stabilization and institutional transformation which also showed favourable improvements. In 1999, the share of government sector fell upto 64 per cent of industrial and 99 per cent of agricultural production. In the same year the share of processing industry in the gross output of production declined up to 77.9 per cent and that of extractive industry increased by 2.3 times, i.e., 22.1 per cent as against 9.6 per cent in 1995. The proportion of capital intensive branches of industry and power industry increased by more than twice and of the fuel industry by more than 3 times. The rapid development of engineering industry resulted in the sharp increase in the volume of production output under new nomenclature (automobile, manufactured goods of radio-electronics, electrical engineering and technology etc.) This led to an increase in its share in the industry up to 13.9 per cent. The most noticeable trend of structural reconstruction seemed to have been the growth of industrial infrastructure establishments etc.

In the present situation when the economic liberalization policy of Uzbekistan is being determined on the basis of State programmes towards building up a progressive structure of economy, the priority must be given to those branches and kinds of activity which would ensure the introduction of achievements of science and technological policy into production and the minimum growth of demands in new production resources. The country's participation in micro-economic relations on the basis of equal rights would further enable it to achieve steady rate of economic growth.

At the same time the structural ameliorations in the national economy in favour of progressive branches cannot be an effective factor for long-term economic growth if they are not accompanied by development of other branches of economy. Otherwise the growth of individual branches and spheres of management at the cost of others may finally lead to economic recession due to the emergence of extreme structural disproportions. The negative process in the economy as a consequence of instability in the economic development may further grow due to low level development of different branches and poor diversification of the economy.

It should further be emphasised that during economic liberalization, the balanced economic growth does not reproduce the established structure of economy at all. It presupposes differentiated dynamics of growth in various branches and sectors of economy depending on the priority of developmental plans for ensuring the progressive changes, and also satisfying the system of public requirements. In this connection the radical reorganization of the structure of different branches of national economy and its social and technological reorientation are the decisive conditions for building up efficient self-reliant national economy.

It is to be pointed out that the preferential development of the labour-intensive production based on the latest achievements of science and technological policy should become the main goal of structural ameliorations in the industrial sector. In perspective there must be provision for the growth in sectors like electronic and radio industry, instruments and machine tool making industry and also a further growth in the light and food industry. At this time the development of science-intensive branches requires additional expenditure in order to carry out NIOKR acts as an important direction for upgrading the structure of industrial production. Besides, speedy development of processing industry ensures diversification of economic structure towards the growth of labour productivity which is the major pre-requisite for extensive industrialization as well. The diversification of economy may thus lead to strengthening relations among different branches of industry as well as expanding the market for interim and final production.

21

Tajikistan: Problems of Social Development

KH. UMAROV and J. MAKHMADSHOEV

The great accomplishment of Tajikistan in developing not only its economy and society but also the human factor has been to a large extent related to implementation of the ideological concept of the Communist party. However, the concept that only the Communist society is capable of developing economies of developing countries needs to be examined in the light of its impact on overall economy.

In the pre-1990 period, the progress achieved in Tajikistan reveals that it increased the possibilities of overall social development. It was first of all reflected in increasing the average monthly salaries. During 1965-1990 period, it increased by 2.16 times, including 2.47 times in industry and 2.37 times in agriculture. However, the rate of growth of salaries was low while compared to the rate of increase in gross domestic product, national income and basic production assets. Such disproportion was planned and corresponded to the unrealistic Communist concept, i.e., maintaining higher rate in production of

* Translated from the original Russian into English by Sushmita Bhattacharya.

basic production assets than the production of consumer goods. The level of salaries was adjusted to the commodity offer which depended on production of consumer goods and services. Still, the state paid more attention to the development of material base of the so-called non-production sector (education, health care, culture, sports, etc.).

Here, the obvious contradiction comes out. Considering the higher rate of growth in the basic assets in the last 20 years of the Communist regime, a change occurred in the structure of the so-called utilization of national income for consumption and accumulation, which resulted in favour of consumption. The share of the latter increased from 66.8 per cent to 75.5 per cent and correspondingly the share of the fund of accumulation decreased from 33.2 per cent to 24.4 per cent. Such changes were related to the demographic boom in the republic of Tajikistan. In accordance with social guarantees the state had to ensure total employment, minimal wages, housing, free education, medical care, etc. Since the rate of natural growth of population in Tajikistan was several times higher than the average rate in the former USSR, the Union government had to find additional resources for the republic of Tajikistan in the union budget itself. Therefore, the volume of transfers from the union budget into the republican one grew notably during the Soviet period.

The main role in this accomplishment was played by public consumption funds (current expenses on development of sectors of public services, pensions and social aid). It also corresponded to the ideological concept of Communist regime, according to which preference was given not to personal but public consumption. With regard to personal consumption, the course was taken to leveling the volume and structure of personal consumption. As we know, this course was fatal for the entire political structure, because it was unnatural. But after the collapse of the USSR all these trends and tendencies came to a stand still.

Liberalization of economy without proper preparatory work, complete severance of economic ties with Russia and other member countries of CIS, the undeclared economic blockade by Uzbekistan, and the civil war with all its effects brought an abrupt decline in the living standards of the people as well as a catastrophic fall in major indicators of social development. Despite the declared and widely promoted accomplishments in the economic growth, the social development index still continues to decline. It was announced in 1999 that the percentage of poverty level in Tajikistan was as much as 83.5 per cent. Lately, official statements indicate the figure as being 85 per cent.

A study carried out by the State Agency for Statistics (now the *Goskomstat*) and by the Center for Strategic Studies of Administration of President of Republic of Tajikistan in collaboration with UNDP and the World Bank covered 14,000 people in 125 settlements. The degree of representation in this selective study was very high. The study shows that one third of population of the country belongs to the category of very poor and 20 per cent to the category of "poorest", i.e., those whose income is equivalent to $ 1.075 (the level of purchasing ability) per day. Out of total number of people surveyed, 50 per cent did not consume meat products during a particular year, and 85 per cent did not have access to confectionery.

However, some figures obtained through the study seem to be doubtful. The question arises, while the rate of unemployment is shown to have reached the level of 65 per cent to 70 per cent and the average salary is $ 9.5, then why only 20 per cent of population falls under the category of the "poorest", i.e., having only $ 1.075 a day? In this case, their monthly income would amount to just $ 32.25, or 83 *Somoni* a month. Considering this, the poverty situation of the country would look different.

Tajikistan has the lowest level of living standards among the countries of the CIS. It is demonstrated in the data on average salary of the population. The salary in Tajikistan in 1999 equalled to $ 9.5, in Azerbaijan – $ 45, in Armenia – $ 33, in Belorussia – $ 74, in Kazakhstan – $ 98, in Kyrgyzstan – $ 23, in Moldova – $ 27, in Russia – $ 76, in Uzbekistan – $ 67 and in Ukraine – $ 46.[1]

Officials in Tajikistan cite reasons for poverty as a result of destruction and losses due to the civil war in Tajikistan. However, civil wars took place also in Azerbaijan, Armenia and Moldova, but such decline in living standards as in Tajikistan has not been observed in these countries. During the period 1999-2000, there was also a decline in the income of the population. As per the latest data, the average salary is equal to $ 8.7, which is 8.5 per cent lower than what used to be two years ago.

Expansion of economic space is also taking place in the country. According to official data, expenditure of the richest households exceeds expenditure of the poorest ones by four times. At the poorest households, expenses on food make 79 per cent of the family budget. The above study shows that in the last decade there has been a steady rise in demands of various needs which are met through natural production and humanitarian assistance.

It is hard to believe the information that the range of difference in expenditure between the richest and the poorest is four times. Indirectly it is demonstrated by the data on the salary level in the different sectors of economy. The salary in the field of credits and state insurance exceeds the salary of workers of collective farms by almost ten times, while the salaries of workers of health care, physical culture and social security exceed by 11 times.[2] If one adds here the "shadow" income then the difference becomes overwhelming, especially if we take into account the income from corruption and drug business.

It is generally admitted that in rural areas the poverty level is significantly higher than in the cities. About 77 per cent of the population live in rural areas. According to a survey conducted in 1999 on the level of living standard of the population, 18.6 per cent of the urban population belonged to the category of very poor as against 24.4 per cent of the rural population. However, 18.5 per cent of the urban population belonged to the category of the poorest along with 81.5 per cent of the rural population. Poverty is prevalent in the extreme forms in rural territories. In some regions of the country, several cases of malnutrition have also been noticed, thereby coming close to famine.

The purchasing ability of the average monthly salary too remains low. In Dushanbe and other cities of the country, the prices of major food products remain low in comparison with cities in other countries because of low purchasing ability of the population. But, even despite the low prices, the purchasing ability of average monthly salary in Tajikistan remains the lowest among CIS countries.

In 1999, the average monthly salary in Dushanbe was equal to 31 kgs. of bread (in Tashkent 151 kgs., in Minsk 231 kgs.), or 56 kgs. of milk (in Tashkent 128 kgs. and in Minsk 605 kgs.), or 8 kgs. of meat (in Tashkent 18 kgs. and in Minsk 61 kgs.), or 4 kg of butter (in Tashkent 10 kgs. and in Minsk 45 kgs.), or 16 kgs. of sugar (in Tashkent 32 kgs. and in Minsk 131 kgs.), or 94 kgs. of potatoes (in Tashkent 100 kgs. and in Minsk 129 kgs.)[3]. The overwhelming majority of the population is not capable of paying for communal services (electricity, gas, water, sewage, garbage, etc.). It is not likely that the situation will improve in near future. It is, therefore, one of the reasons for the failure of some enterprises which ultimately contributed much to the economic crisis.

The inadequate purchasing ability of the population and the low productivity of natural production in rural areas influenced consumption of food in the country. According to a random survey, average consumption of bread products per person has been recorded as 176.4 kgs. (the highest among the CIS), rice – 18 kgs., potatoes – 30 kgs., vegetables – 46.8 kgs., meat – 7.2 kgs., eggs – 36 pieces, milk – 44.4 kgs., vegetable oil – 10.8 kgs., sugar, including confectionery – 7.2 kgs. When the figures are compared with the data on Kazakhstan it has been found that in 1999, consumption of bread products per person was 200 kgs., potatoes – 87 kgs., vegetables – 65 kgs., meat – 41 kgs., milk and dairy products – 187 kgs., eggs – 37 pieces, sugar – 18 kgs. and vegetable oil – 11 kgs. Except for bread, consumption of other food items in Tajikistan is lower than that of Kazakhstan. It is but natural that it creates protein and calorie deficiency in human organism, and thus results in retarded development of children both physically and mentally.

The obvious imbalance in nutrition of the population of Tajikistan is evident when compared to nutritional data of advanced countries. Germany can be taken as an example where per capita consumption of bread is 74 kgs., potatoes – 75 kgs., meat and meat products – 92 kgs., milk and dairy products – 421 kgs. and eggs – 225 pieces. Simple comparison of the nutrition at the level of the population in Germany and Tajikistan shows that due to low income in Tajikistan, consumption takes place just for physical survival.

The dynamics of low purchasing ability of population is subject to the practical absence of indexation of salaries. Besides, the Government does not take into account the minimum subsistence level and the cost of the consumer basket. Until now, the Parliament has not adopted laws on minimum subsistence level or consumer basket or indexation of income. Had the country adopted such laws, the government would have faced various kinds of difficulties. The problem, however, remains whether to implement or not these laws. In case of the failure to implement the approved Parliamentary documents, the government fears that it would lose its face and prestige among the people. And if the laws are implemented, all revenues of state budget would be spent on salaries. The only activity, which can be carried out in this direction, is the periodical revision of salary. Here, one might encounter two phenomena: (*a*) periodical revision of minimal salary and (*b*) revision of salary by sectors. The latter, however, is relevant only for employees of budget-supported sector.

In Tajikistan, during 1992-2001 the minimal salary was revised 11 times and 5 times during 1995-2001 alone. Uzbekistan carried out such revision in the same period 24 times, Kazakhstan – 27 times, Belorussia – 23 times, Russia – 17 times[4]. As for the revision of salary sectorwise, such revision has always been annihilated by inflation. In the year 2000, before adoption of the new budget, a decision was made on the salary raise in the social sector (education, culture and health care) by an average of 40 per cent. The authors of the new budget and naturally the government too set the target of inflation level to be 27 per cent in 2000 and 12.7 per cent in 2001. However, summary of results of the whole year showed that the actual level of inflation in 2000 was 60 per cent. Thus, the effect of such action was below zero. Even when increase in nominal salary is considered, the real wages in 2001 were lower than the previous year.

As regards pensioners, in the last decade the retirement age of this category of population had a tendency to decline. At present, their share in total population is 6.2 per cent. It is lower than the figure in other countries of Central Asia, and much lower than in other countries of CIS. In Tajikistan there are 92 pensioners among every 1,000 people, in Uzbekistan – 122, in Russia – 266 and in Kazakhstan – 179. It means that the economic burden of this category of population upon the state budget or pension fund remains low. Nevertheless, the level of pension in Tajikistan remains the lowest in CIS and is equal to $ 3.1. In the neighbouring Uzbekistan, it is equal to $ 26.4, in Turkmenistan – $ 12.5, in Kyrgyzstan – $ 12.9, in Russia – $ 19.4 and in Belorussia – $ 24.1. Recently, a decision was made in Tajikistan to increase the amount of minimal pension which is now equal to $ 1.8.

In the last few years, pension has lost its importance as the source of survival for more than half-a-million people. While in 1995 the pension formed 50 per cent of average salary, in 2000 this index decreased to 32 per cent. The other type of social protection of the population is the monetary compensation for the poor. The government developed such a program. In accordance with this program, the volume of state financing for monetary compensation in 2000 was equal to 2 billion Tajik *Rubles*, or 6 million *Somoni* (about $ 2.55 million). About 1 million people were supposed to be benefited by such compensation (less than 20 per cent of the population). But real payments were much lower as people simply did not apply for it because of its small size ($ 0.21 per month). Only 5 per cent of the population received this very insignificant compensation.

The transformation has had negative impact on the development of system of education. The state financing of education is limited mainly to paying the very low salaries to the personnel. In 1995, average salary in this sphere was $ 4.0, in 1996 — $ 5.2, in 1999 — $ 5.9. The salary of professor of university was $ 10.6. All other expenditures: repair of school buildings, printing textbooks and purchase of equipment are covered through loans of Islamic Development Bank, Asian Development Bank or the World Bank, or through programs of humanitarian assistance. Therefore, they are of limited nature and are not able to meet real needs of the system of education. A significant part of expenditure is compensated through collecting fees from the parents. But these funds cannot cover one-tenth of expenditure on repair of school buildings and school equipment.

The system of vocational education is in the state of complete collapse. Closure of industry and construction work led to a decrease in the demand for qualified labour, and shortage of budget resources led to reduction in financing which contributed to complete termination of activities. The so-called system of training combines also ceased to exist. These combines used to provide vocational training to students of secondary schools in accordance with the Soviet concept of general polytechnic school.

A very alarming problem for secondary schools is outflow of teachers for work in other countries, because the average salary of a teacher is not enough to earn even bread for his family. In rural areas, there are almost no male teachers of active working age left. They all are in Russia, Kazakhstan, and Ukraine on low prestige non-qualified works. According to some sources, the hitherto well known professors of physics, chemistry and biology now work as cleaners and porters.

As a whole, secondary education is losing its importance because of inadequate development of labour market and also due to practical absence of demand for qualified personnel. This is the reason for the low level of school attendance. The elementary schools cover about 97 per cent of children, while the initial stage of secondary school has 85 per cent of children. Each year, the number of school students who do not wish to continue education in senior secondary school is increasing. At schools, lyceums and universities corruption is widespread due to the low level of salaries. Bribes are common for tests and examination as well as for admission to prestigious faculties. The practice of sale of secondary school certificates and university diplomas is also common.

The system of protection of health of the population is in a more dramatic state. Because of inadequate budget, numerous disproportions have formed in this sector. At present, there is an excess of medical institutions, beds, and personnel. At the same time, there is shortage of funds for paying salary (even though it is the lowest among all other sectors of the economy), for purchasing expendable materials, for nutrition of patients, procurement of medicines and medical equipment. There is a significant gap between the budget for medical services and the real cost of services. The per capita budget expenditure for health care in 2001 has been planned as 3.44 *Somoni* or $ 1.43, i.e., $ 0.13 per month. Besides, the budget expenditure for development of this system has been shrinking due to inflation. In 2001, the planned budget expenditure for development of health care was just 8.5 per cent, much lower than the previous year.

Until now, the damage inflicted to health-care system during the civil war has not been repaired. The system of emergency medical assistance has not been rehabilitated. The majority of district hospitals have neither the ambulances nor the means of communication. Majority of the hospitals and polyclinics do not have ultrasonic equipment; there is not a single computer tomograph (CT scanner) in the whole country, no lythotrinic machines, not a single magnetic resonance imager (CMRI). The hospitals and polyclinics receive equipment through humanitarian aid programs. But, such assistance cannot provide all city and district medical facilities with the necessary equipment, including the means of emergency medical assistance. The equipment made during Soviet times is getting out of order and cannot be used anymore.

As it was already noted, the salaries of employees of medical institutions are the lowest in the country. Moreover, it has the tendency to reduce. In 1995, the average monthly salary of medical staff was $ 3.8, in 1996 — $ 4.2, in 1997 — $ 3.8, in 1998 — $ 3.6 and in 2000 — $ 3.56. The extremely low level of salary of health personnel is the reason for their outflow. There is a dramatic decline in the quality of health services and widespread corruption prevails in this sector.

At present, there is a very serious problem of access of the poor section of the population to medical services. The cost of surgical operations and post-operational care is very high, and the categories of "very poor" and "poorest" of the population are practically not able to pay. Many deaths among poor families are reported to be due to the shortage of finance to pay for necessary operation.

Following the example of advanced countries some high-level officials in health care service as well as some economists lent their support for introduction of the scheme of self-sustainability and development of the private sector. But, implementation of such proposals encounters poverty and the low paying ability of the population. Services by private medical institutions will then be used by corrupt government bureaucracy, mafia-type business circles, drug dealers, employees of international organizations and joint ventures with foreign capital.

After the disintegration of the USSR, the structural needs of ecological character changed greatly. The closure of industrial enterprises resulted in abrupt reduction in volume of toxic substances processed by refuse-treatment facilities. The figure obtained shows that in 1990 it was 492,000 tons, in 1995 – 60,600 tons and in 1999 – 42,100 tons. The volume of such substance fell to 11.7 times during the period between 1990 and 1999. Most of the ecologically harmful industries are now not functioning. The degree of contamination of water by chemicals fell drastically, which is explained by the equally rapid reduction in the use of mineral and organic fertilizers, practically complete refusal of pesticides in agriculture. In the last ten years, supply of mineral fertilizers to the agricultural sector fell from 240,000 tons to 23,200 tons, i.e., more than 10 times. Accordingly, use of organic fertilizers was reduced from 950,000 to 262,500 tons. This somehow proved to be beneficial as far as protection of environment is concerned.

Thus, in Tajikistan extreme poverty has already brought in a social catastrophe. Elimination of poverty is an extremely complicated task. It has been calculated that eradication of extreme poverty would require 20 times increase in the current level of state expenditure on the social sphere. For nearly 10 to 15 years, resolving this issue seems impossible. In the last decade, the state lacked sufficient resources to support protection of environment and maintain rational use of natural resources. The budget showed a trend towards reduction. In 1995, the state spent on this sector $ 0.32 million; in 1996 — $ 0.51 mln, in 1997 — $ 0.30 mln, in 1998 — $ 0.23 mln, in 1999 — $ 0.12 mln. Naturally, this funding is miserable, compared to the real needs in this area.

However, problems of a different nature do appear here. Due to poverty, people who have not been able to buy fuel and electricity, resort to mass cutting of not just nearby forests but fruit and decorative trees as well. The high-valued archa, pistachio and almond orchards are being destroyed. The percentage of land covered with forest fell in the last ten years from 3.5 per cent to 3.0 per cent. Reproduction of forest is a very slow process. Due to cutting of forests, the mudslide flows have become frequent and their destructive strength has increased. Natural calamities in Tajikistan has thus assumed global character like rapid melting of glaciers, reduction in the volume of discharge of water in the rivers of Aral sea basin, etc. In order to tackle the situation effective international assistance is urgently required because these problems cannot be resolved through budgetary means.

REFERENCES

1. *Data of the General Confederation of Trade Unions.*
2. *Annual statistics of Republic of Tajikistan.* Dushanbe, 2000, p. 69.
3. *Data of the General Confederation of Trade Unions*, 1999.
4. *Data of General Confederation of Trade Unions*, 2001.

22

Ecology and Development in Central Asia

SHODIMUROD DUSTOBOEV

At the beginning of 21st century the world community, including the Central Asian Republics, has entered the transition phase to a new civilization that demands steady socio-economic development as alternative to speedy economic growth. First of all, new ecological concepts such as the concept of steady growth, ecological prosperity, ecological safety and others have now assumed importance.

All this is connected with the inseparable nature of the linkage between the problems of environmental protection and economic, social, political and other problems of social development. These problems are fundamentally inter-related and inter-dependent, and they cannot be solved by separating one from the other. The environmental protection is not a prerogative of only the nature conservation bodies but it requires a change in the direction of development and formation of a new system of values on the basis of existing nature of ecological index of social development and also keeping in view the ecological factor in all kinds of human activities.

---

* Translated from the original Russian into English by Sushmita Bhattacharya.

The problem of cardinal change in the quality of development is assuming particular urgency and is taking both regional and global character in view of the following circumstances:

Firstly, the hasty use of natural resources by mankind and exhaustion of raw materials and fuel and energy resources went on without any indepth consideration of the mysteries inherent in nature and natural laws. Consequently-man, made technology that negates the forms of life in nature gave rise to conflict which came up between technology and ecology.[1] This led to using of the entire huge mass of the natural resources by mankind for the purpose of production. However, only 1.5 to 2 per cent is transformed into finished products, while as the remaining is turned into industrial and domestic waste products.

In the Republic of Tajikistan the total amount of solid industrial waste products by the year 1998 reached up to 250 mln. tons, storage of which occupies 1,000 hectares of land area. The mining industry enterprises alone contributed to more than 190 mln. tons of toxic waste products that have negative impact on environment and are piled up in the depots, dumping yards and other places. As far as solid domestic waste products are concerned these amount to around 5.5. to 6 mln. tons per year throughout the Republic causing great damage to the natural environment.

During the entire course of their existence homosapiens have cut down two thirds of the forests and destroyed more than two hundred species of animals and plants. The supply of oxygen to the atmosphere has come down and as a result of wrong management of agriculture almost two hundred million hectares of cultivable land have degraded.[2] About 3,00,000 hectares of land or 30 per cent of cultivable fertile land of Tajikistan face degradation due to destruction and over exploitation of drainage and irrigation systems, and also due to sharp cuts in funds earmarked for their repair and maintenance.

Secondly, entire world including the Central Asian Republics is in pursuit of fast economic growth and as a result of merciless consumption of natural resources 300 million tons of carbon dioxide, 150 million tons of sulphur dioxide, 50 million tons of nitrous oxides,[3] and also a huge quantity of fluoric compounds, mercury and other toxic substances are discharged into the atmosphere each year. The total volume of estimated discharged polluting substances in 1970 was 19 milliard/billion tons and by the year 2000 it had risen up to 50 milliard/billion tons.[4] Moreover, an analysis of the available data on the generation of hazardous waste products throughout the world provides evidence of extremely unequal share of the states in polluting the planet by their industrial waste products. The enterprises of the United States produced by the end of 1980s about 270 mln. tons of hazardous waste products per year, the share of the European countries particularly the member of EEC was roughly 25 mln. tons, and the East European countries had a share of about 20 mln. tons. As against this, hazardous waste products generated by rest of the countries of the world together were not more than 15 to 18 mln. tons.[5]

The lack of uniformity in production entailed a marked difference in the non-uniformity of consumption in different regions and countries of the world. At present 20 per cent of the richest section of the world population contributes to 83 per cent of the aggregate wealth of the world, while 20 per cent of the poorest section has less than 1.5 per cent share (an average American consumes aluminium: 34, copper: 45, phosphate raw materials: 58, petroleum: 45, natural gas: 184 and meat 10 times more than, say, an Indian).[6]

In the Republic of Tajikistan, according to the data of the State Statistical Committee of the Republic, the discharged amount of harmful substances to the atmosphere declined by more than three times during the period, 1991-2000, i.e. from 100.5 thousand tons to 29.6 thousand tons. The chemical components discharged in the atmosphere from permanent establishments got reduced in following manner: carbon dioxide—from 42.9 to 20.2, sulphuric anhydride – from 17 to 1.4, nitric oxide—from 7.1 to 1.1, hydro-carbon – from 2.1 to 0.1 and others—from 1.7 to 0.2 (in thousand tons). The analysis of the above-stated data and the ecological condition of the Republic indicates that the sharp decline in the amount of discharged substances in the atmospheric air during the last 10 years is mainly due to the decline in the level of utilization of the production capacities in the industrial undertakings.

On the other hand, due to difficult financial position of the country (connected with the disintegration of the former Soviet Union and disruption of the co-operative economic relations among the industrial enterprises, and also as a consequence of the civil war), there is no potential available to renew the stock of obsolete technological equipment as well as the ecological technique. In the first instance, with regard to the dust and gas cleaning plant, if the total amount of discharged harmful substances in the atmosphere is reduced, it is natural that the potential use of that technique and technology will also go down, which could improve the ecological condition of the air in the Republic. The percentage of polluting substances picked up by the dust and gas cleaning equipment varies from 51 per cent to 84 per cent. Discharge of harmful substances by one inhabitant of the Republic in 1998 was recorded as 18 kgs., as against 23 kgs by a resident of Dushanbe city.

The essence of the matter is that at present more than 70 per cent of the total volume of gaseous discharges in the atmospheric air is contributed by motor transport. The total number of automobiles in the Republic in 1998 was 2,34,012. Main causes behind the negative impact of the gaseous discharges coming out of motor transport are the use of ethylated petrol and low quality fuel, violating the norms of technical maintenance and repair work, and absence of devices to control the toxic level and measure the level of smoke of exhaust gases etc. The last factors having negative impact on the environment by means of motor transport are also connected (other than technological reasons) with the low living standard of the people and economic power of the country, owing to which the people are not in a position to purchase modern, ecologically less harmful expensive technique (modern car), and also to buy more purified and costly motor fuel.

Thirdly, there has been a direct organic link between the poverty of the people and low economic potential of both the people and the state in solving the ecological problems and maintaining steady development. In other words, the lower is the level of economic potential of the country and its people, the lesser is the means the country will have to arrange and introduce less polluting or non-polluting ecologically less harmful techniques and technology. On the other hand, due to the lack of sufficient resources like coal and other means of fuel and energy, particularly in the rural areas, people in order to meet their consumption need are forced to destroy forests and make irrational use of land and water resources etc. This may also lead towards imbalance in the ecology and degradation of forest economy as well as land and water resources.

Apart from poverty alleviation and resolving ecological problems one of the global problems also concerns with the problems of providing a sizeable section of the population with fresh drinking water as well as water for irrigation. This concern applies also to the Central Asian republics, and even to such a country like the Republic of Tajikistan which has abundant water resources.

Central Asia occupies an area of 12,27,000 sq. kms. stretching 1,150 kms from north to south and 2,350 kms from west to east. The total land of Central Asia suitable for irrigation is about 15 million hectares out of which 12 million hectares is suitable for growing cotton. These lands are located approximately 9 million hectares on the Amu Darya basin and 6 million hectares on the basin of the river Syr Darya. Substantial development of irrigated farming in the region is possible only by regulating the flow of these rivers, by constructing large and small hydro-electric stations, and also by more rational and scientific consumption of them in Uzbekistan, Turkmenistan and Kazakhstan. Despite the fact that the largest portion of water (almost 80%) gets accumulated in the territories of Tajikistan and Kyrgyzstan, its predominant portion (more than 85%) is consumed in Uzbekistan, Turkmenistan and Kazakhstan. For instance, the total utilization of the water from Zarafshan that originates in the territory of Tajikistan, is done by Uzbekistan. The water use for irrigation and drinking needs in the Central Asian Republics is closely connected with the population growth. While in 1959 only about 22 million people lived in the whole region, it has now reached the mark of 55 millions. In the Republic of Tajikistan itself the population figure rose from 2 to 6 millions and there is still a tendency to grow. By 2010 it is expected that population in Central Asia will reach the figure of 65 to 70 million people.

It is to be noted that in Tajikistan, beginning from 1970 onwards, there has been a deficit of water for irrigation in the Kulyab zone and Gissar valley. The water level of the river Kofarnighan also decreased thus creating acute shortage of drinking water in Sogd region. Besides, shortage of drinking water can be attributed to (*a*) the irregularity in the distribution of water as well as supply of running water for the population of the entire Republic, and (*b*) surface water especially in the villages where major chunk of the population live, remains scanty and so unfit for water supply. Thus protection and rational use of water resources still remain one of the most important directions for ensuring steady development of the country. Installation of new water purification machines and ensuring the supply of running water in the villages are the main tasks to be undertaken urgently. Besides, there is also need to strike a balance between water resources and technology by ensuring their rational use in the whole of Central Asia.

Thus, one may conclude that:

(*a*) protection of environment is one of the organic elements for overall development in Central Asia;

(*b*) development not only demands regulating market economy but also ecologically viable production and environment friendly new techniques which could ensure minimum negative impact and maximum healthy environment by improving the quality of water, air and soil; and

(*c*) national programs of steady development in the Central Asian Republics must be worked out with the involvement of population by taking into account the above-mentioned criteria in order to satisfy the needs of future generations.

REFERENCES

1. For further details see Dustboyev, *Ecological and Economic Problems of Chemicalization of Production in Tajik SSR*, Dushanbe, 1990.

2. Arustamov, E.A., (ed.), Safeguarding of the Vital Activities, M., 2000, p. 200.
3. Dustboev Sh., *op. cit.*, p. 29.
4. Mazur, I.M., Moldavanov, O.I., *The Course of Engineering Ecology*, M. Vysshaya Shkola (High School), 1999, p. 6.
5. *Action Programme: Agenda for 21st Century*, Geneva, 1993, p. 37.
6. World Commission, *Environment and Development of our Common Future*, Oxford, 1991, p. 383.

Contributors

A. Urinov teaches at the Ferghana State University, Uzbekistan.

Ajay Patnaik teaches at the School of International Studies, Jawaharlal Nehru University, New Delhi.

Akhmadali Gafurov is Professor of Economics, Farghana State University, Uzbekistan.

Anita Sengupta is Fellow at the Maulana Abul Kalam Azad Institute of Asian Studies, Kolkata.

Bulat Sultanov, former Director, Center for Foreign Policy and Analyses, Almaty is a diplomat from Kazakhstan.

D. Hakimov teaches at the Ferghana State University, Uzbekistan.

Devendra Kaushik is UGC Professor Emeritus and the Chairman, Executive Council, Maulana Abul Kalam Azad Institute of Asian Studies, Kolkata.

Fatih Teshabaev, former Uzbek Ambassador to USA and UK is the Special Adviser to the UN Representative in Uzbekistan, Tashkent.

J. Makhmadshoev is from Dushanbe, Tajikistan.

K. Warikoo is Director, Central Asian Studies Programme, Centre for South, Central & South East Asian Studies, School of International Studies, Jawaharlal Nehru University, New Delhi.

Khazi Mohd. Umarov is the Chief Researcher, Centre for Social Problems of Mankind, Academy of Sciences, Dushanbe, Tajikistan.

Laura Yerekesheva is associated with the Center for Foreign Policy and Analysis, Almaty, Kazakhstan.

Leila Muzaparova is associated with the Center for Foreign Policy and Analysis, Almaty, Kazakhstan.

Mahavir Singh is Director, Maulana Abul Kalam Azad Institute of Asian Studies, Kolkata.

Mahmudjon N. Sabirov is the Chairman, Executive Council, Inter State Council of Kazakhstan, Kyrgyzstan, Tajikistan and Uzbekistan, Bishkek.

Mohammad Monir Alam teaches at University of Jammu, Jammu.

Ondjik Musayev is First Deputy Chairman of the National Movement, Council of The National Revival of Turkmenistan and First Deputy of the Political Council of the Democratic Party of Turkmenistan.

P.L. Dash teaches at the Centre for Central Eurasian Studies, University of Bombay, Mumbai.

R.G. Gidadhubli is former Professor at the Centre for Central Eurasian Studies, University of Bombay, Mumbai.

Rafis Abazov is associated with the Centre for Social Research, National Academy of Sciences, Kyrgyzstan, Bishkek.

S.P. Singh is Professor and Head, Department of History, L.N. Mithila University, Darbhanga, Bihar.

Mrs. Sheel K. Asopa is Fellow, Maulana Abul Kalam Azad Institute of Asian Studies, Kolkata.

Shodimurod Dustoboev works at the Academy of Sciences of the Republic of Tajikistan, Dushanbe.

Shri Prakash teaches at the Academy of Third World Studies, Jamia Millia Islamia, New Delhi.

Mrs. Suchandana Chatterjee is Fellow at the Maulana Abul Kalam Azad Institute of Asian Studies, Kolkata.

Mrs. Sushmita Bhattacharya is Fellow, Russian Language & Literature Programme, Maulana Abul Kalam Azad Institute of Asian Studies, Kolkata.